T0291901

Design for Health

Applications of Human Factors

Design for Health
Applications of Human Factors

Edited by

Arathi Sethumadhavan
Microsoft, Redmond, WA, United States

Farzan Sasangohar
Texas A&M University, College Station, TX, United States

ACADEMIC PRESS

An imprint of Elsevier

Academic Press is an imprint of Elsevier
125 London Wall, London EC2Y 5AS, United Kingdom
525 B Street, Suite 1650, San Diego, CA 92101, United States
50 Hampshire Street, 5th Floor, Cambridge, MA 02139, United States
The Boulevard, Langford Lane, Kidlington, Oxford OX5 1GB, United Kingdom

Notices
Knowledge and best practice in this field are constantly changing. As new research and experience
broaden our understanding, changes in research methods, professional practices, or medical
treatment may become necessary.

Practitioners and researchers must always rely on their own experience and knowledge in evaluating
and using any information, methods, compounds, or experiments described herein. In using such
information or methods they should be mindful of their own safety and the safety of others,
including parties for whom they have a professional responsibility.

To the fullest extent of the law, neither the Publisher nor the authors, contributors, or editors,
assume any liability for any injury and/or damage to persons or property as a matter of products
liability, negligence or otherwise, or from any use or operation of any methods, products,
instructions, or ideas contained in the material herein.

British Library Cataloguing-in-Publication Data
A catalogue record for this book is available from the British Library

Library of Congress Cataloging-in-Publication Data
A catalog record for this book is available from the Library of Congress

ISBN: 978-0-12-816427-3

For Information on all Academic Press publications
visit our website at https://www.elsevier.com/books-and-journals

Publisher: Nikki Levy
Acquisitions Editor: Joslyn Chaiprasert-Paguio
Editorial Project Manager: Barbara Makinster
Production Project Manager: Bharatwaj Varatharajan
Cover Image and Layout Designer: Karen Chappell
Elsevier Designer: Christian Bilbow

Typeset by MPS Limited, Chennai, India

Dedication

This book is dedicated to my Dad who taught
me to dare. I miss him every day.

Arathi Sethumadhavan
September 7, 2019

To Diyana, Diyako, and Elmira!

Farzan Sasangohar
September 7, 2019

Contents

    Joseph A. Cafazzo

    Introduction   47
    Designing a system, not a product   48
    Health care is opaque   51
    Observerships and research ethics   52
    Case study: when product design is not enough—the vital
        signs project   54
    Change management, Lean, and implementation science   57
    The service design approach   58
    Case study: service design a heart-failure-management
        app for patients   59
    Conclusion   63
    References   63

4. **Design for eHealth and telehealth**   67
    Dena Al-Thani, Savio Monteiro and Lakshman S. Tamil

    Introduction   67
    Functional and nonfunctional requirements   69
    Design and prototyping   72
    Case study: heart failure readmission prevention   73
    System operation   75
    Contextual and cognitive support   75
    Clinical study: a pilot trial   76
    Design guidelines   77
    Conclusion   84
    References   84

5. **Design of mobile health technology**   87
    Plinio Pelegrini Morita

    Introduction   87
    Design guidelines   92
    Case study: understanding user behavior in the wild
        through real-world data   95
    The prototyping   95
    Data-driven design   98
    Conclusion   100
    References   101

6. **Design for effective care collaboration**   103
    *Patrice Dolhonde Tremoulet, Susan Harkness Regli
    and Ramya Krishnan*

    Challenges in care coordination   105
    Design guidelines   107

Section 2
Healthcare systems

7.   Design for critical care

D. Kirk Hamilton

8.   Design for emergencies

Yuval Bitan

9.   Design for resilience

Lisa Sundahl Platt

Section 3
Special population

17. Design of health information and communication technologies for older adults   341

Christina N. Harrington, Lyndsie Marie Koon and Wendy A. Rogers

List of contributors

Dena Al-Thani College of Science and Engineering, Hamad Bin Khalifa University, Doha, Qatar

R. Arnold Drexel University College of Medicine, Philadelphia, PA, United States

Alessandra N. Bazzano Tulane University School of Public Health and Tropical Medicine, New Orleans, LA, United States; Taylor Center for Social Innovation and Design Thinking, Tulane University, New Orleans, LA, United States

Natalie C. Benda Weill Cornell Medicine, New York, NY, United States

Yuval Bitan Ben-Gurion University of the Negev, Be'er Sheva, Israel

Russell J. Branaghan Arizona State University, Tempe, AZ, United States; Research Collective, Tempe, AZ, United States

Joseph A. Cafazzo Healthcare Human Factors, University Health Network, Toronto, ON, Canada; Wolfond Chair in Digital Health, University Health Network, Toronto, ON, Canada; Institute of Health Policy, Management and Evaluation, University of Toronto, Toronto, ON, Canada; Institute of Biomaterials and Biomedical Engineering, University of Toronto, Toronto, ON, Canada

Luiz H. Cavalcanti Department of Human-centered Computing, IUPUI School of Informatics and Computing, Indianapolis, IN, United States

Allen R. Chen Armstrong Institute for Patient Safety and Quality, Johns Hopkins University School of Medicine, Baltimore, MD, United States; Departments of Oncology and Pediatrics, Johns Hopkins University School of Medicine, Baltimore, MD, United States

Victor P. Cornet Department of Human-centered Computing, IUPUI School of Informatics and Computing, Indianapolis, IN, United States

Carly Daley Department of BioHealth Informatics, IUPUI School of Informatics and Computing, Indianapolis, IN, United States; Parkview Mirro Center for Research and Innovation, Parkview Health, Fort Wayne, IN, United States

L. Bryant Foster Research Collective, Tempe, AZ, United States

D. Kirk Hamilton Texas A&M University, College Station, TX, United States

Christina N. Harrington Communication Studies, Northwestern University, Evanston, IL, United States

Emily A. Hildebrand Research Collective, Tempe, AZ, United States

Richard J. Holden Department of Medicine, Indiana University School of Medicine, Indianapolis, IN, United States; Regenstrief Institute, Indianapolis, IN, United States

Ashley M. Hughes Department of Biomedical and Health Information Sciences, College of Applied Health Sciences, University of Illinois at Chicago, Chicago, IL, United States

Jina Huh-Yoo College of Computing and Informatics, Drexel University, Philadelphia, PA, United States

D.J. Karavite Department of Biomedical and Health Informatics, Children's Hospital of Philadelphia, Philadelphia, PA, United States

Sadaf Kazi Armstrong Institute for Patient Safety and Quality, Johns Hopkins University School of Medicine, Baltimore, MD, United States

Lyndsie Marie Koon College of Applied Health Sciences, University of Illinois at Urbana Champagne, IL, United States

Ramya Krishnan ECRI Institute, Plymouth Meeting, PA, United States

Rachel E. Mason Department of Epidemiology and Biostatistics, School of Public Health, University of Illinois at Chicago, Chicago, IL, United States; Department of Biomedical and Health Information Sciences, College of Applied Health Sciences, University of Illinois at Chicago, Chicago, IL, United States

Ranjana K. Mehta Industrial & Systems Engineering, Texas A&M University, College Station, TX, United States

K.M. Miller National Center for Human Factors in Healthcare, MedStar Health, Washington, DC, United States

Nicole L. Mollenkopf Armstrong Institute for Patient Safety and Quality, Johns Hopkins University School of Medicine, Baltimore, MD, United States; Johns Hopkins University School of Nursing, Baltimore, MD, United States

Enid Montague DePaul University, Chicago, IL, United States

Savio Monteiro Quality of Life Technology Laboratory, Erik Jonsson School of Engineering and Computer Science, University of Texas at Dallas, Richardson, TX, United States

Plinio Pelegrini Morita School of Public Health and Health Systems, Faculty of Applied Health Sciences, University of Waterloo, Waterloo, ON, Canada; Institute of Health Policy, Management and Evaluation, University of Toronto, Toronto, ON, Canada

N. Muthu Department of Biomedical and Health Informatics, Children's Hospital of Philadelphia, Philadelphia, PA, United States

Joseph K. Nuamah Industrial & Systems Engineering, Texas A&M University, College Station, TX, United States

Mustafa Ozkaynak College of Nursing, University of Colorado, Denver, CO, United States

Sun Young Park School of Information, University of Michigan School of Art and Design, Ann Arbor, MI, United States

Amit Parulekar Department of BioHealth Informatics, IUPUI School of Informatics and Computing, Indianapolis, IN, United States

Lisa Sundahl Platt Florida Institute of Built Environment Resilience, Department of Interior Design, College of Design Construction and Planning, University of Florida, Gainesville, FL, United States

Blaine Reeder College of Nursing, University of Colorado, Denver, CO, United States

Susan Harkness Regli University of Pennsylvania Health System, Philadelphia, PA, United States

Wendy A. Rogers College of Applied Health Sciences, University of Illinois at Urbana Champagne, IL, United States

L.C. Schubel National Center for Human Factors in Healthcare, MedStar Health, Washington, DC, United States

Lakshman S. Tamil Quality of Life Technology Laboratory, Erik Jonsson School of Engineering and Computer Science, University of Texas at Dallas, Richardson, TX, United States

Patrice Dolhonde Tremoulet Rowan University, Glassboro, NJ, United States; ECRI Institute, Plymouth Meeting, PA, United States

Rupa S. Valdez University of Virginia, Charlottesville, VA, United States

Shirley D. Yan Johns Hopkins Bloomberg School of Public Health, Baltimore, MD, United States

About the editors

Arathi Sethumadhavan

Arathi Sethumadhavan is the Head of User Research of Ethics & Society in Cloud + AI at Microsoft, where she is responsible for bringing the perspectives of traditionally disempowered and neglected communities into shaping products. Key technology areas include AI across speech, computer vision, face recognition, and mixed reality. Prior to joining Microsoft, she worked at Medtronic, where she provided human factors leadership to multiple products in the Cardiac Rhythm and Heart Failure portfolio, including the world's smallest pacemaker. She has also spent several years investigating the implications of automation on air traffic controller performance and situation awareness. She has published numerous articles on a range of topics from patient safety, affective computing, and human—robot interaction, has delivered nearly 50 talks at national and international conferences, and been recognized by the American Psychological Foundation, the American Psychological Association, and the Human Factors and Ergonomics Society. She has a PhD in Human Factors Psychology from Texas Tech University and an undergraduate degree in Computer Science from Calicut University.

Farzan Sasangohar

Farzan Sasangohar, PhD, is an Assistant Professor of Industrial and Systems Engineering as well as Environmental and Occupational Health at Texas A&M University. He is also a Scientist and Assistant Professor at the Houston Methodist Hospital's Center for Outcomes Research and Department of Surgery. Prior to joining TAMU, he worked as the Manager of Design Research at TD Bank and as a Research Scientist at MIT AeroAstro. He has experience in designing, developing, and evaluating human-systems in different domains such as aviation, process control, surface transportation, finance, and health care. He has received a PhD in Mechanical and Industrial Engineering from the University of Toronto in 2015, an SM in Engineering Systems from MIT in 2011, an MASc and BCS in Systems Design Engineering and Computer Science from the University of Waterloo in 2010 and 2007, and a BA in Information Technology from York University in 2009. He has authored more than 100 peer-reviewed publications and his research, teaching, and service have received national and international recognition. His research interests include remote health and performance monitoring, system resilience and safety, and user-centered design.

Preface

Healthcare has seen significant transformation in recent years, primarily due to technological advances that have pushed the capabilities of care. For example, electronic health records are replacing paper medical records, artificial intelligence systems are being used to augment clinical decision-making, robotics is changing the way surgeries are being performed, mobile health apps are encouraging patient self-care, and miniaturizations of components are making medical devices smaller, less invasive, and more advanced. While technological advances have pushed the capabilities of care, these have also increased the complexity of tasks, environments, and human-system interaction. Consequently, today's healthcare is not as safe as it should be. Preventable medical errors are unfortunately a leading cause of death across the world. Perceived complexity of health-care tasks and environments are surpassing health-care personnel's cognitive and physical limitations, placing the patients' and caregivers' health at risk. The discipline of human factors can help by examining the interaction among the humans and other elements in the health-care ecosystem.

The goal of this book is to provide a comprehensive look at critical and emerging issues in healthcare and patient safety. We have read and been inspired by many good textbooks in this field. At this formative stage, however, we missed real appreciation for the application and impact of human factors science until we started working as practitioners, educators, and academicians. This motivated us to use a case study approach to illustrate diverse applications of "human factors" to complex health-care issues in real-life contexts. The book also uses the Design for X methodology to provide specific design guidelines in a wide range of health-care contexts, tools and technologies, and population-dependent criteria (Xs) that must be considered in the design of safe and usable health-care ecosystem.

This book has been a collaborative feat in the truest sense. We believe our complementary backgrounds in Psychology and Engineering as well as our collective work experiences in academia and industry are reflected well in a cohesive product that is well-suited for a wide range of audiences.

This text is a multiauthor book, comprising 17 chapters. The authors include renowned practitioners and academics, from different disciplines, who bring a unique, multidisciplinary approach to problem-solving in the complex domain of healthcare. Each chapter starts with an introduction and a focused review of literature on a specific topic, followed by a set of practical human factors guidelines. Each chapter then presents one or two case studies that demonstrate how some of the guidelines and principles are used for the design, evaluation, or improvements to: specific tools, devices, and technologies (Section 1), health-care systems and environments (Section 2), and applications for special populations (Section 3). This specific structure and perspectives offered in this book will be beneficial to practitioners in health-care settings as well as those in medical device and consumer health industries. This book can also be adopted as a textbook for courses focusing on health-care human factors, public health, nursing, industrial and systems engineering, health safety, and applied psychology.

Chapter 1, Designing for medical device safety, provides an overview of a process for incorporating a human factors design approach into medical device development. They then discuss how contextual inquiry, participatory design, prototyping, formative testing, and validation usability testing can be used to design a total artificial heart. This chapter will serve as an excellent foundation for those, working in the medical device space, who want to learn to integrate human factors into product development.

With many stakeholders such as patients, physicians, nurses, and pharmacists involved in the prescription, processing, and monitoring of medications, medication errors are unfortunately common. Chapter 2, Designing for medication safety, describes challenges with medication reconciliation—the process of gathering patients' medication history and using that information in subsequent points of care—and provides guidelines to minimize these challenges. They then review how observations, cognitive task analysis, user analysis, and field experiments can be employed to uncover complexities in performing medication reconciliation.

Chapters 3−5 center around digital health, which includes mobile health, eHealth, and telehealth. With technology being increasingly used to manage chronic illnesses and promote well-being, these chapters are a great addition to this book. Chapter 3, Design for digital health, applies the human-tech ladder framework to digital health and emphasizes the importance of considering team interactions as well as political and organizational elements in addition to the psychological and physical needs of users, during the design process. Chapter 4, Design for eHealth and telehealth, describes the importance of requirement gathering and prototyping when designing for eHealth and telehealth systems. The authors then provide guidelines for the design of a telehealth system aimed at patients with congestive heart failure. Chapter 5, Design of mobile health technology, discusses how different types of mobile health solutions have transformed self-monitoring by patients as well as remote monitoring by care providers. He then describes the role of a user-centered design process, visual appeal, and persuasive design in the development of a mobile health app for asthma.

Chapter 6, Design for effective care collaboration, the last chapter in Section 1, focuses on the need of tools to enhance the communication of clinical information between different health-care providers. They then demonstrate how participatory design and heuristic evaluation were applied to improve care coordination in emergency situations and electronic health records postvisit summaries.

Chapters 7–14 use a systems perspective to document guidelines and case studies related to several complex health-care systems that continue to challenge health-care system designers, practitioners, and researchers. Such challenges have led to an unprecedented appreciation for system-level constructs and methods to understand the complexity imposed by such systems. Chapter 7, Systems design for critical care, discusses the increasing level of perceived complexity in intensive care environments and illustrates the importance of considering various systems design criteria using a comparative analysis of two intensive care units at Johns Hopkins. Chapter 8, Design for emergencies, discusses the importance of taking cognitive load into account when designing for emergency responders. Then the author uses a three-pillar framework (operator–equipment–environment) to discuss guidelines for supporting responders' work in mass casualty incidents. Chapter 9, Designing for resilience, introduces the notion of resilience in healthcare and uses the adaptive capacity performance hierarchy to illustrate increased resilience through improved robustness and adaptation, using two case studies.

Chapter 10, Designing for collaborative work, discusses the importance of team science in a dynamic health-care environment and provides guidelines on creating a collaborative infrastructure, teamwork training, and tools to improve collaboration. Their case study demonstrates team culture change in a psychiatric setting. The growing prevalence of burnout among health-care professionals has been associated with three different albeit interconnected constructs: stress, fatigue, and workload. Chapter 11, Design for stress, fatigue, and workload management, provides a review of these "Big 3," their impact on various health-care workers, and an accessible summary of assessment methods and system-level heuristics to mitigate them. In Chapter 12, Design for cognitive support, the authors provide an overview of cognitive processes and resources (e.g., attention, perception, and working memory) that play a critical role in clinical decision-making. Their case study illustrates the application of several heuristics and guidelines to the design of a clinical decision support system for sepsis. Chapter 13, Design for improved workflow in health care, provides a good summary of qualitative methods for understanding and improving workflow in complex health-care environments. The authors use a case study of emergency departments to discuss the application of their workflow improvement guidelines. Chapter 14, Design for self-care, discusses emerging trends in self-care, including tools and technologies, physical activity and nutrition, knowledge acquisition and transfer, and medication management. This chapter provides several solutions to address the current barriers in self-care and shows the application of some of these guidelines in a case study of heart failure self-care.

Chapters 15–17 capture what we view as population-specific grand challenges in healthcare. For anyone who wishes to embrace inclusion, which is empowering all individuals regardless of their abilities, and improve equity in healthcare, Chapter 15, Design for inclusivity, will be an excellent resource. The authors provide best practices along with applied examples of creating health-care designs that are inclusive of various populations. Authors in Chapter 16, Design for global health, discuss a very important topic, global health. They demonstrate how a human-centered design approach can be used to increase modern contraceptive use among adolescent girls in Africa. The projected growth of the older population will pose challenges to health-care providers. Chapter 17, Design of health information and communication technologies for older adults, focuses on the topic of aging and describes how information and communication technologies can be used as a resource for health management, by taking into consideration age-related impairments.

We sincerely thank those authors who contributed to this book. This would not have been possible without their dedication to the field. We thank students and colleagues who helped review the book chapters: Jacob Kolman, Arjun Rao, Ethan Larsen, Carl Markert, Changwon Son, Jukrin Moon, Samuel Bonet Olivencia, and Karim Zahed. We would also like to express our gratitude and appreciation to all our teachers, particularly Frank Durso, Stacey Scott, and Birsen Donmez, who continue to inspire us. Last, but certainly not least, we would like to thank our parents, Sethumadhavan, Girija, Farah, and Parviz for teaching us the importance of education and for being our relentless supporters.

Arathi Sethumadhavan and Farzan Sasangohar

Section 1

Devices, tools, and health care IT

Chapter 1

Designing for medical device safety

Russell J. Branaghan[1,2], Emily A. Hildebrand[2] and L. Bryant Foster[2]
[1]*Arizona State University, Tempe, AZ, United States,* [2]*Research Collective, Tempe, AZ, United States*

Introduction

Medical devices diagnose, prevent, monitor, treat, alleviate, or compensate for disease or injury (World Health Organization, 2018). They range from thermometers to left ventricular assist devices and include hospital beds, infusion therapy instruments, pulse oximeters, implantable devices, such as pacemakers, and some mobile apps (Branaghan, 2018). They even include in vitro diagnostic products, such as lab equipment, reagents, and test kits (United States Food and Drug Administration [FDA], 2018).

The importance of medical devices is rising due to several factors, including advances in technology, increases in lifestyle-associated disease (Menotti, Puddu, Maiani, & Catasta, 2015; Weisburger, 2002), and an aging population. For example, the world's population of people 65 years and older increases by approximately 850,000 every month (Kinsella & Phillips, 2005), and half of the people who have ever reached the age of 65 are alive today (Rowe & Kahn, 2015). As a result, focusing on the safety and usability of medical devices can improve human health drastically.

Medical devices developed with human factors (HF) principles and methods not only make devices easier to learn, more efficient to use, more satisfying, and better able to fit into peoples' lives, but they also reduce the likelihood of physical or psychological injury to patients, caregivers, and health-care providers (Wiklund & Weinger, 2011). The HF and patient safety literatures are replete with cautionary tales of death at the hands of use error. These stories play out in a predictable manner, with well-meaning users accidentally operating devices incorrectly, with tragic results. Typically, although the user was blamed, the device itself made the error possible. For example, Wachter (2012) describes an incident reported in Smetzer, Baker, Byrne, and Cohen (2010), in which an obstetric nurse accidentally connected an opiate

Design for Health. DOI: https://doi.org/10.1016/B978-0-12-816427-3.00001-4

pain medication intended for an epidural to a mother's IV line. The lines and bags for the IV and epidural lines were so similar that the nurse simply confused them, resulting in the mother's death.

In another example, provided by Zhang, Patel, Johnson, and Shortliffe (2004), a nurse, trying to program an infusion pump to deliver 130.1 mL/h, pressed the appropriate keys "130.1" but failed to realize that the decimal point on the device only works for numbers up to 99.9. Consequently, the pump ignored the decimal point and delivered the drug at 10 times the intended rate—1301 mL/h. These problems are not limited to a few devices but are more common than most people realize, with issues identified on insulin pumps, ablation systems, automated external defibrillators, duodenoscope reprocessing, and many more (United States Food and Drug Administration [FDA], 2016a).

Recognizing the gravity of this problem, this chapter provides an overview of HF as it relates to medical device design. It introduces the reader to the importance of HF, the process and methods of HF design and evaluation, and where these activities fit into a product development process. Following this, several principles of good HF design are provided. Applied with care, these principles can reduce many of the common HF problems in medical device design. Finally, a case study involving the design of a total artificial heart (TAH) is provided. This case study illustrates the application of these methods and guidelines to a real-world medical device.

Human factors design process

The HF design process involves an early and constant focus on users and their tasks to ensure that the device fulfills, and hopefully even improves, users' needs for safety, efficiency, effectiveness, and satisfaction. However, good designs do not emerge fully formed from solely considering users' needs. Good design involves redesign. That is, it develops through an iterative process which not only identifies user needs but also involves end users in the development and design-validation process.

In this section, methods and a process for implementing an HF design approach are provided. Regulatory bodies and standards organizations (such as the International Standards Organization [ISO], US Food and Drug Administration [FDA], European Conformity, and Association for the Advancement of Medical Instrumentation [AAMI]) have become instrumental in providing standards and guidance (see AAMI, 2009; United States Food and Drug Administration [FDA], 2016a,b; ISO, 2015) for executing these processes. Fig. 1.1 summarizes the information commonly found in these standards by representing the three main steps required for incorporating HF into medical device design and development. Ensuring compliance with the required regulatory standards and guidance is an important consideration in any medical device design.

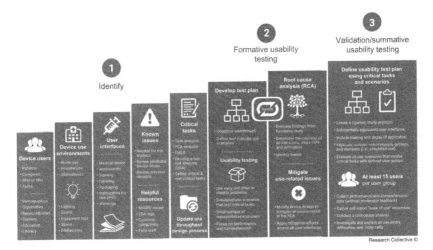

FIGURE 1.1   Process for incorporating HF into medical device design and development. *HF*, Human factors.

Identify device users, environments, interfaces

Device users

The first step in an HF design process is to identify and understand users, including their behaviors, needs, desires, capabilities, and limitations. This is critical for designing medical devices appropriately. For example, a user interface (UI) may need to be completely different for physicians and elderly patients. Begin to understand all the potential users by asking questions such as

- Who purchases the device?
- Who receives the device?
- Who unpacks the device?
- Who sets up the device?
- Who uses the device? Are there different users for different tasks?
- Who cleans, reprocesses, or provides maintenance for the device?
- Who disposes of the device?

Once these questions have been answered and the user groups are clearly defined, a second set of questions can help identify each user group's characteristics, abilities, and limitations, such as

- Do the users have physical or cognitive limitations?
- What is their level of education?
- Do they require specialized training?
- What is their emotional state when using the device?
- Are they in a state of panic because the device is used only in a state of emergency?

Device environments

The next step considers where the device is used. Different environments have unique characteristics; these distinctions greatly influence how a device is used, and these influence many aspects of its design. For example, there would likely be different design considerations for a device used in an outpatient clinic versus the one used in a patient's home. Specifically, users in health-care facilities are likely to be able-bodied, trained medical personnel. The use environment is likely to be well-lit and sanitized, with easy access to electrical power. This is not true of home environments. Patients at home may have a variety of physical and cognitive deficits. Homes are designed for comfort, intimacy, entertainment, and socialization. They are not, however, designed for medical devices.

Questions that can be helpful in identifying and characterizing intended use environments include the following:

- Where will each end user interact with the device?
- What is the lighting like?
- How about ambient noise?
- How much space do users have?
- How hot or cold does each environment get?
- What other equipment is also in the environment?

Device interfaces

Finally, to understand how users may interact with the device, it is important to identify all the device interface components. The term "UI" is often thought to mean a "graphical UI (GUI)," such as the screen on the device in Fig. 1.2. However, for medical devices, all elements that a user interacts with when using the device comprise the "device UI." The device UI therefore includes the packaging of the device and related equipment or accessories, any additional labeling provided on the device, the accompanying instructions for use (IFU), any hardware features, such as physical buttons, knobs, or levers, and of course, the GUI (Food and Drug Administration, 2016b). An HF design process should be applied to each component of the device interface.

Methods for identifying users, environments, and interfaces

HF applies knowledge and methodologies from human sciences to improve the match between people and their products by characterizing the users, their environments, and how they will interact with the device (e.g., Lee, Wickens, Liu, & Boyle, 2017). Two common methods include the following:

- *Contextual inquiry*

This is the process of observing and interviewing users in their use environments to reveal insights about their interactions with the device (Beyer & Holtzblatt, 1997). Contextual inquiry is a method that was derived from

FIGURE 1.2 The C2 Hospital Driver provides pneumatic power to the SynCardia temporary TAH from implantation through patient recovery in the hospital. *C2*, Companion 2; *TAH*, total artificial heart.

ethnography, a practice adapted from the field of anthropology, where researchers would study different cultures by immersing themselves in the culture for months or years at a time (Merriam, 2009). When designing medical devices, this type of observational work can be accomplished by observing surgical procedures, shadowing physicians or nurses during rounds, or performing a ride-along with emergency medical technicians (EMTs).

- *Interviews*

Aside from performing interviews in context (see the previous section), end users can also be interviewed individually or in groups to reveal insights about their interaction with a device (Kuniavsky, 2003). In addition, interviews are helpful for discussing in-depth scenarios and critical situations that occur infrequently and/or that are difficult to observe (Merriam, 2009). Interviews can be designed to be structured, semistructured, or free form, depending on the overall goals of the inquiry, and can be conducted in any location.

Identifying risks

Identifying potential risks with medical device design helps to ensure that devices do not cause harm to patients, caregivers, or health-care providers. It also helps to anticipate the ways in which the device could foreseeably be misused, enabling the medical device manufacturer to redesign that part of the product or to develop mitigations to prevent those risks from occurring. This section describes methods for identifying those potential risks.

Critical tasks and known issues

A critical task is the one which, if performed incorrectly or not performed at all, would or could cause serious harm to the user or to a patient. Harm can include injury (both physical and emotional), discomfort, and even a delay in or lack of therapy (Story, 2012; United States Food and Drug Administration [FDA], 2016b). Critical tasks should be determined from the severity of outcomes or consequences resulting from potential use errors, using some variation of a risk analysis. Any task that could lead to harm, regardless of the likelihood of occurrence, should be defined as a critical task (Story, 2012). For devices that have predicate or similar devices already available in the marketplace, analyzing known hazards is another step to identifying potential critical tasks of the device as well as to ensure that the device is not repeating the same mistakes that have already occurred previously.

Method for identifying critical tasks and known issues

Identifying critical tasks involves breaking down all the potential ways that a user will interact with the device. Once all of the use-related tasks have been identified, it is important to consider the key perceptions, cognitive components, and behaviors (i.e., actions) that a user would need to complete in order to successfully perform each task. For any task where a user could foreseeably commit an error that could lead to a negative consequence (e.g., patient or user harm and delay in therapy), a plan needs to be in place for how to eliminate or mitigate that risk. Different approaches for identifying critical tasks include the following:

- *Task/Perception, cognition, action (PCA) analysis*

A task analysis is a process that identifies all of the steps and substeps involved in using or interacting with a device (Kuniavsky, 2003). For each substep, the PCA components are defined (Zhang et al., 2004). That is, any perceptual or cognitive processes as well as actions required for a user to complete a task can be used to understand where breakdowns in human interaction can occur. For example, if a person needs to hear an alarm in order to determine that a device is malfunctioning, the alarm must be designed so that it is at an appropriate decibel level and has a distinct enough sound to alert users appropriately.

- *Failure mode effects analysis (FMEA)*

An FMEA is another method for determining critical tasks (Israelski & Muto, 2004). An FMEA is typically developed by brainstorming possible usage scenarios for a given device that could lead to a "failure mode." For each failure identified, an estimate is made of its occurrence, severity, and detection. Then, an evaluation is made of the necessary actions to be taken to minimize the negative consequence associated with the failure (Stamatis, 2003).

The FDA guidance for medical device HF provides a thorough list of resources for identifying known issues (Food and Drug Administration, 2016b), including current device users, journals, proceedings from professional meetings, and adverse event reports.

Formative usability process

Once the intended users, environments, devices interfaces, and use risks have been identified and design mitigations are in place, the device should be evaluated to ensure that the design is meeting the needs of the intended users in the intended use environments. The findings from those evaluations can then be used to iterate upon the design of the device. This routine comprises the formative usability process—design, evaluate, and repeat (Redish et al., 2002).

The formative usability process can be conducted at any stage in the development process. In fact, performing formative testing with rough prototypes early in the design phase can help to identify potential issues early in the design when modifications are cheap. As the device design is iterated on, continued formative testing will make it unlikely that usability problems will persist in later stages of product design and development. Methods for performing formative evaluations including the following:

- *Participatory design*

This method involves users in the design process and provides a forum for designers and device developers to interact, work with, and better understand end users (Sanders & Stappers, 2008; Sanders & William, 2002). Participatory design can be achieved in a number of ways, using velcro or foam modeling, sketching, and collaging (Hanington & Martin, 2012; Sanders & William, 2002). Regardless of the approach, the overall goal is for users to be actively involved in the design process by communicating and visualizing their needs.

- *Expert reviews*

Although involving users in the formative evaluations is critical, expert reviews by expert practitioners can be employed to complement user research in the medical-device-design process. One common and easily implemented method is a heuristic analysis, where a small set of HF experts will evaluate a device's UIs against HF design principles to identify usability and safety issues (Nielsen, 1994; Zhang, Johnson, Patel, Paige, & Kubose, 2003).

Another commonly used and effective method is the cognitive walkthrough, where HF experts identify usability issues by working through a series of tasks related to the device from the "perspective" of an end user (Polson, Lewis, Rieman, & Wharton, 1992).

- *Usability testing*

One of the most effective methods for evaluating device interfaces is by performing usability tests, where representative users conduct realistic tasks with the medical device in a simulated environment of use. The data from usability testing often includes success/failure rate, frequency and type of errors, time on task, and user responses to perceived ease-of-use and satisfaction (Rubin & Chisnell, 2008). During formative usability testing, it is important to focus on evaluating performance on critical tasks to ensure that users can perform those correctly. Wiklund and Weinger (2011) advise preparing and testing for the worst case scenario, including a difficult environment of use, for users who are not well trained, and thus under stress, and/or are not technologically sophisticated. Similarly, Rubin and Chisnell (2008) recommend preparing for the worst by including a few "least competent users" (LCUs) during formative usability tests. LCUs are end users who represent the least skilled person who could potentially use the device. The reasoning is simple: if the least expert group is successful with the device, most other groups will likely be successful as well.

Otherwise, it is important to identify users who are representative of the actual users of the product. To ensure that usability test results are valid, it is important to recruit participants based on the end users' characteristics, such as education level, training, technical sophistication, and age defined during the "identify" stage. Further, as devices are often used by several different types of end users, separate usability tests should be conducted with each group. Fortunately, for a formative study, only 5–7 end users per user group are needed to participate, as they will identify the majority of usability issues (Faulkner, 2003).

Finally, formative usability studies are a critical tool in preparing for validation testing. Some tasks are difficult to simulate and require props, mannequins, confederates, or special codes to trigger events. Preparing for validation testing can require several iterations of task materials, environment, and instructions. Conducting formative studies provides an opportunity to iterate on those study components prior to the validation study.

Validation testing

The goal of validation testing is to demonstrate through usability testing that the medical device can be used safely and effectively by the intended users, in the intended use environments. Validation testing is the final step in the HF design process before launching a medical device on the market.

There are several characteristics of a validation usability test which differentiate it from a usability test that would be performed during the formative stage. First, market-ready versions of the device, labeling, and training should be included in the study. In addition, realistic training needs to be provided to study participants to mimic the level of training that will be available to users when the device is on the market.

The number of participants will differ from formative testing as well. While guidance documents indicate that manufacturers should be responsible for making their own determinations of the necessary number of test participants in the validation study, the FDA HF guidance does specify a minimum of 15 participants per end user group.

The goal of the validation study is to demonstrate that use-related risks are minimized to an acceptable level. This is accomplished by having representative users' complete critical tasks via realistic simulated-use scenarios. Note that some critical tasks cannot be simulated. In this case, comprehension questions are appropriate for assessing users' understanding of the critical information. Depending on the device, it may be reasonable to provide users with resources they would normally have access to in real life, should they need additional information or help (e.g., helpline).

Three types of data will typically be collected during a validation study: participant performance, knowledge task comprehension accuracy, and qualitative interview responses. The performance, knowledge, and qualitative data collected are synthesized and analyzed to understand and describe the root causes of any observed use errors or difficulties that participants encountered. The details leading to the use error, what users said about it, and what they did will help to determine the root cause. The root cause is ultimately what determines which component of the interface was responsible for the use error. For example, the root cause should not be that the user was not paying attention, or the user was distracted, or the user was ignorant. Following this analysis, device designers will need to determine what potential harm- and risk-control measures, if needed, may be taken to mitigate resulting risks due to observed use errors. If the formative usability process was done correctly, it would have helped to identify and mitigate use errors early on in the development life cycle. While use errors on critical tasks do not necessarily mean the device cannot pass muster with FDA, it will always come down to the level of risk associated with any use errors. If the use-related risk is still high, the HF design process will need to be reevaluated and, in some cases, repeated.

The activities described previously provide a robust process for designing usable medical devices; the ones that address user needs, improve ease of use, and reduce use error. On the other hand, many HF issues identified in formative and validation testing could be eliminated simply by following the design principles outlined next. These principles are provided not because they obviate the need for implementing an HF process (they do not) but because following them can make the HF process substantially more efficient.

Enable simple interactions

Even advanced technology can be made simple to use; and simplicity can improve safety. Start by providing only the functionality users need and avoid feature creep (Page, 2009; Rust, Thompson, & Hamilton, 2006). This reduces clutter, making items easier to locate. Next, streamline frequent and important activities by eliminating unnecessary steps. Then facilitate legibility and readability by making displays, labels, and texts that are easy to read from the typical distance of use. Provide consistent and familiar placement of information, labeling, color coding, and device behavior. Further, provide sensible grouping of interface items, since placing related items close together tends to facilitate learning of the UI (Branaghan, Covas-Smith, Jackson, & Eidman, 2011). Finally, where appropriate, support side-by-side comparisons of information. This reduces cognitive load because users do not need to maintain information in memory as they navigate between pages or screens.

Design for the environment of use

Effectiveness and safety of the medical device are influenced by the environment in which the device is used. Some environments are loud and hectic, whereas others are quiet. Make sure to understand, characterize, anticipate, and design for the intended environment of use. Do not forget to assess the usability of the device in the representative conditions of use.

Also, consider that devices, originally designed for medical environments, may eventually be used in patient homes (Bitterman, 2011; National Research Council, 2010). This is a concern, because professional health-care environments often have good lighting and ample space ideal for medical equipment. This can be quite different than the home environment, which can be cluttered, with low light, carpeting, cords, children, pets, and other things that get in the way of using the device.

Avoid physical strain and repetitive motion

Wiklund and Weinger (2011) point out that many medical procedures are repetitive, sometimes causing cumulative trauma stress. For instance, laparoscopic surgery is less painful than open surgery for patients, but it is more demanding for surgeons, leading to fatigue and discomfort. During laparoscopic surgery the surgeon holds a more static posture for a longer period of time, causing accumulation of lactic acid and toxins, and subsequent cumulative trauma disorder (Lowndes & Hallbeck, 2014; Supe, Kulkarni, & Supe, 2010).

Wiklund and Weinger (2011) advise to reduce the number of repetitive motions and the force required to operate a device. Also, eliminate pressure points and facilitate the use of neutral joint positions.

Provide timely and informative feedback

Provide informative feedback, enabling users to understand the device's status at all times (Lewis & Norman, 1995; Maglio & Kandogan, 2004; Nielsen, 1994). Despite the best efforts from medical-device manufacturers, device errors and failures occur periodically, and it is important to make users aware of these errors and failures. Ensure that errors are communicated effectively, and recovered from quickly, taking care to guide the user through error resolution. As a rule, in an error situation, a UI should convey: what went wrong, why it went wrong, what the user should do about it, and how to get additional information.

Design with accessibility in mind

Designers often design for able-bodied people by default, perhaps because they are not familiar with the needs of all users or because they do not know how to accommodate them. Human abilities are widely variable, partially due to physiological factors, and also due to differences in experience, motivation, and expectations. This is compounded by age and disability. Medical device users will vary in size, shape, physical ability, intellectual ability, reading ability, technical experience, and so on (Story, Schwier, & Kailes, 2009). Some users will have physical, sensory, or cognitive difficulties. For example, some may have a visual impairment, making it difficult for them to read small fine text. Others may have peripheral neuropathy making it difficult for them to discriminate different textures on button surfaces. It is important to make devices accessible to a wide range of users. Clarkson, Coleman, Keates, and Lebbon (2013) advocate for implementing inclusive design principles that focus on designing for the needs of all people. In essence, the approach is to change the definition of the user at the beginning of the design process to include a wider range of capabilities.

Do not overrely on training and instructions for use

Medical device manufacturers are often too optimistic about the effectiveness of training and IFU in helping users learn how to use new devices (Wright, Creighton, & Threlfall, 1982). Often, these materials are not available to users, especially home health-care providers who travel from one place to another. Finally, even when provided, users are often too busy to read through IFU's or engage in training (Morrow, Leirer, & Sheikh, 1988).

Design with user emotions in mind

Medical devices need to appeal to people emotionally and esthetically (Norman, 2004). Devices with appealing design suggest higher quality, which can generate greater confidence in the user. Well-designed and esthetically pleasing devices can be less intimidating than poorly designed products. They are more likely to facilitate user satisfaction and may look friendlier and reduce anxiety among patients. One example of emotional design, described by Kelley and Kelley (2013), involved redesigning the diagnostic imaging experience for GE Healthcare. Diagnostic imaging with MRI can be intimidating to children, with big machines, confined spaces, and scary noises. One industrial designer, Doug Dietz, recognized this problem, conducted observational research at a day care center, and interviewed experts at a children's museum. This led him to design an adventure, rather than a machine. The Pirate's Adventure uses environmental design and props to make the experience more fun. This resulted in a substantial increase in patient satisfaction, reduction in anxiety, and made it easier for children to stay still during the imaging, preventing doctors from needing to repeat scans.

Not every product can be turned into a Pirate's Adventure, but most products can be improved by implementing an HF process. Next, a case study involving the design of a TAH is discussed. The case study serves to illustrate the HF design process as well as the design principles described previously. In addition, it serves to illustrate the multidisciplinary nature of good design. SynCardia, the manufacturer, worked with an HF firm (Research Collective), an industrial design firm (Farm Design), and a product development firm (Sunrise Product Development). The success of the product hinged on the ability of these groups to work together.

Case Study: SynCardia

Every 10 minutes, a new name is added to the list of patients waiting for an organ transplant in the United States. As the list already has more than 120,000 names, most patients will be waiting months or even years before a donor organ becomes available. Unfortunately, many die while waiting. Each day, 22 people in the United States die while awaiting a donor organ. The problem is that there simply are not enough donors to meet the demand.

SynCardia Systems, LLC makes the world's most widely used temporary TAH. The TAH is implanted into patients suffering from end-stage heart failure to keep them alive and healthy while awaiting a donor heart. The TAH circulates blood in the body through a connection to a driver that provides pneumatic, pulsatile pressure. After the TAH is implanted, patients are connected to the Companion 2 Hospital Driver (Fig. 1.2).

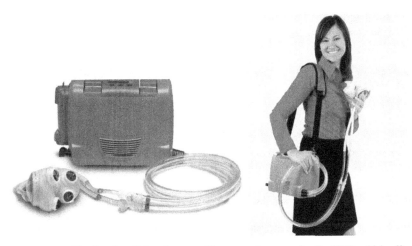

FIGURE 1.3 The Freedom Driver is a portable pneumatic pump for the TAH, which offers increased mobility. Patients who meet discharge criteria can then be released from the hospital to live at home with their families and friends, while they wait for a matching donor heart. *TAH*, Total artificial heart.

After a patient becomes clinically stable, they can be switched to the Freedom Driver (Fig. 1.3), a smaller, lighter pneumatic pump that allows them to be released from the hospital to enjoy active and independent lives at home, while they wait for a matching donor heart.

In 2016 SynCardia implemented a human-centered design strategy to create the next-generation Freedom Driver. This approach began with deepening their understanding of the Freedom Driver users, developing prototypes based on users' needs and desires, and evaluating the prototype designs through user research (see Fig. 1.4 for the evolution of the prototype designs). The final step will be to demonstrate the device's usability through validation usability testing.

Phase 1: Contextual inquiry and participatory design

SynCardia's first step was to conduct user research to understand the needs and desires of device users, which included patients, caregivers, and clinicians. SynCardia performed contextual inquiry research by visiting nine current and former Freedom Driver patients in their homes and 16 clinicians including ventricular assist device coordinators, cardiologists, and cardiology nurses in the hospitals where they work (Fig. 1.5).

Conducting contextual inquiry research in the users' natural setting allowed SynCardia to observe the way users performed device-specific tasks, document the tools and equipment they used to accomplish those tasks, discuss critical instances that occurred in the past, and identify their

Foam model	Appearance model	Functioning prototype
Formative study 2	Formative study 3	Formative study 4

 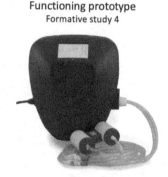

FIGURE 1.4 Foam models were used in formative studies to obtain feedback from patients and clinicians about the ideal shape for the next-generation driver, the orientation and size of the graphical-user interface, the location and style of batteries, the location of the driveline port, and more.

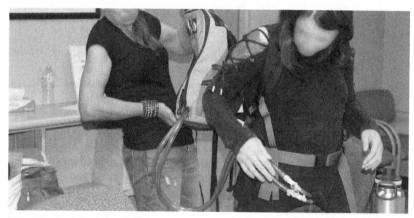

FIGURE 1.5 A patient and her caregiver demonstrate how they prepare to leave the house with the current Freedom Driver.

troubleshooting techniques and work-arounds. The findings from the contextual inquiry provided SynCardia with a detailed list of design criteria for the next-generation Freedom Driver. Findings include the following:

- *Simplify the process of transferring patients from one driver to another:* To do so, the current driver's drivelines have two connectors that must be swapped simultaneously. Swapping drivers is a high-risk task often performed under stressful circumstances when the driver has malfunctioned. Potential harm to the patient includes loss of consciousness or death. Sometimes, the patient has already lost consciousness and a caregiver is responsible for making the swap on his or her own. Patient participants in the study described instances where they had to perform a driver swap in a car, a restaurant, or at a sporting event. The next-generation driver should simplify the process of transferring a patient from one driver to another. The transfer should be able to be performed with one hand within 2 seconds.

- *Provide timely feedback about the status of the pump, batteries, and alarms:* The current driver's LCD display provides important information about the pump's status, but it is small and lacks a backlight. Many patients said that they kept a flashlight by their bed so that they could check their pump's status in the middle of the night. The small font and poor contrast on the LCD made it difficult for patients to check the pump's status when the driver was more than 3 ft away. In addition, the small display does not provide the user with any additional information about the driver's battery status or alarm. The next-generation driver should include a GUI to display the status of the pump and batteries as well as provide alarm descriptions.

- *Provide actionable and easily recognizable instructions on the device*: The current driver does not provide any textual information to accompany an audible alarm. Patients and clinicians described situations where a lack of information about an alarm caused extreme anxiety. One patient said that he was flown by helicopter to a hospital 30 miles away because of a high alarm on the driver. He felt fine, and the driver seemed to be functioning, but the alarm gave him great concern so he called for emergency assistance. In the hospital, he was transferred to another driver, and it was later determined that the cause of the alarm was the failure of a backup system, and was thus not life threatening. He could have transferred to his backup driver at home with much less anxiety and without an expensive emergency flight. Alarm sounds should be unique to the driver, capture patients' and caregivers' attention, and display messages that explain the problem and provide a solution.

Clinician participants also took part in a participatory design exercise, where they were asked to draw their ideal Freedom Driver GUI. SynCardia used the results of this research to create design criteria that would improve the user experience and usability of the next-generation Freedom Driver GUI. A key finding of the participatory design exercise was the clinicians' desire for the GUI to display waveforms, similar to the Companion 2 Hospital Driver, that provide deeper information about the driver's performance. In addition, clinicians' drawings included a display with the ability to manage the driver's settings, including the TAH beat rate (Fig. 1.6). On the current Freedom Driver, clinicians set the beat rate by turning a screw on the back of the driver. The process takes several minutes as the clinician turns the screw, waits for the driver to settle in on the new beat rate, then evaluates if the beat rate is appropriate or should be adjusted again. If a

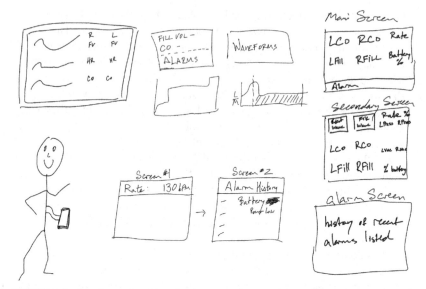

FIGURE 1.6 Drawings created by clinicians who work with Freedom Driver patients when asked to create their ideal Freedom Driver graphical user interface as part of a participatory design exercise.

clinician wants to set the beat rate to a specific value, it may take several attempts, turning the screw clockwise, then counterclockwise until the clinician is able to set the beat rate on that number.

With the design criteria set by the contextual research, SynCardia set out to create prototypes of the next-generation driver, GUI, batteries, and driveline connectors that could be evaluated in formative studies. SynCardia refined the design of the driver's UI elements through prototyping and formative studies with the goal of creating a next-generation Freedom Driver that minimizes potential harm and is easier for patients to live with than the current driver.

Phase 2: Graphical user interface wireframe prototype and formative study 1

As digital displays can be created faster than physical products, SynCardia first set out to make decisions about the GUI. SynCardia wanted to obtain feedback from expert users to determine the optimal size of the display. The display needs to be visible in a wide range of environments (home, hospital, outdoors, etc.) and clearly present information about the driver's status, alarm messages, and battery status. A unique wireframe prototype was created using Adobe XD for each of the possible display sizes (4.3″, 5″, and 7″) (Fig. 1.7).

The prototypes were placed on a tablet and interaction was added to allow users to navigate through the wireframes and perform the task of changing the driver's beat rate. Eight expert clinicians participated in the

FIGURE 1.7 Interactive GUI wireframe prototypes were presented on a tablet. *GUI*, Graphical user interface.

formative study. They performed the task of changing the beat rate and provided feedback about the content displayed on each display size. The study showed that users prefer to see the waveforms when making changes to the beat rate. The 4.3″ display was too small to provide all that contents on the screen at once. The clinicians liked the amount of information provided on the 7″ display but worried that the large display would cause the driver to be bigger and heavier. The 5″ display was determined to be the perfect size. It was big enough for users to see the waveforms when changing the beat rate and would not increase the size and weight of the driver.

Once the screen size was chosen, the focus for the GUI was to make the displayed content visible, legible, and understandable. There were a number of considerations that were taken when determining the characteristics of the display. The bond rule was applied, which states that the height of the letter is set to 0.007 times the viewing distance when both the viewing distance and the letter height are in the same units (Lee et al., 2017). Mixed-case text was used since all-caps is difficult to read, especially in long strings. Mixed-case text, on the other hand, offers a wider variety of word shapes, providing more sensory information that is more easily processed. A high-contrast display, with dark text on a white background contributed to legibility, making the display easy to read even when viewed by older patients and caregivers. Care was taken to minimize the amount of clutter in the display.

Roboto-Regular font, a sans-serif font, was chosen due to its familiarity with users and ease of reading on a computerized display (Lee et al., 2017). Since patients regularly need to read values that indicate the driver's status from a distance of 48 in., and with possible glare, a 30-point font size was chosen for those values. The GUI was refined and evaluated through subsequent formative studies.

Phase 3: Foam models, driveline connector prototypes, and formative study 2

SynCardia created three foam model driver prototypes (Fig. 1.8) and a prototype of the new driveline connector (Fig. 1.9) based on the design criteria determined through the contextual inquiry and participatory design exercise with experienced users.

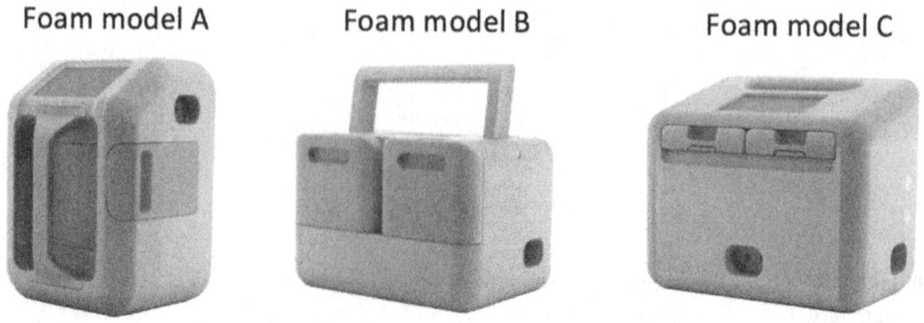

Foam model A   Foam model B   Foam model C

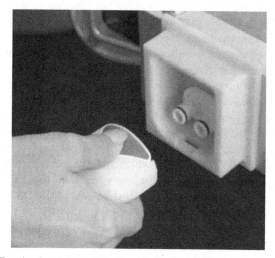

FIGURE 1.8 Foam models used in the second formative study to obtain users' feedback about the size, shape, and the location of batteries, handles, and driveline ports.

FIGURE 1.9 Functional prototype of the new driveline connector.

The foam models and driveline connector were evaluated with a mix of patients, caregivers, and clinicians in a second formative study (Fig. 1.10). The results of this study indicated that the shape of all three foam models would be uncomfortable for patients to carry. Experienced patients and caregivers said that the driver is almost always in a backpack worn by the patient. Therefore the driver should be taller and narrower to fit the shape of a patient's back. The study also revealed that the batteries and GUI should be placed on the top of the driver. Patients prefer to change the batteries when the driver is on the ground or on a table. In either location, the patient would be positioned above the driver so that the batteries would be most accessible on top of the driver. Similarly, a display on the top of the driver, angled as shown in Foam Model A, would be the easiest to see when the driver is at or below eye level. The driveline port should be low on the driver. All patients talked about getting their drivelines caught on things,

FIGURE 1.10 A former patient and his caregiver provide feedback about the shape and size of the foam models in formative study 2.

such as door handles and the corner of countertops. Keeping the driveline port low makes it easier for the patient to keep the drivelines close to their body and reduce uncomfortable snags. The usability of a new driveline connector prototype was also evaluated in this formative study. Participants were asked to transfer the drivelines using a mocked up driver port. Time on task and errors were documented as they performed the swap. All participants were able to perform the swap in less than 1.5 seconds with no errors; SynCardia's goal was for users to complete the swap in 2 seconds or less.

Phase 4: Appearance models, battery prototypes, alarm messages, and formative study 3

In the third formative study, participants evaluated two unique appearance models and foam prototypes that were painted to give the appearance of a finished product (Fig. 1.11), battery prototypes (Fig. 1.12), and alarm messages.

The previous study provided conclusive evidence that the driver's display and batteries should be positioned at the top of the driver, and both appearance models were designed accordingly. However, the models were designed to obtain additional feedback about users' preferences for the overall shape. In the previous formative study, users said that they wanted a driver that was shaped to fit more comfortably in a backpack. The shape of the appearance models was taller and slimmer than the original foam models. The results of the study revealed that the participants preferred the shape of appearance model 2 as it felt more comfortable when worn in a backpack, and the placement of the batteries allowed for quicker access (Fig. 1.13).

This formative study also evaluated five battery prototypes. Batteries with a loop had better usability results than the batteries that required users to pinch or squeeze. This result was expected because pinching is a fine motor skill, whereas grasping is a gross motor skill recruiting more muscles. Batteries with a large loop to accommodate fingers of all sizes were created and evaluated in subsequent formative studies.

Appearance model 1   Appearance model 2

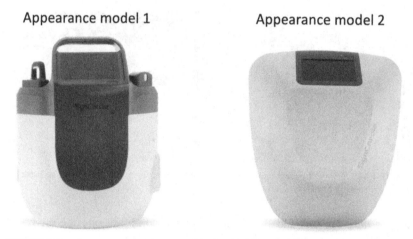

FIGURE 1.11   Appearance models are used in the third formative study to obtain users' feedback about the size, shape, and the location of batteries, handles, and driveline ports.

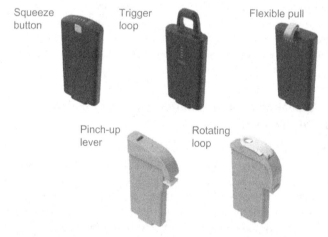

Squeeze   Trigger   Flexible pull
button   loop

          Pinch-up   Rotating
          lever   loop

FIGURE 1.12   Battery prototypes that allowed users to provide feedback about various handle and grip styles.

FIGURE 1.13   Two clinicians discuss the placement of the batteries on an appearance model in formative study 3.

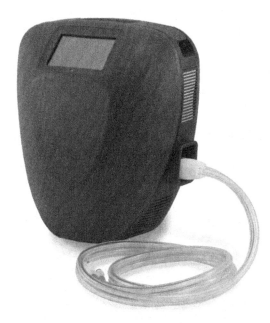

FIGURE 1.14 The functional prototype that contained working pump mechanism, a touchscreen graphical user interface, and alarm sounds and messages.

Messages were developed to explain each possible situation that would cause an alarm to occur. The alarm messages provide the user with the reason for the alarm and instructions for resolving the problem. The messages are written in plain language, for example, "The Driver is getting hot. Make sure the Driver is not covered and has sufficient airflow." The messages do not contain error codes that do not help the user solve the problem, for example, "Error #405." The alarm messages were evaluated to ensure comprehension by each user group.

Phase 5: Functional prototype, auditory alarms, and formative study 4

With the overall shape of the driver decided, SynCardia put the working pump components and GUI into a fully functional prototype (Fig. 1.14). Another formative study was performed with this functional prototype to reevaluate the usability of the process of transferring a patient from one driver to another, setting driver parameters using the touchscreen, and responding to alarms and error messages (Fig. 1.15). Usability was evaluated by documenting participants' successes, difficulties, and use errors when performing tasks. There were no use errors on any of the 21 tasks completed by the 12 participants. This result was achieved by having evaluated all the tasks in the previous formative studies with lower fidelity prototypes.

This formative study also included an evaluation of the auditory alarms. The purpose of auditory alarms on the next-generation Freedom Driver is to bring

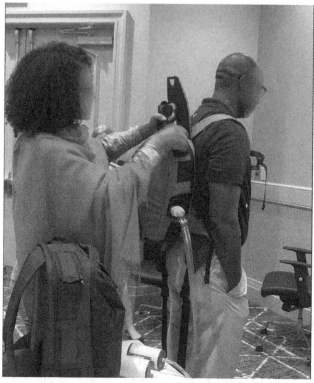

FIGURE 1.15   A former patient and his caregiver replace the batteries in the prototype driver in formative study 4.

attention to the display, where additional information about the alarm and steps to resolve the alarm are provided. The next-generation driver will have two levels of auditory alarms, a low and a high alarm. A low alarm indicates that the device needs attention, but nothing must be done immediately. For example, when the driver's batteries are depleted to 20% remaining, the driver will sound the low alarm and display a message informing the user of the low batteries and prompting the user to replace them. A high alarm indicates that action is needed right away, for example, when the driver malfunctions, the patient must be transferred immediately to the backup driver. The two alarms are designed to be discriminable from each other through the use of volume, frequency, envelope (e.g., a rising sound or a constant sound), and rhythm. The high alarm is louder and the tempo is higher than the lower one. To facilitate audition in a range of environments, the high alarm uses both high and low frequency sounds. The high alarm is designed to be 15–30 dB above the expected ambient noise expected in patients' homes, hospitals, outdoors, in restaurants, etc. Although the alarm is loud, it is not overly startling due to its use of a rise time that starts low and increases quickly. The alarms were triggered at various times in the formative study, and during each time, the users responded appropriately.

Phase	Purpose	Findings	Design recommendations based on human factors principles
Contextual inquiry and participatory design	Understand user needs, desires, limitations, and environments of use	Transferring patients from one driver to another is a high-risk task often performed under stress	The process of transferring patients from one driver to another must be easy
		The current driver does not provide clear status feedback	The driver should provide clear status feedback at all times
		The current driver does not provide instructions to remedy alarms	The driver should clearly explain why alarms occur and provide troubleshooting instructions
		Setting the driver beat rate is difficult and requires the use of tools	The driver should provide a simple process for clinicians to set the beat rate accurately without tools
Graphical user interface wireframe prototype and formative study 1	Evaluate the graphical-user interface information architecture	Clinicians prefer to see waveforms on the display that indicate TAH performance	The display size should be 5" diagonally to provide enough space for clinical information while remaining light
		A 5" display is the smallest size that still provides clinicians with important information about TAH performance	The graphical user interface should provide waveforms using line weight and typeface visible from 4'
			The graphical user interface should use a sans-serif 30-point font
Foam models, driveline connector prototypes, and formative study 2	Evaluate driver shape and handle, battery, display, and port placement	Participants all perform a driver swap effectively, but the latch mechanism on the prototype caused slight delays	The button on the driveline connector should be salient and provide haptic feedback when depressed
		Participants need the driver to be stable to avoid being knocked over and damaged	The driver should have a wide base to provide stability on multiple surfaces
		Participants prefer a display that is angled so that it can be seen when the driver is below or at the same height as the user	The driver should have an angled display

(Continued)

(Continued)

Phase	Purpose	Findings	Design recommendations based on human factors principles
Appearance models, battery prototypes, alarm messages, and formative study 3	Evaluate driver shape and handle, battery, display, and port placement as well as alarm messages	Participants preferred the driver that felt more comfortable when worn in a backpack	The driver should be shaped like a human back—wider at the top and narrower at the bottom
		Participants preferred batteries that had a large loop that facilitated quick removal from the driver	Batteries should provide a large grasping loop that accommodates a wide range of finger sizes
		Alarm messages were clear and all participants responded to them appropriately	Alarm messages should state the problem and clear steps to remedy the problem
Functional prototype, auditory alarms, and formative study 4	Evaluate the look and feel of a functioning driver and assess comprehension of audible alarms	Participants successfully responded to all alarms and successfully transferred from one driver to another	The driver connector that has been refined since formative study 2 appears to meet all requirements for usability to ensure safe transfers from one driver to another
		Participants could distinguish high alarms from medium alarms and alert tones	Alarm tones should be 15–30 dB above ambient noise and include both high and low frequencies

TAH, Total artificial heart.

Next steps

SynCardia's next step will be to complete the engineering and design of the next-generation Freedom Driver and all accompanying UI components (training, IFU, etc.). They will conduct another formative usability study with the completed product to determine if there are any additional usability problems. Once any remaining usability issues have been addressed, SynCardia will perform a final validation usability study to demonstrate that the intended users can safely and effectively use the next-generation Freedom Driver.

Conclusion

First, incorporating HF principles and methods into medical device design can reduce the likelihood of physical or psychological injury to patients, caregivers, and health-care providers. Second, HF can help to create devices that are easier to learn, more efficient and satisfying to use, and better suited to fit into peoples' lives. When implemented early in design, the application of HF principles can lead to a more streamlined development process— avoiding costly time delays when it becomes apparent that a device does not meet user needs or could lead to unnecessary injury or death.

References

Association for the Advancement of Medical Instrumentation (AAMI). (2009). *ANSI/AAMI HE75 human factors engineering - Design of medical devices.*

Beyer, H., & Holtzblatt, K. (1997). *Contextual design: Defining customer-centered systems.* Elsevier.

Bitterman, N. (2011). Design of medical devices—A home perspective. *European Journal of Internal Medicine, 22*(1), 39–42.

Branaghan, R. J. (2018). Human factors in medical device design: Methods, principles and guidelines. *Critical Care Nursing Clinics, 2,* 225–236.

Branaghan, R. J., Covas-Smith, C. M., Jackson, K. D., & Eidman, C. (2011). Using knowledge structures to redesign an instructor–operator station. *Applied Ergonomics, 42*(6), 934–940.

Clarkson, P. J., Coleman, R., Keates, S., & Lebbon, C. (2013). *Inclusive design: Design for the whole population.* Springer Science & Business Media.

Faulkner, L. (2003). Beyond the five-user assumption: Benefits of increased sample sizes in usability testing. *Behavior Research Methods, Instruments, and Computers, 35*(3), 379–383.

Hanington, B., & Martin, B. (2012). *Universal methods of design: 100 ways to research complex problems, develop innovative ideas, and design effective solutions.* Rockport Publishers.

International Standards Organization (ISO). (2015). *Medical devices - Part 1: Application of usability engineering to medical devices.*

Israelski, E. W., & Muto, W. H. (2004). Human factors risk management as a way to improve medical device safety: A case study of the therac 25 radiation therapy system. *The Joint Commission Journal on Quality and Safety, 30*(12), 689–695.

Kelley, T., & Kelley, D. (2013). *Creative confidence: Unleashing the creative potential within us all.* Crown Business.

Kinsella, K. G., & Phillips, D. R. (2005). *Global aging: The challenge of success* (Vol. 60, No. 1, p. 3). Washington, DC: Population Reference Bureau.

Kuniavsky, M. (2003). *Observing the user experience: A practitioner's guide to user research.* Elsevier.

Lee, J. D., Wickens, C. D., Liu, Y., & Boyle, L. N. (2017). *Designing for people: An introduction to human factors engineering.* CreateSpace.

Lewis, C., & Norman, D. A. (1995). Designing for error. In R. M. Baeker, J. Grudin, W. A. S. Buxton, & S. Greenberg (Eds.), *Readings in human–computer interaction* (2nd ed, pp. 686–697). Morgan Kaufmann.

Lowndes, B. R., & Hallbeck, M. S. (2014). Overview of human factors and ergonomics in the OR, with an emphasis on minimally invasive surgeries. *Human Factors and Ergonomics in Manufacturing & Service Industries, 24*(3), 308–317.

Maglio, P. P., & Kandogan, E. (2004). Error messages: What's the problem? *Queue, 2*(8), 50–55.

Menotti, A., Puddu, P. E., Maiani, G., & Catasta, G. (2015). Lifestyle behaviour and lifetime incidence of heart diseases. *International Journal of Cardiology, 201,* 293–299.

Merriam, S. B. (2009). *Qualitative research: A guide to design and implementation.* John Wiley & Sons.

Morrow, D., Leirer, V., & Sheikh, J. (1988). Adherence and medication instructions review and recommendations. *Journal of the American Geriatrics Society, 36*(12), 1147–1160.

National Research Council. (2010). *The role of human factors in home health care: Workshop summary.* National Academies Press.

Nielsen, J. (1994). Heuristic evaluation. In J. Nielsen, & R. L. Mack (Eds.), *Usability inspection methods.* New York: John Wiley & Sons.

Norman, D. A. (2004). *Emotional design: Why we love (or hate) everyday things.* Basic Civitas Books.

Page, T. (2009). Feature creep and usability in consumer electronic product design. *International Journal of Product Development, 9*(4), 406–428.

Polson, P. G., Lewis, C., Rieman, J., & Wharton, C. (1992). Cognitive walkthroughs: A method for theory-based evaluation of user interfaces. *International Journal of Man-Machine Studies, 36*(5), 741–773.

Redish, J. G., Bias, R. G., Bailey, R., Molich, R., Dumas, J., & Spool, J. M. (2002). *Usability in practice: formative usability evaluations-evolution and revolution. CHI'02 extended abstracts on human factors in computing systems* (pp. 885–890). ACM.

Rowe, J. W., & Kahn, R. L. (2015). Successful aging 2.0: Conceptual expansions for the 21st century. *The Journals of Gerontology: Series B, 70*(4), 593–596.

Rubin, J., & Chisnell, D. (2008). *Handbook of usability testing.* Wiley.

Rust, R. T., Thompson, D. V., & Hamilton, R. W. (2006). Defeating feature fatigue. *Harvard Business Review, 84*(2), 37–47.

Sanders, E. B. N., & Stappers, P. J. (2008). Co-creation and the new landscapes of design. *Co-Design, 4*(1), 5–18.

Sanders, E. B. N., & William, C. T. (2002). Harnessing people's creativity: Ideation and expression through visual communication. In J. Langford, & D. McDonagh (Eds.), *Focus groups: Supporting effective product development* (pp. 137–148). New York: CRC Press.

Smetzer, J., Baker, C., Byrne, F. D., & Cohen, M. R. (2010). Shaping systems for better behavioral choices: Lessons learned from a fatal medication error. *The Joint Commission Journal on Quality and Patient Safety, 36*(4), 152–AP2.

Stamatis, D. H. (2003). *Failure mode and effect analysis: FMEA from theory to execution.* ASQ Quality Press.

Story, M. F. (2012). The FDA perspective on human factors in medical device software development. *Presented at: 2012 IQPC Software Design for Medical Devices.* Europe Munich, Germany —February 1, 2012. Available at: https://www.fda.gov/media/83044/download.

Story, M. F., Schwier, E., & Kailes, J. I. (2009). Perspectives of patients with disabilities on the accessibility of medical equipment: Examination tables, imaging equipment, medical chairs, and weight scales. *Disability and Health Journal, 2*(4), 169—179.

Supe, A. N., Kulkarni, G. V., & Supe, P. A. (2010). Ergonomics in laparoscopic surgery. *Journal of Minimal Access Surgery, 6*(2), 31.

United States Food and Drug Administration (FDA). (2016a). *List of highest priority devices for human factors review: Draft guidance for industry and Food and Drug Administration Staff.* https://www.fda.gov/downloads/MedicalDevices/DeviceRegulationandGuidance/ GuidanceDocuments/UCM484097.pdf. Retrieved April 15, 2019.

United States Food and Drug Administration (FDA). (2016b). *Applying human factors and usability engineering to medical devices.* https://www.fda.gov/downloads/MedicalDevices/ .../UCM259760.pdf. Retrieved October 31, 2018.

United States Food and Drug Administration (FDA). (2018). *Is the product a medical device?* https://www.fda.gov/medicaldevices/deviceregulationandguidance/overview/classifyyourdevice/ucm051512.htm. Retrieved September 16, 2018.

Wachter, R. M. (2012). *Understanding patient safety* (2nd ed.). New York: McGraw-Hill Medical.

Weisburger, J. H. (2002). Lifestyle, health and disease prevention: the underlying mechanisms. *European Journal of Cancer Prevention, 11*, 1—7.

Wiklund, M. E., & Weinger, M. B. (2011). General principles. In M. B. Weinger, M. E. Wiklund, & D. J. Gardner-Bonneau (Eds.), *Handbook of human factors in medical device design.* New York: CRC Press.

World Health Organization. (2018). *Medical device - Full definition.* <http://www.who.int/medical_devices/full_deffinition/en/> Retrieved September 16, 2018.

Wright, P., Creighton, P., & Threlfall, S. M. (1982). Some factors determining when instructions will be read. *Ergonomics, 25*(3), 225—237.

Zhang, J., Johnson, T. R., Patel, V. L., Paige, D. L., & Kubose, T. (2003). Using usability heuristics to evaluate patient safety of medical devices. *Journal of Biomedical Informatics, 36* (1—2), 23—30.

Zhang, J., Patel, V. L., Johnson, T. R., & Shortliffe, E. H. (2004). A cognitive taxonomy of medical errors. *Journal of Biomedical Informatics, 37*(3), 193—204.

Further reading

Kieras, D. E., & Bovair, S. (1984). The role of a mental model in learning to operate a device. *Cognitive Science, 8*(3), 255—273.

Loftus, G. R. (1985). Evaluating forgetting curves. *Journal of Experimental Psychology: Learning, Memory, and Cognition, 11*(2), 397.

Chapter 2

Designing for medication safety

Sadaf Kazi[1], Allen R. Chen[1,2] and Nicole L. Mollenkopf[1,3]
[1]Armstrong Institute for Patient Safety and Quality, Johns Hopkins University School of Medicine, Baltimore, MD, United States, [2]Departments of Oncology and Pediatrics, Johns Hopkins University School of Medicine, Baltimore, MD, United States, [3]Johns Hopkins University School of Nursing, Baltimore, MD, United States

Designing for medication safety

One of the most common interventions in health care is medication use. Although simple when contrasted against interventions such as surgery, the high incidence of adverse drug events (Bates et al., 1995; Bates, 1997) highlights the complexity and risk inherent in the medication-use process. This process comprises multiple interconnected stages: prescribing, order processing, dispensing, administration, and monitoring (Institute for Safe Medication Practices, 2018). Not only is there considerable variation in how steps are executed across stages (Pevnick, Shane, & Schnipper, 2016), but the interconnected nature of the stages may also mean that errors made in one stage often have a cascading effect on subsequent stages (Carayon et al., 2014).

The involvement of many stakeholders (e.g., patients, physicians, nurses, medical assistants, pharmacists, and pharmacy technicians) results in frequent handoffs throughout the medication-use process. Poor communication during handoffs can result in inefficiencies and errors (Arora, Kao, Lovinger, Seiden, & Meltzer, 2007; Petersen et al., 1994). Technology, such as decision support tools and electronic health records (EHR), can facilitate information sharing and decision support, and replace handwritten charts and fax machines to order medications. However, insufficient consideration of design challenges that arise in human−automation interaction (Parasuraman, Sheridan, & Wickens, 2000) may result in risks in the use of these technologies to safely accomplish tasks in the medication-use process (Koppel et al., 2005).

Medication errors during care transitions

Errors can occur at any point in the medication-use process. At care transitions, however, the medication-use system is especially vulnerable to

Design for Health. DOI: https://doi.org/10.1016/B978-0-12-816427-3.00002-6
31

problems that can lead to errors and harm. For example, Boockvar et al. (2004) found that adverse drug events that occurred during care transitions were implicated in hospital readmissions from nursing homes. Care transitions present diverse vulnerabilities to the medication-use process, including temporary medication changes made to the care plan becoming permanent during transitions, or medications failing to be reordered correctly, and unavailability or inaccuracy of the prior medication list. These problems demonstrate the importance of shared information and knowledge about the patient in devising the care plan. A formal process to assess medications at transitions points, known as medication reconciliation, is viewed by professional, regulatory, and standard-setting agencies as essential to minimize preventable harm and errors.

Medication reconciliation

The Joint Commission (2006) defines medication reconciliation as assembling the "best possible medication history, and using this list to provide correct medication to the patient at all points of care." The medication reconciliation process consists of (1) gathering a patient's "home" list of medications currently being taken, (2) comparing that list to the medications that are currently prescribed for that patient at the transition point, and (3) utilizing medication information to inform prescribing at the current point in time, as well as in the future.

The list of home medications informs subsequent parts of the medication reconciliation process. "Home" may refer to the patient's home, or any setting in which the patient receives care prior to the transition. In the inpatient setting, transitions could include hospital admission, transfer between different levels of care (e.g., critical care and intermediate care) or care provider teams, and hospital discharge. In the community setting, patients may transition between a variety of provider types (e.g., primary care provider and specialist), setting types (e.g., outpatient surgery center), or even multiple pharmacies.

Assembling the medication list from home and the current setting of care requires specialized skills. This responsibility has historically fallen to the prescribing physician. However, because gathering this information can be difficult and time-consuming, there is now greater involvement of nonphysician providers with varying levels of medication knowledge, such as nurses, medical assistants, pharmacy technicians, and pharmacists, in obtaining the home medication list. In inpatient settings, nursing involvement at error-prone stages during care transitions, including gathering the medication list at admission (White et al., 2011) and verifying the medication list at discharge (Pronovost et al., 2003), has translated to improved rates of medication reconciliation.

It is noteworthy that involving pharmacists and pharmacy technicians not only improves the completion rate of medication reconciliation but also, more importantly, the completeness and quality of the medication history elicited from the patient (Pevnick et al., 2018; Varkey et al., 2007), and doing so is cost effective (Karnon, Campbell, & Czoski-Murray, 2009). These improvements can be attributed to the specialized medication knowledge of pharmacy staff and the substantial time spent in collecting medication histories. Depending on the study, this time may range between 20 and 40 minutes, but collecting the medication histories of medically complex patients can also be as high as almost 80 minutes (Pevnick et al., 2018).

The final step of medication reconciliation is prescribing medications to meet the current and future needs of the patient. This entails resolving differences, if they exist, between medication lists, prescribing appropriate medications based on current illnesses and patient-related factors (e.g., physiologic and pathophysiologic parameters, adherence to medication, medication cost, and access to pharmacy), updating the medication list, and communicating the updated medication list with the patient.

Challenges with completing medication reconciliation

Quality of medication reconciliation

Despite being recognized as a formal component of high quality health care by various organizations in the United States since the mid-2000s (The Joint Commission, 2006; Patient Protection and Affordable Care Act, 2010), there remains disagreement about what constitutes safe, accurate, and high-quality medication reconciliation. Initial efforts to improve medication reconciliation focused on improving performance rates without always considering the quality of the process (Pevnick et al., 2016). For example, it is possible to increase the compliance rates of medication reconciliation in some EHRs by checking a single box that indicates completion of the process. The ideal medication history, however, requires elicitation and documentation of multiple details about home and clinic medications: medication name, dose, frequency, and time of last dose for prescribed and over-the-counter (OTC) supplemental medication, in addition to an assessment of the patient's understanding of and ability to manage their medications (Pevnick & Schnipper, 2017). It is possible for prescribers to bypass these details and yet check the box indicating completion of medication reconciliation (Kazi, Khunlertkit, & Chen, 2017).

Multisource verification

It is critical to forego reliance on a single source and instead collate and synthesize information about the home medication list from multiple sources, such as medication bottles, prescription notes, and pharmacy dispensing information. This is because unitary sources of information, by themselves, may not accurately capture the home medication list (Hummel, Evans, & Lee, 2010; Lee, Nishimura, Ngu, Tieu, & Auerbach, 2014). However, limitations in availability of multiple sources of information, and time required to gather this information, make it difficult to achieve multisource verification.

Involvement of multiple stakeholders

When multiple stakeholders are involved in assembling the home medication list, the time at which each health-care provider engages with the medication list to accomplish medication reconciliation may not be arranged in a logical, linear manner to positively impact medication safety (Pevnick et al., 2016). For example, the pharmacist may assemble the admission medication history after medication orders have been written by the physician. Orders written without eliciting a complete medication history may have the risk of omitting information or medications important to the patient's profile.

Technology design

The design of technology required to accomplish medication reconciliation may not conform with providers' knowledge, workflow, and expectations. For example, Van Stiphout et al. (2015) found that EHR design did not provide an option to document the side effects of medication. Instead, the only option was to document this information in an "allergies" box. In addition, integrating details across disparate sources (e.g., current and previous medication lists on the electronic medical record (EMR), pharmacy records, the patient, and pill bottles) may adversely affect the completion of medication reconciliation (Hummel et al., 2010). Information access costs, including difficulties in the availability or access of details about medication at the point of care, may hinder obtaining information that is essential in completing medication reconciliation.

Design guidelines for medication reconciliation

Substantial progress has been made in the development of processes and tools to reduce challenges with performing high-quality medication reconciliation. We classify these developments as supporting two distinct stages involved in medication reconciliation: (1) assembly of the home medication list, and (2) performing the reconciliation process between distinct lists. Principles to support list assembly focus on strengthening larger, macro-level aspects of the organization. Guidelines to support the reconciliation process focus on interface design.

Assembling the home medication list

- Provide general training about roles and responsibilities of all stakeholders in assembling the medication list in addition to providing training on role-specific duties. For example, Wright et al. (2017) trained nurses in eliciting and documenting medication history on the EHR, whereas physicians were trained in reviewing the history, documenting medication reconciliation, and generating an after-visit summary, and medical assistants were trained in printing the summary and generating the next appointment.
- Use local unit-based champions to help support redesigned roles and responsibilities of stakeholders (Wright et al., 2017).
- Use just-in-time training to reinforce the use of electronic tools to assemble the medication list (Wright et al., 2017).
- Write medication lists in a manner to support multistakeholder comprehension (Saleem, Herout, & Wilck, 2016).
- Support search for medication-related information during list assembly (e.g., interaction profile of medications, supporting search for medications with ambiguous spellings, and alert to look-alike and sound-alike medications [Horsky & Ramelson, 2016]).
- Support consolidation of information from multisource verification (Van Stiphout et al., 2015).
- Provide a venue to compile salient points and challenges about the medication list and to communicate these points to the prescriber who will complete medication reconciliation.
- Alert other team members about incomplete aspects of the assembled medication list to avoid reduplication of information-gathering efforts. For example, Hummel et al. (2010) proposed flagging patients who had incomplete medication histories to set off a targeted search of the missing information. Relatedly, in our own work, we found that it may be useful to get cues about aspects of the list that are incomplete or are relying on input from other providers for completion (Kazi et al., 2017).

Performing reconciliation

- The ordering of each unique medication list on the prescriber interface should correspond to the patient's journey in the system, that is, begin from the intake list and end with the discharge list (Plaisant et al., 2013; Plaisant, Wu, Hettinger, Powsner, & Shneiderman, 2015).
- Provide the user the option to group the medication list according to therapeutic category (Plaisant et al., 2013, 2015) or disease condition (Bitan et al., 2019).
- Use spatial cues to highlight similarities and differences between lists. For example, the Twinlist interface (Plaisant et al., 2013) inserted the

greatest distance between unique medications from intake and discharge lists, and arranged common medications in the center.

- Support recognition over recall when two lists need to be compared by presenting them side by side. Having lists on separate screens will require memorization and recall from the first list to the second (Horsky & Ramelson, 2016).
- Alert users to redundancies and discrepancies in dose, frequency, and routes of medications from different lists, for example, through grouping or highlighting (Kramer et al., 2016; Plaisant et al., 2013, 2015).
- Present options to indicate uncertainty about medication because of lack of details (e.g., "Clarify" button by Kramer et al. [2016]).
- Present piecemeal information to support information processing and decision-making during distinct stages of the reconciliation process. For example, Plaisant et al. (2013, 2015) first presented the alphabetized intake and discharge lists next to each other. Second, identical medications between the lists were spatially moved closer. Third, unique medications were moved further away. Fourth, differences between similar medications were highlighted. Finally, the display was compacted by categorizing and moving medications based on uniqueness and redundancies.
- Lengthy lists that require scrolling to reach the end of the list may result in users forgetting to reconcile medications at the bottom of the list. This was resolved by Plaisant et al. by leaving the last step (signing off) at the end of the list, requiring the user to scroll down.
- Provide feedback that a medication has been successfully managed (e.g., background color change in Kramer et al. [2016]).
- Recognize the tasks that medication lists are used in while building in design features to also support the list assembly and reconciliation. For example, prescribers may elicit medication information when the patient is verbalizing the problem list of symptoms but forget to later reconcile these medications. Integrating strategies to reduce the resulting prospective memory and postcompletion errors (e.g., encoding specific details about the context in which tasks have to be performed; Kazi, Durso, & Thomas, under review) may help in improving the rate of medication reconciliation.

Case study: medication reconciliation

Although there is a theoretical framework for what constitutes medication reconciliation, the best practice outlining how to carry out the process, the optimal personnel, and technology support remains unclear. Our study aimed to uncover the current state of the system of performing medication reconciliation and test its concordance with the best practices (e.g., documenting details about medication and prioritizing high-risk steps) in an outpatient setting.

Methods and design

We used several human factors methods to uncover the complexities in performing medication reconciliation. A human factors psychologist (author SK) conducted *direct observations* of 10 health-care providers (including attending physicians, fellows, nurse practitioners, and nurses) and two medical assistants to understand the process of medication reconciliation during outpatient visits. These direct observations were a vehicle to conduct cognitive task analysis (CTA) and user analysis.

CTA involves analyzing discrete steps involved in any process with a special focus on the goals, activities, skills, cognitive demands, errors, and strategies involved in accomplishing any task (Crandall, Klein, & Hoffman, 2006; Militello & Hutton, 1998). CTA is a valuable tool in revealing when information needs arise in the medication-reconciliation process, and shortcuts, workarounds, and strategies that experts (e.g., attendings and nurse practitioners) and novices (e.g., fellows) use to satisfy these needs at different steps in the process (e.g., consulting with other stakeholders, such as patients, nurses, and medical assistants; accessing information on the EHR). The observations focused on understanding stages during the patient visit when elements of medication reconciliation were performed, stakeholders who were involved in assembling the list of home and clinic medications, stages at which the stakeholders were involved and roles and responsibilities at each stage, information needs of stakeholders, and artifacts that were used to support the assembly of the list. CTA was also used to investigate cognitive challenges in interacting with interfaces (e.g., uncertainties in location of relevant information, searching for medication information, integrating information from multiple sources, and documenting information relayed by the patient).

Understanding discrete steps in the process also helps understand characteristics of stakeholders and users who are involved in the process. *User analysis* (Dillon & Watson, 1996) can be helpful in understanding the profiles of users of the system. This includes analyzing individual differences in characteristics, such as education level, domain knowledge, experience, skills, and abilities, which may influence how users interact with the system. In our study, we defined users not only as health-care prescribers, such as physicians and nurses, but also providers who supported prescribers, including pharmacists and medical assistants, and patients. Once we understand the cognitive demands of the task of medication reconciliation, as well as characteristics of users in the system, we can analyze whether users have the necessary knowledge, skills, and abilities to effectively perform their roles.

Finally, we conducted a *field experiment* on 18 oncology providers (five attending physicians, seven fellows, one physician assistant, and four nurse practitioners) from an academic medical center to understand how prescribers accomplished medication reconciliation in the outpatient setting. The experiment was designed to capture the workflow involved in assembling the complex medication history for a *standardized patient* in oncology. We collaborated with subject matter experts in oncology and pharmacy to design elements to increase the realism of our field experiment. First, an oncologist (author AC) created a fictional medical profile for the standardized patient on the EHR test environment. The profile contained the medical and oncologic history, oncology treatment plan, and medications. To test skills in eliciting and documenting a nuanced medication history, we also programmed errors into the profile, including wrong medication, wrong frequency, and medication omissions. The participants in our study could interact with all parts of the EHR related to this standardized patient profile. Second, we created a script that the standardized patient (author NM) could follow to respond to any medication-related questions by the study participants.

Participants were asked to complete medication reconciliation in the EHR and were tested individually in empty patient rooms. All sessions were observed by a human factors psychologist (author SK), who recorded the details elicited for each medication, time taken to reconcile each medication, and whether participants detected and corrected dose and frequency errors on the medication list. In addition, other general observations, such as which sections of the EHR were accessed to complete medication reconciliation, task-switching behaviors, and general workflow of performing medication reconciliation, were also recorded. Although participants were told that the study was to understand the workflow of medication reconciliation, we did not inform them about the specific metrics that we were interested in. At the end of the experiment, participants were administered the system usability scale (Brooke, 1996) to investigate the usability of the EHR in supporting medication reconciliation.

Results

Our primary metric for the field experiment involved assessing the quality of medication reconciliation, including completion of details deemed essential by the Joint Commission and Institution for Safe Medication Practices (ISMP), and time on task. We also used a human systems integration (HSI) approach to frame the combined findings from the CTA, user analysis, and field experiment. The HSI perspective was detailed by the United States Air Force (2009) and recognizes the following nine components: manpower, personnel, training, human factors engineering, safety, environment, occupational health, survivability, and habitability. For the purpose of our study, however, only the first five of these components were relevant. Table 2.1 list

TABLE 2.1 Human systems integrations considerations in medication reconciliation.

HSI component	Description	Considerations for medication reconciliation
Manpower	The number and types of distinct personnel that are available to operate, maintain, and support the system	• Which stakeholders (including patients and health-care providers) are available to participate in completing medication reconciliation? • How many distinct types of health-care providers (e.g., prescribers, nonprescribers) are essential to ensure safe and high-quality medication reconciliation? • Which providers are the most cost-effective in safely and accurately performing medication reconciliation?
Personnel	The knowledge, skills, aptitudes, experience levels, and abilities required to operate and maintain the system	• What knowledge, skills, aptitudes, experience, and abilities are essential to perform high-quality medication reconciliation? • Knowledge of medications and how they are used (e.g., dosing and frequency; McDonald, Mansukhani, Kokotajlo, Diaz, & Robinson, 2018) • Ability to elicit (from patients and other sources) a reliable list of current/home prescription and OTC medications, dietary supplements, including details about how the medication is being taken (e.g., dose, frequency, route, and time of last dose) • Ability to determine accuracy of information elicited from the patient (e.g., does the regimen make sense?), whether based on current knowledge, or the ability to research drug references or other electronic or physical sources • Operate the EHR to obtain and document a reliable medication list and perform reconciliation • Understanding of workflow and roles of personnel
Training	The instruction and resources required by personnel with the requisite knowledge, skills, and abilities to competently perform their job	Training on how to effectively perform medication reconciliation should include (Keogh et al., 2016) • What information sources should be accessed (e.g., patient/family, pharmacy benefits information, and community pharmacy records) • How to use electronic tools (e.g., EHR and health information exchanges) to obtain and document medication information • Which types of information to collect (e.g., prescription and OTC medications and drug allergy information)

(Continued)

TABLE 2.1 (Continued)

HSI component	Description	Considerations for medication reconciliation
		• How to use interview techniques (e.g., use of open-ended questions) to effectively elicit medication information from patients • Understanding of local workflows, including of roles and responsibilities of personnel involved in medication reconciliation process
Human factors engineering	Applying knowledge about human capabilities and limitations to design, develop, modify, and evaluate systems with a goal toward optimizing human systems performance	• Individual factors (e.g., physical and cognitive capacities and limitations of key stakeholders involved in the medication reconciliation process) • Task factors (e.g., complexity, need to integrate information from multiple sources; involvement of multiple stakeholders, specialized knowledge, drug–drug interaction, and managing alerts) • Technology design (e.g., visual layout of the EHR, information availability and ease of access, EHR opacity, and medication alerts) and artifacts (e.g., pill bottles and paper prescriptions) • Operational conditions (e.g., time pressure to complete patient visit and limited access to information from primary care physician) • Physical environment (e.g., design of patient room making it difficult to display home medication list to the patient) • Organizational factors (e.g., rules from regulatory bodies, including local institutional, state, and national, international organizations)
Safety	Design and operational characteristics to minimize the likelihood of accidents or mishaps to operators that threaten system survivability	How do components of the medication reconciliation system interact to ensure patient safety? (Cohen, 2007) • Does the system provide detection methods (e.g., system redundancies) to make errors obvious to personnel so they can be corrected before causing patient harm? • Are strategies aimed at preventing, mitigating, or working around errors (Durso, Ferguson, et al., 2015)? • Does the system have the ability to recognize when an error reaches a patient so as to quickly mitigate patient harm? • Is the system simplified (e.g., removal of unnecessary steps) and standardized (e.g., the best method to accomplish steps outlined and consistently used by personnel) to support safety?

Note: Descriptions of HSI components were adapted from the Air Force Human Systems Integration Handbook: Planning and Execution of Human Systems Integration. *EHR,* Electronic health records; *HSI,* human systems integration; *OTC,* over-the-counter.

HSI considerations that can inform design recommendations for medication reconciliation.

Despite providers being drawn from the same specialty (i.e., oncology), there was considerable variation in how the medication list was assembled. Instead of being guided by the category of medication (e.g., cancer vs non-cancer), the interface design determined the medication details that were elicited. Providers were more likely to elicit dose and frequency for medications that had to be newly added to the EHR than for medications that were already present in the EHR (Kazi et al., 2017).

The observations and simulations also made it apparent that the current system of medication reconciliation is complex and prioritizes efficiency over quality. Indeed, with operational constraints, such as limited patient visit time, work force constraints, and EHR design limitations, it may be challenging to perform high-quality medication reconciliation. However, it is also possible to leverage the complex nature of interactions and interdependencies between the components of the medication reconciliation system to improve its quality.

An HSI perspective is broader than a human factors perspective in its consideration of multi-system influences on human performance, and appreciation for dynamics that arise from interactions between systems (Durso, Boehm-Davis, & Lee, 2015). We use this perspective to highlight essential considerations that can enhance the quality of medication reconciliation (see Table 2.1). Manpower and personnel considerations focus on availability, knowledge, skills, attitudes, and abilities to perform medication reconciliation, such as basic medication knowledge, ability to navigate drug information sources, skill in patient interview techniques, and an understanding of medication reconciliation workflows and roles of personnel.

Personnel considerations can help inform training requirements to ensure that diverse personnel can perform essential tasks in medication reconciliation. Although pharmacists and pharmacy technicians possess knowledge that make them ideal for participating in this step, their availability is limited, particularly in the ambulatory clinic setting. In community settings, clinical staff medical assistants with no-to-low formal training in medications and medication-use principles may assist in the process of obtaining, verifying or modifying home medication lists, provided they have completed 5 hours of order entry training, which does not specifically include medication orders (Shane, 2016). Training should be based on documented workflows, should include didactic and experiential elements, as well as demonstration of competency prior to personnel working independently in the medication reconciliation process (Pevnick & Schnipper, 2017). Human factors engineering (Carayon et al., 2014; Carayon, 2006) investigates how interactions between components of the sociotechnical system (e.g., individual stakeholders, task factors, technology, operational condition, physical environment, and organization factors) impact outcome measures, such as safe and high-quality medication reconciliation.

A medication reconciliation system that is resilient to errors can be built through multiple layers of safety. It would be ideal to design the system to prevent the occurrence of errors. When prevention is not possible, strategies should be available to mitigate the effect of the error or work around the error without threatening system safety (Durso, Ferguson, Kazi, Cunningham, & Ryan, 2015). The system should be capable of detecting signs of impending errors (e.g., alerting about error-prone medication regimens for complex patients) or phases when the system enters states of low resilience so that stakeholders can take corrective action to minimize the effects of the error. In ecological systems, early warning signs of low resilience include critical slowing down and slowed recovery from challenges (Scheffer et al., 2009). Applied to medication safety, this may mean slowed detection of and recovery from errors made in assembling the medication list or reconciling medication, similar types of errors being repeated, and reduced capacity to manage new challenges in the medication reconciliation system (e.g., unavailability of access to historical medication information). The ability to detect errors, for example, through event-reporting systems can help in maintaining transparency about error rates and trends in errors (Leape, 2002).

Conclusion

Medication reconciliation entails eliciting complex information about medications and reconciling divergent information with a goal toward accurately prescribing medications. This system comprises multiple components: stakeholders, the built environment, task and work characteristics, compliance with accreditation and regulatory elements, etc. These components interact with each other, are influenced by the design of the system in which they are contained, and shape the performance and safety of the overall system. Although pharmacist-elicited medication history can help alleviate some challenges with medication reconciliation, because of resource constraints, it is not feasible to rely solely on pharmacists. It is important to strengthen other parts of the system to accomplish safe medication reconciliation. One way to do this is by using decision support to aid the elicitation and integration of information that is essential to completing reliable medication reconciliation (Plaisant et al., 2015).

Technological advances hold the promise of addressing safety and efficiency concerns in medication safety. However, without an appreciation of human factors issues, technology may not only increase the complexity of the medication reconciliation process but also worsen existing problems. Using an HSI approach can help generate new insights into drivers of adverse events, offer unique solutions to alleviate longstanding problems, and help in designing systems that are relatively resilient to errors. When applied to medication reconciliation, the HSI perspective can not only add to our understanding of specific features of technology design that may aid health-care professionals in obtaining, verifying, and reconciling medications but also inform details about staffing, personnel characteristics, and training requirements that can improve both the safety and efficiency of the medication reconciliation process.

References

Arora, V., Kao, J., Lovinger, D., Seiden, S. C., & Meltzer, D. (2007). Medication discrepancies in resident sign-outs and their potential to harm. *Journal of General Internal Medicine, 22* (12), 1751–1755. Available from https://doi.org/10.1007/s11606-007-0415-x.

Bates, D. W. (1997). The costs of adverse drug events in hospitalized patients. *JAMA: The Journal of the American Medical Association, 277*(4), 307. Available from https://doi.org/10.1001/jama.1997.03540280045032.

Bates, D. W., Cullen, D. J., Laird, N., Petersen, L. A., Small, S. D., Servi, D., & Hallisey, R. (1995). Incidence of adverse drug events and potential adverse drug events. Implications for prevention. ADE Prevention Study Group [see comments]. *JAMA, 274*(1), 29–34. Available from https://doi.org/10.1016/S1075-4210(05)80011-2.

Bitan, Y., Parmet, Y., Greenfield, G., Teng, S., Cook, R. I., & Nunnally, M. E. (2019). Making sense of the cognitive task of medication reconciliation using a card sorting task. *Human Factors.* Available from https://doi.org/10.1177/0018720819837037.

Boockvar, K., Fishman, E., Kyriacou, C. K., Monias, A., Gavi, S., & Cortes, T. (2004). Adverse events due to discontinuations in drug use and dose changes in patients transferred between acute and long-term care facilities. *Archives of Internal Medicine, 164*(5), 545–550. Available from https://doi.org/10.1001/archinte.164.5.545.

Brooke, J. (1996). SUS: A "quick and dirty" usability scale. In P. W. Jordan, B. Thomas, B. A. Weerdmeester, & A. L. McClelland (Eds.), Usability Evaluation in Industry. *London.* Taylor and Francis.

Carayon, P. (2006). Human factors of complex sociotechnical systems. *Applied Ergonomics, 37* (4), 525–535. Available from https://doi.org/10.1016/j.apergo.2006.04.011.

Carayon, P., Wetterneck, T. B., Rivera-Rodriguez, A. J., Hundt, A. S., Hoonakker, P., Holden, R. J., & Gurses, A. P. (2014). Human factors systems approach to healthcare quality and patient safety. *Applied Ergonomics, 45*, 14–25. Available from https://doi.org/10.1016/j.apergo.2013.04.023.

Cohen, M. R. (2007). Causes of medication errors. In M. R. Cohen (Ed.), *Medication errors* (pp. 55–66). American Pharmacists Association.

Crandall, B., Klein, G., Klein, G. A., & Hoffman, R. R. (2006). *Working minds: A practitioner's guide to cognitive task analysis.* Cambridge, MA: MIT Press.

Dillon, A., & Watson, C. (1996). User analysis in HCI – The historical lessons from individual differences research. *International Journal of Human Computer Studies, 45*(6), 619–637. Available from https://doi.org/10.1006/ijhc.1996.0071.

Durso, F. T., Boehm-Davis, D. A., & Lee, J. D. (2015). *A view of human systems integration from the academy. APA handbook of human systems integration* (pp. 5–19). Washington, DC: American Psychological Association.

Durso, F. T., Ferguson, A. N., Kazi, S., Cunningham, C., & Ryan, C. (2015). Strategic threat management: An exploration of nursing strategies in the pediatric intensive care unit. *Applied Ergonomics*, *47*, 345–354. Available from https://doi.org/10.1016/j.apergo.2014.09.002.

Horsky, J., & Ramelson, H. Z. (2016). Cognitive errors in reconciling complex medication lists. *Annual Symposium Proceedings. AMIA Symposium*, *2016*, 638–646. Available from https://doi.org/10.1007/s00107-007-0192-6.

Hummel, J., Evans, P. C., & Lee, H. (2010). Medication reconciliation in the emergency department: Opportunities for workflow redesign. *Quality and Safety in Health Care*, *19*(6), 531–535. Available from https://doi.org/10.1136/qshc.2009.035121.

Institute for Safe Medication Practices. *Key elements of medication use*. (2018). Retrieved January 1, 2019, from <https://www.ismp.org/ten-key-elements>.

Karnon, J., Campbell, F., & Czoski-Murray, C. (2009). Model-based cost-effectiveness analysis of interventions aimed at preventing medication error at hospital admission (medicines reconciliation). *Journal of Evaluation in Clinical Practice*, *15*(2), 299–306. Available from https://doi.org/10.1111/j.1365-2753.2008.01000.x.

Kazi, S., Durso, F. T., & Thomas, R. (under review). Prospective memory in dynamic environments: The role of uncertainty.

Kazi, S., Khunlertkit, A., & Chen, A. (2017). Can simulation improve EMR implementation? Application to medication reconciliation. *Proceedings of the International Symposium on Human Factors and Ergonomics in Health Care*, *6*(1), 255–258. Available from https://doi.org/10.1177/2327857917061058.

Keogh, C., Kachalia, A., Fiumara, K., Goulart, D., Coblyn, J., & Desai, S. P. (2016). Ambulatory medication reconciliation: Using a collaborative approach to process improvement at an academic medical center. *Joint Commission Journal on Quality and Patient Safety*, *42*(4), 186–192. Available from https://doi.org/10.1016/S1553-7250(16)42023-4.

Koppel, R., Cohen, A., Abaluck, B., Localio, A. R., Kimmel, S. E., & Strom, B. L. (2005). Role of computerized physician order entry systems in facilitating medication errors. *JAMA*, *293* (10), 1197–1203.

Kramer, H. S., Gibson, B., Livnat, Y., Thraen, I., Brody, A. A., & Rupper, R. (2016). Evaluation of an electronic module for reconciling medications in home health plans of care. *Applied Clinical Informatics*, *7*(2), 412–424. Available from https://doi.org/10.4338/ACI-2015-11-RA-0154.

Leape, L. L. (2002). Reporting of adverse events. *The New England Journal of Medicine*, *347* (20), 1633–1638. Available from https://doi.org/10.1056/NEJMNEJMhpr011493.

Lee, K. P., Nishimura, K., Ngu, B., Tieu, L., & Auerbach, A. D. (2014). Predictors of completeness of patients' self-reported personal medication lists and discrepancies with clinic medication lists. *Annals of Pharmacotherapy*, *48*(2), 168–177. Available from https://doi.org/10.1177/1060028013512109.

McDonald, D., Mansukhani, R., Kokotajlo, S., Diaz, F., & Robinson, C. (2018). Effect of nursing education on optimization of medication reconciliation in the pediatric emergency department. *Journal of Pediatric Pharmacology and Therapeutics*, *23*(3), 203–208. Available from https://doi.org/10.5863/1551-6776-23.3.203.

Millitello, L. G., & Hutton, R. J. B. (1998). Applied cognitive task analysis (ACTA): a practitioner's toolkit for understanding cognitive task demands. *Ergonomics*, *41*(11), 1618–1641. Available from https://doi.org/10.1080/001401398186108.

Parasuraman, R., Sheridan, T. B., & Wickens, C. D. (2000). A model for types and levels of human interaction with automation. *IEEE Transaction on Systems, Man, and Cybernetics – Part A: Systems and Humans*, *30*(3), 286–297.

Patient Protection and Affordable Care Act. (2010). *Public Law, 111*(48), 759−762.

Petersen, L. A., Brennan., Troyen, A., O'Neil, A. C., Cook, F. E., & Lee, T. H. (1994). Does housestaff discontinuity of care increase the risk for preventable adverse events? *Annals of Internal Medicine, 121*, 866−872.

Pevnick, J. M., & Schnipper, J. L. (2017). Exploring how to better measure and improve the quality of medication reconciliation. *Joint Commission Journal on Quality and Patient Safety, 43*(5), 209−211. Available from https://doi.org/10.1016/j.jcjq.2017.02.003.

Pevnick, J. M., Nguyen, C., Jackevicius, C. A., Palmer, K. A., Shane, R., Cook-Wiens, G., ... Bell, D. S. (2018). Improving admission medication reconciliation with pharmacists or pharmacy technicians in the emergency department: A randomised controlled trial. *BMJ Quality and Safety, 27*(7), 512−520. Available from https://doi.org/10.1136/bmjqs-2017-006761.

Pevnick, J. M., Shane, R., & Schnipper, J. L. (2016). The problem with medication reconciliation. *BMJ Quality and Safety, 25*(9), 726−730. Available from https://doi.org/10.1136/bmjqs-2015-004734.

Plaisant, C., Chao, T., Wu, J., Hettinger, A. Z., Herskovic, J. R., Johnson, T. R., ... Shneiderman, B. (2013). Twinlist: novel user interface designs for medication reconciliation. *AMIA Annual Symposium Proceedings, 2013*, 1150−1159. Retrieved from https://www.ncbi.nlm.nih.gov/pmc/articles/PMC3900136/.

Plaisant, C., Wu, J., Hettinger, Z. A., Powsner, S., & Shneiderman, B. (2015). Novel user interface design for medication reconciliation: An evaluation of Twinlist. *Journal of the American Medical Informatics Association, 22*(2), 340−349. Available from https://doi.org/10.1093/jamia/ocu021.

Pronovost, P., Weast, B., Schwarz, M., Wyskiel, R. M., Prow, D., Milanovich, S. N., ... Lipsett, P. (2003). Medication reconciliation: A practical tool to reduce the risk of medication errors. *Journal of Critical Care, 18*(4), 201−205. Available from https://doi.org/10.1016/j.jcrc.2003.10.001.

Saleem, J. J., Herout, J., & Wilck, N. R. (2016). Function-specific design principles for the electronic health record. *Proceedings of the Human Factors and Ergonomics Society*, 578−582. Available from https://doi.org/10.1177/1541931213601133.

Scheffer, M., Bascompte, J., Brock, W. A., Brovkin, V., Carpenter, S. R., Dakos, V., ... Sugihara, G. (2009). Early-warning signals for critical transitions. *Nature, 461*(7260), 53−59. Available from https://doi.org/10.1038/nature08227.

Shane, R. (2016). Why "Universal Precautions" are needed for medication lists. *BMJ Quality and Safety, 25*(9), 731−732. Available from https://doi.org/10.1136/bmjqs-2015-005116.

The Joint Commission. Using Medication Reconciliation to Prevent Errors. (2006). *Joint Commission Journal on Quality and Patient Safety, 32*(4), 230−232. Available from https://doi.org/10.1016/S1553-7250(06)32030-2.

United States Air Force. (2009). *Air force human systems integration handbook: Planning and execution of human systems integration.* Brooks City-Base, TX: Directorate of Human Performance Integration.

Van Stiphout, F., Zwart-Van Rijkom, J. E. F., Maggio, L. A., Aarts, J. E. C. M., Bates, D. W., Van Gelder, T., ... Ter Braak, E. W. M. T. (2015). Task analysis of information technology-mediated medication management in outpatient care. *British Journal of Clinical Pharmacology, 80*(3), 415−424. Available from https://doi.org/10.1111/bcp.12625.

Varkey, P., Cunningham, J., O'Meara, J., Bonacci, R., Desai, N., & Sheeler, R. (2007). Multidisciplinary approach to inpatient medication reconciliation in an academic setting. *American Journal of Health-System Pharmacy, 64*(8), 1−12. Retrieved from http://10.0.8.98/ajhp060314.

White, C. M., Schoettker, P. J., Conway, P. H., Geiser, M., Olivea, J., Pruett, R., & Kotagal, U. R. (2011). Utilising improvement science methods to optimise medication reconciliation. *BMJ Quality & Safety, 20*(4), 372–380. Available from https://doi.org/10.1136/bmjqs.2010.047845.

Wright, T. B., Adams, K., Church, V. L., Ferraro, M., Ragland, S., Sayers, A., ... Lesselroth, B. J. (2017). Implementation of a medication reconciliation assistive technology: A qualitative analysis. *AMIA Annual Symposium Proceedings. AMIA Symposium, 2017*, 1802–1811. Retrieved from https://www.ncbi.nlm.nih.gov/pmc/articles/PMC5977680/.

Chapter 3

Design for digital health

Joseph A. Cafazzo[1,2,3,4]

[1]*Healthcare Human Factors, University Health Network, Toronto, ON, Canada,* [2]*Wolfond Chair in Digital Health, University Health Network, Toronto, ON, Canada,* [3]*Institute of Health Policy, Management and Evaluation, University of Toronto, Toronto, ON, Canada,* [4]*Institute of Biomaterials and Biomedical Engineering, University of Toronto, Toronto, ON, Canada*

Introduction

Digital health is a contemporary term that attempts to encompass, and perhaps even supersede, the terms *eHealth, mHealth, telehealth,* and *telecare* in taxonomy. Its use is to avoid the largely synonymous and overlapping terms that have caused confusion at times in both academia and in practice. The term "digital health" is more often used in North America, in media, and even some professional associations (Canada Health Infoway, 2018).

With this context, the intent of this chapter is to go beyond the design of electronic health records (EHRs) and mobile health apps, to where design of the broader scope of digital health is needed for successful use in the doctor's office, the specialist's clinic, the hospital ward, and at home. Other chapters in this book offer details on the techniques needed to design a great product. Here instead I will broaden the scope of design techniques to be more encompassing of the entire experience, including implementation issues that are typically the most common reasons for failure of any product launch (Gagnon et al., 2012).

The failure of digital health interventions has become increasingly acute. Commentary in both peer-reviewed and gray literature has been recently pointing to the poor execution of health information technologies as being a major ill in health care. The "promise" has been largely unfulfilled, and the blame laid at the feet of health care practitioners; characterized as luddites who cannot adapt to technological innovations (Kellermann & Jones, 2013). The truth of the matter is that health care practitioners are the users of the most advanced, sophisticated technologies in any industry. This includes the advanced diagnostic and therapeutic devices, which are far more technologically complex than any EHR system. The outcomes of health information technology adoption have been so mixed, and often poor, that it is being

Design for Health. DOI: https://doi.org/10.1016/B978-0-12-816427-3.00003-8

47

cited as a cause for clinician burnout (Collier, 2017; Shanafelt et al., 2016). In addition, a new health profession has emerged as a result: the scribe. Scribes are tasked to shadow clinicians, documenting their work in the EHR, while the clinicians themselves have all but given up. How damning an outcome of the use of a technology is one that creates work for a user that already has too much and adds cost to a health system that was seeking savings through its use?

Increasingly, blame is directed at health information technologies themselves, and how seemingly tone-deaf their design has been when implemented into care environments. Although usability issues are often cited as a major aspect of why there is poor uptake and utility of health information technology, it is being recognized that the design problems extend well beyond the product itself. Workflows in health care are increasingly being disrupted as a result of the introduction of health information technology (Ratwani et al., 2018). Arguably, this could be considered a good thing, given the perceived inefficiencies in health care. However, it would also assume that there was a deliberate design process, which encompassed all aspects of the user experience when the technology was introduced, including workflow. Instead, most implementations use change management techniques to convince, cajole, and nudge the user into acceptance. In change management the "change" refers to people and not to the system being designed (Van de Maele, 2015). Change management undoubtedly has its place in implementation, but far too often it is used to patch a poor user experience brought on by a poorly designed technology, or even well-designed technology that does not consider or respect the workflow in the setting.

To address this challenge, I will cover actual case studies of how the design of digital health interventions needs to be taken out of the designer's comfort zone; that is, well outside of the focus group, workshop, and studio setting and into the clinic and people's homes. The good news is that those exceptional skills that designers have honed over the years are still relevant here, no matter the context. In fact, naiveté of seemingly complex medical environments could be considered an asset in the design of health technologies when it comes to improving experiences, if not the product itself.

Designing a system, not a product

For the purposes of this chapter, I will examine more systemic aspects of the design of digital health interventions, given how encompassing the term is intended. For that, I need a more formal approach to the design problem. One way of doing that is to use a theoretical framework—often used in academia, but rarely in practice. Theoretical frameworks can often ground the design work in evidence, rather than in a less rigorous "gut" approach. They can frame a problem so thoroughly that it can be used as a guide for the design team. Not much in design is by the numbers or formulaic, nor should it be for a creative process, but the aspects that can be captured through such a framework could be useful if only as a reminder of the design goal and of any missed steps in the process toward that goal.

For design in digital health, I need to consider aspects of the system that one might think are well outside of the domain of the designer. This is largely because health care can seem esoteric—how does one design for a domain requiring years of postgraduate education to learn, and still many more years for proficiency? Further, how does one design for a system that has elements of complex physical, chemical, or behavioral science? This complexity can often paralyze the designer and the design process, with a constant anxiety of not knowing enough about the subject.

Health care delivery can be highly heterogeneous as well. Beyond the regulations, guidelines, and policies, health care organizations and practitioners have a great deal of latitude in care delivery (Swensen et al., 2010). The same hospital can have differing processes to admit patients to their various internal specialty clinics, on the mere perception (rather than reality) that needs differ. Organizations may also document the care delivered within these clinics differently, with entirely incompatible health record systems, and even transition and discharge of patients differently. Therefore a well-designed product does not translate well from one hospital to another, or even from one clinic to another in the same hospital. Clearly, I need to think of designing for health care actors and environments differently than I do for more homogenous workplaces.

Most designers tend to limit their focus to the product, the interaction, or a specific experience; the "unit of analysis" in academic terms. It is the "what" or "for whom" of the design. There can be folly in an approach focused solely on outputs or goals. However, it is important not to lose sight of the goal of your design; the framing of the problem needs not to lose sight of the higher order, systemic confounders. In a domain as complex as health, the foci of design should consider these high-order units of analysis, or the potential confounders of the design.

There are a number of example design research frameworks that are similar in how they break down complexity and confounders. This includes the *four orders of design* by Buchanan, which frames a hierarchy from the domains of communications (signs and symbols), to product design (objects and artifacts), to interactions (service design), and to systems and environments (organizational design) (Buchanan, 1992, 1999). Similarly, Jones mapped the design process to "challenge complexity" in the hierarchy of (1) traditional design, (2) product/service design, (3) organization/transformational design, and (4) social transformational design (Jones, 2014).

Rather than defining a hierarchy in terms of design domains, the *human-tech ladder* is a theoretical framework that captures this design complexity in the form of the *unit of analysis* of the design, from a human factors

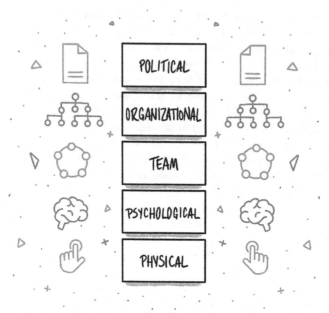

FIGURE 3.1   The human-tech ladder. *Modified from Vicente, K. J. (2004). The human factor: Revolutionizing the way I live with technology. Vintage Canada. Illustration by Adam Badzynski.*

engineering perspective (Vicente, 2004). Created by Vicente during his time as a human factors engineering professor at the University of Toronto, the framework is both familiar and bold in what it suggests are the conceptual domains of any design process (Fig. 3.1).

Most designers would be both familiar with and comfortable in the lower rungs of the human-tech ladder, which include the *physical* and *psychological* aspects of design. These particular aspects are important considerations when designing a product, be it a medical device or a mobile health app for asthma. In the physical domain an infusion pump needs to be light enough with a comfortable handle for a nurse to move it from one unit to another, and to mount it to an IV pole, at or above the height of a patient in bed. Psychologically and cognitively, the same infusion pump needs a simple way to be programed to avoid making medication errors, one of the most common adverse events related to technology in health care (de Vries, Ramrattan, Smorenburg, Gouma, & Boermeester, 2008). For an asthma self-care app, the design needs to be physically accessible when someone has a flare up, and psychologically it needs to manage and nudge users to use their control inhaler, even while asymptomatic.

Beyond the bottom two rungs, I am seemingly going beyond a product. But dealing with *team* aspects of products is not so unfamiliar to most designers either, especially when considering the design of a secure messaging service, or an EHR system that assumes use by clinical teams, or even interactions that extend to the patient electronically.

However, the nature of the team dynamics, which includes individual roles, workflows, and other interaction touchpoints, is often imposed on the product design. The care and effort of your product design appear to now be subjected to the seemingly arbitrary design of how the team that uses it actually operates. The rigor of the design process for medical devices is often imposed on regulations, whereby design decisions require a formal validation process to ensure safety. However, once handed to the clinical team that uses it, there is no such rigorous design and validation process on how the team works, what their work processes entail, and how they will apply the technology.

The design of a product could be more effective, and the experience improved, if the team dynamics, interactions, and workflows were also part of that design. This becomes more apparent at the organizational and political rungs of the human-tech ladder. Elements, such as working conditions, staffing levels, and other environmental effects, are all aspects that could factor into the design. One should consider how well would your product perform if the nurse-to-patient ratio was half of what you had assumed in its design; consider that a busy cancer center that has several times the volumes that a clinic in the community might have; or the qualifications of who is using your technology differ from what was intended.

When considering the elements at these higher levels, I am designing a sociotechnical system, not just a product. These top three rungs, the high-order aspects of the system, need to be considered in the design of digital health technologies too, despite how intangible and inaccessible they may be to the designer.

Health care is opaque

The *team* aspects of the human-tech ladder need to be observed to be understood. Insights cannot be easily elucidated through interviews or focus groups. Paradoxically, most professionals who are experienced and proficient at what they do cannot verbally articulate how they work with the level of detail necessary for the designer. In educational circles, this is known as the *paradox of expertise*, and it is the same phenomenon that hinders an expert in a particular subject matter unable to properly instruct a student on that subject (Morita & Cafazzo, 2016). To be able to understand your subject's work and their work setting, direct observation is necessary to obtain design insights into any product or service that they will use. This is even more important in health care that contains dozens, if not hundreds, of esoteric specialties and subservices that contribute to overall delivery of care. This is at the root of the complexity of designing for health.

Unfortunately, health care settings are increasingly becoming opaque to the designer. Design residency was at a time more common. But design insights are difficult to obtain with increasingly restrictive privacy policies and regulations. It is now more difficult to get access to patients and health care providers to interview, let alone to observe interactions with technology and each other. These observations are necessary to understand the nature of the work and workflows, and to identify interaction touchpoints. Unlike health care, most consumer products and services are relatively easy to access, with designers even actively participating in field observations as a form of autoethnography (O'Kane, Rogers, & Blandford, 2014). In the general consumer space, it is not difficult for a designer to walk through the process of renting a car, buying personal home insurance, or buying and setting up the latest smartphone in order to gain insights to redesigning those particular experiences. Conversely, designers in health care receive inputs often second- or third-hand. The results are telling and often poor (Karsh, Weinger, Abbott, & Wears, 2010).

Not surprisingly, these barriers to the insights at the *team* level are such that designers too often limit their work to the lower rungs of the human-tech ladder, with predictably poor results (Karsh et al., 2010). Simply conducting interviews with staff and patients will not be enough to overcome this design-research gap. Gaining access to the team and their work environments can be achieved by closely partnering with stakeholders who value the design process and the designer's contributions. The extra effort is not just desirable, it is a necessity.

Observerships and research ethics

The design research process in health care is so wrought with policy and regulation that it warrants special attention and planning. If access to a health care setting is needed, a formal application for an observership is often needed. The application would require a sponsor, usually a division head or chief, to approve your application. Unless the designer is doing work directly for the organization, approval is unlikely. Sponsored access through a company that has a business or research relationship with the health care setting is the most likely avenue to obtain this approval otherwise. It takes time to establish these relationships, and a rationale needs to be stated as to why the observership is needed. One should be prepared to make repeated attempts to justify access since design research is an atypical rationale. A record of immunization and privacy training may also be required for approvals for an observership.

Beyond the ability to observe generally, design research often requires access to the actors that are the subject of the design. These include patients, clinicians, and support staff. Interviews, surveys, focus groups, or any other form of interaction with these actors may subject the designer to the additional requirement of a research ethics review. An organization's institutional review board (IRB) would review a formal protocol application detailing how the actor will be recruited, how consent will be obtained, and how data will be used. The IRB will scrutinize the ethics of the proposed research and weigh the risks and benefits of work being conducted. There is particular scrutiny when patients are involved in the research and, if it is done for commercial purposes, where there may be a conflict of interest. The language and framing of the rationale need to be stated in neutral terms as to not show bias as to its scientific merit or otherwise. You are justifying your inquiry and not the potential outcomes of the design research. At the same time, you must state the intent of the research that it is to inform the design of a product and service and that it *may* lead to better outcomes and experiences for the user.

Where an application for an observership may only take days or weeks of effort, an IRB application can take several months. This is the very reason why so little design research is conducted in health care. Many design firms cannot fathom the effort for such an undertaking. Of course, the outcome of the design process suffers as a result. The only tactic to employ is to plan ahead and not be too pedantic about the sequencing of the design process. There is no reason why you cannot conduct design research throughout the design process, using it to inform conceptual thinking and prototypes. You should be careful though that your inquiry does not deviate from the IRB protocol that you submitted, as you will be forced to submit an amendment that will delay your work once again. It is best to keep your protocol balanced between detail (which the IRB will expect) and flexibility (that you will need to deal with the unexpected). With projects that have tight timelines, you need to get creative on how the design research gets used, even if it is delayed through the approval process, just as long as one does not forget its importance altogether.

Design for digital health guidelines

- Given that failures largely occur at implementation, the heterogeneity of health care delivery requires *the scope of design* to consider *the delivery of a service*, rather than solely the digital health product within a service.
- Seemingly innocuous issues *at the team and organizational levels* can negatively affect the implementation of digital health products. Hence, frameworks, such the *human-tech ladder*, demonstrate the needed *scope of the system design* of digital health interventions.
- The tactics used in *service design* emphasize *all touchpoints* of the patient experience, *not just those that involve the digital health product.*
- Consequently, design discovery *requires direct observation* of the health care delivery environment, mapping the interaction of actors within the system of touchpoints that affect the patient experience. *Second-hand insights are often*

(Continued)

(Continued)

too coarse in detail to sufficiently design for such complex and esoteric environments in health care.
- *Additional planning is required* in designing for health care settings to obtain the required access for *observerships,* unlike most consumer product design.

Case study: when product design is not enough—the vital signs project

There is no better way to demonstrate the importance of design research than a case study of how a seemingly well-designed product failed when implemented clinically.

In the case of the "vital signs" project the problem to be solved was not an easy one. There is a certain subgroup of inpatients that are complex to manage and often slip through the cracks of the system; not sick enough to be admitted to the intensive care unit, but too sick to be cared for in general ward, where staff are less experienced in dealing with a complicated case and where there may be no continuous monitoring of vital signs to alert staff to a deteriorating patient. What often occurs, sadly, is an adverse event known as "failure-to-rescue," where a patient deteriorates over time and requires an unplanned intervention, admission to the ICU, or expires as a result of the inaction of clinical staff (Ghaferi & Dimick, 2015). The harm might have been avoided if noticed hours or even days earlier. The reasons why nursing staff do not notice this often slow patient deterioration are complex but can be partially attributed to a recency effect or bias (Croskerry, 2002), whereby the nurse does not expect a patient to deteriorate to the point of coding or requiring an escalation.

Perhaps a more attributable cause is how vital signs are recorded and interpreted. Patients in these general wards typically only get a spot check of their vital signs on a 4-hour or 8-hour basis. As nurses are on 8- or 12-hour shifts, they may only see one or two sets of data points on their paper chart, unless the chart is well designed (they are usually not), or they seek out that information deliberately. An electronic system of documentation does not guarantee any more ease of access to more data points or better saliency of patient trends. Without a historical trend over the previous few days, it may be difficult for a nurse to detect marked changes in the patient condition. Even if the nurses had well-designed systems (paper or electronic) to make the trending more salient, this detection would still be entirely dependent on a nurse's cognition and behavior. The system has a single point of failure, that of human fallibility.

To prevent failure-to-rescue adverse events, early warning scores (EWSs) have been used with some notable success (Prytherch, Smith, Schmidt, &

Featherstone, 2010; Stenhouse, Coates, Tivey, Allsop, & Parker, 2000). An EWS is a computation of risk of deterioration based on numeric vital sign readings and scored nursing observations. Above a certain threshold, the EWS would indicate an escalation to the care the patient is receiving. This would start with a clinician from the "outreach" team or other specialty, who would be called for an urgent consult.

A manual calculation of an EWS would be too time-consuming and wrought with potential error. An electronic calculation would be obvious, assuming electronic documentation of the elements required. However, capturing vital sign readings from vital signs monitors has a complexity and cost to it, with little chance of interoperability with the hospital EHR.

Direct manual documentation into the EHR was a possible alternative approach. As part of the design research, a field study was conducted of the prevailing nursing practice of documentation at the point of care (Yeung, Lapinsky, Granton, Doran, & Cafazzo, 2012). Sites were chosen so that both paper-based and electronic documentation could be observed. Perhaps unsurprisingly, it was found that it generally takes longer for nurses to document electronically. These nurses would also avoid entering vital signs directly into the EHR and would rather document on scrap paper and enter the readings into the EHR later in their shift, or at its conclusion. This delay in entering the vital signs electronically would not suit our objectives of generating an EWS to intervene before the patient deteriorates. The computers in the patients' rooms were found to be inconveniently located, required a login process, and were generally disruptive to nurse workflow. It was simply much easier for the nurses to log in once and batch-enter the readings while seated at the nursing station.

This highlighted the challenge of electronic documentation: it is very difficult to beat pen and paper for convenience and speed, despite the advantages otherwise. Informed by the research, I attempted to optimize the way nurses document in an electronic system such that they would not feel the need to use paper as an interim step. The data-entry method needed to be at the point of care so that readings could be transcribed directly from the vital signs monitoring screen. A mobile phone application was considered to be an optimal means. Tablets were dismissed, as they were not pocketable and would often end up resting on surfaces, and misplaced, as nurses performed tasks that required two hands.

What eventually transpired was a rigorous iterative user-centered design approach conducted over countless hours of user experience design (UXD) work with nursing staff to help create an app to allow easy entry of vital signs (Yeung, 2009).

It included a clever way to document respiratory rate, a particularly difficult vital sign to capture. Not part of the capability of the vital signs monitor, the process of determining respiration rate traditionally required the nurse to count the number of breaths over a 15-second period by observing the patient's chest expanding and contracting. They would then derive breaths per minute by multiplying their count by 4. Instead, the app allowed the nurse to simply tap on the screen every time they observed the patient take a breath. The app would automatically calculate the rate by determining the time interval between the taps. The nurses loved the convenience of this feature during successive iterations of usability testing and feedback. Other data-entry features for pain scores and for transcribing values from the vital signs monitor were also well received. Into the final stages of development, it was felt that the electronic documentation through this vital signs app was as close to optimized as possible to the simplicity and efficiency of paper and pen. The EWS calculation and alerting system was also thoroughly designed and tested. It was on to implementation.

Unfortunately, that is where the design process ended for this project. What transpired next was a series of serious miscalculations as to how certain one can be of a successful outcome with what appears to be a very well-designed product using all of the prevailing design processes and wisdom (Gopal, 2011).

The project was introduced to nursing staff through the hospital's nursing informatics staff. These are specially tasked nurses who assist staff with all forms of EHR-related work and were thought to be ideally suited to introduce the vital signs application. It was left to these specialists to plan the implementation, including orientation, training, and supporting the nursing staff using the application. Much of this was done through weekly team meetings, where the staff could be addressed as a group. Initially, it appeared that the pilot was going well. Readings were being received for more than 90% of cases. Technical issues appeared minimal. Then, suddenly, it began to unravel.

Nursing informatics staff continued to orient and train successive groups of nurses as to the details of why I was doing this work and what the desired outcome will be. Nothing was scripted in this respect, and a few misplaced words during a few orientation sessions were enough to doom the project. It turns out that during one such session, the project was described as "experimental," "research," and the efforts of a "Master's student." To jaded nursing staff that had been through many pilot quality improvement and EHR implementation projects, these words had a different meaning: "optional," "not part of the standard of care," "I don't need to do this." In addition to this factor, it was later learned that the hospital added a layer of security onto the iPhones being used that required the nurses to log into the phone as well as the vital sign applications, and the login credentials differed in each case. As well, unbeknownst to the design team, infection control added a protective phone case that partially obstructed the software keyboard that made login and data entry difficult.

The rate of data capture plummeted to 66% as word got around the units that the nature of the project was not for clinical care, and the mounting fatigue and inconvenience of multiple logins and frustrating data-entry errors due to the obstructing phone case. Patients complained of nurses who were found texting in front of them instead of attending to them. The rate of data capture fell to 42% in the evenings. The use of the system was so low at this point that it could not be used reliably as a means to calculate EWS and avoid failure-to-rescue adverse events as intended.

The premise that the system was not for clinical care was, in fact, false. The intent was always to make this tool the standard of care if it could be realized in terms of feasibility, but the project would never be able to recover from this messaging to ever determine it. In the defense of the nursing informatics staff, who described the project in such a way that discouraged the use of the tool, they were not incorrect in the characterization, but it was a lesson that it is the design of the entire experience of the end user, beyond the product, that determines the success of a system. The design process was so concerned about the interactions that revolved around the app itself that it was not fully appreciated that the experience of the nursing staff extended well beyond the thin layer of glass of their iPhones.

It is not to say that all of these problems encountered during implementation were unforeseen. They could have been anticipated in any complex clinical environment with nursing staff, patients, and a bit of technology. There were any number of approaches and disciplines that could have mitigated the problems in this implementation or could have easily avoided them altogether.

Whatever approach could have been taken, however, should have been considered a further extension of the original design problem, and not simply the staging from product design to implementation. In the end, it was clear that the design of this system was never completed and that the design problem to be solved delved much further beyond the software and hardware and the interactions therein. Consideration of the dynamics of the team, organization, and policy came into play that were never considered in scope for the design, or rather that it would be handled by more traditional methods of implementation.

Change management, Lean, and implementation science

The semantics of the technique used in the design and implementation of technology can be daunting to the uninitiated, and occasionally frustrating to those who embrace the dogma of design. If you were to do a thorough taxonomy of the aspects, features, processes, techniques, and philosophy behind most prominent design and implementation disciplines, you would find a degree of overlap. There will always be arguments of what should be used when, or if at all. For those who define their professions as such, they can at times feel threatened when their particular discipline is critiqued, marginalized, or not given its due.

But as the complexity of the system that is being designed increases, it is inevitable that the designer will cross paths with other professions, disciplines, and those using techniques that are trying to solve the same problem they have. The requisite argument will ensue as to which technique is best suited to address the problem, but it serves the greater goal to find what is common about the approaches.

The service design approach

Introducing the use of service design into health care should be obvious in an industry that is ostensibly a service. But with change management and Lean so predominant in health care, and a more academic implementation science approach also in the mix, there is little opportunity for a new discipline to take hold. There is also the valid argument that health care would simply benefit from a traditional UXD approach. What about creating an entirely new perspective in patient experience design (Meloncon, 2017)?

The user-centeredness common to nearly all of these approaches is what is most important, and design in digital health in particular could benefit from picking from what technique suits one best for the problem at hand, regardless of the discipline. *Service design* borrows from other design and implementation disciplines and techniques, which does not make it any less derivative than those from which it borrows. Most importantly, it emphasizes and focuses the user experience *in its totality*, and by formal definition, *a holistic view* (Zomerdijk & Voss, 2010).

With service design, one's design abilities extend to less tangible aspects of the system than a physical product. It also applies to high-order rungs of the human-tech ladder of *team* and *organization*. Thus there are aspects that lend themselves particularly well to health care and addressing its complexity.

One such technique in service design is the use of the *service blueprint* (Stickdorn & Schneider, 2011). In many respects, blueprinting is not unlike workflow mapping using Unified Modeling Language activity diagrams and swim lanes identifying the actors of the system. However, service blueprinting uniquely characterizes interactions with actors and artifacts. Taking the *unit of analysis* as the patient, it employs a theater metaphor by delineating *front-of-stage* interactions as those that are apparent to the recipient of the service. The *back-of-stage* interactions are characterized as those aspects in support of the delivery of the service hidden from patient view. Finally, there are *support processes*, which might include the higher order organizational and policy aspects required to deliver the service.

Service blueprinting follows the staging of the service over time, and of particular importance, it identifies the patient *touchpoints*. Borrowed from interaction design, a touchpoint is defined as any interaction with the service. The challenge capturing the touchpoints for your particular design work is determining the form of the interaction and the level of granularity. The interaction can be everything from the greeting of the patient in the waiting room to logging into their heart failure management app on their phone. The granularity can be as coarse as the hospital visit or the fine-grained interaction of an aide escorting the patient to the imaging department. It is left to the experience of the design team to determine the appropriateness of the breakdown of the interactions, based on the amount of time, effort, and budget. The inventory of these touchpoints can be mapped along the entire longitudinal experience of the patient.

By determining the present state of the service, e.g. the longitudinal workflow, the interactions, and the touchpoints, requires direct observational techniques. No amount of interviewing, workshopping, or conducting focus groups will allow an unvarnished view into the details of the service as it is currently delivered. This is especially important in a health care setting, where the tasks can be esoteric and specialized. As such, using the AEIOU method of ethnographic observation is particularly well suited for conducting service design (Euchner, 2014). It frames and organizes your observations into activities, environments, interactions, objects, and users, which are the elements needed in capturing the extent of the service.

Once you have captured an inventory of these touchpoints, they require a design process of their own, using techniques that depend on the form of interaction and the artifacts that need to be created. The challenge is not to treat the touchpoints as separate and discrete, but to coordinate and orchestrate their design for a consistent, delightful experience.

A simplified service blueprint is shown in Fig. 3.2, depicting a high-level, coarse representation of the touchpoints and interactions, and back-of-stage processes. As the blueprint can be used in the research phase of the design to capture the current state of the service, it can also be used to define the future state, acting as a guide for the net new touchpoints that would require design and those that require redesign.

One drawback to this technique can be that it is for the blueprinting of the "customer" experience traditionally, or the patient experience in the context of health care, and not necessarily of the care provider of the service. The clinician experience is of great importance too if the service is going to viable, especially when there is the introduction of a new technology. Clinicians have been inundated over the years with digital tools that were apparently designed with improving their experience and have not done so. There is no doubt that a well-designed service is our goal, but unless the designer elevates the clinician experience throughout the design of touchpoints, the service blueprint approach will not carry the design forward any further than any other technique.

Case study: service design a heart-failure-management app for patients

With that caveat, this technique was used for extending the design of the heart failure management system, *Medly*, into practice in a busy urban teaching hospital. The challenge with such systems in the past is that they often

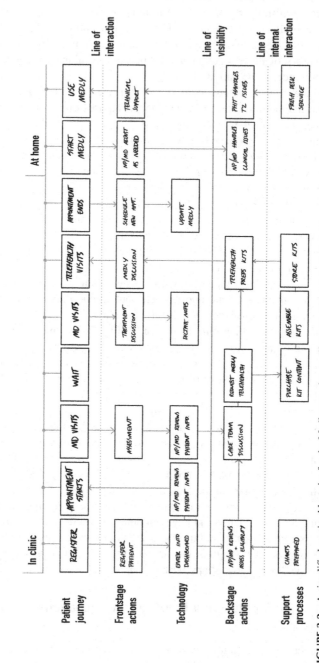

FIGURE 3.2 A simplified service blueprint for the Medly experience. *Illustration by Adam Badzynski.*

could not get past the piloting phase. Although the design of the product was not always optimal either, the difficulty was designing the system as a service to be delivered by a specialty heart function clinic.

The objective of the *Medly* system is to monitor vital signs and symptoms of heart failure patients from their home and intervene as needed to avoid an unnecessary hospitalization. This patient population is among the highest in utilization of health services and is rehospitalized as much as 50% of the time within 6 months (O'Connor, 2017). Many of the rehospitalizations are avoidable, and the patients generally suffer more from these unnecessary admissions. Technologies to acquire the vital signs and symptoms have existed for many years, but more recent designs centered around the use of a mobile phone application have emerged as a more ubiquitous, cost effective way of acquiring and transmitting the data. A Bluetooth blood pressure monitor and weight scale avoids manual entry, ensuring data integrity and providing convenience for the patient. The data is typically stored and displayed in the clinic. Depending on the sophistication of the system, patients who appear to be deteriorating can be identified well before the patient needs a readmission. However, this may be an entirely manual process for the clinical staff to determine.

The process of implementing such a system in busy clinic has been a challenge. It often requires dedicated staff to identify amenable patients, onboard and train them on the technology, provide follow up as necessary while being monitored, and to retrieve and inventory the equipment when the use is discontinued. The number of patients that can be supported by a single clinician can vary, but it is often considered too costly to be sustainable. As a result, in many health care settings, the use of such digital tools is still not common. Again, this is a design problem that encompasses both the *team* and *organizational* levels of the human-tech ladder.

The objective then of the service design process for *Medly* was not only to provide the patient with optimal experience, but to streamline the service such that it was viable and sustainable for the clinic to deliver and for the organization to support. Through many hours of direct observation, interviews, and huddling, a current state was obtained. The next step was to extend the *Medly* product to a future state for use in the clinic, essentially transforming it from a product to a service. The Medly blueprint depicted in Fig. 3.2 is greatly simplified for the purposes of illustration. The actual future-state blueprint includes dozens more touchpoints.

What was also somewhat daunting to the design team was the breadth of the interaction channels that encompassed a future-state *Medly* service. These channels included face-to-face, by phone, by website, by app, and by interactive voice response (IVR) system. The IVR was used for automated voice messages to the patient to remind them to take readings when they missed a day. The challenge was to make this cohesive; a singularly consistent and positive experience for the patient, and at the same time making it viable for the clinic to deliver. As well, the number of back-of-stage staff delivering the service was diverse, including cardiologists, nurse practitioners, staff nurses, and clerical staff. In addition, support staff for technical support and onboarding were captured in the blueprint. Organizationally, there were little or no financial incentives for the use of such technology, given the current funding model. The concern was that the most costly component in the introduction of such a service was not the technology, but the cost of additional staff workload. Hence, a design constraint was ensuring that utilization of clinical staff was minimized.

In designing a future-state inventory of the touchpoints, some artifacts were created that seemed counterintuitive to the implementation of a digital tool. The designers created a number of paper-based forms to avoid the burdensome electronic systems that are often not where they need be when you need them. The design of an onboarding slip, much like a paper-based prescription, served as a more natural way for the clinician to quickly define the parameters needed to set up the patient's account. An electronic means of entering this information at this point in the workflow would simply slow the process.

Paper-based manuals and tip sheets were provided to the patients for convenience rather than hunting for information online or calling the clinic. The clinicians themselves were scripted to describe what *Medly* is and why they are asking patients to enroll.

The application itself was designed so that patients could self-manage their symptoms, when appropriately alerted. The workflow and escalation process was designed so that only about 20% of the alerts were left to the clinic to address. Patients who were comfortable with technology could use their own phone and their own devices, greatly reducing the cost of deployment. Tuning the clinic staffing levels evolved over time. It was first thought that the responsible cardiologist should address the alerts. When it was realized that this could not be sustainable given their workload, nurse practitioners were used. The refinement of the alerting algorithm created the opportunity that in the end a staff nurse with training in heart failure management could manage the majority of the alerts, with the balance being escalated to the nurse practitioners or cardiologist.

The result was a clinician-to-patient ratio that was several times higher than any system currently available, with an optimized patient experience. Both of these outcomes were important and needed, as one without the other would not have been viable or sustainable.

This outcome was not achieved without iteration, just as any user-centered design process would demand for a product development. Iteration with service design is more difficult to simulate though, with soft launches with a limited number of patients being the most practical approach to test early prototypes of the service.

Conclusion

For such a design process to happen, it required a level of specialization, commitment, and embeddedness on the part of the designer. This notion of residency within health care settings, with easy access to clinicians and their patients, is a positive trend that is noteworthy in many health care organizations. The embedded designer is not exactly ubiquitous, but the value can be easily articulated now that the risk of failed implementations is intolerable. With digital health interventions being increasingly more integrated into practice, including being prescribed as a therapeutic, there is a clear need to view the design of the system more broadly than I have in the past. It is unlikely that I will see the mainstreaming of digital health as a standard of care without more thoughtful, comprehensive design practice. In drawing on a technique that is intuitive for the problem at hand, and by simply dropping the mystique of the design technique itself, the designer has the opportunity to define a system that transcends narrow definitions of what is expected of them. So too, will be the broader opportunities for design that will undoubtedly follow for a health care industry so much in need.

References

Buchanan, R. (1992). Wicked problems in design thinking. *Design Issues*, *8*(2), 5−21.

Buchanan, R. (1999). Design research and the new learning. *Design Issues*, *17*(4), 3−23.

Canada Health Infoway. (2018). *What is digital health*. Retrieved May 14, 2019, from <https://www.infoway-inforoute.ca/en/what-we-do/benefits-of-digital-health/what-is-digital-health> Accessed 14.05.19.

Collier, R. (2017). Electronic health records contributing to physician burnout. *CMAJ: Canadian Medical Association Journal = Journal de l'Association Medicale Canadienne*, *189*(45), E1405−E1406. Available from https://doi.org/10.1503/cmaj.109-5522.

Croskerry, P. (2002). Achieving quality in clinical decision making: Cognitive strategies and detection of bias. *Academic Emergency Medicine: Official Journal of the Society for Academic Emergency Medicine*, *9*(11), 1184−1204. Available from https://doi.org/10.1197/aemj.9.11.1184.

de Vries, E. N., Ramrattan, M. A., Smorenburg, S. M., Gouma, D. J., & Boermeester, M. A. (2008). The incidence and nature of in-hospital adverse events: A systematic review. *Quality & Safety in Health Care*, *17*(3), 216−223. Available from https://doi.org/10.1136/qshc.2007.023622.

Euchner, J. (2014). The art and science of design: Interviews with Tom MacTavish, Anijo Mathew and Kim Erwin: Three professors from the Institute of Design at the Illinois Institute of Technology talk with Jim Euchner about the tools of design thinking. *Research-Technology Management*, *57*(3), 10. Available from https://doi.org/10.5437/08956308X5703003.

Gagnon, M.-P., Desmartis, M., Labrecque, M., Car, J., Pagliari, C., Pluye, P., ... Légaré, F. (2012). Systematic review of factors influencing the adoption of information and communication technologies by healthcare professionals. *Journal of Medical Systems*, *36*(1), 241−277. Available from https://doi.org/10.1007/s10916-010-9473-4.

Ghaferi, A. A., & Dimick, J. B. (2015). Understanding failure to rescue and improving safety culture. *Annals of Surgery, 261*(5), 839−840. Available from https://doi.org/10.1097/SLA.0000000000001135.

Gopal, A. (2011). *Reducing "failure-to-rescue" events through enhanced critical care response teams (Masters Thesis).* University of Toronto. Available from http://hdl.handle.net/1807/30609.

Jones, P. H. (2014). Systemic design principles for complex social systems. In G. S. Metcalf (Ed.), *Social systems and design* (Vol. 1, pp. 91−128). Tokyo: Springer Japan. https://doi.org/10.1007/978-4-431-54478-4_4.

Karsh, B.-T., Weinger, M. B., Abbott, P. A., & Wears, R. L. (2010). Health information technology: Fallacies and sober realities. *Journal of the American Medical Informatics Association: JAMIA, 17*(6), 617−623. Available from https://doi.org/10.1136/jamia.2010.005637.

Kellermann, A. L., & Jones, S. S. (2013). What it will take to achieve the as-yet-unfulfilled promises of health information technology. *Health Affairs, 32*(1), 63−68. Available from https://doi.org/10.1377/hlthaff.2012.0693.

Meloncon, L. K. (2017). Patient experience design: Expanding usability methodologies for healthcare. *Communication Design Quarterly Review, 5*(2), 19−28. Available from https://doi.org/10.1145/3131201.3131203.

Morita, P. P., & Cafazzo, J. A. (2016). Challenges and paradoxes of human factors in health technology design. *JMIR Human Factors, 3*(1), e11. Available from https://doi.org/10.2196/humanfactors.4653.

O'Connor, C. M. (2017). High heart failure readmission rates. *JACC: Heart Failure, 5*(5), 393. Available from https://doi.org/10.1016/j.jchf.2017.03.011.

O'Kane, A. A., Rogers, Y., & Blandford, A. E. (2014). *Gaining empathy for non-routine mobile device use through autoethnography. Proceedings of the SIGCHI conference on human factors in computing systems* (pp. 987−990). New York: ACM. <https://doi.org/10.1145/2556288.2557179>.

Prytherch, D. R., Smith, G. B., Schmidt, P. E., & Featherstone, P. I. (2010). ViEWS—Towards a national early warning score for detecting adult inpatient deterioration. *Resuscitation, 81*(8), 932−937. Available from https://doi.org/10.1016/j.resuscitation.2010.04.014.

Ratwani, R. M., Savage, E., Will, A., Arnold, R., Khairat, S., Miller, K., ... Hettinger, A. Z. (2018). A usability and safety analysis of electronic health records: A multi-center study. *Journal of the American Medical Informatics Association: JAMIA, 25*(9), 1197−1201. Available from https://doi.org/10.1093/jamia/ocy088.

Shanafelt, T. D., Dyrbye, L. N., Sinsky, C., Hasan, O., Satele, D., Sloan, J., & West, C. P. (2016). Relationship between clerical burden and characteristics of the electronic environment with physician burnout and professional satisfaction. *Mayo Clinic Proceedings. Mayo Clinic, 91*(7), 836−848. Available from https://doi.org/10.1016/j.mayocp.2016.05.007.

Stenhouse, C., Coates, S., Tivey, M., Allsop, P., & Parker, T. (2000). Prospective evaluation of a modified Early Warning Score to aid earlier detection of patients developing critical illness on a general surgical ward. *British Journal of Anaesthesia, 84*(5), 663P. Available from https://doi.org/10.1093/bja/84.5.663.

Stickdorn, M., & Schneider, J. (2011). *This is service design thinking: Basics, tools, cases* (p. 373) Amsterdam: Wiley, BIS Publishers.

Swensen, S. J., Meyer, G. S., Nelson, E. C., Hunt, G. C., Jr, Pryor, D. B., Weissberg, J. I., ... James, B. C. (2010). Cottage industry to postindustrial care—The revolution in health care delivery. *The New England Journal of Medicine, 362*(5), e12. https://www.nejm.org/doi/full/10.1056/NeJMp0911199.

Van de Maele, D. (2015). *Change management is now service design.* Retrieved from https://medium.com/@davevandemaele/change-management-is-now-service-design-3374e3b21b44.

Vicente, K. J. (2004). *The human factor: Revolutionizing the way we live with technology.* Toronto, ON, Canada: Vintage Canada.

Yeung, M. S. (2011). *Enhancement of critical care response teams through the use of electronic nursing-mediated vital signs surveillance* (Master of Health Science) (2009). University of Toronto. Retrieved from < https://tspace.library.utoronto.ca/handle/1807/19006 >.

Yeung, M. S., Lapinsky, S. E., Granton, J. T., Doran, D. M., & Cafazzo, J. A. (2012). Examining nursing vital signs documentation workflow: Barriers and opportunities in general internal medicine units. *Journal of Clinical Nursing, 21*(7−8), 975−982. Available from https://doi.org/10.1111/j.1365-2702.2011.03937.x.

Zomerdijk, L. G., & Voss, C. A. (2010). Service design for experience-centric services. *Journal of Service Research, 13*(1), 67−82. Available from https://doi.org/10.1177/1094670509351960.

Chapter 4

Design for eHealth and telehealth

Dena Al-Thani[1], Savio Monteiro[2] and Lakshman S. Tamil[2]

[1]*College of Science and Engineering, Hamad Bin Khalifa University, Doha, Qatar,* [2]*Quality of Life Technology Laboratory, Erik Jonsson School of Engineering and Computer Science, University of Texas at Dallas, Richardson, TX, United States*

Introduction

The skyrocketing healthcare cost and the insufficient healthcare manpower have been an impetus for the changing paradigm in healthcare, especially for managing chronic conditions, follow-up care, general wellbeing, and rural care with more emphasis on patient-centric health management. Patient-centric management involves people taking shared responsibility for their health outcomes. The tools necessary to achieve this include an electronic health record (EHR), sensor devices for gathering physiological information relevant to the particular illness, contextual presentation of information to both patients and doctors, and optimized communication and involvement of healthcare personnel. All these components should be integrated into a system for easy use by both the patients and the healthcare providers. The Quality of Life Technology Laboratory at the University of Texas at Dallas has developed such an integrated system that can be used easily via the web. The system is called "HygeiaTel," and it is used here as an example to describe the design of the next-generation telehealth system. This powerful telehealth system is capable of providing, anywhere and anytime, health service at a reduced cost. Telehealth per se is not a new concept (Roine, Ohinmaa, & Hailey, 2001); consultation and second opinion via email, telephone, and facsimile had been already in existence.

The systems in place now are less synchronous and are more tuned toward doctor-to-doctor consultation than patient-to-doctor consultation. Recently, there are videoconferencing systems established around the globe for teleconsultation between doctors and patients. Though these telehealth centers provide some telecare, they do not transform one's living room into a virtual doctor's office. The future systems will provide such a virtual

Design for Health. DOI: https://doi.org/10.1016/B978-0-12-816427-3.00004-X

67

experience of a doctor's office for the patients right in their living rooms (Devasigamani, McCracken, & Tamil, 2013; Monteiro, Gupta, Nourani, & Tamil, 2011; Saeed et al., 2009).

A glimpse of the future of the telehealth is shown in Fig. 4.1. The changing demographic patterns of the world show a declining potential-support ratio especially among the developed countries. Support ratio is an index developed by the United Nations to describe the number of people available to provide support for people older than 65 years of age or younger than 16 years of age. This number has been steadily declining from 12 in 1950 to 9 in 2009 and is expected to decline further to 4 in 2050. Also, in the future, the younger population will be found more in the currently underdeveloped countries while the aging population will be overwhelming in the developed countries. Considering the future demographics of the world, Fig. 4.1 is a potential architecture of the future healthcare system where telehealth can play a vital role in alleviating the imbalance of available younger population to care for the elderly. A pilot trial of the "HygeiaTel" system was conducted on 12 congestive heart failure (CHF) patients at a rural hospital in Texas, United States, with the intent to keep them at their homes and prevent them from returning to the hospital or the emergency room for at least 30 days after the initial treatment for CHF. The trial was successful and provided rich information on the design aspects of a successful telehealth system. The lessons learned in the design of "HygeiaTel" telehealth system forms the core of this chapter. Fig. 4.2 provides an overview of "HygeiaTel."

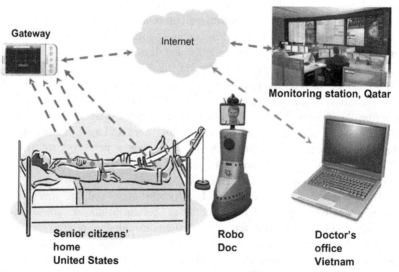

FIGURE 4.1 The future telehealth application.

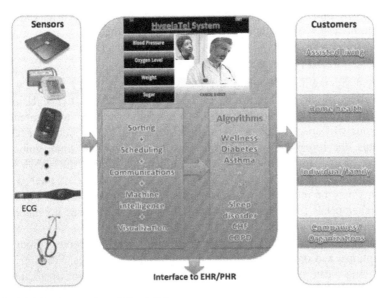

FIGURE 4.2   An overview of HygeiaTel.

Functional and nonfunctional requirements

When designing for eHealth and telehealth, the requirement gathering and prototype design stages need to be centered around patients, clinicians, and the healthcare system (Boehm & Basili, 2005; Sommerville, 2011).

Functional requirements explain how the system behaves while nonfunctional requirements represent the system's constraints. Functional requirements include the main purpose of the product. A functional requirement of the "HygeiaTel" system is that it should be capable of connecting patients to healthcare professionals anywhere and anytime. This is a high-level requirement which can be broken down into a number of requirements such as an online appointment system, a live display of a patient's vital signs in the doctor's portal, payment system, and so on. Nonfunctional requirements would include the compatibility of the sensors integrated to the portal, the system performance, and the portal's design and usability.

Requirement gathering for telemedicine system

When planning the requirement gathering process for an interactive telemedicine system, the designer should think first about the type of data that must be gathered. In such a study it is usual to use a combination of qualitative and quantitative techniques. For example, if you need to know how engaged the patients are with a specific system, you may need to look at the system logs. If you plan to design an entirely new system for clinical use, you may need to interview the clinicians and perhaps observe them.

Interviews and focus groups

When designing for telehealth the researcher will typically interview the main users of the system, which will be clinicians and patients. Using a semistructured interview approach is preferable, whereby a researcher's questions will arise out of the discussion, depending on the course it takes. For this, the researcher will need to develop an interview topic guide. A number of challenges arise with this technique. Scheduling interviews with clinicians can be extremely difficult given the busy nature of their work. Patients may be reluctant to discuss topics relating to their health. Thus the researcher needs to frame the questions in a way which does not interfere with the patients' privacy.

Focus groups are helpful when it comes to exploring people's thoughts, perceptions, and opinions about introducing new technologies. Focus groups have long been used in health services research (Institute for Clinical Evaluative Science, 1999). Their use can result in rich data content and allow the researcher to explore unexpected and new ideas.

Observational studies

Observations are currently the most popular data collection technique when designing an interactive telehealth or eHealth system. Given the richness of the data collected, researchers in the field favor it over other techniques. The main method for collecting data is taking field notes. Video and audio recording may also be used. However, video and audio recording in healthcare settings may be rather restricted due to the need to maintain patients' privacy. Observational techniques are often coupled with surveys to assess satisfaction, usability, performance, or cognitive load. Observational studies are very time consuming. They may take months or years and, in some cases, would need a sizable team of researchers. In addition, clinicians are usually reluctant to perform observational studies, as this kind of study is unlike clinical trials where a study protocol is very well structured and prepared. In addition, observational studies tend to be less structured and are often considered to be exploratory studies.

Existing system log data

Data logs of telehealth systems are extremely helpful for investigating usage patterns, participant engagement, usability issues, users' information needs, and much more. These logs also enable a researcher to understand a user's behavior during observational studies. Such data logs may already be in place for security and privacy reasons, or the researcher may need to ask the development team to add these logs. In some cases, it might be hard to implement a mechanism for keeping logs. For example, you might not have access to the back end of the system you are studying. In such a scenario, you may record the screen and use video analysis software to annotate the videos and manually create the logs.

Studying documentations

Another technique of requirement gathering, in the context of telehealth or eHealth, is reviewing documentation. This can include doctors' notes and reports, patients' charts, and other related documents which provide the designer with a rich source of information. By studying such documents the designer will have a good understanding of the context of the work, the type of data collected, and action required. This method also avoids the need to meet with clinicians or medical professionals, which is a challenging aspect of other techniques.

Participatory design

There is a growing interest in the application of this method in the health domain (Greenbaum, 1993); participatory design (PD) ensures the acceptance of eHealth or telehealth system, as the users are involved in the design and development stages. One main challenge that could affect the success of such a project is the ability to bring all the stakeholders together. However, companies such as Coloplast and Kaiser Permanente had successfully implemented this technique in their design and development activities. Therefore applying such a process with a commercial partner might be helpful.

Andersen, Bansler, Kensing, and Moll (2017) collaborated with two commercial companies to develop an eHealth prototype into a full commercial system. In the project, called SCAUT, they conducted a series of PD workshops with 60 cardiac device patients. In the workshops the patients' relatives, cardiologists, nurses, and lab technicians were involved alongside a project team that included software developers, designers, and researchers. The workshops were conducted in a number of settings including patients' homes, and cardiologists' clinics and meeting rooms. One of the main aims of SCAUT is to improve patients' and clinicians' engagement when using remote monitoring of patients with an implanted electronic cardiac device. On the completion of the project the team discussed the challenges of applying PD. Patients' and clinicians' disagreements were one of the main challenges highlighted in this research work, because the perceptions, backgrounds, interests, and goals differ from one type of user to another. Thus the researcher needs to find common ground between patients, clinicians, and other system users from which to start the discussion. In most projects the aim of conducting PD workshops is to introduce new technologies into the clinicians' workflow. Thus some clinicians might feel unwilling to be involved, as they may view the integration of technology as a burden and will, therefore, push for some features to be removed.

Design and prototyping

The design and prototyping stages follow the requirement gathering stage. The first stage in the design phase is referred to as the conceptual design, in which "the requirements are transformed into a conceptual model" (Sharp, Rogers, & Preece, 2007). A conceptual design should outline the purpose of the system and the concepts whereby the users would interact with it. The concepts include the type of interface, the type of interaction, the metaphor used, and the domain of the system. To develop the conceptual design the designer would need to analyze the data gathered from the previous stage and the list of functional and nonfunctional requirements produced.

Once the conceptual design is defined and discussed with the various stakeholders (including the patients, clinicians, and medical professionals) the design team will have a more concrete and detailed idea of the design. The process of discussing the design is also iterative, in which a new design suggestion is discussed in each iteration. The design team can then come up with a concrete design. A concrete design involves the look and feel of the system, the design of the screen, the information visualization, the layout of the screens, the interaction type, and more. The following stage is the prototype production. Prototypes are a version of the system that allows designers to collect feedback from the stakeholders. Prototypes can be developed at any time during the system development's life cycle. At the early stages, a low-fidelity prototype can be produced. A low-fidelity prototype can simply be a paper drawing illustrating what the system would look like. Later on, in the product's life cycle, the user can be introduced to the high-fidelity prototype. A high-fidelity prototype is a functional prototype, whereby the user can actually perform the tasks. However, a functional prototype is not considered to be a full system. A prototype can represent a full set of features that are not yet functional. This is referred to as a horizontal prototype (Nielsen, 1987), while a vertical prototype can represent one or more features that are fully functional. Depending on the data that the designer aims to collect, and the stage of the system's development, the designer must choose between different types of prototypes. Developing and assessing the prototype with users in the telemedicine domain has a number of benefits (Patel, Kannampallil, & Kaufman, 2015). It allows for early validation with patients and medical professionals. It allows both patients and medical professionals to take an active part in the development and hence enables easy adoption. The designer and developer will have the opportunity to understand the critical context such as patient's home, doctor's office, and outdoor. Most importantly, studies in the field of human computer interaction (HCI) have long shown that such an approach has a major impact on the success of the project (Hix & Hartson, 1993).

Case study: heart failure readmission prevention

HygeiaTel is a web-based telehealth system capable of providing connectivity anywhere and anytime to patients and healthcare professionals. It is based on client/server architecture and incorporates three different but interconnected portals: one for patients, one for healthcare providers such as doctors and nurses, and one for real-time monitoring stations. A schematic of the architecture and the important components of the system are shown in Figs. 4.3 and 4.4, respectively (Tamil, 2009). This Internet-based system is highly scalable and is capable of thousands of simultaneous connections (Saeed et al., 2009). Security and privacy are incorporated as an integral part of the design. There are two layers to the architecture: the data layer and the management layer. The data layer provides a seamless data path to audio/video, EHR, and medical devices. The management layer provides device management, login and security management, and billing management.

Cross-platform compatibility and flexibility are important design features. HygeiaTel allows healthcare providers to use any Internet-connected computer: a desktop, a tablet, or a smartphone. The monitoring stations can use all of these devices except smartphone. If the number of patients monitored is large, then the Internet bandwidth to the monitoring station should also be proportionally large. The patient-side device should have additional Bluetooth connectivity, as it acts also as a gateway to the medical devices used for vital signs measurement. Giving doctors the capability to measure

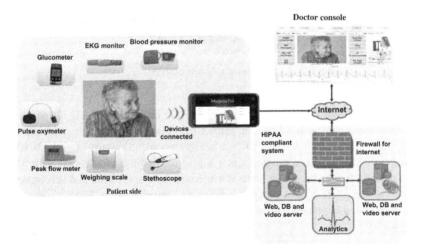

FIGURE 4.3 HygeiaTel telehealth system.

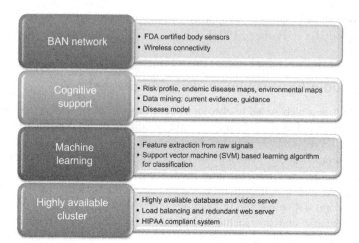

FIGURE 4.4   Components of HygeiaTel system.

FIGURE 4.5   Snapshot of patient web portal (Monteiro, 2015).

patients' vital signs remotely produces a virtual clinic-like setting. Also, the same devices can be used by the patient to periodically measure vital signs and post them automatically to the health record (Monteiro et al., 2010; Monteiro, 2015). These readings, in conjunction with prediction algorithms, can provide feedback, advice, and alarm when necessary. This is a secondary usage of the system as a chronic care management system. Fig. 4.5 shows the view of the patient portal where the vital sign measurements are also displayed.

The vital sign measurements are also posted in the server, enabling access by doctors and monitoring stations. Fig. 4.6 gives the view of a monitoring

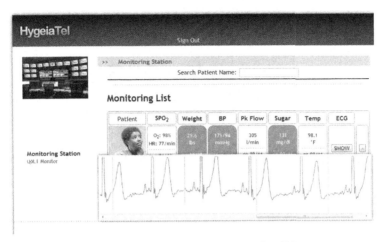

FIGURE 4.6   Snapshot of monitoring station web portal (Monteiro, 2015).

station portal where a nurse or a technician can remotely monitor a large number of patients from a single location and act when necessary.

System operation

When a patient wants to see a doctor online, s/he goes to the patient web portal and chooses one of the available Internet doctors based on physician profile and specialty. Then the payment system appears and requests the patient to pay for the service using a credit card, and as soon as the payment transaction is over, the patient and the doctor are connected via video and audio. The doctor can request the patient to take his vital signs if the patient has the required devices. The readings will be automatically available and visible in the doctor's portal for the doctor to see. The doctor can request blood and other test results including X-ray and MRI, which the patient can obtain from an independent laboratory and post in the EHR. The doctor has the contact information for all the pharmacies and laboratories in the vicinity of the patient and so can send the prescription directly for pharmacy delivery or patient pickup. At the end of the session the doctor can post a report to the EHR as well as forward it to the patient's email.

Contextual and cognitive support

The telehealth system described here can provide contextual as well as cognitive support. The system is able to locate the whereabouts of the patient using GPS or Internet or by asking the patient to enter a physical address. Then, using this information, the contextual agent collects weather and disease outbreak information and presents it to the doctor. This is important

FIGURE 4.7   Doctor's portal showing the weather and location of the patient (Monteiro, 2015).

information for a remotely located doctor to understand the environment of the patient and to diagnose the patient's illness correctly. Fig. 4.7 shows the doctor's web portal view of the weather and location of the patient. The system can also incorporate patient's positional information (e.g., sitting or standing) to contextualize vital sign information. This system also incorporates cognitive support for doctors and patients based on machine learning. This cognitive support system can provide trend and predictive information that can help the doctor with the diagnosis and the patient with the management of the disease.

Clinical study: a pilot trial

HygeiaTel telehealth platform was tested to see whether it can successfully prevent patients from emergency room admission or hospital readmission within 30 days of discharge from the original CHF episode. The statistics show that normally 25% of the discharged patients would be readmitted within 30 days. In our clinical study, 12 patients, discharged after a CHF episode from a rural hospital in Texas, were chosen as subjects. These patients were provided the HygeiaTel telehealth platform and peripheral devices such as weighing scale, blood pressure meter, glucose meter, and oximeter. After some training by case nurses, the patients measured their vital signs periodically and answered a questionnaire about their health. These data were automatically uploaded to a server where it was available for processing and viewing. The case nurse working remotely managed these patients and prevented all of them from readmission for 30 days (Baldwin, Black, & Hammond, 2013). This study, in addition to proving the usefulness of this telehealth system, has also pointed out the deficiency and the needed improvements to the system. The list of lessons learned and the design aspects that the future generations of telehealth systems should have are valuable outcomes of the pilot trial. Such a pilot trial is very important in designing any eHealth or telehealth system. The information it provides can be used to refine the current version as well as add additional features in the future versions of the system.

Design guidelines

Predictive analytics

Scalability of the system is an important feature; the system should be able to support hundreds of thousands of patients simultaneously. Human healthcare providers cannot monitor such a large patient population carefully. Algorithms should provide the first level of triaging, thus making the healthcare providers more efficient and also decreasing the need for large numbers of healthcare providers to manage a large patient population. HygeiaTel has preliminary predictive analytics based on machine learning and answer set programming. This has been developed and tested, initially for diabetes and CHF, and can be extended for all other chronic conditions. Predictive analytics are algorithms that predict the future behavior or trend of a dynamic system using statistical machine learning or data-mining techniques by analyzing the current and historical data. Though the field is still in its infancy, the predictive analytics are successfully used in many areas such as business, financial services, insurance, and fraud detection. One of the successful applications of predictive techniques in the financial arena is the well-known credit scoring scheme. The FICO score for credit rating that people receive is based on the historical and the current data on people. FICO-like scoring can also be computed on the health status of people if appropriate past and present health data are available (Wu & Coggeshall, 2012). For example, CHF management involves measurements of the following vital health signs: weight, blood pressure, blood oxygen, blood sugar (in some cases) and answers to the standard CHF questionnaire. These data form the set of attribute values. The CHF management has three class labels; doing well is denoted by GREEN, a worsening state by YELLOW, and doing poorly by RED, though finer classes can be added by expanding the class labels. The problem consists in computing the conditional probability distribution for all the classes at a given time. CHF management is a dynamic system with evolving states with time. Dynamic Bayesian Networks (Doucet, Freitas, & Gordon, 2001) are a temporal and time-aware probabilistic graphical model that allows us to represent a complex and dynamic system such as the CHF management. Dynamic personalized probabilistic models that take into consideration the disease state as measured by the sensors and other environmental factors can be added by expanding the attribute set. A particle filtering algorithm (Murphy, 2002) is used to estimate the conditional probability for all disease classes. The algorithm can be integrated into the remote monitoring system. The output of the system, depending on the class label, can be a notification to the patient, or a trigger for a focused educational video/instruction to the patient, or a notification to the doctor/nurse depending on the protocol programmed in the system (Monteiro, 2015). The important attributes of the predictive analytics for eHealth or telehealth application are personalization and time awareness of the data. The latest data should be used in creating the classifier, and this process should be continuous and dynamic, thus providing a self-learning environment for the machine learning system.

Personalized instruction and education for behavior modification

Behavioral modification is the key to the success of managing chronic care conditions. It is well established in psychology literature that feedback and education can help in behavioral modification. The responsibility of managing chronic conditions such as CHF mostly lies with the patients. Experience shows that a well-informed patient can behave responsibly. However, general education on a health topic becomes boring when repeated, and also the patients, in general, have trouble figuring out the instructions relevant to their current state of the disease. An effective way to educate the patients is to provide the right information, relevant to the context, just at the right time. The remote monitoring platform has an algorithm that works in conjunction with the predictive analytics algorithm to pop up context-relevant educational material. The reasons for a disease state predicted by the predictive analytics are analyzed by another algorithm that considers the details of the different sensor readings and their historic values. Prerecorded educational instructions for different disease states are stored in the remote monitoring platform, and relevant education material pops up when the algorithm prompts it to do so (Monteiro, 2015).

The most recent research in artificial intelligence (AI) can be used to help patients to modify their behavior. Intelligence has two components: (1) learning from examples, experiences, and patterns to formulate rules and (2) using these rules to perform reasoning. The field of AI attempts to automate both processes. Thus we would like to learn automatically from examples (machine learning), as well as be able to perform reasoning automatically given a set of rules (automated reasoning). Both machine learning and automated reasoning should be used for the purpose of behavior modification. Machine learning can be primarily used to compute the normal range of vitals for a given patient. Automated reasoning can capture the thought processes of the healthcare provider and automate the series of decisions based on the provider's knowledge of the patient's current state, history, and vitals.

Patients' vitals can be recorded automatically using peripherals that communicate via Bluetooth technology to the telehealth platform. So, for example, if a patient's blood pressure turns out to be elevated, then a caregiver may tell the patient to take his/her blood pressure medication, if not taken in the last few hours. If the patient has taken it in the last few hours, the caregiver may tell the patient to lie down for an hour and then measure again. There may be an alternative drug that the caregiver may ask the patient to ingest. The AI embedded in the telehealth platform can automate this thinking process. Thus instead of a healthcare provider giving these instructions, the AI program embedded in the telehealth platform can instruct the patient regarding what actions to perform. Fig. 4.8 shows the automated reasoning and plan creation for chronic care management such as CHF (Monteiro, 2015).

HygeiaTel's automated reasoning AI component is based on nonmonotonic reasoning (Chen et al., 2017, 2018; Chen, Marple, Salazar, Gupta, & Tamil, 2016). Nonmonotonic reasoning is needed because actions have to be taken not just based on what has been done in the past or what has happened in the past but also based on what has not been done or has not happened. For example, a patient may be prescribed the drug, but only if he/she is not found to be allergic to, say, acetaminophen. Standard automated reasoning systems are unable to handle such negation in a coherent manner. However, the nonmonotonic formalism for AI that is used in the system allows for elegant handling of such negation. That is a unique value proposition; by handling negations it can emulate commonsense reasoning of the caregiver better than any other reasoning technology. It can do so in a consistent

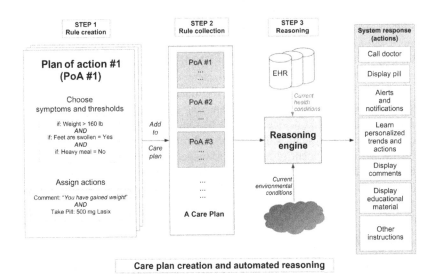

Care plan creation and automated reasoning

FIGURE 4.8 Automated reasoning and plan care creation for chronic disease management CHF (Monteiro, 2015). *CHF*, Congestive heart failure.

manner, that is, without producing any contradictions, something that is much harder for other AI technologies. Nonmonotonic reasoning can also handle default reasoning that is commonly used in medical treatment. In default reasoning, there is a default rule that is applied under normal conditions, but then there are exceptional situations when special rules have to be invoked. For example, a patient with high blood pressure and high heart rate is given Warfarin by default. However, an exception is invoked if the patient is already taking aspirin, in which case a different course of action has to be followed. The nonmonotonic reasoning method is also able to handle incomplete information, which is often the case in practical scenarios. Thus telehealth systems can be extended with advanced automated reasoning that captures the logic and rules that a caregiver employs (based on reading of the vitals, the current situation of the patient, past history, and information entered in EHR) so that a patient can be encouraged to modify his/her behavior based on instructions generated by the telehealth system, thereby reducing the demand on the caregiver's time.

Telehealth element management system

The universal deployment of a telehealth system hinges upon the ability to provide remote management and calibration of devices, ease of setup, safety, security, and reliability. The traditional network management protocols such as Simple Network Management Protocol (SNMP) cannot be used throughout the management plan, and so a structured element management framework for remote telehealth devices named telehealth element management system (TEMS) (Thomas & Tamil, 2011) should be developed. TEMS revolves around two main ideas: the organization and efficient communication of relevant functional information of the remote medical equipment. By taking advantage of the extensibility of SNMP, we can remotely gather data from telehealth equipment to aid in its element management functions such as fault, configuration, accounting, performance, and security management. This is very different than remotely managing physical and networking information of a networked device, such as IP routers and/or switches, via a network management system, which is the traditional use of SNMP. TEMS also includes the development of a unique Management Information Base (MIB), named Telehealth Sensor MIB. This can be developed as a separate module and integrated with existing telehealth platforms. Fig. 4.9 shows the sensor management web portal in HygeiaTel (Monteiro, 2015).

Security and privacy

Security and privacy are extremely important for the successful acceptance of telehealth systems by both the patients and the healthcare providers (Lim, Oh, Choi, & Lakshman, 2010). The security and privacy should be

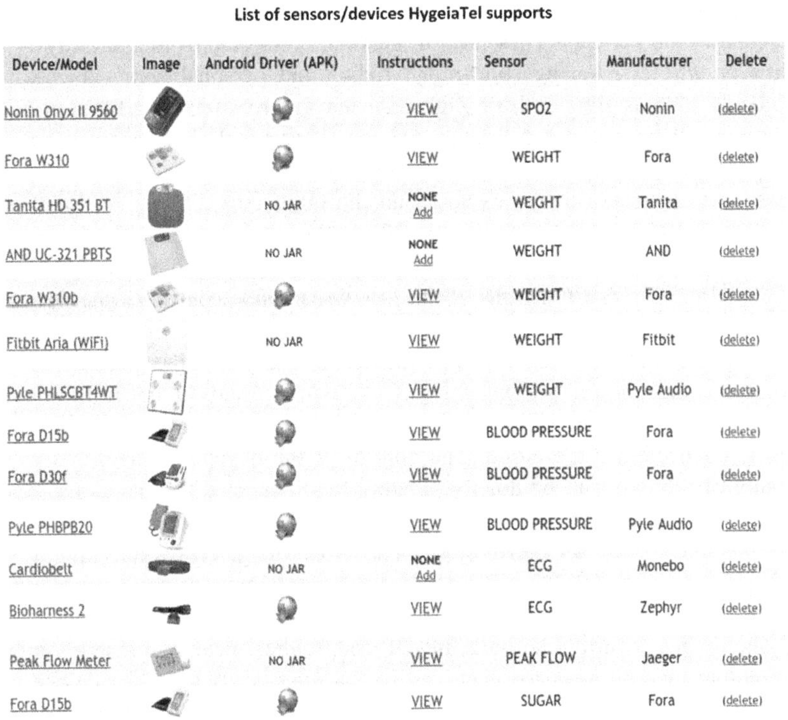

List of sensors/devices HygeiaTel supports

Device/Model	Image	Android Driver (APK)	Instructions	Sensor	Manufacturer	Delete
Nonin Onyx II 9560			VIEW	SPO2	Nonin	(delete)
Fora W310			VIEW	WEIGHT	Fora	(delete)
Tanita HD 351 BT		NO JAR	NONE Add	WEIGHT	Tanita	(delete)
AND UC-321 PBTS		NO JAR	NONE Add	WEIGHT	AND	(delete)
Fora W310b			VIEW	WEIGHT	Fora	(delete)
Fitbit Aria (WiFi)		NO JAR	VIEW	WEIGHT	Fitbit	(delete)
Pyle PHLSCBT4WT			VIEW	WEIGHT	Pyle Audio	(delete)
Fora D15b			VIEW	BLOOD PRESSURE	Fora	(delete)
Fora D30f			VIEW	BLOOD PRESSURE	Fora	(delete)
Pyle PHBPB20			VIEW	BLOOD PRESSURE	Pyle Audio	(delete)
Cardiobelt		NO JAR	NONE Add	ECG	Monebo	(delete)
Bioharness 2			VIEW	ECG	Zephyr	(delete)
Peak Flow Meter		NO JAR	VIEW	PEAK FLOW	Jaeger	(delete)
Fora D15b			VIEW	SUGAR	Fora	(delete)

FIGURE 4.9   Sensor management web portal in HygeiaTel (Monteiro, 2015).

considered from the start during the architecture and the design phase; retro-fitting security or privacy requirements after the product is developed will be a big challenge. The development team that does functional requirements should also develop requirements for security and privacy of the system. It should start with the threat modeling, examining the security and privacy features, the features that can cause security breaches, and those features that can cause trust or privacy breaches. The threat modeling should start with modeling of the application, listing of the threats, and then listing the threat mitigation strategies, followed by the test cases for validating each of the mitigation strategies. In order to optimize the whole telehealth or eHealth system for security and privacy, the system should be divided into zones: device, gateway, cloud, and service. Zoning provides an easier way to seg-ment the solution; each zone has its own data, authentication, and authoriza-tion. Each zone is separated by a trust boundary that represents the transition of data from one source to the other, and during this transition there can be threats such as spoofing, tampering, repudiation, information disclosure, denial of service, and elevation of privileges, and they should be modeled (Shahan & Lamos, 2018).

The device zones are made up of wearable devices or medical devices attached to the patients. These are, in general, connected to the gateways via wires or wirelessly using short-range radios and personal area networking protocols such as Bluetooth or Zigbee. In the future with the advent of 5G, they may all be connected through 5G via IP protocol. The gateway zones comprise the gateways and all their connected devices. A gateway has two sides, one connected to the devices and the other connected to a cloud via Wi-Fi or 3G/4G and in the future via 5G. In the case of telehealth, this gateway can be a special appliance with communication and processing facilities or a smartphone. The functions of the gateway include control of the device, communication of the data received from the device to the cloud, and edge processing of the data. The cloud zone includes the cloud, the gateways, and the devices attached to the gateways. The cloud normally is not in the same space as the gateways. Multiple gateways that are geographically separated can be connected to the cloud. The control of the device, storage, and processing of the data can be done separately but connected via the cloud. The service zone is any software component that connects to the devices via gateway or cloud. They act under their identity toward gateways and clouds to store data, analyze data and autonomously issue commands and controls the devices.

The device security can be achieved using either security tokens—which are unique identity keys for each device that can be used by the device to communicate with the gateway—or the cloud, or by implementing an on-device X.509 certificate and private key which permits authentication as a part of transport layer security (TLS). Internet connection between the devices, gateway and the cloud are secured using TLS. In the security architecture of the HygeiaTel system shown in Fig. 4.10, secure socket layer (SSL) was used, but going forward TLS 1.2 should be used for more secured connection. Cloud security can be guaranteed using device identity registry and policy-based authorization of security keys. In the service zone, efforts should be made so that all software components are secure. For example, machine learning-based decision makings are becoming prevalent in medicine; adversaries can corrupt the machine learning models by intentionally sending wrong data inputs. This adversarial machine learning can become a serious problem for automated decision-support systems in medicine. Security measures to overcome adversarial machine learning should also be a part of the security design in the future. There are government-mandated regulations such as the Health Insurance Portability and Accountability Act of 1996 (HIPAA) in the United States that dictate the privacy and security requirements of health information. The European Union's Directive on Data Protection and Canada's Personal Information Protection and Electronic Documents Act (PIPEDA) are similar regulations for health information in Europe and Canada respectively. Telehealth and eHealth systems should conform to all relevant jurisdictional regulations.

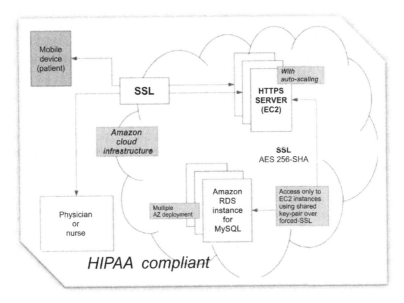

FIGURE 4.10   Security architecture of HygeiaTel System (Monteiro, 2015).

Usability

The software user interface must be usable by its target audience. Default values for the parameters must be selected so that they are a good choice for the majority of users. In order to have a usable system, the user needs to be at the center of the design and evaluation process. The move within healthcare from being physician-focused to being more patient-focused has led to the development of many mobile and wearable devices to support the patient-centric healthcare model. HygeiaTel is designed with patients and clinicians in mind. The aim is to provide the user with a seamless and engaging experience. With only a few clicks a patient can book an appointment with a doctor or input his/her own vital signs.

The interface also provides an interactive portal for nurses and technicians to remotely monitor a large number of patients. A benefit of the different visualization techniques is that the designer can support nurses and technicians by building a sophisticated platform. The platform can provide nurses and technicians with an overview of their patients and then allow them to drill down to a specific patient. The patients' data can be presented in a variety of ways from simple time charts (Badgeley et al., 2016) to complex maps (Araújo, Mejova, Aupetit, & Weber, 2017). The way the data is presented can have a huge impact on how clinicians comprehend the data and thus on whether they are able to make accurate medical decisions. The visuals should support the clinician's decision-making and diagnosing capability. Therefore it is crucial to take into account clinicians' and patients' feedback when designing the visual interface to be adopted. Looking into the most effective visualization techniques to be adopted in the system can bring about huge benefits to patients, clinicians, and healthcare institutions (Gotz & Borland, 2016).

Conclusion

The telehealth system described here has successfully gone through limited testing with rural patients in Texas, United States. The design principles discussed here are based on the lessons learned from the deployment of the system and the feedback received from both patients and healthcare providers. Telehealth will be an accepted complimentary healthcare system in the future. There are certain areas of the medicine that can be handled more easily via telehealth. Chronic care management, psychiatry, follow-up care, and general wellbeing are some of them. The first generation of the telehealth system described here incorporates vital signs measurement and cognitive and contextual information support. The second generation of telehealth system incorporates predictive analytics, personalized and context-relevant patient education for behavioral modification, element management, security, and privacy, thus making it one of the most advanced systems in this field. The future generation telehealth platforms should incorporate augmented reality and should be highly scalable, reliable, and easy to deploy.

References

Andersen, T. O., Bansler, J. P., Kensing, F., & Moll, J. (2017). From prototype to product: Making participatory design of mHealth commercially viable. In A. M. Kanstrup, A. Bygholm, P. Bertelsen, & C. Nøhr (Eds.), *Participatory design & health information technology* (pp. 95–112). IOS Press.

Araújo, M. L. D., Mejova, Y., Aupetit, M., & Weber, I. (2017). Visualizing health awareness in the middle east. In: *The proceeding of eleventh international AAAI conference on web and social media* (pp. 725–726).

Badgeley, M. A., Shameer, K., Glicksberg, B. S., Tomlinson, M. S., Levin, M. A., McCormick, P. J., ... Dudley, J. T. (2016). EHDViz: Clinical dashboard development using open-source technologies. *BMJ Open, 6*(3), pe010579.

Baldwin, K. M., Black, D. L., & Hammond, S. L. (2013). Hospital-based post-discharge community case management —Podium presentation. In: *ANCC pathway to excellence conference.*

Boehm, B., & Basili, V. R. (2005). Software defect reduction top 10 list. *Foundations of Empirical Software Engineering: The Legacy of Victor R. Basili, 426*(37), 426–431.

Chen, Z., Marple, K., Salazar, E., Gupta, G., & Tamil, L. (2016). A physician advisory system for chronic heart failure management based on knowledge patterns. *Theory and Practice of Logic Programming, 16*(5–6), 604–618.

Chen, Z., Salazar, E., Marple, K., Das, S. R., Amin, A., Cheeran, D., ... Gupta, G. (2018). An AI-based heart failure treatment adviser system. *IEEE Journal of Translational Engineering in Health and Medicine, 6*, 1–10.

Chen, Z., Salazar, E., Marple, K., Gupta, G., Tamil, L., Cheeran, D., ... Amin, A. (2017). Improving adherence to heart failure management guidelines via abductive reasoning. *Theory and Practice of Logic Programming, 17*(5−6), 764−779.

Devasigamani, R., McCracken J., & Tamil, L. (2013). Maximizing profits by integrating telehealth consultations in private practices. In: *Proceeding of the American telehealth conference, ATA 2013*, Austin, TX, May 5−7.

Doucet, A., Freitas, N. de, & Gordon, N. (Eds.), (2001). *Sequential Monte Carlo methods in practice*. New York: Springer.

Gotz, D., & Borland, D. (2016). Data-driven healthcare: Challenges and opportunities for interactive visualization. *IEEE Computer Graphics and Applications, 36*(3), 90−96.

Greenbaum, J. (1993). A design of one's own: Towards participatory design in the United States. In D. Schuler, & A. Namioka (Eds.), *Participatory design: Principles and practices*. Hillsdale, NJ: Lawrence Erlbaum.

Hix, D., & Hartson, H. R. (1993). *Rapid prototyping of interaction design*. Developing user interfaces (pp. 249−281). New York: Wiley Professional Computing.

Institute for Clinical Evaluative Science. (1999). Focus groups in health services research at ICES. In: *ICES publication no 99-02-TR*. Ontario, Canada.

Lim, S., Oh, T. H., Choi, Y. B., & Lakshman, T. (2010). Security issues on wireless body area network for remote healthcare monitoring. In: *Proceeding of the IEEE international conference on sensor networks, ubiquitous, and trustworthy computing* (pp. 327−332). IEEE.

Monteiro, Natarajan, S., Saeed, A., Banerjee, S., Gupta, G., Nourani, M., & Tamil, L. (2010). An internet based telemedicine platform with cognitive support. In: *Proceeding of the building partnerships and pathways to address engineering grand challenges conference*, El Paso, TX, Feb. 8−10, 2010.

Monteiro, S. (August 2015). *An intelligent telemedicine platform with cognitive support for chronic care management* (Ph.D. dissertation). Richardson, TX: University of Texas at Dallas.

Monteiro, S., Gupta, G., Nourani, M., & Tamil, L. (2011). HygeiaTel: An intelligent telemedicine system with cognitive support. In: *Proceeding of the first international workshop on mobile systems, applications, and services for healthcare, mHealthSys-2011*, Seattle, WA, Nov. 1.

Murphy, K. (2002) *Dynamic Bayesian networks: Representation, inference and learning* (Ph.D. dissertation). UC, Berkeley, CA: Computer Science Division.

Nielsen, J. (1987). Using scenarios to develop user friendly videotext systems. In: *Proceedings of the NordData87, Joint Scandinavian Computer Conference*.

Patel, V. L., Kannampallil, T. G., & Kaufman, D. R. (Eds.) (2015). *A multi-disciplinary science of human computer interaction in biomedical informatics. In. Cognitive informatics for biomedicine* (pp. 1−7). Springer.

Roine, R., Ohinmaa, A., & Hailey, D. (2001). Assessing telemedicine: A systematic review of the literature. *Canadian Medical Association Journal, 165*(6), 765.

Saeed, A., Faezipour, M., Nourani, M., Banerjee, S., Lee, G., Gupta, G., & Tamil, L. (2009). A scalable wireless body area network for bio-telemetry. *Journal of Information Processing Systems, 5*(2), 77−86.

Shahan, R., & Lamos, B. (2018). IoT security architecture. Available from <https://docs.microsoft.com/en-us/azure/iot-fundamentals/iot-security-architecture> Retrieved 13.05.19.

Sharp, H., Rogers, Y., & Preece, J. (2007). *Interaction design: Beyond human-computer interaction* (2nd revised ed.). Chichester; Hoboken, NJ: John Wiley & Sons.

Sommerville, I. (2011). *Software engineering* (9th ed.). Boston, MA: Addison-Wesley.

Tamil, L. S. (2009). Pervasive health care and healthcare technologies. In: *Proceedings of the 2009 IEEE international conference on multimedia and expo, ICME 2009*, New York City, June 28–July 2. IEEE 2009.

Thomas, J. W., & Tamil, L. S. (2011). Element management system framework for a remote telemedicine sensor environment. In: *Proceeding of the second annual AMA-IEEE medical technology conference*. Boston, MA.

Wu, J., & Coggeshall, S. (2012). *Foundations of predictive analytics*. Boca Raton, FL: Taylor and Francis.

Chapter 5

Design of mobile health technology

Plinio Pelegrini Morita[1,2]
[1]*School of Public Health and Health Systems, Faculty of Applied Health Sciences, University of Waterloo, Waterloo, ON, Canada,* [2]*Institute of Health Policy, Management and Evaluation, University of Toronto, Toronto, ON, Canada*

Introduction

Mobile health (mHealth) technology is commonly defined as "the practice of eHealth assisted by smartphones, which are used to capture, analyze, process, and transmit health-based information from sensors and other biomedical systems" (Sasan, 2015). eHealth is a broader concept defined by the delivery of healthcare services and useful information to patients, family members, and healthcare providers through the use of electronic devices and communication. The general definition of mHealth includes a wide range of products and technologies that can be used for collecting data from individuals, ranging from apps to help manage chronic conditions to smartwatches that measure heart rate in conjunction to a smartphone app. mHealth provides a new way to collect patients' health information either through the use of sensors (e.g., wearables, internal phone sensors, Internet of Things [IoT], wireless devices) or through self-reported data collected through mobile apps (questionnaires, self-reported values that are collected by non-connected devices and later reported in the app) (Free et al., 2013; Goyal, Morita, Lewis, et al., 2016; Steinhubl, Muse, & Topol, 2015). Examples of wearables can be found in Fig. 5.1.

mHealth devices normally use smartphones as a gateway to collect data from patients in remote (e.g., rural or isolated) or home settings, enabling a more comprehensive assessment of patients' health, the deployment of self-management programs that empower patients to be more involved in their care, and the shift from acute care to community care. Current technology monitors patients' health continuously, with the added benefit of informing clinicians about patient conditions in near-real-time.

Design for Health. DOI: https://doi.org/10.1016/B978-0-12-816427-3.00005-1

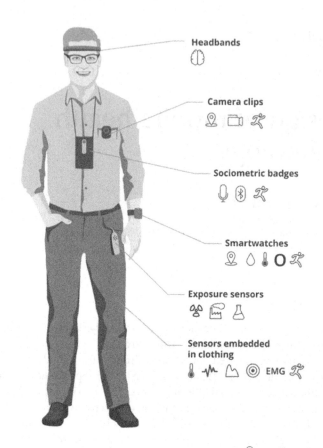

FIGURE 5.1   Examples of mobile health devices.

Wearables are sensors built into form factors that can be carried on your body to collect information about your health and about your well-being. Wearables have been extensively used to monitor physical activity, sleep, heart rate, falls, and balance issues, among others (Piwek, Ellis, Andrews, & Joinson, 2016). The uniqueness of wearable devices is in the ability for users to carry them and enable health monitoring 24/7—a transformative shift worth discussing and categorizing to better frame the design guidelines and case study next.

The new world of mHealth

mHealth technology has changed our approach to health monitoring, leading to a new model that empowers patients to be involved in their own care, while also changing how clinicians interpret our health (Free et al., 2013; Goyal, Morita, Lewis, et al., 2016; Goyal, Morita, Picton, et al., 2016; Morita et al., 2019). Before the advent of mHealth, clinicians were only able to evaluate their patients by measuring health conditions in the clinic, through results of laboratory and clinical tests, and through self-reported information provided by patients and family members during clinic visits. mHealth has enabled clinicians to have a better insight into patients' health though the collection of more frequent and richer data from patients being monitored, providing continuous and near-real-time data about the condition being monitored (Morita et al., 2019). mHealth apps enable remote patient monitoring, empower patients to self-manage their diseases, and provide useful educational content to the end users. Other examples of mHealth apps include personal health records (PHRs) as a channel for patients to access their medical records and educational platforms that deliver tailored content. Table 5.1 presents a sample of types of mHealth solutions that are available on the market for patients and clinicians alike.

Wellness versus clinical practice

It is important to highlight the distinction between using mHealth for clinical practice and using these same technologies for wellness and well-being

TABLE 5.1 Examples of mHealth solutions and their use.

Technology	Examples	Function
Mobile health apps	WellDoc Shire OnePath Mobile App bant 30 Days MyFitnessPal	Support the collection of data through mobile sensors, self-reported data, questionnaires, and others
Wearable devices	Fitbit Apple Watch Garmin	Collect health information through direct monitoring of your activities or vital signs
Internet of Things	Withings Aura Smart Sleep SystemBedditWireless blood pressure cuffs	Nonwearable devices that collect health information through sensors in your home

self-monitoring (Gagnon, Ngangue, Payne-Gagnon, & Desmartis, 2016; Steinhubl et al., 2015). The current use of these technologies for clinical practice is still in its infancy, and most of the use of mHealth apps and wearables end up falling into the consumer-level technology category. Consequently, individuals are either self-monitoring or self-managing their chronic conditions without the supervision of a physician, or they are using the technology to monitor fitness levels and for self-understanding. From a design perspective, it is important to consider the final application of the app or wearable being designed. The features to be embedded into the app should be well aligned with how the technology will be used by different types of user, ensuring that user need and limitation are considered when selecting features for the app.

Currently, mHealth apps are not fully integrated into the healthcare system as a component of patient care (Gagnon et al., 2016). One of the main reasons for this limitation is the skepticism from clinicians to use this data for clinical decision making due to the lower quality of the data and high level of uncertainty. For example, when a reading is provided by a wireless scale, there is no guarantee that the data is coming from the patient being monitored, and the quality of the data is usually lower than data collected by clinical-grade scales and measured using well-established protocols in the clinic.

Within this space, one of the largest movements supporting the use of mHealth data for better patient self-understanding is a community self-identified as Quantified Self (Swan, 2012). This community focuses on the development of apps, algorithms, and APIs to extract data from mHealth and wearables to enable patients to build a better understanding of their own health (Quantified Self, 2019; Swan, 2012).

Types of mHealth solutions

In addition to the different use scenarios described above, designers should also be aware of the different types of mHealth solutions available on the market, some of their characteristics, and challenges in the design of these solutions. Some examples presented next should give the readers an idea of the possible mHealth solutions:

PHRs—These apps provide patients access to their medical records, presented as a web-portal or mobile app, with a wide range of types of information displayed (e.g., medical notes, lab results, medical images). The main design challenge with PHRs is the sheer amount of information available in electronic medical records and the fact that PHRs can only provide access to a small subset of variables of the larger system. Designers should spend significant effort with information architecture to ensure that the large amounts of data are presented to the users in a meaningful and organized structure, avoiding the paradox of choice, which will be discussed later in this chapter.

In addition, PHRs provide access to confidential patient information, so privacy by design should be incorporated into the design of the technology, following HIPAA guidelines (U.S. Department of Health & Human Services, 2019) (see Chapter 10, Designing for collaborative work, for more details). My HealtheVet is an example of a successful PHR system, providing access to pharmacy systems, appointments, and health records (HealtheVet, 2019).

Apps for self-management of chronic conditions—mHealth can be designed to support patients interested in self-managing their chronic conditions. Apps designed for this purpose should focus on promoting positive behavior change focused on enabling patients to monitor their own health and improving their lifestyles. An important methodology in this space is persuasive design (see below), where a set of features can be incorporated into the app design to guide indented behaviors. Designers involved in the development of these apps should focus on understanding the user behavior that they are trying to target. Medly (Ware, Ross, Cafazzo, Laporte, & Seto, 2018) and breathe (Morita et al., 2019) are some examples of successful mHealth apps for supporting patients with different types of chronic diseases.

Remote patient monitoring and telehealth apps—Seniors living independently and patients in the community with chronic diseases often need to collect health data using portable medical devices to send a stream of data for healthcare providers to support their care. Patients with diabetes, for example, need to constantly monitor their levels of blood glucose using portable glucometers. This information is critical for patients to provide to their physician, and the responsibility for collecting and compiling the information often falls on patients and family members. mHealth can be designed to support these patients, providing tools for the collection of symptoms, medication intake, measurements taken, and automatic data collection from connected devices. Designers developing apps of this type should incorporate features that can remind patients of their schedule, provide patients with an easy and straightforward interface to collect data, and engagement mechanisms to bring patients back to the app when more data is needed from them. Examples of portable medical devices include, for example, continuous glucose monitoring devices and connected blood pressure monitors.

Health and well-being—A large majority of mHealth apps on the market promote and support self-monitoring one's fitness levels and well-being. These apps aim at providing insights about everyday activity levels, food intake, and weight, among other variables. They also serve as a platform for users to collect data, provision of algorithms to provide more in-depth insights about users' data, a platform to share progress with others, and a social media engine to highlight how performance compares to that of peers. Designers developing apps of this type should have in mind that the users of these platforms are already engaged and that the common frequent users of the platform do not normally represent the larger population, as these are usually more engaged, self-driven, and committed to a healthier lifestyle. Apps in this category include, but are not limited to, MyFitnessPal (Under Armour, 2019) and the <30 Days app (Goyal, Morita, Picton, et al., 2016).

Wearables—As hardware attached to the user's body, wearables provide a sensor platform to collect user-level data including heart rate, physical activity, sleep, and skin conductance. Wearables will have a limited user interface embedded into the device, so this type of mHealth presents additional challenges for designers as it will normally require the design of a more complex user interaction, the design of an accompanying smartphone app, and the industrial design of the wearable itself. Designers working with the design of wearables should consider the importance of esthetics and visual appeal, as wearables will normally be incorporated with the user's outfit and consequently require a more in-depth analysis of the style preferences of the user base. Fitbit (Fitbit, 2019) and the Apple Watch (Apple, 2019a) are some examples of widely used wearables capable of collecting relevant health data.

Healthcare IoT—Homes are becoming loaded with connected sensors capable of monitoring our health. Ranging from simple wireless scales measuring our weight (e.g., Withings Body or Fitbit Aria) to more complex devices that can monitor the everyday chores of individuals living with dementia, several new sensors are being developed and integrated into health monitoring platforms every day. Designers working with Healthcare IoT will be focusing on the industrial design of the device, with a great focus on maintaining adherence and ensuring users are using the sensors regularly. Widely used IoT devices that we have at home capable of monitoring our health include wireless scales, smart pillboxes, and fall detection systems.

Design guidelines

Considering the types of mHealth presented above and the intended use of the mHealth solution being designed, several factors need to be considered to ensure proper uptake both from patients and healthcare providers alike. The design of any mHealth solution will follow user-centered design principles and methodologies in which, through an iterative process, designers will revise the design of the solutions based on user feedback (design tools presented in the use-case), the user performance measured through in-app analytics (analytics tools presented in the use-case), and usability issues identified through cognitive walkthroughs and usability testing (Wiklund, Kendler, & Strochlic, 2011). Only through full cycles of complete user-centered design, it is possible to minimize user interaction issues and maximize the benefit to the final user.

As with any user-centered design process, the design activities will start at the collection of user requirements. Designers should spend a significant amount of time understanding how patients manage their chronic conditions or monitor their health, understanding what their needs are, and identifying the optimal way to support patients and healthcare providers before starting the prototyping activities. A proper understanding of what the patients or final users of the app/wearable need will lead to designers actually designing mHealth that can benefit patients. Therefore it is important to:

- *consider the environment in which the user is going to be using the technology* (e.g., forgetting that clinicians will be using gloves when interacting with a smartphone may severely impact the rate of adoption);
- *consider the type of care that the patient is receiving*, as patients that are under constant surveillance by their clinicians will use self-reporting features more frequently than patients that are not (Morita et al., 2019);
- *consider the type of device the patient is using*, as the choice of iOS, Android, or Windows will define which functions are available for developers, the types of users that will be using the app, and the variety of devices that will have to be designed for;
- *consider the limitations of the end-users*, as, for example, seniors with cognitive and motor limitations may struggle to use the app if it is designed for smaller devices like smartphones; and
- *consider the lifestyle of the user*, designing apps for healthy, well-fit users who are looking for opportunities to improve their fitness levels requires a very different approach from designing for patients with chronic conditions (see the section "Persuasive design"). Other important considerations include the ideal times to reach out to the patients (Morita et al., 2019), which can be determined using in-app analytics.

Function and features for mHealth apps

mHealth apps share a list of common features that over the years have demonstrated value to the end users. While not an exhaustive list, the following represents the majority of functions normally present:

- Sensor integration—Wearable and healthcare IoT integration allows mHealth apps to collect user/patient data directly from home.
- Journaling—Component of an mHealth app that allows users to log symptoms, thoughts, food intake, medication intake, notes, and more.
- Questionnaires—Features to collect self-reported data from users in the form of questions and narratives.
- Reminders—Component that allows users to set up reminders for medication, adherence to the use of the mHealth app, and other tasks.
- Educational components—Educational content presented in multiple formats as, for example, text, video, or games.
- Gamification—Tools to keep users engaged with the mHealth app/treatment, while coming back to monitor their health and compete with peers.

- Social media—Social channels for users to share their progress, compete with others, and receive support from peers.

Importance of visual appeal and following design guidelines

mHealth apps running on smartphones need to be aligned with current design standards and guidelines. End users will expect the same level of design quality as they would from other apps in their phone. Since larger companies such as Google and Apple invest strongly in the design of their apps, innovators in the mHealth space must strive to design apps that also satisfy those same design standards. These companies usually publish design guidelines that can be used by app designers to align their apps to the platform standards. Apple has organized their guidelines in their Human Interface Guideline library (Apple, 2019b), while Google publishes their material in the Material Design library (Google, 2019).

Persuasive design

A significant portion of designing mHealth technology is focused on fostering positive behavior change and ensuring certain behaviors are performed by the user (Goyal, Morita, Lewis, et al., 2016; Morita et al., 2019; Uddin et al., 2016). Persuasive design in healthcare is a methodology aimed at providing small incremental behavioral changes to drive users to healthier lifestyles (Oinas-Kukkonen & Harjumaa, 2009). For example, apps that monitor blood glucose levels are designed to ensure that users collect glucose level measurements daily. Within this scenario, as designers, it is important to consider persuasive design as a design tool focusing on driving behavior (Oinas-Kukkonen & Harjumaa, 2009). Designers of mHealth technology can leverage persuasive design to incorporate features that not only ensure positive user experience but also modify the necessary behaviors targeted by the intervention.

Paradoxes of health technology design

Throughout the design of mHealth technology, innovators need to be aware of the paradoxes of health technology design and the potential impact on the final product, to avoid misalignment between final user needs and the app or wearable that is being developed (Morita & Cafazzo, 2015). The paradox of expertise describes how subject matter experts may not represent the actual final users of the technology. Individuals engaged in the design of new solutions are normally expert users and have different mental models from the main end user. For example, a patient advocating for the development of new tools to monitor their asthma may be very familiar with smartphone technology and wearables. Hence, when interviewing these individuals during the user-needs assessment, designers need to be cognizant of the different level of technology savviness, ability to self-manage, and the mental models around how their asthma flare-ups operate.

Designers are often tempted to incorporate as many features as possible in the app to target as many users' needs as possible. The paradox of choice (Schwartz, 2004) explains how users, when overloaded with options, do not make the right decisions and feel overwhelmed, resulting in attrition. It is important to include features that satisfy the user needs and to incorporate a set of features that achieve the goals of the app or wearable, while keeping it simple and manageable by the user. Designers must be careful not to overdesign an app, incorporate too many functionalities and features, and target too many user needs. The best mHealth tools on the market are simple, focus on the very specific user needs, and deliver value with a minimal number of features.

The last paradox is the paradox of preference versus performance (Morita & Cafazzo, 2015). Designers have the opportunity to incorporate very interesting, engaging, and shiny features on apps that will potentially raise the interest and skew the preference of users. However, that does not mean that those features and design solutions will lead to the best performance when users are interacting with the app. An overdesigned app may attract users and result in users preferring a solution that does not have the highest performance. For this reason, it is always important to evaluate the designs using usability testing with well-established performance metrics, as only asking users about their preference may result in the selection of solutions that do not necessarily reflect their optimal user performance.

Case study: understanding user behavior in the wild through real-world data

The science of data-driven design (Morita et al., 2019) relies heavily on the collection of solid analytic indicators that can help us understand how people are using the apps. Some of these apps included *breathe*, an mHealth app designed to help patients with asthma (Morita et al., 2019) (Fig. 5.2); and <30 Days (Goyal, Morita, Picton, et al., 2016) an mHealth app designed in collaboration with the Heart and Stroke Foundation of Canada to help Canadians care for their heart health (Fig. 5.3). Figs. 5.2 and 5.3 provide examples of the importance of the stylistic and esthetic guidelines presented above to ensure the development of an mHealth app that is appealing and engaging to the final end users.

The prototyping

Prototyping tools are critical for the design of mHealth apps, as they provide a customized environment for creating the design assets, as well as a

FIGURE 5.2 Breathe, an mHealth app designed to support patients with asthma.

FIGURE 5.3 The Heart and Stroke Foundation of Canada <30 Days app.

platform for testing ideas and user interface with potential end users. The initial stages of prototyping exercise will likely be on paper, using sketches to organize the ideas and to share the thoughts with subject matter experts and representative users. As the fidelity of prototypes evolves, so will the tools that will be used to design the app. Platforms such as Adobe Illustrator or Sketch provide very comprehensive platforms for designers to convert lower fidelity prototypes into medium-to-high-fidelity prototypes. Figs. 5.4 and 5.5 provide examples of high-fidelity prototypes of breathe and the <30 Days app.

The prototypes need to be tested with representative end users and will need to be converted into interactive prototypes that could be presented to participants to allow the users to navigate through the different screens and

FIGURE 5.4 Screenshots from breathe showcasing the importance of esthetics, the design of simple and streamlined interfaces, and the most common features of mHealth technology.

to experience the app being designed. Through cognitive walkthroughs and usability testing, user performance metrics and user feedback can be collected to be used in the next iteration of the design (Wiklund et al., 2011). The prototyping software available on the market provides the necessary tools for easily transitioning from designing to user testing.

While many of these platforms have been on the market for years, it is important to search for the current gold standards and recent prototyping

FIGURE 5.5 The <30 Days app.

software. The design community is extremely active and collaborative, so always search for the best tool available at the moment. Some examples of prototyping tools that have been available on the market for several years include, but are not limited to Adobe Illustrator (Adobe, 2019), InVision (InVision, 2019), Axure (Axure, 2019), and Sketch (Sketch, 2019). InVision, for example, provides a comprehensive platform for transforming static assets (e.g., screenshots of the app being designed) into interactive prototypes that can be loaded on a smartphone and given to participants for user testing.

Data-driven design

The common approach to user-centered design focuses on evaluating the performance of and collecting feedback from representative users in controlled laboratory usability tests (Morita & Cafazzo, 2015; Wiklund et al., 2011). While a critical phase of a solid user-centered design process, usability testing only provides opportunities for improvement prior to the final deployment of the mHealth app in the real world.

Monitoring the performance of the app or wearable being designed, in the real world, is just as important as conducting iterative design cycles, cognitive walkthroughs, and usability testing. Even the most rigorous iterative design process is not able to generate a perfect app free of user interaction issues. Usage analytics have provided insights about how often users were actually using the different features of the <30 Days app and which challenges were being completed more often (Goyal, Morita, Picton, et al., 2016), which have provided insights about how to move forward with the new version of the app and about how to design the new set of challenges that would be incorporated on the new app.

In addition, unforeseen factors at the time of the design may impact the usage of the app in the real world, as, for example, changes in workflow or work environment in which the app will be used (e.g., poor color choice or font size for apps that will be used outside under the sun) or unforeseen interactions with novel technologies added to the care process. Therefore it is important to monitor how users are interacting with the technology to help identify potential barriers to successful uptake. The best way to achieve this objective is to implement usage analytics tools in the mHealth solution being developed, as these tools can provide insights about how and when people are using mHealth solutions, how often features are being used, and the flow between different sections of the app. It is virtually impossible for designers to predict all the possible scenarios that are going to be seen in the real world, as many of these issues only become salient when the technology is actually exposed to the real world. Through novel usage analytics engines available on the market, it is now possible to evolve the field of data-driven design, by leveraging the usage analytics as a design input.

While evaluating *breathe*, our team observed several interesting behavioral patterns that have been used in the next iteration of the platform. For example, we observed the effects of reminders on user adherence to the mHealth intervention. When looking at the login data plotted by time of day, we could see a significant increase in frequency after reminders were sent at 7:00 p.m. (Fig. 5.6). The same effect is sustained over time, where users are still responding to the reminders even after 12 months of the intervention (Fig. 5.7). It is also possible to observe, for example, that there is an increase in app usage in the early hours of the day (5:00–10:00 a.m.). All this information can be used to inform future reminders and the engagement

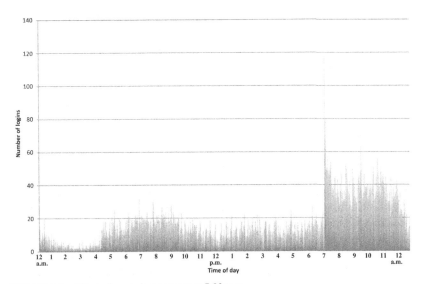

FIGURE 5.6   Effect of reminders sent out at 7:00 p.m.

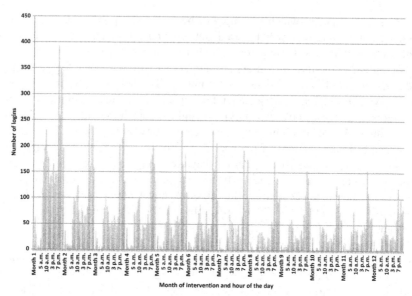

FIGURE 5.7 Sustained effect of reminders after 12 months. Reminders were sent out to patients at 7:00 p.m.

component of the app, targeting users when they are most active in using the mHealth app.

It is important to remember that there are means of collecting user behavior information (e.g., analytics, ethnographic probes) that can lend insights on how users are actually using the product in the real world. Behavioral information is critical to indicate how users are actually using the app in a noncontrolled setting, but such effort requires careful planning of indicators (e.g., Analytics Platform for Effective Engagement Evaluation [APEEE]; Pham et al., 2018) and the use of analytics tools as, for example, Mixpanel, Flurry Analytics, and Google Analytics.

Conclusion

Behavioral information is critical for mHealth technology designers to better understand how their users are interacting with the app. One important message is that the design process of an app does not end at deployment. It is our responsibility to continuously iterate on the design to achieve a product that addresses the patient needs. There are currently platforms on the market that have been specifically designed for this purpose, as in the case of the APEEE (Pham et al., 2018).

Over the years, the development of initiatives to evaluate mHealth technologies has given us several lessons:

- Implement usage analytics in the app from the beginning. The data will teach the designers very important lessons about how the users are using the technology.
- Do not think that the design efforts have ended once the app or wearable has hit the market. There will be several iterations of product designs that will be necessary based on the usage data being collecting.
- Explore the data without biases; there will always be unexpected insights from the data that has been collected.

Due to the rapid evolution of technology, designers in the mHealth space need to be prepared to quickly iterate on the design of their app and to leverage lessons learned from how users are actually using the app in the next design cycles. This data-driven design principle has the potential of providing critical and contextual information about deficiencies in the design that would not have been caught in a usability lab.

References

Adobe. (2019). Adobe illustrator. Retrieved from <https://www.adobe.com/ca/products/illustrator.html>.

Apple. (2019a). Apple Watch. Retrieved from <https://www.apple.com/ca/watch/>.

Apple. (2019b). Human interface guidelines. Retrieved from <https://developer.apple.com/design/human-interface-guidelines/>.

Axure. (2019). Axure. Retrieved from <https://www.axure.com/>.

Fitbit. (2019). Fitbit. Retrieved from <https://www.fitbit.com/en-ca/home>.

Free, C., Phillips, G., Galli, L., Watson, L., Felix, L., Edwards, P., . . . Haines, A. (2013). The effectiveness of mobile-health technology-based health behaviour change or disease management interventions for health care consumers: A systematic review. *PLoS Medicine*, *10*(1). Available from https://doi.org/10.1371/journal.pmed.1001362.

Gagnon, M. P., Ngangue, P., Payne-Gagnon, J., & Desmartis, M. (2016). M-Health adoption by healthcare professionals: A systematic review. *Journal of the American Medical Informatics Association*, *23*(1), 212−220. Available from https://doi.org/10.1093/jamia/ocv052.

Google. (2019). Material design. Retrieved from <https://material.io/design/>.

Goyal, S., Morita, P. P., Lewis, G. F., Yu, C., Seto, E., & Cafazzo, J. A. (2016). The systematic design of a behavioural mobile health application for the self-management of type 2 diabetes. *Canadian Journal of Diabetes*, *40*(1), 95−104. Available from https://doi.org/10.1016/j.jcjd.2015.06.007.

Goyal, S., Morita, P. P., Picton, P., Seto, E., Zbib, A., & Cafazzo, J. A. (2016). Uptake of a consumer-focused mHealth application for the assessment and prevention of heart disease: The <30 Days study. *JMIR MHealth and UHealth*, *4*(1), e32. Available from https://doi.org/10.2196/mhealth.4730.

HealtheVet. (2019). HealtheVet portal. Retrieved from <https://www.myhealth.va.gov/mhv-portal-web/home>.

InVision. (2019). InVision. Retrieved from <https://www.invisionapp.com/>.

Morita, P. P., & Cafazzo, J. A. (2015). Challenges and paradoxes of human factors in health technology design. *JMIR Journal of Human Factors*, *3*(1), 1−7. Available from https://doi.org/10.2196/humanfactors.4653.

Morita, P. P., Yeung, M. S., Ferrone, A., Taite, A. K., Madeley, C., Stevens-Lavigne, A., & Licskai, C. (2019). A patient-centered mobile health system that supports asthma self-management (breathe): Design, development, and utilization. *JMIR MHealth and UHealth, 7* (1), e10956. Available from https://doi.org/10.2196/10956.

Oinas-Kukkonen, H., & Harjumaa, M. (2009). Persuasive systems design: Key issues, process model, and system features. *Communications of the Association for Information Systems, 24* (1), 28.

Pham, Q., Graham, G., Lalloo, C., Morita, P. P., Seto, E., Stinson, J. N., & Cafazzo, J. A. (2018). An analytics platform to evaluate effective engagement with pediatric mobile health apps: Design, development, and formative Evaluation. *JMIR MHealth and UHealth, 6*(12), e11447. Available from https://doi.org/10.2196/11447.

Piwek, L., Ellis, D. A., Andrews, S., & Joinson, A. (2016). The rise of consumer health wearables: Promises and barriers. *PLoS Medicine, 13*(2), 1–9. Available from https://doi.org/10.1371/journal.pmed.1001953.

Quantified Self. (2019). Quantified self. Retrieved from <https://quantifiedself.com/>.

(2015th ed). Sasan, A. (Ed.), (2015). *Mobile health: A technology road map* (Vol. 5). Berlin, Germany: Springer. Available from https://doi.org/10.1007/978-3-319-12817-7.

Schwartz, B. (2004). *The paradox of choice: Why less is more.* New York: Ecco.

Sketch. (2019). Sketch. Retrieved from <https://www.sketch.com/>.

Steinhubl, S. R., Muse, E. D., & Topol, E. J. (2015). The emerging field of mobile health. *Science Translational Medicine, 7*(283), 1–12. Available from https://doi.org/10.1126/scitranslmed.aaa3487.

Swan, M. (2012). Sensor mania! The Internet of Things, wearable computing, objective metrics, and the quantified self 2.0. *Journal of Sensor and Actuator Networks, 1*(3), 217–253. Available from https://doi.org/10.3390/jsan1030217.

U.S. Department of Health & Human Services. (2019). Health information Privacy. Retrieved from <https://www.hhs.gov/hipaa/index.html>.

Uddin, A. A., Morita, P. P., Tallevi, K., Armour, K., Li, J., Nolan, R. P., & Cafazzo, J. A. (2016). Development of a wearable cardiac monitoring system for behavioral neurocardiac training: A usability study. *JMIR MHealth and UHealth, 4*(2), e45. Available from https://doi.org/10.2196/mhealth.5288.

Under Armour. (2019). MyFitnessPal. Retrieved from <https://www.myfitnesspal.com/>.

Ware, P., Ross, H. J., Cafazzo, J. A., Laporte, A., & Seto, E. (2018). Implementation and evaluation of a smartphone-based telemonitoring program for patients with heart failure: Mixed-methods study protocol. *Journal of Medical Internet Research, 20*(5). Available from https://doi.org/10.2196/resprot.9911.

Wiklund, M. E., Kendler, J., & Strochlic, A. Y. (2011). *Usability testing of medical devices.* Boca Raton, FL: CRC Press.

Chapter 6

Design for effective care collaboration

Patrice Dolhonde Tremoulet[1,2], Susan Harkness Regli[3] and
Ramya Krishnan[2]
*[1]Rowan University, Glassboro, NJ, United States, [2]ECRI Institute, Plymouth Meeting, PA,
United States, [3]University of Pennsylvania Health System, Philadelphia, PA, United States*

Both patients and clinicians benefit from effective interclinician communications that support care collaboration. The need for tools that facilitate effective communication among health-care providers is increasing (Bellew et al., 2017; Jones et al., 2017; Reimer, Alfes, Rowe, & Rodriguez-Fox, 2018; Salen, 2017). First responders and emergency department personnel who care for trauma patients are focused primarily on providing treatment, making it difficult for them to share or record clinical data about their patients. In mass casualty scenarios, capturing patient data is even more challenging. Meanwhile, patients in acute care typically receive support from a team of clinicians who need to coordinate amongst themselves; when these patients are discharged, outpatient providers need access to clinical information about the patients' recent acute care visits. Acute care is increasingly provided by hospitalists or urgent care providers who have not met their patients prior to treating them and need records that provide rapid understanding to inform treatment. The urgent care organizations where care is received may not even be in the same care network as patients' primary care providers. Moreover, patients with complex health conditions are often followed by many different specialists whose interactions with, and care for, these patients must be coordinated. Electronic health records (EHRs) have the potential to facilitate clinical communication and collaboration among the different providers who interact with patients. Unfortunately, EHRs currently do not often perform this function very well (Chao, 2016; McMurray et al., 2013; Slager, Beckstrom, Weir, Del Fiol, & Brooke, 2017).

Design for Health. DOI: https://doi.org/10.1016/B978-0-12-816427-3.00006-3

In an era when many different clinicians contribute to acute care for a single patient, effective clinical communication requires the following (Regli et al., 2010):

- Gathering and recording relevant patient data upon intake—when patients first present for acute care or are treated by first responders.
- Maintaining patient information throughout an acute care episode, including adding updates with new data, documenting interpretations and decision-making rationale, and organizing patient information so it can easily be shared among care teams.
- Preparing for discharge by generating documentation about the recent encounter that includes information clinicians will need to coordinate outpatient care.

This chapter presents two case studies that illustrate how human factors research can help address current shortfalls in how health-care information is collected, stored, distributed, and analyzed. Both efforts focus on helping to improve clinical communication, but they address different current challenges using different methods. The first case study describes a participatory design effort to improve mechanisms for capturing information in a digital format that can be easily stored, shared, understood by multiple audiences, and analyzed by multiple systems. In this project, we engaged multiple military medical subject matter experts (SMEs) by eliciting knowledge, ideas, and feedback from them throughout the entire process of designing and testing a novel software prototype. This software, which runs on mobile devices, enables users to easily collect, organize, update, and share patient data during casualty situations (Regli, 2012). While this project focused on developing software to be used by military medical providers, the use case for the prototype includes tasks of civilian health providers, such as first responders and emergency care providers, who must document patient information in parallel with rapidly assessing and treating patients.

The second case study addresses the challenge of assessing usability of documents generated by acute care providers' EHR systems, with an eye toward improving their effectiveness for care coordination. Unlike the first effort, which involved creating a prototype of a novel technology-based solution, the second effort focused on a heuristic evaluation in which clinical and human factors experts identified usability issues with the products of existing technologies. This effort not only confirmed the need for a better design of those technologies, beginning with eliciting user needs and developing new requirements, but also provided some general recommendations to improve EHR systems so that these generate documentation that more effectively communicates clinical information about patients recently discharged from acute care settings to the outpatient providers who will care for them (Tremoulet et al., 2018).

Challenges in care coordination

Several years ago, we noted in our research that many of the problems that hamper basic understanding about patient conditions, as well as efforts to understand patterns of health incidents in individuals and groups, are analogous to the challenges associated with capturing and disseminating military tactical intelligence: "At the small unit level out on patrol, details are not often reported in a way that can be shared or analyzed across geography and time (different medical information systems make sharing and aggregating for analysis difficult), reported data is described differently by different people (different terminology in different organizations and different record fields in different EHR systems), data is not easy to share among units (hard to share patient data between offices, hospitals, states)" (Regli et al., 2010). Ten years later, US health providers' abilities to share patient data are still often very limited, though there is a greater awareness that EHR systems do not support seamless sharing of patient data among providers (Adler-milstein & Pfeifer, 2017; Mello, Adler-milstein, Ding, & Savage, 2018; Zelmer et al., 2017) nor have they enabled researchers to aggregate and analyze population data (Iroju, Soriyan, Gambo, & Olaleke, 2013; Khennou, Khamlichi, & Chaoui, 2017). Recognizing the significance of this problem, the US Centers for Medicare & Medicaid Services recently renamed its "EHR incentive programs" to "Promoting interoperability programs" and allocated funding to support integration between EHR systems (Centers for Medicare and Medicaid Services, 2018). This is a positive development, but it will take significant time and effort for this work to get done (Benson & Grieve, 2016). In the meantime, it remains difficult to share patient information among providers using different EHR systems.

Though the work that is described in this chapter's first case study was performed nearly a decade ago, the problems it addresses—loss of information due to difficulties capturing and sharing data about patients treated by first responders prior to arriving at an acute care facility—are very much relevant today (Goldberg et al., 2017; Zhang, Sarcevic, & Bossen, 2017). Despite the proliferation of mobile devices that could be applied to capture patient data at point of injury and during transport, many first responders either use paper forms to record patient data or orally communicate information when delivering patients, leading to significant information loss (Carter, Davis, Evans, & Cone, 2009; Cuk, Wimmer, & Powell, 2017; Duckworth, 2016; Shelton & Sinclair, 2016). Similarly, when patients are transferred to hospital emergency departments from skilled nursing facilities, clinics, and other urgent care settings, such as smaller outlying hospitals, a significant amount of patient information can be lost (Bellew et al., 2017; Reimer et al., 2018). One recent study showed that a mobile app was superior to paper for triage in ER (Savatmongkorngul, Yuksen, Suwattanasilp, Sawanyawisuth, & Sittichanbuncha, 2017) and an older effort showed the value of using mobile devices to capture patient data in a simulated civilian mass casualty event (DeMers et al., 2011). In general, however, simply translating forms to digital formats will not fully address the challenge. In fact, there is solid evidence that EHRs contribute to information loss by inhibiting health providers' abilities to construct a complete patient story (Chao, 2016; Varpio et al., 2015) and that the time required to keep EHRs up-to-date represents a burden for outpatient primary care providers that makes them especially vulnerable to burnout (Downing, Bates, & Longhurst, 2018; Webber, Schaffer, Willey, & Aldrich, 2018).

Of course, assuming care for incoming trauma patients is only one of many situations where providers need rapid access to well-organized and meaningful clinical information about their patients. Each day, patients in acute care who stay in the same location will be cared for by two to three teams, with transitions of care occurring during regularly scheduled shift changes (Rauch, 2018; Salen, 2017). Other patients may need to be transferred to higher or lower acuity care units, resulting in a different type of within-acute-care-facility care transitions (Abraham, Nguyen, Almoosa, Patel, & Patel, 2011; Hoonakker et al., 2018; Zakrison et al., 2016). Finally, when patients are discharged, their care is transitioned from a team of inpatient providers to one or more outpatient providers. EHRs and health information exchanges (HIEs) have the potential to improve care collaboration and consequently patient care by allowing seamless information exchange and access to richer patient health information (Gordon, Bernard, Salzman, & Whitebird, 2015; Menachemi, Rahurkar, Harle, & Vest, 2018). However, currently design and implementation challenges, not to mention lack of interoperability between systems, prevent these technologies from enhancing care collaboration (Chase et al., 2014; Cifuentes et al., 2015; McMurray et al., 2013; Sockolow et al., 2014). In some cases, EHRs and HIEs effectively impede care collaboration (Chao, 2016; Slager et al., 2017; Varpio et al., 2015).

Though there are still far too many instances where it is difficult to share patient information across different units of a single facility (Holmgren, Patel, & Adler-Milstein, 2017; Kulshrestha & Singh, 2016), a more common challenge is sharing clinical information about patients among providers working for different organizations that use their own EHR systems (Everson & Adler-Milstein, 2018; Slager et al., 2017). A 2017 study found that fewer than 1/3 of US hospitals can find, send, and accept information for patients who receive care somewhere else (Holmgren et al., 2017). Moreover, when a hospital does share a patient's data, it rarely provides that data in a structured format that can be easily integrated into the receiving organization's health information systems (Holmgren et al., 2017).

Discharge from acute care is a transition that is particularly vulnerable to information loss. Part of the problem is that few inpatient providers realize that the discharge summaries generated by their facilities' EHR systems are often not immediately available to the outpatient providers who will follow up with discharged patients. In many cases, outpatient providers end up relying on the after-visit summaries given to patients upon discharge to obtain information about recent acute care visits (Gorry, 2017). Recognizing that this situation could put patients at risk of adverse events due to ineffective information transfer, we recently conducted a heuristic evaluation of after-visit summaries from the perspective of outpatient physicians who must rely upon them to obtain information about recent acute care visits (Tremoulet et al., 2018). This work is described in the second case study in this chapter.

Design guidelines

Based upon our experience working on the two use cases previously summarized, we developed eight guidelines for designing and evaluating tools that are used to support care coordination by communicating clinical information about patients. These are as follows:

1. *Accommodate ALL users' language/expression styles.* Designing spoken language understanding technology requires specifying grammars and identifying a complete vocabulary so that the technology can recognize different ways of expressing the same thing. Developing after-visit summaries (AVS) that are useful to both patients and clinicians requires using precise terms that are meaningful to clinicians AND providing definitions of these terms that are understandable to patients/caregivers.

2. *Use consistent terms, labels, and wording.* This is a best practice, related to a well-known user interface design heuristic (consistency and standards—Nielsen, 1994b). Applications that support care coordination should not only use consistent, standard wording to communicate messages to their users, they should also remind clinical users to use standard terminology when providing information that will be used to generate reports or documents about recent medical care.

3. *Organize applications so that they support users' mental models for conveying patient information.* Military first responders are trained to populate a standard report with a specific organization of information, so electronic reporting solutions must be able to present captured information in the same order as a conventional report, while allowing speakers to provide information in any order, and cuing them for required fields after parsing their utterances. For clinicians entering daily progress note data, EHRs should support both of the two most commonly used sequences for entering data (SOAP—subjective data, objective data, assessment, and plan; and APSO—assessment, plan, subjective data, and objective data). They should also allow organizations to customize the order in which information is displayed.

4. *Minimize clicks, button presses, commands, and other interactions so users can focus their attention on generating useful content rather than on*

navigating the application. Data entry needs to be as seamless as possible, but the applications should provide guidance/prompts to ensure that all relevant data is entered.

5. *Provide previews or actual views of reports or documents containing information entered into applications.* Users need to be able to see how the information they enter will be organized and formatted in final document versions. These views should be accompanied by short reminders that reports/documents may be viewed by multiple different parties (other clinicians, patients/caregivers) with different levels of understanding and information needs. Similarly, users should be able to review newly entered information for correctness and completeness, which, in the case of a spoken language understanding system, may entail having the system play back what it "heard" before finalizing data entry based upon speech.

6. *Make it easy to edit data, but track user identification and date/time of all edits.* Previews and summaries can help users identify errors or omissions, and it must be easy to address them, but it is also important to keep track of which users entered what data at what time.

7. *Make data access transparent.* All members of a patient's care team should have access to the patient's data, including the patient, any associated caregivers, and physicians from different health systems. Care team members should be able to see who has access to the data, when the data was last accessed, and by whom it was accessed.

8. *Provide role-based views.* Since the information needs of different members of a patient's care team will vary based on their roles, having multiple views will allow users fast access to the most relevant information. Making the information searchable is another way to improve rapid access.

Case study 1: Creating a prototype to facilitate clinical communication in emergency situations

When multiple people are injured simultaneously, first responders must quickly decide whom to treat first, under high stress, and with little information. In these situations, first responders are challenged to document medically relevant information, including mechanism of injury, demographics, and medical interventions performed. As patients are transferred from the point of injury to acute care facilities, there is a high risk of information loss. In 2012 we initiated a participatory design effort that yielded an innovative demonstration prototype, called C4ISR-Med, which illustrated how mobile technologies could help enhance military first responders' medical situational awareness and facilitate the collection and sharing of medical information (Regli, 2012). A separate effort showed that mobile devices could be used to support collection and sharing of data about patients during a civilian mass casualty situation (DeMers et al., 2011).

Participatory design approach

One of the keys to this prototype development effort was engaging military medical and tactical SMEs early and often. A retired Major General and physician from the US Army served as a consultant for the entire effort. Not only was he a source of expertise about military health-care providers, he also supplied significant assistance in shaping the vision for this effort and facilitated access to active duty SMEs, by helping arrange for our team to visit several military medical facilities.

For example, our team traveled to Ft. Gordon, GA, to speak with representatives of the Regional Training Site—Medical (RTS-Med). RTS-Med is part of the 3rd Medical Training Brigade, Medical Readiness Training Command. During our visit, we met with SMEs with Combat Lifesaver and Medical Communications for Combat Casualty Care training expertise. We reviewed current battlefield technology capabilities and limitations and conducted interviews with medics to determine how spoken dialogue could best be used to enter values into the Tactical Combat Casualty Card, a medical reporting form.

We also traveled to the Army Medical Department (AMEDD) Center and School at Ft. Sam Houston in San Antonio, TX. The center is where the AMEDD formulates its medical organization tactics, doctrine, and equipment, and the school is where the army educates and trains all its medical personnel. We observed medics in various stages of training. Afterward, several program instructors (active duty medics themselves) fielded our questions regarding how medics were trained, the equipment they carried, and how they used it along with how they performed their duties on the battlefield.

Finally, we visited medical facilities in Germany to observe operations and speak with additional SMEs. At Ramstein Air Force Base, we observed preparations for an Aeromedical evacuation mission to/from Bagram and the offloading of patients when the mission was completed (at the time wounded were transported from Afghanistan to Ramstein and then back to the United States). The team had the opportunity to interview both Aeromedical evacuation and Critical Care Air Transport Team members; the former care for more patients and those who are less critical and more stable, while the latter care for fewer, extremely ill casualties, who are similar to intensive care unit patients. One of the many things we learned during this trip was that the crews must stop patient care in flight so that they can enter data into EHRs and print them in time for landing. Team members were also able to meet with care providers, including nurses, surgeons, and respiratory technicians who work in Landstuhl Regional Medical Center.

These trips included a mix of field observations, structured interviews, and interactive feedback sessions where we shared ideas for usage scenarios and design concepts with the SMEs and obtained their reactions and advice to improve our designs and overall vision. Conversations with SMEs during the trips and follow-up email exchanges revealed that significant information exists that, if captured and shared, could (1) aid the first responders in assessing situations and (2) enhance patient outcomes and medical health records. The knowledge garnered from these interactions was used to create and refine a future concept of operations—including realistic test scenarios—to iteratively develop the user interfaces of our prototype solution and to model a field medic's dialogue with the system. Involving experts in all aspects of design, implementation, and testing increased the likelihood of user relevance and acceptance for the technology solution.

Solution overview

Despite a federal requirement for electronic reporting at ground level, the medic's primary responsibility is saving lives, so documentation takes a back seat. We learned several priority requirements from our interactions with SMEs:

1. The medic's hands are busy treating patients; data entry needs to be accomplished in a primarily hands-free manner.
2. The time from arrival on scene to moving the patient to a transport vehicle can be as short as minutes. The primary goal is to get the patient quickly out of the area so that neither the patient nor the medic remain in the combat area.
3. The amount of information transferred can be extremely small. Even just having basic information about injuries, medication, and a few vital signs is a vast improvement over having no information captured.

The C4ISR-Med prototype leveraged mobile devices and advanced speech technology to encourage electronic reporting during application of treatment while minimizing distraction from life-saving activities. The prototype software ran on a wide variety of Android OS-based hardware, providing multiple form factors to fit different contexts of use, including small form-factor Android watches (complete with GPS and Wi-Fi capability), small and large phones, and tablets. The future concept of operations that we codeveloped with SMEs assumed the following apportionment of equipment:

- All personnel wear small, unintrusive physiological sensors and either wear smartwatches or carry phones that wirelessly collect important vital signs data generated by the sensors.
- The medic wears a smartwatch to receive alerts and to activate speech processing and carries a phone for review of vitals and for processing speech into combat casualty reports. (Speech is captured using a Bluetooth microphone, wired microphone, or by speaking directly into the phone.)

- The squad leader carries a phone for lightweight blue force tracking and status review as well as digital entry of nine-line report.
- The transport medic has a phone and/or tablet that can be used to review vitals and to review, update, and create new reports.

The concept of operations for using our prototype in the field includes collecting baseline pulse oximetry, breathing rate, and respiration measurements for each individual in varying operational conditions prior to deployment, to determine thresholds that might indicate injury. During deployment, C4ISR-Med automatically collects and shares vital signs data with combat medics. When team members' vitals go below the predetermined thresholds, the medic receives an audio alert that indicates he should look at his watch to review who is injured (names in red) and where they are located in relationship to his position (Fig. 6.1).

If a medic can get to an injured person immediately, there is no opportunity to review any other information before starting treatment. If, however, the medic has time (e.g., while in transit), he/she can take out his/her phone to review the vitals of the patients (Fig. 6.2) or see where everyone is on a map (Fig. 6.3).

The medic may begin or continue documentation at any point while administering treatment. To begin entering data, the medic taps twice anywhere on the smartwatch to start speech processing on the phone. Any information known about the patient from a preentered profile (e.g., allergies) and current date and time will be automatically populated in the report. If vital signs data are available from body-worn sensors, they are also automatically put into the report. The medic's speech is parsed by the system into a report based on the format of an existing paper report form (Fig. 6.4). The prototype enables reporting to be done with minimal interaction so the responder's hands can be free for treatment. (Currently, field medics may resort to writing injury and treatment details on medical tape or laminated cards, if they

FIGURE 6.1 Display on smartwatch worn by medic who can review injured personnel identity, location, and severity of injuries.

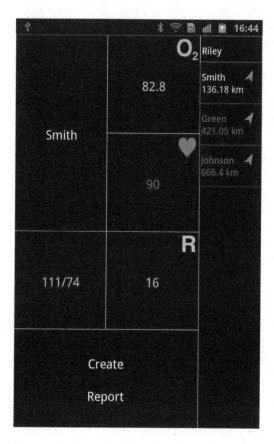

FIGURE 6.2 Smartphone display for medic who can select a name and review that person's vitals.

have them available. C4ISR-Med replaces the need to write by providing a speech-based reporting of injury and treatment data.)

When a transportation vehicle arrives, all reports are transferred to a tablet in the vehicle, which enables users to monitor vitals from the wearable sensors, review reports, and make updates during transport, for example, changes in patient status or additional treatments provided. Finally, the reports are automatically transferred to the acute care facility when the transport vehicles get close enough to access the facility's network, so that preparations for treatment can begin as soon as possible.

As reports come in, the acute care facility staff can review them (Fig. 6.5) and begin to prepare resources and personnel to be ready to treat the incoming patients as soon as they arrive. All data about point of injury and transit incidents, treatments, and patient vitals are available in easy-to-import digital format, parsed into records with tagged fields indicating what was entered for injury type, treatment, and medication. These records are valuable not only for the long-term care of individual patients but also for data analysis of treatments and medicines versus patient outcomes.

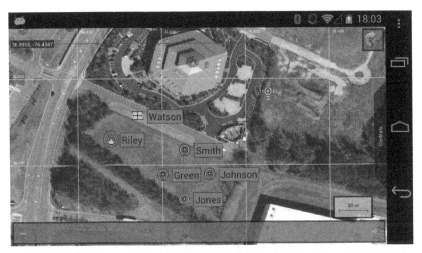

FIGURE 6.3 Smartphone or tablet display for medic or squad leader who can review position and status of entire team.

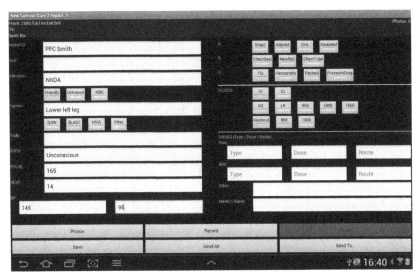

FIGURE 6.4 Smartphone or tablet display summarizing report created based upon spoken input. If the user has time and is safe, the report can be edited through the touchscreen.

Discussion

The human factors research activities conducted as part of this effort, which entailed frequent interaction with military medical SMEs, enabled us to develop realistic test scenarios and design, improve, and demonstrate the

FIGURE 6.5 One possible way to display the reports that are sent to the hospital when the transport vehicle gets close enough for wireless transmission. The data can be easily imported into different applications for review. This view was created to demonstrate the capabilities of our prototype solution.

utility of software for mobile devices that facilitate the collection, management, and sharing of combat casualty data.

Since the C4ISR-Med effort was completed, ownership of smartphones has steadily increased worldwide (Pew Research Center, 2016, 2018), and smartwatches like the one featured in our demonstration have become more popular (NPD Group, Inc., 2017). In fact, it is now very common for individuals to upload applications that enable them to access work email and perform other job functions on personal mobile devices. Meanwhile, tablets much more powerful than those we used in our demonstration are relatively inexpensive, so it is plausible to envision civilian first responders using some mix of personally owned phones and tablets mounted in vehicles to digitally capture and share patient data. Most would likely welcome the availability of an app that they could leverage and use in lieu of paper to generate patient records (Cuk et al., 2017).

Naturally, a successful effort to create technology that could replace paper reports currently used by most first responders, and supplement the oral reports given to emergency department personnel, would require recruiting several first responders to serve as SMEs who would help shape and refine an overall vision and the user interfaces of different solution components, just as we engaged military SMEs to support the C4ISR-Med effort. It is certainly possible to adapt some of the software created under that project to create a new solution, but the adaptation would have to be guided by input and feedback from the target end users in order to produce a useful and usable solution.

Moreover, some of the lessons learned from C4ISR-Med could also be applied to the improvement of EHRs. Switching from paper to electronic records does not automatically make the process of creating a new record or updating an existing one easier. Many researchers have pointed out that the workload associated with documenting patient care can increase when practices switch from paper to electronic records (Benda, Meadors, Hettinger, & Ratwani, 2016; Meigs & Solomon, 2016). Others seeking to understand rising rates of physician burnout report that the burden of interacting with EHR systems is a significant contributing factor (Gregory, Russo, & Singh, 2017; Shanafelt, Dyrbye, & West, 2017). Our second case study explores how the modules within these systems that generate medical documents could be redesigned to help better support outpatient providers.

Case study 2: Redesigning "after-visit summaries" to better support clinical communication

Unlike the C4ISR-Med prototype, most commercial EHR systems cannot export data in a form that can be easily imported or otherwise shared with other systems (Holmgren et al., 2017; Lim, Jarvenpaa, & Lanham, 2015). Though most EHR systems can generate discharge summaries, which communicate clinical information about patients' recent acute care visits, difficulties sharing patient data within and across facilities frequently prevent outpatient providers from receiving these documents prior to follow-up visits (Jones et al., 2017; Solan, Sherman, DeBlasio, & Simmons, 2016). This has led outpatient physicians to sometimes rely on patient-facing discharge documents, often called "after-visit summaries" or "AVS," to obtain clinical information, even though these documents were not designed for this purpose (Gorry, 2017). Other names for AVS include discharge instructions, patient instructions, clinical summaries, or summary of care documents.

Since the integration work needed to enable providers to seamlessly transfer patient information to providers who use different EHR systems will require significant time and effort, in the short-to-medium term it is advisable to adapt discharge documentation so that it can do a better job in supporting care coordination (Bansard, Clanet, & Raginel, 2017; Newnham et al., 2017). As a first step, to obtain data to guide this adaptation, we conducted a heuristic evaluation to assess how well AVS currently support care coordination. The results of our evaluation confirmed our suspicion that AVS do not fully meet the needs of outpatient physicians who must rely on them to obtain information about recent acute care visits; hence we recommend a participatory design effort where outpatient care providers and patients are both involved in developing more specific requirements for the content, structure, and organization of discharge documentation as a next step. However, acute care facilities do not need to wait for a participatory design effort to be completed to improve the usability of their AVS; they may use the general recommendations that we identified based upon our evaluation to redesign the templates their EHR systems use to generate AVS.

Novel approach to heuristic evaluation

We worked with clinicians and human factors experts affiliated with two different hospitals to create four simulated discharge documents, which were populated with patient data based on two publicly available use cases created by the National Institute of Standards and Technology (Lowry et al., 2012). Using simulated documents eliminated the need to protect actual patient data, kept our reviewers blind to the hospitals that shared copies of their documents, and made it easier to replicate our study. The simulated documents were reviewed by clinicians to ensure that they were representative of the actual paperwork that would be provided to patients/caregivers upon discharge.

In addition, we created a set of 17 *medical document usability heuristics* after reviewing the heuristics commonly used to assess medical devices (Zhang, Johnson, Patel, Paige, & Kubose, 2003), software user interface usability heuristics (Nielsen, 1994b; Shneiderman, 2010), heuristics for assessing online documentation (Kantner, Shroyer, & Rosenbaum, 2002), and published guidance on producing clear, concise writing generally (Centers for Disease Control and Prevention, 2009; Plain Language Action and Information Network, 2011) and comprehensible medical writing specifically (Badarudeen & Sabharwal, 2010; Burke et al., 2014; Centers for Medicare and Medicaid Services, 2010; Agency for Healthcare Research and Quality [AHRQ], 2011). The originators of heuristic evaluation recommend developing heuristics specific to the item being assessed (Nielsen & Molich, 1990). We organized the 17 heuristics into 5 categories: readability, comprehensibility, minimalism, content, and organization (Tremoulet et al., 2018).

Typically, heuristic evaluations are conducted by having three to five experts independently identify and rate the severity of usability issues (Nielsen, 1994a; Nielsen & Molich, 1990). Instead, we constructed four teams; each comprised a human factors expert and an outpatient physician (either currently practicing or retired). The team approach facilitated productive conversations that allowed the human factors expert to understand the clinical significance of the violations and helped the teams come up with potential solutions for improving AVS usability. It also reduced the amount of time that we required from the clinicians, by eliminating the ~3 hours of time needed to train them to conduct evaluations alone. Since the four teams each assessed all four documents independently of the other teams, we believe that the majority of the significant problems were identified. Ratings were developed based upon the 5-point scale initially articulated by the originators of heuristic evaluation (Nielsen & Molich, 1990) and subsequently used to assess how usability of medical devices impacts patient safety (Zhang et al., 2003): 0 = not an issue, 1 = cosmetic only, 2 = minor issue, 3 = major issue, and 4 = catastrophic issue.

Evaluation results

The teams identified a total of 224 unique usability problems across the 4 simulated AVS. Average severity rating across all identified issues was 2.57 (between minor and major). Although there was considerable variability in how information was presented between the two hospitals that participated in our study, we found several common types of issues that were deemed to have a negative impact upon usability from the perspective of a primary care physician offering follow-up care, as well as some unique issues within each document. AVS from both hospitals had heuristic violations ranging in severity from mild (cosmetic) to catastrophic (dramatically impairs use), and each document contained violations of at least two heuristics in each of our five heuristic categories.

Most of the issues that were rated catastrophic were associated with violations of content heuristics; however, several of our experts indicated that the formatting, structure, and organization were so problematic that the documents are hard for anyone to use (Tremoulet et al., 2018). Suggestions for improving AVS varied. Clinicians were concerned largely with the content, but all expert reviewers noted several areas they felt would be confusing to patients. These included unclear patient instructions, using billing terminology rather than lay terminology (or medical terminology) to describe a particular condition, listing medications that need to be discontinued instead of just those that are to be continued or started, having important information undifferentiated and embedded in larger sections or blocks of text, and using inconsistent language (e.g., referring to the patient alternatively as "person" and "patient").

Recommendations to improve electronic health record–generated after-visit summaries

We considered the common themes among our participants' suggestions for improvement, along with the severity ratings that they assigned to identified usability issues, to generate several general recommendations for improving EHR-generated discharge documents so that these are both more useful as a tool for clinical communication and more useable by patients and caregivers. Recognizing that AVS may be used to bridge a communication gap between inpatient and outpatient providers, our top five recommendations for acute care organizations are to work with EHR vendors to fulfill the following tasks:

1. *Ensure that clinical information needed by the outpatient physician who will provide follow-up care is included in AVS.* At a minimum, AVS should include the six items that the Joint Commission mandates be included in discharge summaries: reason for hospitalization, significant findings, procedures and treatments provided, patient's condition at

discharge, patient/family instructions, and attending physician's signature (Kind & Smith, 2008). Other critical clinical information that should be included are patient medical, surgical, and family history and pending test results.

2. *Place information provided specifically for clinicians in a separate, clearly labeled section (or clearly labeled subsections).* Since outpatient providers may need to use AVS to obtain information about a patient's acute care visit, discharging clinicians should have the option to insert additional information directed toward the outpatient providers into one or more clearly marked sections, so both patients and clinicians can easily recognize text directed toward clinicians.

3. *Establish a standardized order and format for presenting different information in discharge documents,* with patient diagnoses explained upfront and multiple diagnoses clearly differentiated and defined. (Ideally the recommended ordering of information should be determined based on input and reviews by multiple outpatient providers.)

4. *Use consistent font size, font type, indents, and spacing throughout the document.* The standardized format should include standard header and subheader content and format. Not only will following this recommendation improve readability of documents and allow outpatient providers to easily find the information most relevant to them, it also gives vendors and acute care organizations the opportunity to differentiate their documents from those generated by other systems through a unique style.

5. *Ensure that the headers and footers contain only meaningful information,* such as the patient's name, age, the date the document was printed, and page numbers.

These recommendations are consistent with recent work describing how discharge documents provided by acute care providers and AVS provided by outpatient providers can be improved to become more useful and usable by patients and caregivers (Federman et al., 2017; Nguyen, Kruger, Greysen, Lyndon, & Goldman, 2014; Ruth, Geskey, Shaffer, Bramley, & Paul, 2011; Sarzynski et al., 2016). They are also consistent with several of the practical recommendations on how hospital discharge summaries could be improved to make them more usable by outpatient physicians, which were compiled in a 2015 review article (Unnewehr, Schaaf, Marev, Fitch, & Friederichs, 2015).

Discussion

For the foreseeable future, we expect that AVS will continue bridging gaps in communication between inpatient and outpatient providers, so we recommend that facilities providing acute care should work with EHR vendors to redesign the portion of the systems that produces discharge documentation to better support care coordination. Using the general guidance listed previously to guide adaptation of the EHR modules that generate AVS would not only enable these documents to better support care coordination, it would also make them more usable for patients and caregivers. In addition, acute care organizations could easily apply the technique we developed for conducting heuristic evaluations to assess and develop specific recommendations for improving their AVS.

We further recommend that EHR vendors and/or acute care providers sponsor a participatory design effort where human factors engineers elicit ideas and feedback from outpatient providers, including both primary care and specialty practices, to develop more specific requirements for AVS, such as the headings and subheadings to use to organize information in the AVS. The knowledge acquired through that effort could lead to much more detailed specifications for the content, structure, and organization of AVS yet could still afford vendors and acute care organizations significant freedom to brand their documents by developing unique formatting styles.

Conclusion

These case studies explore how technology can optimize the information that is prepared for and received about patients who are transitioning between different health-care providers. In the first, austere environments and the need to transition multiple patients at once make it hard to capture all the relevant data about each patient. In the second, gaps in both time and space between providers, coupled with lack of interoperability among health information technologies, prevent outpatient providers from receiving useful data about patients' recent acute care visits.

The participatory design activities performed under the C4ISR-Med effort entailed having human factors experts work with SMEs to identify user needs, develop and validate user requirements, and design and test user interaction paradigms, including graphical and audio user interfaces. In contrast, the heuristic evaluation performed under the AVS usability effort was primarily focused on evaluating the products of existing technology; however, this evaluation established a need to generate new requirements and designs for EHR-generated AVS. Moreover, the clinical and human factors experts who participated in the AVS study produced several general recommendations for redesigning the modules in EHR systems that generate AVS.

Both situations demanded creativity in the application of human factors methodologies due to the nature of the clinical environments. For the C4ISR-Med effort, we were not able to regularly get participants into a design lab to interact with our human factors personnel and software engineers. Rather, we had to go to where the participants could be found and work with whatever time and information they were able to share with us.

For the AVS effort, we knew that heuristic evaluations are typically performed early in the process of developing technology; this form of expert review is relatively quick and inexpensive, compared to end-user simulated-use testing, and it typically can identify most major usability issues (Nielsen & Molich, 1990). Knowing that we needed to reduce the amount of time required for busy clinical experts to participate, we adapted the traditional method for conducting heuristic evaluations to include both a human factors expert and a clinician on each review team. This accomplished two goals: it enabled the clinicians to participate within the confines of their schedules and maximized the value of time dedicated to the effort by having their work guided and enhanced by the human factors experts' experience with the process. We believe that this approach of teaming a human factors expert with a clinical expert provides significant benefits to both individuals, enabling each to learn more about the other's area of expertise, leading to better designed health-care technologies.

Conducting human factors work to improve care collaboration in health care presents challenges that require creative solutions. Patient care is of the utmost priority, and design activities have to fit in around that critical activity. Human factors experts running simulations to evaluate usability, for example, might have to skip extensive training of busy clinicians in a new technology and instead have software engineers partner with clinicians to be the "users" in a fast-paced evaluation scenario (Penn Medicine News, 2016). On the other hand, assessing the usability of a device that is typically used in a complex health-care environment, surrounded by other technologies, when one only has access to the device in isolation, could be handled by using a combination of an expert review and a targeted, brief survey sent to clinical users who interact with the technology regularly (Gaev & Tremoulet, 2018). Human factors experts may need to adapt methodologies to enable the most valuable work to be done in the most compressed time windows to accommodate the demands of health care.

While we live in what has been dubbed the "information age," obtaining access to health-care information can be very challenging. In cases of trauma patients, particularly mass casualty scenarios, it is difficult to capture patient data, so it is often lost before it can be recorded. In other cases, so much data is entered into EHRs that it can be hard to find and extract relevant information. Even if information can be easily filtered and organized, barriers, such as lack of interoperability among health information technology systems and incomplete contact information, may prevent providers from accessing information about a patient. Human factors methodologies are needed now more than ever to address challenges in care coordination across the continuum of a patient's care.

References

Abraham, J., Nguyen, V., Almoosa, K. F., Patel, B., & Patel, V. L. (2011). *Falling through the cracks: Information breakdowns in critical care handoff communication*, . *AMIA annual symposium proceedings* (Vol. 2011, p. 28). American Medical Informatics Association.

Adler-milstein, J., & Pfeifer, E. (2017). Information blocking: Is it occurring and what policy strategies can address it? *The Milbank Quarterly, 95*(1), 117−135.

Agency for Healthcare Research and Quality [AHRQ]. (2011). *Tips on writing a report on health care quality for consumers.* Rockville, MD: Agency for Healthcare Research and Quality. https://www.ahrq.gov/talkingquality/resources/writing/index.html. Content last reviewed July 2011.

Badarudeen, S., & Sabharwal, S. (2010). Assessing readability of patient education materials: Current role in orthopaedics. *Clinical Orthopaedics and Related Research, 468*(10), 2572−2580.

Bansard, M., Clanet, R., & Raginel, T. (2017). Proposal of standardised and logical templates for discharge letters and discharge summaries sent to general practitioners. *Santé Publique, 29*(1), 57−70.

Bellew, S., Martin, A., Wang, R., Bellolio, M. F., Walker, L., & Sunga, K. (2017). "What's the next step?" Improving interfacility emergency department transfer handoff communication. *The American Journal of Emergency Medicine, 35*(8), 1194−1196.

Benda, N. C., Meadors, M. L., Hettinger, A. Z., & Ratwani, R. M. (2016). Emergency physician task switching increases with the introduction of a commercial electronic health record. *Annals of Emergency Medicine, 67*(6), 741−746.

Benson, T., & Grieve, G. (2016). *Why interoperability is hard. Principles of health interoperability* (pp. 19−35). Springer.

Burke, H. B., Hoang, A., Becher, D., Fontelo, P., Liu, F., Stephens, M., ... Baxi, N. S. (2014). QNOTE: An instrument for measuring the quality of EHR clinical notes. *Journal of the American Medical Informatics Association, 21*(5), 910−916.

Carter, A. J., Davis, K. A., Evans, L. V., & Cone, D. C. (2009). Information loss in emergency medical services handover of trauma patients. *Prehospital Emergency Care, 13*(3), 280−285.

Centers for Disease Control and Prevention. (2009). *Simply put: A guide for creating easy-to-understand materials.* Atlanta, GA: Centers for Disease Control and Prevention. Retrieved from <https://www.cdc.gov/healthliteracy/pdf/Simply_Put.pdf>.

Centers for Medicare and Medicaid Services. *Toolkit for making written material clear and effective.* (2010).

Chao, C.-A. (2016). The impact of electronic health records on collaborative work routines: A narrative network analysis. *International Journal of Medical Informatics, 94*, 100−111.

Chase, D. A., Ash, J. S., Cohen, D. J., Hall, J., Olson G. M., & Dorr, D. A. (2014). The EHR's roles in collaboration between providers: A qualitative study. In: *AMIA annual symposium proceedings* (pp. 1718−1727).

Cifuentes, M., Davis, M., Fernald, D., Gunn, R., Dickinson, P., & Cohen, D. J. (2015). Electronic health record challenges, workarounds, and solutions observed in practices integrating behavioral health and primary care. *The Journal of the American Board of Family Medicine, 28*(Supplement 1), S63−S72.

Centers for Medicare and Medicaid Services. *Promoting interoperability.* (July 31, 2018). Retrieved from <https://www.cms.gov/Regulations-and-Guidance/Legislation/EHRIncentivePrograms/index.html?redirect = /EHRIncentivePrograms/>.

Cuk, S., Wimmer, H., & Powell, L. M. (2017). Problems associated with patient care reports and transferring data between ambulance and hospitals from the perspective of emergency medical technicians. *Issues in Information Systems, 18*(4), 16−26.

DeMers, G., Kahn, C., Buono, C., Chan, T., Blair, P., Griswold, W., ... & Plymoth, A.N. (2011). Secure scalable disaster electronic medical record and tracking system. In: *The 2011 international conference on technologies for homeland security (HST)*. Available from: https://doi.org/10.1109/THS.2011.6107903.

Downing, N. L., Bates, D. W., & Longhurst, C. A. (2018). Physician burnout in the electronic health record era: Are we ignoring the real cause? *Annals of Internal Medicine, 169*, 50−51.

Duckworth, R. L. (2016). Five ways to perfect the patient handoff: It's a perilous transition for the patient; here's how to help it go smoother. *EMS World, 45*(11), 1.

Everson, J., & Adler-Milstein, J. (2018). Gaps in health information exchange between hospitals that treat many shared patients. *Journal of the American Medical Informatics Association, 25*(9), 1114−1121.

Federman, A. D., Sanchez-Munoz, A., Jandorf, L., Salmon, C., Wolf, M. S., & Kannry, J. (2017). Patient and clinician perspectives on the outpatient after-visit summary: A qualitative study to inform improvements in visit summary design. *Journal of the American Medical Informatics Association, 24*(e1), e61−e68. Available from https://doi.org/10.1093/jamia/ocw106.

Gaev, J., & Tremoulet, P. D. (2018). Implementing a program to share user experience data for medical devices. *Proceedings of the Human Factors and Ergonomics Society Annual Meeting, 62*(1), 543−547. Available from https://doi.org/10.1177/1541931218621123.

Goldberg, S. A., Porat, A., Strother, C. G., Lim, N. Q., Wijeratne, H. S., Sanchez, G., & Munjal, K. G. (2017). Quantitative analysis of the content of EMS handoff of critically ill and injured patients to the emergency department. *Prehospital Emergency Care, 21*(1), 14−17.

Gordon, B. D., Bernard, K., Salzman, J., & Whitebird, R. R. (2015). Impact of health information exchange on emergency medicine clinical decision making. *The Western Journal of Emergency Medicine, 16*(7), 1047−1051.

Gorry, T. (2017). Harnessing the power of the EMR to improve written communications. In: *Presentation at "transforming health IT by embedding safety", partnership for health IT patient safety meeting* (Plymouth Meeting, PA).

Gregory, M. E., Russo, E., & Singh, H. (2017). Electronic health record alert-related workload as a predictor of burnout in primary care providers. *Applied Clinical Informatics, 8*(03), 686−697.

Holmgren, A. J., Patel, V., & Adler-Milstein, J. (2017). Progress in interoperability: Measuring US hospitals' engagement in sharing patient data. *Health Affairs, 36*(10), 1820−1827.

Hoonakker, P., Wooldridge, A., Hose, B. Z., Carayon, P., Eithun, B., Brazelton, T., ... Rusy, D. (2018). *Things falling through the cracks: Information loss during pediatric trauma care transitions. Congress of the international ergonomics association* (pp. 479−488). Cham: Springer.

Iroju, O., Soriyan, A., Gambo, I., & Olaleke, J. (2013). Interoperability in healthcare: Benefits, challenges and resolutions. *International Journal of Innovation and Applied Studies, 3*(1), 262−270.

Jones, C. D., Cumbler, E., Honigman, B., Burke, R. E., Boxer, R. S., Levy, C., ... Wald, H. L. (2017). Hospital to post-acute care facility transfers: Identifying targets for information exchange quality improvement. *Journal of the American Medical Directors Association, 18* (1), 70−73.

Kantner, L., Shroyer, R., & Rosenbaum, S. (2002). Structured heuristic evaluation of online documentation. In: *IEEE international professional communication conference* (pp. 331−342).

Khennou, F., Khamlichi, Y. I., & Chaoui, N. E. H. (2017). Evaluating electronic health records interoperability. In: International conference on information and software technologies (pp. 106−118).

Kind, A. J., & Smith, M. A. (2008). *Documentation of mandated discharge summary components in transitions from acute to subacute care. AHRQ patient safety: New directions and alternative approaches* (pp. 179−188). Rockville, MD: Agency for Healthcare Research and Quality.

Kulshrestha, A., & Singh, J. (2016). Inter-hospital and intra-hospital patient transfer: Recent concepts. *Indian Journal of Anaesthesia, 60*(7), 451.

Lim, S. Y., Jarvenpaa, S. L., & Lanham, H. J. (2015). Barriers to interorganizational knowledge transfer in post-hospital care transitions: Review and directions for information systems research. *Journal of Management Information Systems, 32*(3), 48−74.

Lowry, S. Z., Quinn, M. T., Ramaiah, M., Brick, D., Patterson, E. S., Zhang, J., ... , Gibbons, M.C. (2012). (NISTIR 7865) A human factors guide to enhance EHR usability of critical user interactions when supporting pediatric patient care. In: NIST interagency/internal report (NISTIR)-7865.

McMurray, J., Hicks, E., Johnson, H., Elliott, J., Byrne, K., & Stolee, P. (2013). 'Trying to find information is like hating yourself every day': The collision of electronic information systems in transition with patients in transition. *Health Informatics Journal, 19*(3), 218−232.

Meigs, S. L., & Solomon, M. (2016). Electronic health record use a bitter pill for many physicians. *Perspectives in Health Information Management, 13*(Winter), 1d. Retrieved from <https://https://www.ncbi.nlm.nih.gov/pmc/articles/PMC4739443/>.

Mello, M. M., Adler-milstein, J., Ding, K. L., & Savage, L. (2018). Legal barriers to the growth of health information exchange—Boulders or pebbles? *The Milbank Quarterly, 96*(1), 110−143.

Menachemi, N., Rahurkar, S., Harle, C. A., & Vest, J. R. (2018). The benefits of health information exchange: An updated systematic review. *Journal of the American Medical Informatics Association, 25*(9), 1259−1265.

Pew Research Center. *Smartphone ownership rates skyrocket in many emerging economies, but digital divide remains.* (Feb 22, 2016). Pew Research Center. Retrieved from <http://www.pewglobal.org/2016/02/22/smartphone-ownership-rates-skyrocket-in-many-emerging-economies-but-digital-divide-remains/>.

Pew Research Center. *Mobile fact sheet.* (Feb 5, 2018). Retrieved from <http://www.pewinternet.org/fact-sheet/mobile/>.

Newnham, H., Barker, A., Ritchie, E., Hitchcock, K., Gibbs, H., & Holton, S. (2017). Discharge communication practices and healthcare provider and patient preferences, satisfaction and comprehension: A systematic review. *International Journal for Quality in Health Care,* 1−17. Available from https://doi.org/10.1093/intqhc/mzx121.

Nguyen, O. K., Kruger, J., Greysen, S. R., Lyndon, A., & Goldman, L. E. (2014). Understanding how to improve collaboration between hospitals and primary care in postdischarge care transitions: A qualitative study of primary care leaders' perspectives. *Journal of Hospital Medicine, 9*(11), 700−706.

Nielsen, J. (1994a). *Usability engineering.* Elsevier.

Nielsen, J. (1994b). *10 Usability heuristics for user interface design.* Fremont, CA: Nielsen Norman Group. Retrieved from <https://www.nngroup.com/articles/ten-usability-heuristics/>.

Nielsen, J., & Molich, R. (1990). Heuristic evaluation of user interfaces. In: Proceedings of the SIGCHI conference on human factors in computing systems (pp. 249−256).

NPD Group, Inc. *Smartwatch ownership expected to increase nearly 60 percent into 2019.* (2017). Retrieved from <https://www.npd.com/wps/portal/npd/us/news/press-releases/2017/us-smartwatch-ownership-expected-to-increase-nearly-60-percent-into-2019/>.

Penn Medicine News. *Simulations help create the future of healthcare* (Jun 8, 2016). Penn Medicine News. Retrieved from <https://www.pennmedicine.org/news/internal-newsletters/system-news/2016/june/simulations-help-create-the-future-of-health>

Plain Language Action and Information Network. *Federal plain language guidelines.* (2011). Retrieved from <http://www.plainlanguage.gov/howto/guidelines/FederalPLGuidelines/FederalPLGuidelines.pdf>.

Rauch, D. A. (2018). Physician's role in coordinating care of hospitalized children. *Pediatrics, 142*(2), e20181503. Retrieved from <https://pediatrics.aappublications.org/content/126/4/829>.

Regli, S. H. (2012, January). *C4ISR-med battlefield medical demonstrations and experiments.* Retrieved from <http://www.atl.external.lmco.com/papers/2123b.pdf>.

Regli, S. H., Tremoulet, P. D., Samoylov, A., Sharma, K., Stibler, K., & Anthony, L. (2010). Medical intelligence informatics. *Proceedings of the ACM SIGCHI First International Workshop of Interactive Systems in Healthcare* (WISH'2010), Atlanta, GA, p. 145–148.

Reimer, A. P., Alfes, C. M., Rowe, A. S., & Rodriguez-Fox, B. M. (2018). Emergency patient handoffs: Identifying essential elements and developing an evidence-based training tool. *The Journal of Continuing Education in Nursing, 49*(1), 34–41.

Ruth, J. L., Geskey, J. M., Shaffer, M. L., Bramley, H. P., & Paul, I. M. (2011). Evaluating communication between pediatric primary care physicians and hospitalists. *Clinical Pediatrics, 50*(10), 923–928.

Salen, P. (2017). *Transitions of care: Complications and solutions. Vignettes in patient safety— Vol. 1.* InTech.

Sarzynski, E., Hashmi, H., Subramanian, J., Fitzpatrick, L., Polverento, M., Simmons, M., ... Given, C. (2016). Opportunities to improve clinical summaries for patients at hospital discharge. *British Medical Journal of Quality & Safety, 26*, 354–356.

Savatmongkorngul, S., Yuksen, C., Suwattanasilp, C., Sawanyawisuth, K., & Sittichanbuncha, Y. (2017). Is a mobile emergency severity index (ESI) triage better than the paper ESI? *Internal and Emergency Medicine, 12*(8), 1273–1277.

Shanafelt, T. D., Dyrbye, L. N., & West, C. P. (2017). Addressing physician burnout: The way forward. *The Journal of the American Medical Association, 317*(9), 901–902.

Shelton, D., & Sinclair, P. (2016). Availability of ambulance patient care reports in the emergency department. *BMJ Open Quality, 5*(1), u209478–w3889. Available from https://doi.org/10.1136/bmjquality.u209478.w3889.

Shneiderman, B. (2010). *Designing the user interface: Strategies for effective human-computer interaction.* India: Pearson Education.

Slager, S., Beckstrom, J., Weir, C., Del Fiol, G., & Brooke, B. S. (2017). Information exchange between providers during transitions of surgical care: Communication, documentation and sometimes both. *Studies in Health Technology and Informatics, 234*, 303.

Sockolow, P. S., Bowles, K. H., Rogers, M., Adelsberger, M. C., Chittams, J. L., & Liao, C. (2014). Opportunities in interdisciplinary care team adoption of electronic point-of-care documentation systems. *Studies in Health Technology and Informatics, 201*, 371–379.

Solan, L. G., Sherman, S. N., DeBlasio, D., & Simmons, J. M. (2016). Communication challenges: A qualitative look at the relationship between pediatric hospitalists and primary care providers. *Academic Pediatrics, 16*(5), 453–459.

Tremoulet, P. D., Krishnan, R., Karavite, D., Muthu, N., Regli, S., Will, A., & Michel, J. (2018). A heuristic evaluation to assess use of after visit summaries for supporting continuity of care. *Applied Clinical Informatics, 9*(03), 714–724.

Unnewehr, M., Schaaf, B., Marev, R., Fitch, J., & Friederichs, H. (2015). Optimizing the quality of hospital discharge summaries—A systematic review and practical tools. *Postgraduate Medicine*, *127*(6), 630–639.

Varpio, L., Rashotte, J., Day, K., King, J., Kuziemsky, C., & Parush, A. (2015). The EHR and building the patient's story: A qualitative investigation of how EHR use obstructs a vital clinical activity. *International Journal of Medical Informatics*, *84*(12), 1019–1028.

Webber, E., Schaffer, J., Willey, C., & Aldrich, J. (2018). Targeting pajama time: Efforts to reduce physician burnout through electronic medical record (EMR) improvements. *American Academy of Pediatrics*, *142*(1), 611.

Zakrison, T. L., Rosenbloom, B., McFarlan, A., Jovicic, A., Soklaridis, S., Allen, C., ... Rizoli, S. (2016). Lost information during the handover of critically injured trauma patients: A mixed-methods study. *BMJ Quality & Safety*, *25*(12), 929–936. Available from https://doi.org/10.1136/bmjqs-2014-003903.

Zelmer, J., Ronchi, E., Hyppönen, H., Lupiáñez-Villanueva, F., Codagnone, C., Nøhr, C., ... Adler-Milstein, J. (2017). International health IT benchmarking: Learning from cross-country comparisons. *Journal of the American Medical Informatics Association*, *24*(2), 371–379.

Zhang, J., Johnson, T. R., Patel, V. L., Paige, D. L., & Kubose, T. (2003). Using usability heuristics to evaluate patient safety of medical devices. *Journal of Biomedical Informatics*, *36*(1), 23–30.

Zhang, Z., Sarcevic, A., & Bossen, C. (2017). Constructing common information spaces across distributed emergency medical teams. In: *Paper presented at the proceedings of the 2017 ACM conference on computer supported cooperative work and social computing.*

Further reading

Sebastian, S. (2018). *A study on impact of smart phone usage on health of college going students.*

Tremoulet, P. D., McManus, M., & Baranov, D. (2017). Rendering ICU data useful via formative evaluations of trajectory, tracking, and trigger (T3TM) software. *Proceedings of the International Symposium on Human Factors and Ergonomics in Health Care*, *6*(1), 50–56.

Section 2

Healthcare systems

Chapter 7

Design for critical care

D. Kirk Hamilton
Texas A&M University, College Station, TX, United States

Introduction

The hospital intensive care unit, or ICU, is the place where critically ill patients receive care. These are the most vulnerable and high acuity patients with life-threatening conditions, and they receive care from highly trained clinicians who are under nearly continuous stress. Design for these patient units influences patients, their families, critical care nurses, clinical staff, and intensivist physicians alike. Unit design can influence patient outcomes.

This chapter provides a brief overview of critical care, including nursing tasks, technological complexity, issues of safety, human factors, and architectural design guidelines, all leading to system design issues. The concept of system design issues for the ICU is explored, and multiple design criteria are suggested. The chapter concludes with a comparative case study of system design in two units at Johns Hopkins Hospital in Baltimore, Maryland, and some suggestions for the design of future ICUs.

Nurses provide the vast majority of patient care in the ICU (Abbey, Chaboyer, & Mitchell, 2012). Each critical care nurse's shift begins with a report of the patient's status from the nurse completing the previous shift and ends with a report to the oncoming nurse responsible for the next shift. ICU nurses are involved with repetitive cycles of assessment, treatment, and documentation, usually every 1, 2, or 4 hours, depending on patient acuity (Hamilton, 2017a). Multiple technical systems support the work of clinicians in the ICU. Ebright (2004, 2010) describes complex nursing work to include coordinating delivery of care, retrieving clinical information, and supporting family needs. Nurses must compensate for missing information, resources, or medications, defective equipment, and must work within a culture that often lacks effective communication and teamwork.

Overview of critical care

Nursing tasks. Critical care nurses work within an expert clinical team dealing with the sickest patients in the hospital. The work of critical care nurses,

Design for Health. DOI: https://doi.org/10.1016/B978-0-12-816427-3.00007-5

129

directly responsible for 24-hour hands-on patient care, is highly demanding. The patient population is extremely ill and vulnerable (Carayon & Gurses, 2005) and while advances have reduced mortality rates, ICU survivors face consequences for cognitive and psychological functioning (Jackson, Mitchell, & Hopkins, 2015). ICU patients are older and sicker than before, and nurses must deal with the demands of new and changing technical equipment (Bergbom, 2007). The differences between the ICU and a typical acute care patient unit include the need for intensive physiologic monitoring, continuous observation, and the ability to provide rapid intervention when required.

The complexity of nursing care results from continuous attention to the physiologic monitor, the requirement for multiple medication treatments, and the constant potential for a negative change in patient conditions, all due to the patients' high acuity. The heavy workload demand and the frequency of interruption can hinder an ICU nurse's ability to perform the expected tasks. Critical care nurses work with an enormous cognitive burden based on task complexity and the simultaneity of multiple demands (Drews, 2007; Machado et al., 2018; Potter et al., 2005).

Technological complexity. A survey of critical care nurses (Verhulst, 2008) reported that most perceived increases of technology in their unit, and two-thirds noted increases in complexity. There has been a "dramatic increase in the technological complexity of the system and the medical work environment" (Gopher & Donchin, 2014, p. 2). Management of these technologies contributes to nurse workload, influences patterns of movement, and may represent a performance obstacle. Of 116 in the Verhulst study, 41% indicated that adjusting and controlling too many devices kept them from providing essential patient care.

Nurses must adapt to continuously evolving technologies which impact their workloads. ICU nurses interact with and manage numerous technical devices, such as monitors, pumps, ventilators, documentation computers, and other machines. Nurses must deal with both fixed and moveable technical equipment within the patient room. There are software and hardware technologies intended to avoid adverse drug events (Hassan, Badawi, Weber, & Cohen, 2010). Management of these many technologies adds to the cognitive burden on the critical care nurse.

An example of technology nurses must manage is the barcode scanner of medicines and patient wristbands which confirm the correct medicines and patient identity to document the administration of each dose. The scanner is sometimes mobile or can be attached in a fixed location within the room. Although technology interventions are intended to save nurses' labor and time, as in the case of barcodes, it can paradoxically increase the demands on nurse cognition and time.

Technologies can improve nurse workflow, although the nurse may develop a work-around to avoid a negative aspect of its use

(Barcode technology, 2008). In this case, nurses have been observed violating safety protocol by using a duplicate wristband when the barcode scanner would not reach the patient's wristband (Hamilton, 2013).

Critical care safety. High mortality rates are associated with illness in an ICU (Dijkema, Dieperink, van Meurs, & Zijlstra, 2012). In a 2006 study, Valentin et al. (2006) found that on average 38.8 sentinel events occur per 100 ICU patient days. Adverse outcomes are far too common (Wu, Pronovost, & Morlock, 2002) and include medication error, errors of diagnosis and treatment, mistakes during handoff, errors during procedures, infections acquired in the hospital, patient falls, and failure to rescue (Donchin et al., 1995; Pagnamenta et al., 2012; Pham et al., 2012).

Between 5% and 15% of hospital in-patients develop an infection during their admission. In addition, critically ill patients in an intensive care unit (ICU) are 5-10 times more likely to acquire a nosocomial infection than those in general wards (Lim & Webb, 2005, p. 887).

Garrouste-Orgeas et al. (2012), noting the high levels of prescribed pharmaceuticals, reported, "Medical errors and adverse events are very common in ICUs, and among them the most prevalent involve medications" (p. 7). Reducing errors associated with these high levels of medication prescriptions requires vigilance and supportive technologies (Hassan et al., 2010).

The importance of safety and quality has been gaining recognition. Critical care infection rates, including central line infections, catheter-associated infections, and ventilator-associated pneumonia, are being given full attention (Wu et al., 2002). Collection of safety and quality data is contributing to improvement initiatives. A study at the University of Michigan by Wahl et al. (2006) reported that units are documenting measures in an effort to prevent catheter-related bloodstream infections and pneumonia associated with ventilator use.

Three strategies to improve safety in critical care have been proposed by Pronovost, Wu, Dorman, and Morlock (2002): (1) prevent errors from occurring, (2) make errors more visible when they occur, and (3) mitigate harm caused by injuries. ICU nurses are best able to implement each of these proposed strategies, as nurses are closest to the bedside for the majority of care episodes: "Critical care medicine can only be practiced by close observation of the patient *at the bedside*, by contemplation, and by the integration of a large database of evidence-based medicine together with a good deal of humility" (Marik, 2001, p. 3).

Human factors design. There is an extensive amount of technology in the critical care patient room. Industrial designers, human factors engineers, and/ or information technology experts may have developed these devices. The human factors engineer addresses multiple issues in the context of the intensive care environment.

Human factor experts working in health care have a long list of areas in which improvements can be made (Carayon, 2012). The human−computer interface for different devices is vitally important for efficiency and nurse effectiveness. There is a need for improved battery and charger designs. Analysis of the patient bed could lead to advances; a flip-up work shelf at the footboard is an example of a useful innovation, and nurses have suggested a light under the bed, near the foot, to help read data on devices at night. The traditional overbed table will not fit under a modern ICU bed and can only be used at an angle. Despite this, every nurse utilizes one or more of these tables to support their work. A new design would be welcome. To support nurses in a crisis, ergonomic analysis of positioning of the Code Blue alarm, the emergency call system, and their respective cancellation buttons are vitally important.

A significant problem is that most medical devices, such as physiologic monitors, infusion pumps, and electronic health records, are not capable of effectively communicating with other devices. The inability to transmit data from one of these systems to another, or lack of system interoperability, is a significant problem. If every physiologic monitor could directly communicate a patient's vital signs data into the electronic health record, as one example, nurses' time could be saved and errors reduced.

Understanding nurse cognition, especially as it relates to situation awareness, is a potentially fertile area of study. Analysis methods from the field of human factors engineering, including cognitive work analysis (Bisantz & Roth, 2007; Jiancaro, Jamieson, & Mihailidis, 2014) and cognitive task analysis (Vicente, 1995), could be helpful to future researchers and designers.

Systems modeling. There is value in the ability to model a system as part of the design process. Carayon and her colleagues (Carayon & Gurses, 2005; Carayon & Smith, 2000; Carayon et al., 2006) introduced the Systems Engineering Initiative for Patient Safety (SEIPS) theory, a human factors framework addressing health-care settings. The theory proposes that five components of the work system (person, tasks, tools and technologies, physical environment, and organizational conditions) interact with and influence each other. Similar to Donabedian's classic *structure-process-outcome* model (1978), the SEIPS model substitutes the five components of the work system for *structure* in Donabedian's model.

The SEIPS model is helpful in understanding the complex interactions associated with an ICU design. In the context of critical care units, the five SEIPS components are present. They can be seen in the form of (1) nurses, staff, and patients; (2) the tasks of caregiving by nurses and clinicians; (3) the multiple tools, equipment, and medical technologies available; (4) the physical setting of the unit, patient rooms, and their features; and (5) the organizational and procedural protocols that influence the caregiving process. The functional design of systems for an ICU must also conform to the requirements of architectural regulations.

Architectural design guidelines. Regulatory standards in North America set some of the basic parameters of critical care unit design, governing things such as mandatory patient room windows, minimum corridor widths, room sizes, and dimensions around the patient bed. The building code establishes the size of smoke compartments and the allowable amounts of glass in doors and walls within ICUs.

In the United States, the architectural design can involve a local or national building code, such as the International Building Code of the International Code Council (ICC, 2018), state hospital licensing standards, review by the state's Authority Having Jurisdiction (AHJ), and conformance with Joint Commission Accreditation Standards (2018). There are engineering requirements in the Electrical Code and standards for other special conditions, such as medical gas installations. Many states and Medicare require adherence to the prescriptive intensive care requirements of the Facilities Guidelines Institute (FGI) *Guidelines for Design and Construction of Hospitals* (Facilities Guidelines Institute, 2018). The Society of Critical Care Medicine has a voluntary performance-based design guideline (Thompson et al., 2012).

Understanding the work of the ICU, safety issues, and regulatory requirements of critical care design is necessary for successful ICU design. Systems thinking and modeling provide insight into designing, constructing, and operating these facilities.

System design criteria in the intensive care unit

The typical hospital ICU features numerous designed systems, ranging from the physically embedded life support technologies of electric utilities, medical gasses, and alarms, to accommodations for digital systems, such as physiologic monitors and electronic health records. One might ask, *what are relevant system design criteria for the ICU?* The author believes that systems in facilities for critical care must address criteria in these six categories:

- Delivery of life-saving critical care medical interventions:
  - provide continuous life support for the critically ill patient,
  - enable prompt and efficient patient treatment,
  - support situation awareness and a high degree of patient observation, and
  - enhance the contemporaneous documentation of care delivery.
- Safety for patients, staff, and others:
  - enable safe task performance on the part of all clinicians,
  - support patient and staff hygiene,
  - prevent airborne, water-borne, and contact transmission of pathogens, and
  - support the safe disposal of human waste and other waste streams.

- Support for clinical effectiveness:
  - enable effective task performance on the part of all clinicians,
  - allow staff to visualize and be aware of others and their patients,
  - enable accurate patient assessment and physiologic monitoring,
  - support the delivery and accurate administration of medications, and
  - enable care by teams when interventions require it.
- Provision of access to needed resources:
  - support the delivery and availability of frequently utilized supplies, and
  - accommodate needed medical equipment and devices.
- Address the social and family needs of patients:
  - allow for active and supportive involvement of patient families, and
  - provide space and amenities for families in the patient room.
- Preparation for the future and the unexpected:
  - be capable of adapting to changes in treatment protocols,
  - be capable of accommodating the future evolution of medical technology,
  - plan to deal with patients from unexpected disasters, and
  - be capable of continuing to perform during a range of service interruptions.

It is likely that critical care units meeting all of these system design criteria would contribute positively to clinical outcomes and effectively support the work of nurses and physicians. The major influence on the quality of care is, of course, the performance of humans within their environment, so the design is not sufficient to ensure the optimum results. On the other hand, if design can make a difference in safety and quality, an evidence-based design process must be utilized in the interest of improved care (Hamilton & Shepley, 2010).

Case study: a comparison of two intensive care units at Johns Hopkins Hospital, Baltimore

An example of two ICUs at Johns Hopkins Hospital in Baltimore provides a comparative case study (Hamilton, 2017a) revealing how two units in the same organization, constructed at different times, have addressed system design issues and criteria. The author conducted field observations on both units, shadowing critical care nurses on multiple 12-hour day and night shifts. Some systems and configurations are consistent for both, and others reflect design differences. The Weinberg unit is older, and the Zayed unit is the most recent design.

Delivery of life-saving critical care medical interventions

Life support systems. The most common life support system in North American critical care units is the headwall configuration in which the head of the bed is against a wall, which contains the various utilities, medical gasses, and alarms. With the bed as a peninsula off the wall, nurses must move in a horseshoe pattern around the other three sides.

All of the life support systems in the two Johns Hopkins units are variations of the headwall design, configured with the bed parallel to the corridor. The view from the corridor is always toward the side of the patient bed. Rooms are designed so that beds are arranged back-to-back in mirrored configurations to share the common utility and plumbing walls. Lessons from the earlier ICU designs are incorporated into the later headwall designs. Placement of electrical outlets, medical gasses, suction canisters, alarm buttons, blood pressure cuffs, and emergency Ambu bags has been carefully considered, incrementally improving each successive design.

Designs at other institutions sometimes feature beds oriented with the toe toward the corridor, or with a freestanding bed away from the wall. Some institutions have adopted a policy of so-called single-handed rooms, where they are all identically oriented and not back-to-back. The assumption is that standardization will lead to fewer errors, although data do not yet support the claim, and skeptical nurses note that patients can have problems on either side of their body (Pati, Harvey, Evans, & Cason, 2009).

Among other types of life support systems is a power column featuring the utilities, gasses, and alarms wrapped around a narrow vertical column reaching from floor to ceiling, usually positioned diagonally off the head of the bed. An overhead boom system provides all the utilities from above, mounted on pendants from the ceiling, and allows 360° access to the bed while leaving the floor clear (Pati, Evans, Waggener, & Harvey, 2008). There are numerous variants to these models, including systems found in Europe and Asia (Figs. 7.1−7.3).

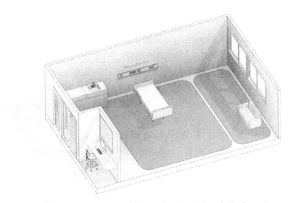

FIGURE 7.1   Headwall life support system. *Illustration by Behzad Yaghmaei.*

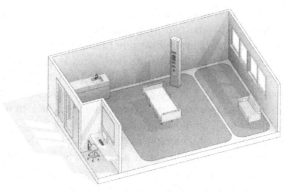

FIGURE 7.2 Power column life support system. *Illustration by Behzad Yaghmaei.*

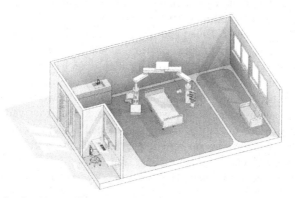

FIGURE 7.3 Overhead boom life support system. *Illustration by Behzad Yaghmaei.*

Safety for patients, staff, and others

Infection control systems. The classic protocol for infection prevention is careful hand hygiene in which the hands are fully washed with soap and water, suggesting a handwashing sink located near the door on the path into and out of the room (Pittet, Allegranzi, & Boyce, 2009). In observations at both ICU units at Johns Hopkins, it is clear that nurses most often use the alcohol gel located at the doorway as they enter and leave the room. Use of the sinks was most often observed when gross soil was on the nurse's hands.

Other protections against infection transmission include filtration of the air handling system and the use of antimicrobial materials on furniture and finishes in the room, along with cleaning protocols. There are readily accessible gloves, gowns, and eye protection for staff and visitors. The two units share the same infection control systems.

Toileting systems. Providing a toilet for extremely ill ICU patients rarely seems to be necessary, yet it is a safety issue. The toilets in these rooms are used more often for waste disposal and that function could easily be better served by a clinical sink. The two units share the same toileting systems.

Nurses have frequently been observed choosing to assist patients eliminating on a blue chuck pad in the bed and then disposing of the pad and waste in a red biohazard bag rather than in the seldom used toilet. This action is a work-around to avoid handling and transporting human waste. One wonders whether a clinical sink or macerator would be a better choice for high acuity patients than a conventional toilet (Apple, 2016).

Support for clinical effectiveness

Decentralized charting alcoves. There has been a trend in ICU design to locate decentralized charting stations near the doorways of patient rooms (Bayramzadeh & Alkazemi, 2014; Fay, Cai, & Real, 2018). The more recently built Zayed unit features decentralized charting alcoves with documentation computers outside pairs of patient rooms. The Weinberg unit does not have such alcoves; nurses charted nearby in stations across the corridor or by positioning a mobile computer in the hallway just outside the room's door. This suggests that nurses find decentralized charting close to each patient a helpful contribution to their charting responsibilities.

Units that feature decentralized charting positions also require some centralized elements. There needs to be a place where a unit clerk can answer the phone and a charge nurse can work, along with a pneumatic tube, medication room, and printers. The central station provides workspace and computers for team members who are not resident on the unit, such as physicians, physical therapists, pharmacists, social workers, chaplains, coders, and any others who may need a temporary place to work. Both the Weinberg and Zayed units have these sorts of centralized features.

Observation of patients. Situation awareness depends upon the ability for staff to observe their patients. Nurses report a desire to see each other's patients in order to respond quickly when help is required (Hamilton, 2017a, 2017b). Windows offering a view of the patient bed provide visualization from decentralized alcoves. Otherwise, visualization and observation of the patient are through glass doors, usually propped open. ICU designs generally use glass doors to provide increased potential for staff to observe patients from corridor positions.

Computer positions and device options. The documentation capability on the Johns Hopkins critical care units includes multiple options. The Zayed unit has access to computer consoles and electronic health records in the decentralized alcoves outside every pair of patient rooms. In addition, staff has access to fixed computers inside the room on the corridor wall, mobile computers on wheels, and tablet computers, as well as computers at two central team stations.

The Weinberg unit, built at an earlier time, does not have decentralized alcoves. The solution in the case of the Weinberg unit is to use mobile computers on wheels in the corridor just outside the room's door, along with a fixed computer in the room just inside the doorway and computers at the central team stations. Clinicians use the mobile computers on wheels and tablet computers in the patient room when necessary.

The lesson from the case study comparison seems to support the widest variation of options for computer documentation and access to medical information. More computers mean more ways to document what is happening, including the high level of activity that accompanies admissions and crisis episodes when several staff members may simultaneously need access to systems.

Support for clinical effectiveness

Technology in the room. One technology issue for the ICU rooms at Johns Hopkins is the use of overhead lifts; they are not available in the Zayed or Weinberg units. Lifting and positioning patients and reducing back injuries among nurses are the potential benefits of ceiling mounted mechanical lifts. The author was somewhat surprised that there were no lifts in the Johns Hopkins ICUs.

Another notable technology for ICUs *not* installed in rooms at Johns Hopkins is the use of a camera linked to a central monitor observation station or telemedicine links. Because Hopkins is a high acuity site and fully staffed, there may not be a need for such technology.

Technology readily available to the room. In addition to the pneumatic tube connection for sending specimens to the lab, centralized unit locations provide for increasingly miniaturized point-of-care laboratory testing (Halpern, 2000). Other technical devices, such as Accu-Chek blood sugar monitors, Doppler ultrasound devices, hypo/hyperthermia temperature control machines, and other portable devices, are located on the unit, ready to deploy.

Supply systems. Every ICU has a system for the delivery and storage of supplies. Many units keep supplies in one or more supply rooms, and nurses must travel back and forth to collect what is needed, returning to keep a small amount in the room. This can mean multiple trips on each shift. Design of the unit and distribution of the supply rooms can mean greater or shorter travel for the nurses. Multiple supply rooms distributed to equalize travel distances provide an answer for nurse efficiency, and units that allow commonly needed supplies to be in the room provide the best access for the bedside nurse.

The policy at Johns Hopkins is to keep frequently needed supplies in carts within the patient room. The logical concept is to have the most frequently needed supplies readily available and close to the point of care, and nurses value the policy and resulting convenience. Some facilities do not stock supplies in the room in order to avoid the need to discard them upon the patient's discharge, but the Johns Hopkins solution is to recycle carts and supplies after a hydrogen peroxide gas decontamination in materials management.

An interesting observation during the author's recent study found that the supply cart location opposite the foot of the bed in the Zayed unit minimized the nurse's travel when compared with the cart location near the doorway at the Weinberg unit (Hamilton, 2017a). If supplies in the room enhance the work of the nurse, supplies at the foot of the bed, equally available to both sides of the bed, are even more effective. Locating a supply cart at the foot of the bed affects the head-to-toe dimension of the room.

Address the social and family needs of patients

Family accommodation. The families are welcome at both the Johns Hopkins ICU units, but there is more space in the newer Zayed unit for a convertible sleeper sofa. The Weinberg unit only had space provided for families in the two large corner rooms and the isolation room. Neither example offers the ideal configuration to support family presence in the ICU.

Preparation for the future and the unexpected

Design and straight corridors. Once the electronic medical record was widely adopted and fairly reliable, architects and their clients were able to develop decentralized charting positions, often in alcoves, that allowed a view into a pair of ICU patient rooms. Nurses and the documentation tasks were moved closer to the patient's bedside. This was apparently a useful and important advance to observation and caregiving.

Unfortunately, the advantage of placing nurses closer to the bedside has allowed many designers to begin adapting their ICU designs to the more rectangular structural footprints of typical acute units, above or below the critical care unit. While this made sense from the standpoint of simplified building and control of construction costs, it has resulted in an unanticipated problem (Hamilton, Swoboda, Lee, & Anderson, 2018). These newer units with straight corridors no longer provide the high visualization of a concentric, fishbowl design where every nurse can be aware of other nurses and their patients. Nurses on these "straight corridor" units describe being afraid because they often feel alone, without backup or support in case of a crisis (Hamilton, 2017b). Nurses on these types of units say they are not aware of what is happening and find it difficult to cover for each other on breaks or trips to get equipment. They feel nervous, expecting they might be blamed if something goes wrong.

The Johns Hopkins case study comparison offers a relevant example. The Weinberg unit is configured as a box shape with two team stations on diagonal corners responsible for 10 beds each. The Weinberg unit, although older with smaller rooms, offers better team communication than the newer Zayed unit. The newer Zayed unit with larger patient rooms features decentralized charting alcoves and straight corridors within the footprint of the acute patient tower. Zayed nurses are widely separated with a minimal view into the rooms of other nurses on the unit.

It would seem that a return to the high visualization form would be desirable for new ICU designs. At the same time, the advantage of decentralized charting which brings nurses closer to the bedside should not be abandoned.

Conclusion: the intensive care unit of the future

A high-performance ICU of the future should address relevant design criteria. Such an ideal unit might be arranged as clusters of 8–10 beds, each in private rooms (Hamilton & Shepley, 2010) organized in a concentric, "fishbowl," or semicircular configuration that enhances caregivers' ability to see each other and their patients (Hamilton, 2017b).

The private rooms would feature an overhead boom life support system delivering medical gasses, electrical power, monitor support, and IV pump capability along with other services to the patient in the bed while providing 360° access to the patient (Pati et al., 2008). The SCCM Guidelines for critical care design use performance requirements for room dimensions, rather than an explicit, prescriptive size (Thompson et al., 2012), so the patient room should be sized for equipment and clinical work around the bed, recognizing that units with higher levels of acuity will require more personnel and equipment.

Back injuries are common among nurses (Ferguson, Grooms, Onate, Khan, & Marrass, 2015). Studies indicate that overhead lifts simplify patient movement and reduce the incidence of nurse injuries (Lee, Faucett, Gillen, Krause, & Landry, 2010). An ideal ICU would have lifts in every patient room. Lifts permit individual nurses to perform tasks that would otherwise require assistance from someone else.

Documentation is a fundamental task for nurses and the clinical team. Today's documentation occurs most often on some type of computer. Decentralized alcoves outside the doorways to pairs of rooms can be used to provide documentation in the electronic health record. Facilities with multiple computer types and locations are supportive of multiple forms of documentation. A computer in the room assists contemporaneous documentation (Hamilton, 2017a).

As described in the case study earlier, positioning needed supplies in the room is a productivity advantage for nurses. The ideal ICU would have a system to resterilize unused supplies upon patient discharge in order to maintain the convenience of material kept at the foot of the bed (Hamilton, 2017a). Locations of supply, medication, and equipment rooms need to be decentralized to the clusters of beds, reducing travel distance for nurses and clinical staff.

To prevent infection, most clinicians use alcohol gel dispensers on the way in and out of the patient room. Dispensers should be located adjacent to the doorway, just inside, outside, or both (Tvedt & Bukholm, 2005). There should be a handwashing sink by the door and another working sink in a counter for nursing tasks (Pittet et al., 2009). In Europe and parts of Canada, macerators are used to safely dispose of human waste instead of risking the spread of pathogens in aerosols when cleaning bedpans in toilets (Apple, 2016; Burrington, 1999).

Numerous studies indicate the value of natural daylight and the diurnal cycle in patient care (Gehlbach et al., 2012; Kelly, Basharati, Swanney, & Beckert, 2014; McKenna, van der Horst, Reiss, & Martin, 2018). The artificial lighting in patient rooms has multiple uses, including general illumination, examination lighting, reading lights, night lights, and task lighting for clinicians. Various lighting that can address all these needs is desired for an ideal room.

An effective method to improve access to specialists includes the use of high-resolution cameras and communication technology (Zhou et al., 2014). Access to a remote e-ICU or tele-ICU center has been shown to improve outcomes, reduce mortality, and lower costs (Breslow, 2007; Khunlertkit & Carayon, 2013). The tele-ICU model includes intensivists, critical nurses, pharmacists, dieticians, physical therapists, and other experts who can consult on the care of ICU patients at remote sites not having access to similar expertise. Some, however, challenge the effectiveness of telemedicine strategies (Thomas, Lucke, Wueste, Weavind, & Patel, 2009).

There is a trend toward patient and family-centered care (Frampton, 2009). Evidence indicates that "family presence" in critical episodes reduces litigation (Flanders & Strasen, 2014). Provision of space for family accommodation is sensible for many reasons, including the ability for family members to assist in caregiving and avoiding errors (Bazuin & Cardon, 2011). A well-designed contemporary ICU should plan for family involvement.

There is ample room for major improvement to outcomes in critical care. Since the design of the complex ICU environment, systems, and technology has an influence on staff performance and patient outcomes, one potential contribution to improvement is collaborative, multidisciplinary design of these units and patient rooms. Attention to research results and thoughtful interpretation of their implications offers the design team an opportunity to improve the numerous decisions associated with system design. We know enough to suggest a best practice or research informed answer for a majority of the major design decisions. It is worth making every effort for the sake of the highly vulnerable patient population at risk in the ICU.

References

Abbey, M., Chaboyer, W., & Mitchell, M. (2012). Understanding the work of critical care nurses: A time and motion study. *Australian Critical Care, 25*, 13–22.

Apple, M. (2016). Toward a safer and cleaner way: Dealing with human waste in healthcare. *Health Environments Research & Design, 9*(4), 26–34.

Barcode technology. (2008). Barcode technology moves to ICU bedside. *Drug Formulary Review, 24*(11), 90–92.

Bayramzadeh, S., & Alkazemi, M. F. (2014). Centralized vs. decentralized nursing stations: An evaluation of the implications of communication technologies in healthcare. *Health Environments Research & Design Journal, 7*(4), 62–80.

Bazuin, D., & Cardon, K. (2011). Creating healing intensive care unit environments: Physical and psychological considerations in designing critical areas. *Critical Care Nursing Quarterly, 34*(4), 259–267.

Bergbom, I. (2007). Editorial. *Intensive and Critical Care Nursing, 23*, 121–123.

Bisantz, A., & Roth, E. (2007). Analysis of cognitive work. *Reviews of Human Factors and Ergonomics, 3*(1), 1–43.

Breslow, M. J. (2007). Remote ICU care programs: Current status. *Journal of Critical Care, 22*, 66–76.

Burrington, M. A. (1999). *An alternative method for human waste disposal. White paper.* Houston, TX: Center for Innovation in Health Facilities.

Carayon, P., & Gurses, A. P. (2005). A human factors engineering conceptual framework of nursing workload and patient safety in intensive care units. *Intensive and Critical Care Nursing, 21*, 284–301.

Carayon, P., & Smith, M. J. (2000). Work organization and ergonomics. *Applied Ergonomics, 31*, 649–662.

Carayon, P. (Ed.), (2012). *Handbook of human factors and ergonomics in health care and patient safety* (2nd ed.). Boca Raton, FL: CRC Press.

Carayon, P., Schoofs Hundt, A., Karsh, B.-T., Gurses, A. P., Alvarado, C., Smith, M., & Brennan, P. (2006). Work system design for patient safety: The SEIPS Model. *Quality and Safety in Health Care, 15*(Suppl. 1), i50–i58.

Dijkema, L. M., Dieperink, W., van Meurs, M., & Zijlstra, J. G. (2012). Preventable mortality evaluation in the ICU. *Critical Care, 16*(2), 309–314.

Donabedian, A. (1978). The quality of medical care. *Science, 200*(4344), 856–864.

Donchin, Y., Gopher, D., Olin, M., Badihi, Y., Biesky, M., Sprung, C. L., ... Cotev, S. (1995). A look into the nature and causes of human error in the intensive care unit. *Critical Care Medicine, 23*(2), 294–300.

Drews, F. A. (2007). The frequency and impact of task interruptions in the ICU. *Proceedings of the human factors and ergonomics society 51st annual meeting 51* (11), 683–686. Available from https://doi.org/10.1177%2F154193120705101117.

Ebright, P. R. (2004). Understanding nurse work. *Clinical Nurse Specialist, 18*(4), 168–170.

Ebright, P. R. (2010). The complex work of RNs: Implications for healthy work environments. *Online Journal of Issues in Nursing, 15*(1), 11.

Facilities Guidelines Institute. (2018). *Guidelines for Design and Construction of Hospitals.* Chicago, IL: American Society of Healthcare Engineering of the American Hospital Association.

Fay, L., Cai, H., & Real, K. (2018). A systematic literature review of empirical studies of decentralized nursing stations. *Health Environments Research & Design, 12*(1), 44–68.

Ferguson, S. A., Grooms, D. R., Onate, J. A., Khan, S. N., & Marrass, W. S. (2015). Low back functional health status of patient handlers. *Journal of Occupational Rehabilitation, 25,* 296–302.

Flanders, S., & Strasen, J. H. (2014). Review of evidence about family presence during resuscitation. *Critical Care Nursing Clinics of North America, 26*(4), 533–550.

Frampton, S. B. (2009). Creating a patient-centered system. *American Journal of Nursing, 109* (3), 30–33.

Garrouste-Orgeas, M., Philippart, F., Bruel, C., Max, A., Lau, N., & Misset, B. (2012). Overview of medication errors and adverse events. *Annals of Intensive Care, 2*(2), 1–9.

Gehlbach, B. K., Chapotot, F., Leproult, R., Whitmore, H., Poston, J., ... van Cautier, E. (2012). Temporal disorganization of circadian rhythmicity and sleep-wake regulation in mechanically ventilated patients receiving continuous intravenous sedation. *Sleep, 35*(8), 1105–1114.

Gopher, D., & Donchin, Y. (2014). Types and causes of medical error in intensive care. In Y. Donchin, & D. Gopher (Eds.), *Around the patient bed: Human factors and safety in health care* (pp. 23–28). Boca Raton, FL: CRC Press.

Halpern, N. A. (2000). Lab/point of care testing. In D. K. Hamilton (Ed.), *ICU 2010: ICU design for the future* (pp. 92–101). Houston, TX: Center for Innovation in Health Facilities.

Hamilton, D. K. (2013). *Doorway to bedside: An exploratory study of nurse interaction with features of the critical care patient room environment.* Unpublished report, Arizona State University.

Hamilton, D. K. (2017a). Navigating the patient room: Critical care nurses' interaction with the designed physical environment (dissertation). Arizona State University.

Hamilton, D. K. (2017b). Is ICU safety threatened by the straight corridor? *Health Environments Research & Design Journal, 10*(2), 101–103.

Hamilton, D. K., & Shepley, M. M. (2010). *Design for critical care: An evidence-based approach.* Oxford: Architectural Press (Elsevier).

Hamilton, D. K., Swoboda, S. M., Lee, J. T., & Anderson, D. C. (2018). Decentralization: The corridor is the problem, not the alcove. *Critical Care Nursing Quarterly, 41*(1), 3–9.

Hassan, E., Badawi, O., Weber, R. J., & Cohen, H. (2010). Using technology to prevent adverse drug events in the intensive care unit. *Critical Care Medicine, 38 Suppl.*, S97–S105.

International Code Council. (2018). *International building code.* Country Club Hills, IL: International Code Council.

Jackson, J. C., Mitchell, N., & Hopkins, R. O. (2015). Cognitive functioning, mental health, and quality of life in ICU survivors: An overview. *Psychiatric Clinics of North America, 38*(1), 91–104.

Jiancaro, T., Jamieson, G. A., & Mihailidis, A. (2014). Twenty years of cognitive work analysis in health care: A scoping review. *Journal of Cognitive Engineering and Decision Making, 8* (1), 3–22.

Joint Commission. (2018). *Comprehensive accreditation manual.* Oak Brook, IL: Joint Commission Resources.

Kelly, P. T., Basharati, S., Swanney, M. P., & Beckert, L. (2014). Predicting diurnal cycle oxygenation in patients with COPD. *American Journal of Respiratory and Critical Care Medicine, 189.*

Khunlertkit, A., & Carayon, P. (2013). Contributions of tele-intensive care unit (tele-ICU) technology to quality of care and patient safety. *Journal of Critical Care, 28*(3), 315e1−315e12.

Lee, S.-J., Faucett, J., Gillen, M., Krause, N., & Landry, L. (2010). Factors associated with safe patient handling behaviors among critical care nurses. *American Journal of Industrial Medicine, 53*(9), 886−897.

Lim, S.-M., & Webb, S. A. R. (2005). Nosocomial bacterial infections in intensive care units. I: Organisms and mechanisms of antibiotic resistance. *Anaesthesia, 60*, 887−902.

Machado, D. A., Figueiredo, N. M. A., Velasques, L. S., Bento, C. A. M., Machado, W. C. A., & Vianna, L. A. M. (2018). Cognitive changes in nurses working in intensive care units. *Revista Brasileira de Enfermagem, 71*(1), 73−79.

Marik, P. E. (2001). *Handbook of evidence-based critical care*. New York: Springer-Verlag.

McKenna, H., van der Horst, G. T. J., Reiss, I., & Martin, D. (2018). Clinical chronobiology: A timely consideration in critical care medicine. *Critical Care, 22*, 124.

Pagnamenta, A., Rabito, G., Arosio, A., Perren, A., Malacrida, R., Barazzoni, F., & Domenighetti, G. (2012). Adverse event reporting in adult intensive care units and the impact of a multifaceted intervention on drug-related adverse events. *Annals of Intensive Care, 2*(47), 1−10.

Pati, D., Evans, J., Waggener, L., & Harvey, T. (2008). An exploratory examination of medical gas booms versus traditional headwalls in intensive care unit design. *Critical Care Nursing Quarterly, 31*(4), 340−356.

Pati, D., Harvey, T., Evans, J., & Cason, C. (2009). *Patient room handedness: An empirical examination*. Dallas, TX: HKS, Inc.

Pham, J. C., Aswani, M. S., Rosen, M., Lee, H. W., Huddle, M., Weeks, K., & Pronovost, P. (2012). Reducing medical errors and adverse events. *Annual Review of Medicine, 63*, 447−463.

Pittet, D., Allegranzi, B., & Boyce, J. (2009). The World Health Organization guidelines on hand hygiene in health care and their consensus recommendations. *Infection Control & Hospital Epidemiology, 30*(7), 611−622.

Potter, P., Wolf, L., Boxerman, S., Grayson, D., Sledge, J., Dunagan, C., & Evanoff, B. (2005). Understanding the cognitive work of nursing in the acute care environment. *Journal of Nursing Administration, 35*(7−8), 327−335.

Pronovost, P., Wu, A. W., Dorman, A., & Morlock, L. (2002). Building safety into ICU care. *Journal of Critical Care, 17*(2), 78−85.

Thomas, E. J., Lucke, J. F., Wueste, L., Weavind, L., & Patel, B. (2009). Association of telemedicine for remote monitoring of intensive care patients with mortality, complications, and length of stay. *The Journal of the American Medical Association, 302*(24), 2671−2678.

Thompson, D. R., Hamilton, D. K., Cadenhead, C. D., Swoboda, S. M., Schwindel, S. M., Anderson, D. C., … Petersen, C. (2012). Guideline for intensive care unit design. *Critical Care Medicine, 40*(5), 1586−1600.

Tvedt, C., & Bukholm, G. (2005). Alcohol-based hand disinfection: a more robust hand-hygiene method in an intensive care unit. *Journal of Hospital Infection, 59*(3), 229−234.

Valentin, A., Capuzzo, M., Guidet, B., Moreno, R. P., Dolanski, L., Bauer, P., & Metnitz, P. G. H. (2006). *Intensive Care Medicine, 32*, 1591−1598.

Verhulst, O. (2008). P258 technology in the ICU; the nurses' point of view. *Critical Care, 12* (Suppl. 2), s206−s207.

Vicente, K. J. (1995). Task analysis, cognitive task analysis, cognitive work analysis: What's the difference? *Proceedings of the Human Factors and Ergonomics Society Annual Meeting, 39*, 534.

Wahl, W. L., Talsma, A., Dawson, C., Dickinson, S., Pennington, K., Wilson, D., . . . Taheri, P. A. (2006). Use of computerized ICU documentation to capture ICU core measures. *Surgery*, *140*(4), 684−690.

Wu, A. W., Pronovost, P., & Morlock, L. (2002). ICU incident reporting systems. *Journal of Critical Care*, *17*(2), 86−94.

Zhou, J., Badawi, O., Hassan, E., Breslow, M., Rosenfeld, B., Lilly, C., & Liu, X. (2014). Long-term intensive care unit (ICU) outcome trends among a nationwide cohort of tele-ICU patients. *Critical Care Medicine*, *42*(12 Suppl.), 360.

Further reading

American Association of Critical-care Nurses. (2005). AACN standards for establishing and maintaining healthy work environments. *American Journal of Critical Care*, *14*, 187−197.

Anderson, J., Gosbee, L. L., Bessesen, M., & Williams, L. (2010). Using human factors engineering to improve the effectiveness of infection prevention and control. *Critical Care Medicine*, *38*(8 Suppl.), S269−S281.

Chulay, M., & Burns, S. M. (Eds.), (2010). *AACN essentials of critical care nursing* (2nd ed.). New York: McGraw Hill Medical.

Dekker, S. (2011). *Patient safety: A human factors approach*. Boca Raton, FL: CRC Press.

Eggimann, P., & Pittet, D. (2001). Infection control in the ICU. *Chest*, *120*(6), 2059−2093.

Endsley, M. R., & Jones, D. G. (2012). *Designing for situation awareness: An approach to user-centered design*. Boca Raton, FL: CRC Press.

Facilities Guidelines Institute. (2010). *Guidelines for design and construction of hospitals and health care facilities*. Chicago, IL: American Society of Healthcare Engineering of the American Hospital Association.

Grass, G., Rensing, C., & Solioz, M. (2011). Metallic copper as an antimicrobial surface. *Applied and Environmental Microbiology*, *77*(5), 1541−1547.

Gurses, A. P., & Carayon, P. (2005). Identifying performance obstacles among intensive care nurses. *Proceedings of the human factors and ergonomics society 49th annual meeting* 49 (11),pp. 1019−1023. Available from https://doi.org/10.1177/154193120504901104.

Hall, K. K., & Kamerow, D. B. (2013). Understanding the role of facility design in the acquisition and prevention of healthcare-associated infections. *Health Environments Research & Design*, *7*(Suppl.), 13−17.

Hamilton, D. K. (2019). Horseshoe, cockpit, and dragonfly: Nurse movement in headwall patient rooms. *Critical Care Nursing Quarterly*, *42*(1), 47−52.

O'Gorman, J., & Humphreys, H. (2012). Application of copper to prevent and control infection. Where are we now? *Journal of Hospital Infection*, *81*(4), 217−223.

Rainey, T. (2000). Clinical context: Treatment protocols, physician roles and intensivist-lead teams. In D. K. Hamilton (Ed.), *ICU 2010: ICU design for the future* (pp. 28−35). Houston, TX: Center for Innovation in Health Facilities.

Rossi, P. J., & Edmiston, C. E., Jr. (2012). Patient safety in the critical care environment. *Surgical Clinics of North America*, *92*, 1369−1386.

Salas, E., Prince, C., Baker, D. P., & Shrestha, L. (1995). Situation awareness in team performance: Implications for measurement and training. *Human Factors*, *37*(1), 123−136.

Sitterding, M. C., Broome, M. E., Everett, L. Q., & Ebright, P. (2012). Understanding situation awareness in nursing work: A hybrid concept analysis. *Advances in Nursing Sciences*, *55*(1), 77−92.

Ulrich, R. S. (1997). A theory of supportive design for healthcare facilities. *Journal of Healthcare Design*, *9*, 3−7.

Chapter 8

Design for emergencies

Yuval Bitan

Ben-Gurion University of the Negev, Be'er Sheva, Israel

Introduction

The young paramedic couldn't foresee the situation she was about to handle on her Saturday morning shift. She already knew very well that work in paramedic services has no routine. In minutes, she might dramatically shift from enjoying a quiet cup of coffee at the station to trying to save lives in another corner of the city. But the scene she was about to witness this morning was different. Not only was this due to the number of casualties that were involved in the train crash, but also because she was the first professional medical support person to arrive at the scene. That meant she was responsible for managing the first few minutes of a chaotic situation.

During the short ambulance drive after her team responded to the 911 calls for help, she reviewed what she had learned at the MCI (mass-casualty incident) training workshop. As a paramedic, she was thinking mainly about how to prioritize the emergency medical treatment for a large number of casualties, but when she looked at the small paramedic field guide she carried in her pocket, she was reminded that as the first paramedic on scene, she would have to manage the operation, at least for the first few minutes, until a more experienced commander will arrive at the scene. The protocol in the field guide reminded her of the tasks she would need to perform. A few minutes later, when her team arrived at the scene, she tried to follow the protocol, but was distracted by the calls for help, the smoke, and all the information that bystanders were shouting at her. "There are many casualties on the other side of the train," "there is a baby on the track over there," "there are casualties that can't get out of the first car".

She opened the MCI kit they had in the ambulance. The tools she found there reminded her of the MCI training that she had taken and helped her focus on the protocol she had to follow. These were simple tools. The incident commander vest marked her as the field officer. The green, yellow, red, and black

Design for Health. DOI: https://doi.org/10.1016/B978-0-12-816427-3.00008-7

147

triage ribbons reminded her of the triage scheme she had to follow. In the paramedic field guide, she found the announcements she had to call using the megaphone, and the printed incident command priority protocol helped her to follow the protocol despite continuous interruptions from other staff members and the dispatch. This was not a simple scene, but the tools that were designed and organized for such incidents led the paramedic through the working protocol she had to follow during the stressful first few minutes, until enough paramedics arrived at the scene and a more experienced commander could take the lead.

This chapter will focus on how to design artifacts for use during emergencies. It will first look at the characteristics of an emergency situation and how this condition affects human performance. Then, the three pillars of emergency systems—environment, human operator, and equipment—and their interaction with each other are elaborated. The last part of this chapter will provide specific design guidelines for emergency systems, demonstrating these principles in a case study implementation.

Human cognition during emergencies

To design for emergencies, it is first necessary to understand the characteristics of emergency situations and how human behavior is affected by these conditions. Emergency situations have many faces. These can range from small emergencies such as a small cut from a kitchen knife when one is making dinner to a bus of 50 tourists that roll off the road in a remote area. The common definition for emergency is that it presents an immediate risk to health, life, property, or surroundings, and it requires urgent intervention to prevent a worsening of the situation and/or immediate palliative care in the aftermath. These unpredictable situations generate ambiguous conditions for the people who are exposed to the emergency.

The most significant feelings that emerge during such situations are confusion and lack of control. The unpredictable situation generates mistrust and fear—feelings that might be amplified in cases of actual life-threatening conditions. In addition, people who experience emergency situations also need to react and to do so swiftly and efficiently. The combination of these frustrating feelings accompanied by time pressure usually results in a high cognitive load and extreme discomfort (Edland & Svenson, 2013; Hwang, 1994).

The term "cognitive load" refers to our cognitive efforts to process, store, and retrieve information that we gain from our surroundings, and high cognitive load often results from an influx of complex and unstructured information. The sudden changes that occur around us during an emergency, and the danger and fear that emerge from a hostile situation all contribute to high cognitive load. The release of stress-related hormones cause increased arousal of the senses. As a result, we observe even higher amounts of information, but our brain struggles to process it all (Hamilton, 1982). This information overload requires more cognitive attention, which again results in high cognitive load.

Decision making under cognitive load

Many studies have investigated how cognitive load affects human performance. These studies support the idea that high cognitive load reduces our ability to plan ahead and make precise calculations. Intensive care units and operating rooms are a good example for work environments that expose clinicians to high workload. Monitor alarms for vital signs generate many signals (some of which are false), which result in cognitive load and time pressure (Bitan, Meyer, Shinar, & Zmora, 2004; Woods, 1995). Tasks that impose a heavy load on short-term memory, such as calculating, planning, and quick decision-making, necessarily impose severe time pressure that also exacerbates this condition (Kahneman, 1973). Studies on behavior under time pressure found, for example, that pedestrians who feel pressured to reach their destination, often adopt riskier behavior, prioritizing convenience over safety (Kadali & Vedagiri, 2013; Kalantarov, Riemer, & Oron-Gilad, 2018).

When experiencing high cognitive load, our analytical thinking mode is suppressed and a spontaneous, intuitive approach becomes dominant. The lack of reasoning and ponderous serial processes generate an effect known as "Attentional Tunneling"—a narrowing of attention and loss of situational awareness that cause us to miss important clues and cues (Wickens, 2005). Since a human operator tends to have limited attention resources, these theoretical models support the idea that cognitive load demands additional attention, and this attention overdemand results in a reduced performance of activities that require higher cognitive functionality (Baddeley, 2003).

These ambiguous situations result in suboptimal decision-making processes both for people who are victims of the emergency situation and for those who come to help them (Klein, 2011). Therefore, ideally, we would prefer that people not have to make decisions during these events. As designers of systems that need to operate during emergencies, our goal is to construct a simple and clear path that will help workers respond to an emergency without any dilemmas or considerations. When we know what we need to do, the feeling of uncertainty defuses, and we can focus on the necessary actions that need to be performed even during the confusion of an emergency. This is the reason that every time we take a plane trip, we are reminded to look for the nearest exit before takeoff and landing. In the unlikely event of an emergency, we will not have to look for the exit—we will know where it is.

Human operators, such as paramedics, may need to perform their duties efficiently under suboptimal conditions such as operating away from standard facilities, sometimes without necessary infrastructure or even electricity, with extensive noise and other distractions, and in some cases amid concern for their personal safety. These complications add to their workload and cognitive stress level. Unlike those who are caught up in the emergency, the decision-making process of people who work in helping organizations during such times involves an additional element affecting their behavior—their experience. These professional workers are brought into the emergency situation and then need to lead and make decisions under confusing conditions that bring on high cognitive load, which may have life-critical implications.

One of the leading models to explain behavior and decision making of experienced professional operators under pressure is the *Recognition Primed Decision Making* model (Klein, 1999). The model describes a process that begins with recognizing the situation, followed by rapid pattern matching and recall of typical solutions that solved similar patterns in the past. The operator then uses the power of mental simulation to evaluate the chosen course of action before initiating the solution. Klein (1999) suggests that one of the key elements in this model is the operator's experience. Experienced operators rely on their intuition to find the typical solution for the pattern they identify. Greenhalgh's (2002) definition for intuition—a rapid judgment, mostly without awareness of the cognitive process that led to it—explains why intuition is so important for decision making under high cognitive load. When we are too busy to invest our attention in the decisions we need to make, intuition is a reliable shortcut.

How to improve the way people perform during emergencies?

Once designers understand the main conditions that affect human behavior during emergencies, and know what to expect from that behavior, they can define guidelines for the interaction we would like them to have when operating devices or following procedures during emergencies. These guidelines will help us to develop tools that fit the expected human behavior during emergencies. Whether these are simple signs, multipurpose electronic tools, or simply priority protocols and checklists, their design should guide the user in how to use them even during the unique circumstances of an emergency.

One of the ways to work efficiently during high cognitive load is to default to automatic actions. An example for such implementation is demonstrated in the way paramedics work during emergencies—they are trained to follow very strict protocols that leave very little room for exertion. The paramedic has to choose the protocol that was designed for the specific clinical situation, but from there on, the protocol guides the paramedic through all the steps and procedures that suit this clinical condition.

Another example of a method that is designed to improve performance during emergencies in commercial aviation is Crew Resource Management (CRM). Originated from research the NTSB and NASA conducted in the early 1970s and that was first published in the NTSB Recommendation

A-79-047 in 1979, the method was designed to improve air-crew performance by focusing on interpersonal communication, leadership, and decision making in the cockpit (Keyes, 1990). The CRM method is concerned not with the technical knowledge and skills required to operate an aircraft but rather with the cognitive skills needed to manage the flight during emergencies. These objectives are translated into detailed protocols that guide a crew not only through the technical aspects of their emergency but also in communication with other team members. Thus this method addresses the foreseen challenges that arise during an emergency, including decreased crew communication, an increase in wrong decisions, and a lower probability of correcting deviations from standard operating procedures. The CRM method ensures that the pilot will have the maximum capacity for the primary task of flying the aircraft and that the workload will be equally distributed among the crew members, maintaining coordination and cooperation through the exchange of information.

How design affects human behavior

"We cannot change the human condition, but we can change the condition the human is operating in" (Reason, 2000) is the main theme for human-centered design. Thus our design approach should focus on the elements that compile the conditions in which someone operates. We can consider two levels of conditions—the physical and the cognitive. For example, on the physical level, since our vision is limited by the physical measurements of our eyes, presentation design can affect the distance at which people will be able to read a sign. On the cognitive level, we know, for example, that noise and interruptions affect decision making. Therefore we can help people improve their ability to make decisions if we can provide a quiet and distraction-free environment.

There are plenty of other examples that can demonstrate how design can affect how humans operate, but before we specifically discuss design for emergencies, we need to look at the system level. We should understand who the actors participating in the setting are, what their interaction is, and which actions can be influenced by our design.

The three pillars of emergency systems

When we design a solution, we need to first look at the entire system, identify the main actors, and understand what affects their behavior. Systems have three main components: the surrounding environment, the human operator, and the equipment. Good design will take the features and limitations of all three pillars into account and the interaction each has with the others. We will first describe these three pillars and then discuss their interactions.

Environment

The environment includes all the features specifying where a system will be operating, such as location, external information sources, organizational characteristics, and even features of the culture. Design quality depends on both how widely and how deeply the huge number of data points related to environment are studied, and how lessons learned are adopted into the design. However, the environment itself cannot be changed or controlled. Although the environment's features are part of our system, we should consider them as an external force that we cannot control. In many cases, system failure has resulted when designers mistakenly thought that they would be able to control the environmental components of the system, but reality proved them wrong. While we cannot change its features, the environment does have influence on how our system operates, and parts of it might be under the control of other systems. It thus needs to be considered as one of the system components.

The environment can sometimes be part of the cause of an emergency and sometimes part of the solution. Consider an earthquake: if a room is not designed to be earthquake resistant, it might not be resilient to the situation and could become a threat to occupants. On the other hand, if this room has features that maintain its resilience in earthquake conditions, it might be a source of shelter.

Human operator

The human operator is a key factor in system performance and efficiency. Even when technology can perform a task independently, and many tasks can be accomplished without human interference, the human operator still has an important role as the monitor, ready to intervene in case the system begins to cross any of its performance borders. The Sheridan 1978 scale, for instance, defines the operator's role in terms of levels of involvement, which has proven useful in systems such as autonomous cars (Sheridan, Verplank, & Brooks, 1978). But defining operator role is only part of the picture. It is also necessary to design the system to fit the user's physical and cognitive abilities and limitations. The study of human—system integration (also known as human factors engineering) provides designers with tools and methods to study the operator's behavior and abilities, along with necessary tasks he or she needs to perform during system operation. This user-centered approach results in instructions for the development of all the interactive equipment elements, including the presentation layer and input methods that allow the operator to capture important information from the other parts of the system and to exert control. Although we call this user-centered design, note that it is the equipment, and not the user, being designed.

Equipment

Thus equipment is the main variable of our system. Equipment can be a man-made apparatus or a process designed to operate with the human operator in the environment as a component of one system. Equipment is the only system component we can actually design or influence, so its design process is most important. However, while the equipment may be considered the heart of the system, designers must never ignore integration with, and interactions among, the two other pillars—who the operator may be and where it will all work (the environment).

The system and the interaction between the three pillars

The three pillars are not independent of each other, and mutual interactions might affect system outcomes. Although only the design of the equipment can be manipulated, failing to examine its interconnection with the two other pillars could cause the entire system to malfunction. For example, the environment and its interaction with the human operator might cause operational challenges with the equipment such as difficulty using the equipment in a dark environment unless there is a feature that assists in finding the controls. A design that accounts for this can help overcome and mitigate such limitations.

On the system level, we need to consider resilience. System designers should expect that the system will not act within its defined boundaries all the time, and an essential consideration is ensuring it functions properly during emergencies. Failures and external forces might push the system out of its comfort zone, and the system should be able to handle these situations without crashing, malfunctioning, or generating unwanted outcomes. Thus when designing for emergencies, resilience is key. Resilience is defined as a system's ability to absorb changes and disturbances and to maintain functionality under both expected and unexpected conditions (Fairbanks et al., 2014). During emergencies, resilient systems should not collapse but continue to operate normally. Since, in our design approach, we can control only the equipment, we should anticipate what could happen in the environment, how the equipment might malfunction, and how the human operator might behave during an emergency, thus designing specific features in the equipment that will make the entire system resilient to extreme conditions. A list of critical elements in our system and a list of dependencies between our system and surrounding systems would highlight features that need to be redundant to support possible failure.

Guidelines for how to design for emergencies

Environment

Although we cannot change this component we need to learn its characteristics and know how it might affect the other pillars in the system during emergency. The environment component of a given system might already have important features that would make it resilient, but for the purpose of this discussion, they will not be considered part of the design process of our system. These features might be designed by other systems, and the present system design needs to take that into consideration as part of the interaction with the environment. However, designers cannot assume that any part of the environment is a feature we can design or configure. Take, for example, the design of a new 911 call center. While the call center design requires a reliable electrical power supply using Uninterruptible Power Supply (UPS) system, the design of the UPS device would not be part of the call center design. The UPS device would be designed as a component in another system, and the call center will employ the UPS "as is." Therefore the UPS will be part of the system's environment.

Human operator

Once we understand the characteristics of the human behavior during emergency and we develop the equipment accordingly, we should focus on training the human operator in using the equipment. The goal is to get to the point where the human can operate the equipment without investing much effort and attention. This will ensure that even under high cognitive load, the operator will be able to perform the necessary procedures. During emergencies people act spontaneously, and emergency design should guide them so they perform the correct actions without planning and thinking. Our ability to change the human operator is limited to training. But training has a small impact during emergencies unless the actions become "automatic," that is, the human no longer needs to think about what to do but instead acts spontaneously (Kahneman, 2011). At this stage the person does not need to divert cognitive resources to this action; therefore it can be done seamlessly even during emergencies.

In order to make this transition into "automatic" procedure, we need to train people until the action becomes a habit. One well-known method for achieving this is by using mnemonics, a common aid for remembering steps and procedures. For example, one of the CRM checklists uses the following easy-to-remember abbreviation to support the crew during emergencies:

P—Pool the facts
I—Identify the problem
L—Look for solutions
O—Operate
T—Take stock

Another training method is through simulation. Klein, in his book *Sources of Power*, concluded that a good simulation can sometimes provide more training value than direct experience. This is one of the reasons why we see more and more professions use simulation tools as part of their training practice.

Equipment

The equipment should be carefully designed following these guidelines:

- *Simplicity*—Design simple user interface that is easy to understand and operate.
- *Independent*—The equipment should not rely on other systems and should have possible redundant connections, so it will not have a single point of failure.
- *Resilience*—Design with the expectation that the equipment might fail—prepare a plan B.

The design for simplicity is the most complicated. This is because human behavior is less predictable than physical failures that result from the environment or internal failures. The design that fits the operator should first allow him or her to control the equipment, providing controls that fit the control task, the environment, and the operator's capabilities. It should encompass not only normal operation but also failure and use errors. An important part of this design is how to inform the operator of the status of the system and what tools he or she will need to control it. The equipment needs to provide the operator with necessary information to assist in control decisions for the system and tools that will allow equipment commands to be sent. A good design will provide all the information that is needed but will not overwhelm the user with too much of it. This information should be relevant to the current system state and the user's capabilities.

Good examples of simple tools that encompass these characteristics are protocols and checklists. These artifacts are easy to follow, require minimal memory and planning, and can be presented using very basic materials.

Case study

This part of the chapter demonstrates how the design principles discussed above can be used in the design of emergency equipment to instruct operation procedures and human behavior during an emergency situation. The *mass-casualty incident* (MCI) example presented at the beginning of the chapter will be used to examine design principles manifested in the MCI kit design. While the kit is not a technology-based tool, basic design concepts fit its unique use.

Mass-casualty incident

Most emergency services define MCI as an emergency incident where the number of casualties exceeds the medical resources that can be allocated to treat those casualties onsite. These events often result from an accident, a sudden attack, or a disaster. Thus the variance between MCIs is greater than their similarity. To overcome this variance, MCI protocols have been developed to provide guidance in managing these chaotic events, where the main goal is to transfer all casualties to concurrent hospitals in the shortest possible time.

MCI protocols guide the emergency medical services (EMS) teams that arrive at the scene to operate quickly and efficiently. Upon arrival to the MCI site the EMS field commander assumes the manager role (Shapira & Shemer, 2002). The first goal is to assess and report the emergency situation. Then a team effort begins, led by the field commander, to apply the MCI treatment procedure, pushing all casualties through three main phases: (1) triage and lifesaving interventions, (2) casualties transported to a designated location where they can receive basic treatment to stabilize their condition with immediate evacuation of critically injured casualties, and (3) evacuation of all casualties according to the triage classifications (Einav et al., 2004). The three pillars can be applied to guide tool development to support the MCI commander during such an incident.

The mass-casualty incident environment

As one can imagine, an MCI environment is extremely chaotic. Emergency services responding to the casualties should expect an environment that is disrupted and disordered, with no systematic functioning or arrangement. Since it is an unexpected situation, most of the people found at the scene will be confused and may provide only partial information about the cause of the event and the location of casualties. Smoke, darkness, and dispersal location might limit visibility and the ability to develop a clear understanding of the scene. Due to these characteristics, the artifacts that the paramedics can use should be readable with minimal lighting and should be short and easy to follow.

Another unique characteristic of the MCI environment is that, unlike other work environments, the operator does not have a work station that can be designed and planned. The location and even the tools might vary between scenes, and the operator will not know much about the work environment before arrival. Accordingly, the paramedics equipment should be mobile in varied terrains and should not rely on external sources of electricity or lighting.

The mass-casualty incident human operator

For emergency services personnel, an MCI is exceedingly stressful because of the lack of necessary resources and the fact that the lives of other people depend on their performance. The operators need to make many decisions and prioritize their actions based on sparse information under very demanding conditions and high cognitive load. The order of the procedures that need to be followed depends on many parameters, and EMS personnel will have to continuously collect additional information about the situation and adjust their decisions accordingly.

Training and preparing EMS personnel for an MCI are challenging because it is difficult to simulate the complication and especially the stress that accompanies an MCI. In most emergency services the MCI commander is trained to manage the event, but since no two MCIs are the same, the commander must be trained to handle many procedures and make many decisions that are unique to the specific MCI. This flexibility requires skills that are challenging to train and prepare for because the varied parameters complicate the task of defining clear advantages and disadvantages for each course of action. MCI simulation is a good tool to train paramedic teams to work during these situations. A realistic simulation will require the paramedics to handle many casualties, with limited resources, and train them not only in providing care but also in managing the MCI operation. This would include following specific protocols that are designed for these events.

The mass-casualty incident management equipment

The need to consider all the aspects of the MCI environment and human operator characteristics during an MCI makes the mission of designing MCI management equipment complex and challenging. The equipment should support the MCI treatment procedure, leading the commander through the three main phases described above. We will examine the equipment the MCI commander is using and demonstrate how it is designed under the constraints of the two other pillars.

The first tool the MCI commander would use is the *paramedic field guide*. This is a small booklet listing the main protocols paramedics need to follow, and it is used to refresh their memory on specific emergency protocols. Since the guide is small and contains information for varied situations, most paramedics always carry it in one of their pockets, so it will always be handy. Although this might seem like a very low-tech solution for information retrieval, the fact that it can be accessed at any time and under any condition (as long as there is a light source) makes it very suitable for the MCI environment.

In addition to the small field guide the MCI commander would have an *MCI kit* to support his/her role and provide the paramedics who arrive at the scene with tools designed specifically for MCIs. In order to act as a commander, the paramedic who takes on this role needs to be easily identified and heard. A *highly visible vest* labeling role (Medical Services Commander) will inform everyone who is in charge. A battery-powered *megaphone* will assist the commander in communicating commands to other paramedics and rescue teams. To help overcome memory limitations during the high workload, the *MCI kit* also includes *incident command priority protocols* with detailed lists of instructions that should be followed during the MCI, along with worksheets and a clipboard.

While paramedics always have to assess their patients' condition, the fact that in an MCI they need to care for more than one patient raises a special need—how to document information about a patient so the next paramedic, who will continue caring for this patient, will have all the information that was already collected about this patient. The *MCI kit* has two simple tools to assist in delivering these important details. The first is a set of permanent markers, and the second, *triage tags* in four colors: *red* (emergency) to mark casualties that need immediate treatment, *yellow* (urgent) for significant injuries that can tolerate a delay in care, *green* (nonurgent) for people who can safely wait for treatment, and *black* for expired casualties. These tags are used to quickly mark casualties' priority after the first assessment. Again, simplicity is an important characteristic in the MCI environment because no special setup is required, and these tools can operate under any conditions. This simplicity also assists the human operator (the paramedic) by serving as a memory aid using a tool that helps in following the MCI protocol (Fig. 8.1):

The equipment the MCI commander is using follow the few basic design principals we discussed earlier in this chapter:

1. They are designed to operate in varied MCI environments, as they are not dependent on resources nor on specific conditions in the environment.

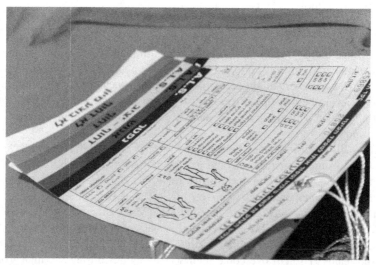

FIGURE 8.1 The MCI triage tags.

2. As these artifacts are not electronic but based on paper and cardboard they are resilient to failure and will function effectively under extreme and unexpected conditions.
3. Taking into consideration the human condition during the MCI, they are very easy to operate and serve the operators as a reminder, leading them through the procedures that need to be done.

Conclusions and implications

While we cannot change the human condition, our design can change human behavior. Design that carefully considers the interaction between the three system components (the three pillars) can generate a system that is resilient to failure and that functions properly even during unexpected circumstances.

The design process should start with a clear definition of the system goals. Next, system boundaries need to be defined—the elements and conditions that will affect the system, and the required functionality that the system will provide during normal and emergency operations. The system boundaries will also define which parts will be included in the design, and which parts the system will receive as part of the environment. Then the design process should identify the environment's effect on the two other components—the human operator and the equipment. The design should emphasize the actions we want the user to do and the features the equipment have to include in order to support the operator in performing those required actions.

To prepare for emergencies, our design should take into account the type of emergency, and the actions required. Then we need to design the equipment in a way that will lead a user to do these actions spontaneously, without needing to make any decisions, and to design the equipment without relying on external resources. Last, but not the least, we need to train operators so they will be able to operate the equipment and achieve the system goals even during emergencies, when human decision-making capabilities are limited.

References

Baddeley, A. (2003). Working memory: Looking back and looking forward. *Nature Reviews Neuroscience, 4*, 829–839. Available from https://doi.org/10.1038/nrn1201.

Bitan, Y., Meyer, J., Shinar, D., & Zmora, E. (2004). Nurses reactions to alarms in a neonatal intensive care unit. *Cognition, Technology & Work, 6*(4), 239–246. Available from https://doi.org/10.1007/s10111-004-0162-2.

Edland, A., & Svenson, O. (2013). Judgment and decision making under time pressure. In: *Time pressure and stress in human judgment and decision making*. Springer Nature: Basel, CH, pp. 27–40. https://doi.org/10.1007/978-1-4757-6846-6_2.

Einav, S., Feigenberg, Z., Weissman, C., Zaichik, D., Caspi, G., Kotler, D., & Freund, H. R. (2004). Evacuation priorities in mass casualty terror-related events: Implications for contingency planning. *Annals of Surgery, 239*(3), 304–310. Available from https://doi.org/10.1097/01.sla.0000114013.19114.57.

Fairbanks, R. J., Wears, R. L., Woods, D. D., Hollnagel, E., Plsek, P., & Cook, R. I. (2014). Resilience and resilience engineering in health care. *Joint Commission Journal on Quality and Patient Safety, 40*(8), 376–383. Available from https://doi.org/10.1016/S1553-7250(14)40049-7.

Greenhalgh, T. (2002). Intuition and evidence—Uneasy bedfellows? *The British Journal of General Practice: The Journal of the Royal College of General Practitioners, 52*(478), 395–400. Available from https://doi.org/10.3399/bjgp12x652382.

Hamilton, V. (1982). *Cognition and stress: An information processing model.* Handbook of stress: Theoretical and clinical aspects (pp. 105–120). New York: Free Press.

Hwang, M. I. (1994). Decision making under time pressure: A model for information systems research. *Information and Management, 27*(4), 197–203. Available from https://doi.org/10.1016/0378-7206(94)90048-5.

Kadali, B. R., & Vedagiri, P. (2013). Modelling pedestrian road crossing behaviour under mixed traffic condition. *European Transport – Trasporti Europei, 55*, 1–17. Available from https://doi.org/10.1016/j.trf.2009.05.002.

Kahneman, D. (1973). *Attention and effort.* Englewood Cliffs, NJ: Prentice Hall.

Kahneman, D. (2011). *Thinking, fast and slow.* London, UK: Macmillan.

Kalantarov, S., Riemer, R., & Oron-Gilad, T. (2018). Pedestrians' road crossing decisions and body parts' movements. *Transportation Research Part F: Traffic Psychology and Behaviour, 53*(October), 155–171. Available from https://doi.org/10.1016/j.trf.2017.09.012.

Keyes, R.J. (1990). *Cockpit resource management. A new approach to aircrew coordination training.* (No. AU/ARI-89-12). AIR UNIV MAXWELL AFB AL AIRPOWER RESEARCH INST.

Klein, G. A. (1999). *Sources of power: How people make decisions.* Cambridge, MA: MIT Press.

Klein, G. A. (2011). *Streetlights and shadows: Searching for the keys to adaptive decision making.* MIT Press.

Reason, J. (2000). Human error: Models and management. *BMJ, 320*(7237), 768–770. Available from http://dx.doi.org/10.1136/bmj.320.7237.768.

Shapira, S. C., & Shemer, J. (2002). Medical management of terrorist attacks. *Israel Medical Association Journal, 4*(7), 489–492.

Sheridan, T. B., Verplank, W. L, and Brooks, T. L. (1978). Human and computer control of undersea teleoperators. (hosted by NASA Technical Reports Server (NTRS): https://ntrs.nasa.gov/search.jsp?R = 19790007441.

Wickens, C.D. (2005). Attentional tunneling and task management. In: *Technical report AHFD-05-01/NASA-05-10.*

Woods, D. D. (1995). The alarm problem and directed attention in dynamic fault management. *Ergonomics, 38*(11), 2371–2393. Available from https://doi.org/10.1080/00140139508925274.

Chapter 9

Design for resilience

Lisa Sundahl Platt
Florida Institute of Built Environment Resilience, Department of Interior Design, College of Design Construction and Planning, University of Florida, Gainesville, FL, United States

What is resilience?

The term *resilience* is one that often conjures up different meanings depending upon its context of use and the individual experiences of the interpreter. Used in everyday parlance, the quality of "being resilient" for most of us evokes a mental image of a person, collection of individuals, or built-system being able to respond in a positive manner to one or a series of crises. Although this simple explanation of the term may be accurate in a very basic sense, it leaves too broad a span of interpretation. Being able to pinpoint resilience may not be compulsory for every circumstance where this quality is potentially relevant. However, in certain human activity settings, the ability to identify the capacity for adaptive response in procedural, technological, or structural frameworks has proven to be quite valuable. Indeed, in safety-critical socio-technical systems, such as health care, the ability to identify and plan for resilience is essential.

Resilience and complexity

When we view a given system's design behavior, the outcome of its response *resilience* is contingent upon how it proactively applies adaptive strategies and available resources to both anticipated and unanticipated system disturbances (Sikula, Mancillas, Linkov, & McDonagh, 2015). We often do not recognize the quality of a system's resilience until it has already either succeeded or failed in its response to an actual crisis. Resilient systems must also learn and evolve from disruptive events allowing them to elevate their procedural knowledge to a new state (Hollnagel, 2014). When performance resilience is a goal, then the elements of a system must optimally sustain their functionality under both expected risk and unexpected emergencies (Fig. 9.1).

Design for Health. DOI: https://doi.org/10.1016/B978-0-12-816427-3.00009-9
161

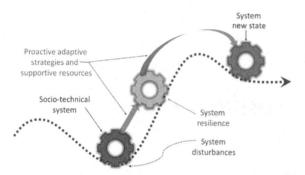

FIGURE 9.1 Diagram of system resilient response to disturbance. *Adapted from Hollnagel (2014).*

To accomplish this mission, systems need to have a unified diverse operational basis that allows them to successfully and seamlessly adjust to different circumstances. This presents an interactive environment where human factors and ergonomics prove to be useful for establishing and measuring potential resilience effectivity of the design of a complex system. The construct of human factors' primary focus is in evaluating how individual people and human activity systems (HASs) respond to external stimuli in various environments and under different situations (Hendrick & Kleiner, 2001). For any socio-technical system to be resilient, it must include some form of human sentience to inform anticipatory response with intelligent input (Hollnagel, 2014). To substantiate this assertion, it is useful to understand something about the early uses of the term resilience along with its progression of applications and meaning.

Inception and development

Dr. Erik Hollnagel, in his article "Resilience Engineering and the Built Environment," indicates that the term "resilience" was first used by Tredgold in 1818, to describe the performance capabilities of structural material. This definition evolved only slightly 40 years later when a description used in a naval report referred to the "modulus of resilience" as a means of assessing the ability of ship construction materials to withstand severe conditions (Hollnagel, 2014).

The term resilience remained within the confines of describing discrete and relatively closed system attributes until the mid-to-late part of the 20th century. At this point, the meaning of resilience was expanded to represent a more emergent rather than static property. In describing the resilience of complex ecologies, with multiple elements impacting system states, Dr. Holling extended the meaning and utility of the concept of resilience. In Holling's interpretation, resilience was meant to represent an ecologically based system's ability to return to a balanced state after a temporary disturbance (Holling, 1973). Holling (1973) also generalized the definition of resilience to characterize a system's abilities to respond to change and disruption and still maintain the same relationships between populations or state variables. This explanation of resilience alludes to a system's capacity to expand its tacit knowledge regarding growth-oriented reaction to unexpected and potential adverse events.

Considering the evolution of resilience as a description of system properties, and its utility to describing complex system behavior, it is perhaps unsurprising that its meaning has become somewhat nebulous. To better understand how a fuzzy property, such as *resilience*, can be applied to principles of complex systems' design, it is important to understand contextual factors driving interpretation and use.

Context

Current scientific applications of the term *resilience* reside in two relatively distinct epistemological areas: psychology and engineering. When we consider the meaning of resilience through the lens of human behavior, it defines the traits and responses of an individual or society that enable them to successfully weather adversity or unanticipated circumstances (Connor & Davidson, 2003). Within the context of systems science or engineering, resilience describes how elements of an operational framework or structure can sustain processes under expected and unexpected events in an efficient manner and evolve to an improved state of function (Hollnagel, 2014) (Fig. 9.2).

Both interpretations are arguably equally nuanced, but clearly different in their intent. One interpretation is more emotionally driven and evokes the tenaciousness of the human spirit. The other explanation suggests the attributes of reliable and dependable systems of support. However, a clear commonality of both descriptions is that resilient "systems," whether human or

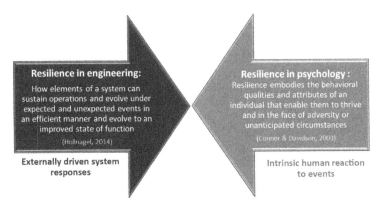

FIGURE 9.2 Dual nature of resilience in socio-technical systems.

engineered, must respond in an adaptive manner to unforeseen events. This connection presents an opportunity for unifying the psychological and engineering definitions of resilience. To be considered resilient, the collective elements of human, engineered, and operative activity systems need to be able to respond in a manner that allows them to maintain optimal function while responding to both internal and external variables impacting them. However, when we consider all the aspects of an individual, group, or organization, it is important to view their resilience potential as something more than just a collection of individual characteristics and behaviors committed to achieving a successful response to system disruption.

The notion of an inclusive approach to gauging systems resilience is especially germane to measuring health-care performance. Health care and its associated environmental components should be considered purposefully as socio-technical Human Activity Systems, or "HAS." The categorization of HAS represents a complex arrangement of symbiotic components that achieve their operational purpose primarily through human action (Checkland, 2000). When we consider both historical and current contexts, health-care delivery has always exemplified the act of humans leveraging environmental resources in some manner to treat illness or enhance human well-being. Despite increasing technological advances, to date, there is not a viable future scenario that will alter this understanding of human health-care delivery's purpose in a substantive way. Given that HAS performance achievement must be based on a systematic design approach (Larsson & Malmsjö 1998), it is useful to have a taxonomy for the development of technical performance measures, or TPM, that can be used to inform resilient health-care support system design.

Designing resilient systems

Resilient design methods

The core construct of judging how resilient a system performs is in understanding how effectively, efficiently, and reliably it responds and adapts to myriad ranges and sources of variation (Hollnagel et al., 2006). A technical classification for assessing resilience engineering performance developed by Woods, which is rooted in cognitive ergonomics, is focused on four conceptual pillars: robustness, recovery, graceful extensibility, and sustained adaptability (Woods, 2015). Since then, this taxonomy for evaluating resilient performance in the design of engineered systems has been expanded, to make it more useful for measuring operational processes and human action representative of resilience (Seager, et al., 2017). Seager characterizes *robustness*, as referring to a system's ability to absorb shocks or stressors from disruption without failing; *recovery*, as describing the characteristic ability of a system to restore resources damaged or impaired by adverse impact; *graceful extensibility*, as the quality of a system to manage in advance of unexpected events to avoid brittle response and catastrophic failures; and *sustained adaptability*, as the acknowledgment and acceptance that none of the aforementioned criteria on its own will be successfully resilient over the long term, regardless of historical success incidence (Seager et al., 2017).

It should be relatively clear how this categorization of system performance criteria could be useful to develop TPM to benchmark actual or simulated system design-dependent performance data. However, it is often useful to have examples of how system TPM can be translated to design-dependent performance and applied to real-world settings. To illustrate these concepts in this chapter, these conceptual pillars of resilient performance have been arranged into an "adaptive capacity performance hierarchy" (Fig. 9.3).

The purpose of applying this taxonomy for categorizing system resilience is to increase its applicability across the continuum of human, technological, and structural subsystems that comprise comprehensive health delivery systems. The aim is that this will help illustrate how the use of resilience engineering-based TPM to guide the development of health system design-dependent performance is not only advantageous but also essential for proactive response to both known and unknown human health and operational-related risk factors.

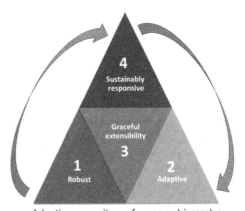

Adaptive capacity performance hierarchy

FIGURE 9.3 Resilience technical performance measures (TPM) adaptive capacity hierarchy. *Adapted from Seager, T. P., Clark, S. S., Eisenberg, D. A., Thomas, J. E., Hinrichs, M. M., Kofron, R., . . . & Aldersono, D.L. (2017). Chapter 3: Resilience and risk: Methods and application in environment, cyber and social domains. In I. Linkov, J.P. Oliveira (Eds.), Redesigning resilient infrastructure research. Springer. Retrieved from <Researchgate.com> and Woods, D. D. (2015). Four concepts for resilience and the implications for the future of resilience engineering.* Reliability Engineering & System Safety, 141, 5−9.

Applications

Designing for robustness

The quality of *robust* performance in a system or subsystem is characterized by its ability to withstand risk regardless of planned or unplanned disturbance. Current statistics on the frequency of nosocomial disease and hospital-acquired infections in the US acute care hospitals alone indicate that there are approximately 722,000 annually reported incidences. These cases result in approximately 75,000 hospital deaths per year (Magill et al., 2014). Currently, many health systems' safe patient-handling procedural models are contingent primarily on behavioral adherence. Examples of these measures, such as increased hand hygiene campaigns, have proven only marginally effective (Shekelle et al., 2013). Current estimates of clinical staff hand hygiene compliance rates in acute care settings have plateaued at about 50% despite widespread education and adoption efforts (Mcguckin & Govednik, 2015).

Implementing environmental design elements that are robust to dangerous pathogen propagation could prove to be viable in stemming the spread of dangerous microbes in health-care environments. A particularly novel innovation, currently under testing and development at the time of this writing, uses biomimetic micropatterning to disrupt the spread of bacteria on treated surfaces (Platt & Greene, 2017).

Case study: Infection prevention by increasing robustness of health-care surfaces

The World Health Organization indicates that hand sanitization is the most effective mechanism for stemming bacterial transmission in industries where dangerous bacterial exposure can lead to detrimental human health and well-being (Pittet et al., 2009). Despite this fact, it has been difficult to ensure people are consistently adhering to good hand hygiene in safety-critical industries (Shekelle et al., 2013). Furthermore, certain studies have indicated that in high-risk industries, such as acute health care, approximately 20% of patient treatment surfaces are not cleaned to baseline standards (Carling et al., 2008). This lack of adherence to safe environmental hygiene standards can sometimes be due to human error issues, such as working memory and signal detection (O'boyle, Henly, & Larson, 2001; Swoboda, Earsing, Strauss, Lane, & Lipsett, 2004; Zhang, Kong, Lamb, & Wu, 2019). This suggests using system design methods that could mitigate the brittle response of relying solely on human behavior as the predominant defense against pathogen transmission. Environmental modifications that served in an automation response role in microbial resistance could perhaps help to moderate the issue of the human error in poor environmental hygiene adherence in industries where dangerous pathogen control is essential.

A biologically inspired microscopic surface pattern called Neoterix ST, under controlled laboratory conditions, has tested resistant to microbial colonization (both attachment and growth) when applied to certain substrates. Coated fabrics, such as polyurethane, that contain Neoterix ST surface topography have demonstrated between 77% and 96% efficacy in resisting the attachment of certain infection-causing bacteria, such as methicillin-resistant *Staphylococcus aureus* in laboratory settings (Sappi North America, ResInnova Labs, & Perfectus Biomed, 2018). The design basis of the Neoterix ST microtopography was derived from surface antifouling research by Dr. Brennan, a materials science and engineering professor at the University of Florida (Sharklet Technologies, Inc., 2017). Dr. Brennan's objective was to create an engineered topography for the US Office of Naval Research that could prevent the settlement of microorganisms on the surface of naval sea-going vessels (Schumacher et al., 2007). Brennan was compelled by researching data on sharks' physical skin attributes that resisted fouling and naturally inhibited microbial growth (Kirschner & Brennan, 2012). He then used his research on the antifouling properties of sharkskin dermal denticles as a foundation for developing a mathematical model for a raised surface pattern with myriad potential applications that could significantly limit the ability of environmental pathogens to colonize on surfaces to which it was applied (Brennan et al., 2010) (Fig. 9.4).

The application of Neoterix ST micropatterning to substrates is done through a release paper transfer process during the product manufacturing process and can be applied to laminate, coated fabric, and acrylic surfaces used in the manufacture of everyday products. This process allows for the creation of a finished product whose surface structure emulates microscopic patterning found on a shark's skin. This innovative approach to resilient

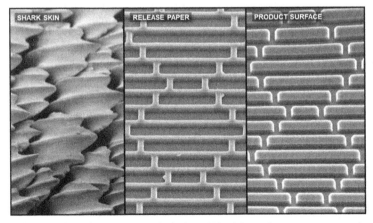

FIGURE 9.4 Microscopic images of shark dermal denticles, release paper topography, and resultant surface micropattern. *Courtesy Sappi North America.*

design for health care might allow real-world applicability of biomimicry-based solutions to naturally limit dangerous pathogen propagation in health-care environments. This approach also brings robustness in that it requires no outside intervention and fits into standard health-care cleaning protocols with the appropriate selection of materials. Given that coated fabrics are often used for upholstery in health-care furnishing, applied finishes, and equipment, this type of robust design intervention may prove to be a useful component in a resilient systems approach, reducing the spread of infection in health and continuing care environments.

Although the strength of resistance to risk in systems response is certainly valuable, it should be clear that additional system abilities are needed to establish resilience. Just being able to avert or mitigate hazard is insufficient to a system being considered as resilient. Indeed, a more appropriate demonstration of resilience would be to co-opt existing resources as well as develop new tools to better adapt to potential system disruption.

Designing for adaptivity

A key indicator of the emergent property of *resilience* is that the system under observation must efficiently and effectively maintain operation during expected and unexpected variation. To be resilient, a human, technological, or operational activity system needs to be functionally adaptive.

Human factors provide an ideal procedural framework for establishing adaptivity to system user requirements. Operational drivers responsive to various uptake and sustained utilization incentives, supportive infrastructure that promotes ease of use, and finally the ability to coalesce its resources in a combinatory way to be responsive to various mutable usage settings all provide a basis to operationalize system adaptivity.

The persuasive experience (PX) theoretical framework was developed to explain the relationship between major systems and individually based factors influencing human behavior (Yu & Li, 2016). Its purpose for development is to theorize how wellness-oriented behavior change process occurs within the use of health-promoting physical activity web-based learning systems. Its potential application utility for ongoing systems design evaluation may prove beneficial in helping to better understand what graphic and haptic user interface factors are necessary to leverage both intentional and unanticipated user behavior change processes.

Case study: Increasing workplace wellness resilience through adaptive persuasive design

Onlife Health (https://www.onlifehealth.com/) is a corporate wellness solution company based in Nashville, Tennessee. The Web-based learning (WBL) and smartphone application interfaces Onlife Health has developed are meant to work as technologically based wellness infrastructure to support their member organizations across the United States. The intent for use of these wellness interfaces is to assist organizations in encouraging employee personal health and well-being with the aims of reducing company insurance expenditures and potentially boosting worker productivity.

In 2017, a human factors study was performed with Onlife Health's WBL and mobile platform with systems users on staff to better understand patterns of corporate wellness-based technology's uptake and sustained use. The objective of this research was to gain clearer insight into what specific WBL and app features were used and deemed helpful by participants of differing health-oriented states of mind, and exercise activity levels, to adopt, apply, and maintain increased physical activity behaviors, and to reduce their personal risk of behavior sensitive conditions, such as cardiovascular disease and its sequelae over time. To mobilize this effort, an online survey was designed that used the PX theory (e.g., Yu & Li, 2016) to investigate the relationship between users' state of mind and behavior (SMB) and their physical activity levels. Following the online survey, independent interviews were conducted with all survey respondents to understand their personal uptake and sustained use of WBL features and associated interactive tools (e.g., apps and wearables) for supporting their own physical activity routines. Open-coding and summative content analysis (Hsieh & Shannon, 2005) were used for content analysis and theme generation within individual participant interviews. The results of interview analyses were then cross-referenced with participant survey responses to see if user decisions in specific WBL feature uptake and use patterns emerged in the PX-SMB categories of study participants. SMB categorizations were: "INTERESTED in improving personal health-related physical activity, but not currently regularly physically active;" "MOTIVATED and currently making plans to improve regular physical activity frequency;" "ENGAGED currently in a physical activity regimen that they perform on a relatively regular basis;" "ADOPTED physical activity as part of daily/weekly practice on a consistent and continual basis." The analysis of participant interview themes and SMB classifications did manifest patterns between group usage and uptake of WBL/app interface feature characteristics (Fig. 9.5).

The interviews revealed that the general WBL resource features used the most by users included those that enabled (1) customization of interface features based on individual preferences, (2) tracking user progress on achievement of individually set health goals, (3) ease of use for physical activity data access and monitoring, (4) synchronization of interoperability with wearables and apps that tracked biometric and physical activity data, and (5) determination of user-health insurance reimbursement accrual of "points" that would contribute to the amount of monetary reimbursement for wellness program participation. The WBL/app interface feature that rose as a preferential and significant theme throughout all interviews, regardless of SMB

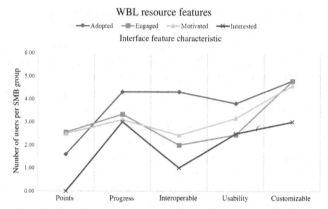

FIGURE 9.5   Study results of Onlife Health's WBL resource use and uptake by different SMB groups. *SMB,* State of mind and behavior; *WBL,* web-based learning. *Corporate identity use courtesy Onlife Health.*

classification, was the importance of users having the ability to customize WBL and app features based on their own user preferences and health goals. In other words, the most preferred system features were the ones that offered the greatest adaptivity to user preference and need (Platt, Li, Bass, & Yu, 2018).

Although this example is reflective of only a small case study, ($N = 33$ participants), in a specific organization, the results present an interesting premise. These outcomes offer a compelling basis for implementing wellness technologies in a way that leverages optimal benefit for both organizations and individual users. Research on corporate wellness programs support that in order to accomplish the aim of a sustainable workplace wellness system, a program developer must do so in a manner that adheres to an organization's vision for cultivating a culture of wellness (Mattke et al., 2013) while concurrently satisfying user psychological need fulfillment (Cable, Edwards, & Zedeck, 2004). Given this consideration of organizational wellness climate on associated program adherence by staff, it might be reasonable to assume that better understanding of the relationships between individual user SMBs and WBL interface features might meaningfully contribute to ongoing workforce wellness technology use. Wellness WBL system features that were *adaptive* to user goals could potentially contribute to sustained system utilization and wellness information application, thus leading to greater possibilities for workplace wellness resilience.

It is important to note that the qualities of *adaptivity* and *robustness* are distinctly different from one another. By means of illustrating this in a very basic manner, we could compare the systems of a suspension bridge and a smartphone. It would be safe to argue that one would consider a suspension bridge a robust system. Well-designed suspension bridges have proven to be able to withstand weather, wear, tear, and at times, even warfare. However, at times we find the undoing of their engineering success to be prompted by their inability to adapt to the previously unforeseen changing nature of transportation vehicle types and traffic patterns (ref. Clifton Suspension Bridge; The Telegraph, July 7, 2009). Conversely, portable technologies, such as those contained on our smartphones, have proven themselves to be infinitely adaptive in nature. Their uses have ranged from geographic information system (GIS) navigation to mobile gaming, from facilitating medical diagnostics to spurring microeconomies in developing nations. In fact, one could argue that the use of these devices as actual "phones" only represents a fraction of their actual value. Smartphones have the capability to be almost infinitely adaptive to their individual user needs and preferences. However, you likely would not want to hit one with a hammer if you plan on using it again. To be fair, there are many aspects of smartphone designs that have proven themselves to be robust to withstand the occasional fumbled drop onto pavement. Suspension bridges, often by their longevity in use, have also demonstrated they have been able to adapt to myriad of different vehicle types with very little change if any to their structural features. The point of this illustration is to articulate what could be considered as their most salient design qualities.

If we were planning to design a system that is truly resilient, we would want to ensure we were combining the qualities of both robustness and adaptivity in the most successful manner possible. The objective would be to confirm that we were considering both present and potential future stressors in engineering for the planned lifespan of our system. We would also attempt to plan for the evolving needs and preferences of our potential system users. Our essential aim in designing a system that is truly resilient should be for its life cycle and utility to "extend" beyond the design basis of its known environment and use as seamlessly as possible. In other words, we would want to leverage the design qualities of robustness and adaptivity in a combinatory manner to create a system with the potential for *graceful extensibility*.

Designing for graceful extensibility

As previously mentioned, when we view the concept of resilience from the lens of psychology, it represents the behavior and affective response attributes of individuals which allow them to flourish in the face of unanticipated circumstances or crisis (Connor & Davidson, 2003). This specific interpretation of human resilience may seem, at first, to be somewhat dichotomous to the definition of "resilience" as it relates to engineering. However, the quality of *graceful extensibility* affords us the opportunity to join the TPM of cognitive and physical ergonomic factors that promote positive user response and acceptance of systems outcomes (Buck, 2009), with the design-dependent performance of environmental conditions meant to support and facilitate *robust* and *adaptive* systems performance. "*Graceful extensibility*" is the quality of system components that have both the capability and capacity to respond with the foresight to unknown unanticipated events. This characteristic of systems resilience thus seeks to engineer infrastructure that is robust to the consequence of surprise events and successful at guiding context specific adaptive human response to avoid potentially catastrophic failures.

Case study: Planning for graceful extensibility through design-development traceability

The process of developing master plans for new construction or renovation is an effort that requires health systems to consider the full scope of stakeholder and operational system needs. Comprehensive design of health system master plans without bringing in human factor specialists and identifying critical stakeholders is obviously possible. In so doing, health system design teams adopt a "bottom-up" linear approach to meeting perceived system requirements by focusing their energies primarily on meeting the basic physical specifications of the system they are charged with designing (Militello, Dominguez, Lintern, & Klein, 2010). However, this process can miss critical functional elements that key stakeholders, such as providers and patients, view as essential to a truly effective system.

Health systems, regardless of their organizational scale, must be designed in a manner to meet the unique needs of their regional constituents. A recommended method for achieving this objective would be to adopt a more "top-down," iterative, and holistic approach to master planning design. This technique allows for thorough problem definition and needs identification along with a framework that provides bidirectional traceability of TPM consequential to "user" (e.g., patient/staff/family) requirements during the conceptual system design phase.

To operationalize this planning concept the health system improvement teams can use human factor analysis (e.g., cognitive and physical ergonomics) and usability assessments to evaluate potential safety and human interaction gaps in the planning process. Planning sessions should include a health system's leadership, design team members, as well as clinical and administrative staff members, and patient and family participants representative of a health system's catchment demography. The goals of these master planning sessions should be to identify and prioritize person-centered (e.g., patient-centered and staff-supportive) requirements (i.e., TPM) that would support positive user-experience outcomes. These TPM can then be cross-referenced with the environment of care (EOC) master plan programmed elements to quantify to what degree design features support essential human-experience/affect outcomes. In other words, the objective of these sessions should be to better understand how critical TPM of personal/psychological resilience could most effectively be supported by resilient design-dependent performance of EOC engineered systems. Fortunately, there is a relatively straightforward way to accomplish this.

A simple tool that can be used by any group of individuals who wish to collectively realize a specific design objective is the "traceability matrix." This process can be used to establish correlations between stakeholder-weighted technical performance measures and associated design-dependent performance (Platt, Bosch, & Kim, 2017). This allows for a diverse group of individuals, with varying backgrounds and experience, to collectively realize comprehensive resilience planning objectives (Table 9.1).

In using this tool, a resilience planning team leads with the "WHYs" (i.e., technical performance measures) of why they think a specific goal needs to be accomplished and then ranks these in terms of importance on a scale of $1-10$ (1 being least important, 10 being most important). Beginning with the "WHYs" in this approach is important because it automatically introduces "purpose" as opposed to merely the "process" of achieving a system performance goal. Evidence supports that most individuals are more likely to commit to adhering to system driven goals they feel are personally meaningful to them and have the potential to directly improve their own circumstances (Latham & Locke, 2007). Next, the team lists the "WHATs" (i.e., design-dependent performance) in the master planning process they think will help them accomplish their objective and then ranks these factors in terms of importance.

Then the process is simply to add the WHAT and WHY and multiply by the rank the participants assign them to get a system's design criteria or process step ordered by importance. The process of weighting technical performance measures and cross-referencing them with the design-dependent performance required to carry them out allows system designers to understand what features should be prioritized during system planning and development (Fig. 9.6).

TABLE 9.1 Med/Surg site example of tracing TPM to design-dependent parameters (DDP) in master plan development.

WHAT		Importance ranking (1 *low importance*–10 *high importance*) WHY								Collective relevance	
		8	7	10	9	10	5	4	6		
		Comfort	Privacy	Clean	Current	Effective	Informative	Personalized	Reassuring		
6	Open nursing station	14	13	32	45	48	33	20	36	241	4
8	Family support areas	48	30	18	34	18	26	36	42	252	3
10	Private patient rooms	54	51	60	57	40	45	42	48	397	1
6	Pt Rm oriented toward nature views	28	13	16	45	16	11	20	24	173	7
5	Various sources of information	26	12	15	42	45	30	27	33	230	5
7	Choice in entertainment options	30	28	17	48	17	24	33	13	210	6
8	Ergonomic furnishings	48	30	54	51	54	13	24	28	302	2
	Relatedness ranking (1 *low relevance*; 2 *moderate relevance*; 3 *high relevance*); cumulative ranking: $(X+Y)*Relevance$										

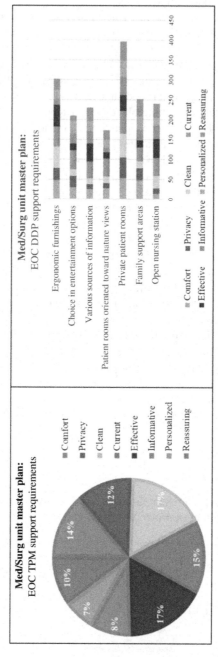

FIGURE 9.6 Master plan design prioritization chart based on traceability matrix outcomes.

In general, this tool affords stakeholders or design teams an improvement or a simple graphic interface to better interpret the relationships between human performance goals and the engineered infrastructure variables that are influencing them. The presentation of a consensus-driven and inclusive picture of designed system elements and human perceptions of positive performance that everyone can understand and discuss builds trust in stakeholders, since everyone involved in the effort has access to the same complete and easy to comprehend data (Khasawneh, Bowling, Jiang, Gramopadhye, & Melloy, 2003). This provides a viable and comprehensive framework for optimizing the potential for *graceful extensibility* in systems design that supports both human capability and operational capacity for systems' response resilience. For a system's design to also be able to *sustainably respond* requires it to also be equipped to take prescient action to myriad and multiple unknown and unknowable circumstances.

Designing for sustainable response

The ability to predict in advance how different interventions are going to impact the operating system and work processes is an ongoing challenge in operations and facility management. In industries that are both safety-critical and highly complex, such as health care, this issue is especially pressing. As the call for increased reliability and resilience in health-care systems' operations heightens, the need for better and more adaptive performance forecasting tools is becoming more relevant. Successfully planning resilient capital improvement initiatives and system sustainability strategies need to simultaneously acknowledge both emerging complexity and emergent system disrupters. This will require a different approach than those historically used for health-care capital planning and improvement purposes.

Case study: Using dynamic modeling in engineering complex systems' sustainable response

"Designing for safety" advocates that approaches using "state of the art [systems] engineering and management" be used when planning facilities where high-risk system activities take place (ANSI/ASSE, 2016). The purpose being to ensure that elements of preventive support are not only included in the ongoing EOC planning but that proactive informational feedforward and feedback mechanisms are embedded into the process to serve as vehicles for continuous improvement within the built environment life cycles (ANSI/ASSE, 2017). System dynamics modeling is an example of an innovative systems engineering technique with great potential for analyzing the longitudinal relationships between care delivery systems and the environmental variables that impact them. Where agent-based modeling is driven by a differential understanding of discrete individual component behaviors, system dynamics is based on the inferential understanding of cumulative integration of collective system component behaviors (Wilensky & Rand, 2015). System dynamics draws from the fields of cognitive and social psychology, organization theory, economics, and other social sciences (Sterman, 2001), to create temporal predictive outcome simulations for operational systems element interactions. The process has had precedent success in environmental planning and project management allowing evidence-based dynamic hypotheses to drive planning decisions, codify cross-disciplinary stakeholder performance outcome criteria, and create models for generating predictive analytics for potential environmental-based design interventions (Elf, Putilova, Von Koch, & Ohrn, 2007; Love, Shen, & Irani, 2002).

The relevance of using system dynamics modeling in planning for health system resilience is in its demonstrated effectiveness in forecasting results of planning decisions (Mawdesley & Al-Jibouri, 2009). This allows health systems' project managers the opportunity to evaluate alternative building strategy reliabilities and, based on simulated outcomes, determine those best suited for adoption into their project plans.

System dynamics generates models based on feedback systems theory (Sterman, 2001). The actual predictive outcome(s) simulation aspect of this systems engineering technique is complicated and often requires specialized training. However, the causal loop diagrams used to inform predictive model construction present an opportunity to incorporate diverse stakeholder participation in operational planning (Fig. 9.7).

The process for developing predictive simulation from models facilitates active and applied stakeholder collaboration in both process and environmental systems design as it allows the modeler to work closely with stakeholder teams to determine the variables that should be considered in systems' frameworks. Increasing the diversity of perspectives in system planning in this manner also augments the potential that the data being used to inform predictive model creation is truly representative of stakeholder population need (Fig. 9.8).

Summing it up

The adoption of applied resilience engineering as a pathway for achieving sustainable quality outcomes has been a relatively recent innovation in

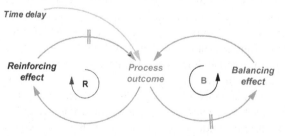

FIGURE 9.7 Example of system dynamics causal loop diagram.

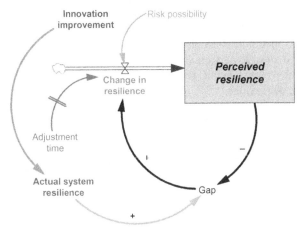

FIGURE 9.8 Example excerpt from system dynamics stock and flow predictive model.

health-care systems improvement (Hollnagel et al., 2006). The primary application of improving resilience in health-care delivery, up to this point, has been in augmenting proactive approaches to care delivery safety (Hollnagel, Braithwaite, & Wears, 2013). Resilient system design's objective is to focus on long-term "chronic" condition management as a holistic approach to achieving reliable system quality, efficiency, and effectiveness (Hollnagel et al., 2006). The application of resilience engineering to complex system improvement is to leverage overlapping performance feedback loops (Dulac, Zipkin, Cutcher-Gershenfeld, Carroll, & Barrett, 2005), to improve adaptive response to hazards (Hollnagel et al., 2006), in order to achieve system equilibrium (Holling, 1973). After reading the explanations of resilience for systems design offered in this chapter, it is hopefully apparent that "designing for resilience" is more than just a potentially viable strategy to improve health systems design efficiency and safety. Indeed, it is a necessary component of the creation of health-care delivery systems that are reliable and sustainably human centered.

Things to remember

1. Because health systems are by nature complex systems, resilience engineering lends itself to designing systems in a way that comprehensively considers the role interactive systems components play in system operational life cycle.
2. Using an adaptive capacity performance hierarchy, such as the one illustrated in this chapter, will allow for the identification and categorization of requisite system component TPM and the development of resilient design-dependent performance (DDP) needed to support them.
3. Easy to use "low-threshold" methods, such as a traceability matrix for codesigning mechanisms that support human capability and operational

capacity for response resilience with health systems stakeholders, can also build uniform group trust in health systems design viability.

4. Using "high-ceiling" methods, such as systems dynamic modeling for predicting long-range design performance outcomes and efficacy, can increase the potential for sustainable response resilience to both known and unknown system disruptions.

Research acknowledgments

Dr. Catherine Bass, PhD Onlife Health; Dr. Amy Blakely, PhD, Sappi North America; Dr. Sheila Bosch, PhD, University of Florida; Michael Greene, Sappi North America; Dr. Huiyang Li, PhD, Human Factors Engineer at Insight Product Development.

Conflict of interest

Lisa Sundahl Platt has in the past worked as a health-care design research consultant for Sappi North America. A case study of the microtopography design their Neoterix ST product is derived from is described in the first case study.

References

Brennan, A. B., Baney, R. H., Carman, M. L., Estes, T. G., Feinberg, A. W., Wilson, L. H., & Schumacher, J. F. (2010). U.S. patent no. 7,650,848. Washington, DC: U.S. Patent and Trademark Office.

Buck, S. (2009). Nine human factors contributing to the user acceptance of telemedicine applications: A cognitive-emotional approach. *Journal of Telemedicine and Telecare, 15*(2), 55–58.

Cable, D., Edwards, J., & Zedeck, S. (2004). Complementary and supplementary fit: A theoretical and empirical integration. *Journal of Applied Psychology, 89*(5), 822–834.

Carling, P. C., Parry, M. M., Rupp, M. E., Po, J. L., Dick, B., Von Beheren, S., & Healthcare Environmental Hygiene Study Group. (2008). Improving cleaning of the environment surrounding patients in 36 acute care hospitals. *Infection Control and Hospital Epidemiology, 29*(11), 1035–1041.

Checkland, P. (2000). *Soft systems methodology: A thirty-year retrospective. Systems research and behavioral science* (pp. S11–S58). Hoboken, NJ: John Wiley & Sons, Ltd.

Connor, K. M., & Davidson, J. R. (2003). Development of a new resilience scale: The Connor-Davidson resilience scale (CD-RISC). *Depression and Anxiety, 18*(2), 76–82.

Dulac, L., Zipkin, F., Cutcher-Gershenfeld, J., Carroll, J., & Barrett, B. (2005). Using system dynamics for safety and risk management in complex engineering systems. In *2005 Proceedings of the winter* simulation conference, 2005 (10 pp.). https://doi.org/10.1109/WSC.2005.1574392.

Elf, M., Putilova, M., Von Koch, L., & Ohrn, K. (2007). Using system dynamics for collaborative design: A case study. *BMC Health Services Research, 7*, 123.

Hendrick, H., & Kleiner, B. M. (2001). *Macroergonomics: An introduction to work system design*. Santa Monica, CA: Human Factors and Ergonomics Society.

Holling, C. (1973). Resilience and stability of ecological systems. *Annual Review of Ecology and Systematics, 4*, 1−23.

Hollnagel, E. (2014). Resilience engineering and the built environment. *Building Research & Information, 42*(2), 1−8. Available from https://doi.org/10.1080/09613218.2014.862607.

Hollnagel, E., Braithwaite, J., & Wears, R. L. (Eds.), (2013). *Resilient health care.* Farnham, Surrey, Ashgate Publishing, Ltd.

Hollnagel, E., Woods, D., & Leveson, N. (2006). *Resilience engineering: Concepts and precepts.* Aldershot, England; Burlington, VT: Ashgate, Print.

Hsieh, H., & Shannon, S. (2005). Three approaches to qualitative content analysis. *Qualitative Health Research, 15*(9), 1277−1288.

Khasawneh, M. T., Bowling, S. R., Jiang, X., Gramopadhye, A. K., & Melloy, B. J. (2003). A model for predicting human trust in automated systems. *Origins, 5.*

Kirschner, C. M., & Brennan, A. B. (2012). Bio-inspired antifouling strategies. *Annual Review of Materials Research, 42*, 211−229.

Larsson, N., & Malmsjö, O. (1998). A model for design of human activity systems. *Systemic Practice and Action Research, 11*(4), 455−479.

Latham, G. P., & Locke, E. A. (2007). New developments in and directions for goal-setting research. *European Psychologist, 12*(4), 290−300. Available from https://doi.org/10.1027/1016-9040.12.4.290.

Love, P. E. D., Holt, G. D., Shen, L. Y., Li, H., & Irani, Z. (2002). Using systems dynamics to better understand change and rework in construction project management systems. *International Journal of Project Management, 20*(6), 425−436.

Magill, S., Edwards, J., Bamberg, W., Beldavs, Z., Dumyati, G., Kainer, M., ... Fridkin, S. (2014). Multistate point-prevalence survey of health care−associated infections. *The New England Journal of Medicine, 370*(13), 1198−1208.

Mattke, S., Liu, H., Caloyeras, J. P., Huang, C. Y., Van Busum, K. R., Khodyakov, D., & Shier, V. (2013). *United States. Department of Labor. Workplace wellness programs study final report.* RAND Corporation. Retrieved from <http://www.rand.org>. February 4, 2017.

Mawdesley, M., & Al-Jibouri, S. (2009). Modeling construction project productivity using systems dynamics approach. *International Journal of Productivity and Performance Management, 59*(1), 18−36.

Mcguckin, M., & Govednik, J. (2015). A review of electronic hand hygiene monitoring: Considerations for hospital management in data collection, healthcare worker supervision, and patient perception. *Journal of Healthcare Management, 60*(5), 348.

Militello, L., Dominguez, C., Lintern, G., & Klein, G. (2010). The role of cognitive systems engineering in the systems engineering design process. *Systems Engineering, 13*(3), 261−273.

O'boyle, C. A., Henly, S. J., & Larson, E. (2001). Understanding adherence to hand hygiene recommendations: The theory of planned behavior. *American Journal of Infection Control, 29*(6), 352−360.

Pittet, D., Allegranzi, B., Boyce, J., & World Health Organization World Alliance for Patient Safety First Global Patient Safety Challenge Core Group of Experts. (2009). The World Health Organization guidelines on hand hygiene in health care and their consensus recommendations. *Infection Control and Hospital Epidemiology, 30*(7), 611−622.

Platt, L. S., & Greene, M. (2017). Increasing patient safety through resilient design: Using human factors engineering and environmental support mechanisms to reduce potentials of hospital acquired infection. In: *International conference on applied human factors and ergonomics* (pp. 3−10). Springer, Cham, Switzerland.

Platt, L. S., Bosch, S. J., & Kim, D. (2017). Toward a framework for designing person-centered mental health interiors for veterans. *Journal of Interior Design, 42*(2), 27–48.

Platt, L. S., Li, H., Bass, C. E., & Yu, K. (2018). Validating persuasive experience (PX) theory: Preliminary results of a case study on a corporate wellness program's web-based learning interfaces. In: *Proceedings of the international symposium on human factors and ergonomics in health care* (Vol. 7, No. 1, pp. 56–63). New Delhi, India: Sage India, SAGE Publications.

Sappi North America, ResInnova Labs, & Perfectus Biomed (2018). *Performance of soiled surfaces.* Neoterix® ST Technology Performance Data. Data used with permission of Sappi NA.

Schumacher, J. F., Carman, M. L., Estes, T. G., Feinberg, A. W., Wilson, L. H., Callow, M. E., ... Brennan, A. B. (2007). Engineered antifouling microtopographies—effect of feature size, geometry, and roughness on settlement of zoospores of the green alga Ulva. *Biofouling, 23*(1), 55–62.

Seager, T. P., Clark, S. S., Eisenberg, D. A., Thomas, J. E., Hinrichs, M. M., Kofron, R., ... Aldersono, D. L. (2017). Chapter 3: Resilience and risk: Methods and application in environment, cyber and social domains. In I. Linkov, & J. P. Oliveira (Eds.), *Redesigning resilient infrastructure research.* Springer. http://dx.doi.org/10.1007/978-94-024-1123-2.

Sharklet Technologies, Inc. (2017). *Inspired by nature the discovery of Sharklet.* Retrieved from: <http://sharklet.com/our-technology/sharklet-discovery/> Accessed 01.03.17.

Shekelle, P. G., Wachter, R. M., Pronovost, P. J., Schoelles, K., McDonald, K. M., Dy, S. M. ... Winters B. D. (2013). *Making health care safer II: An updated critical analysis of the evidence for patient safety practices.* Comparative effectiveness review no. 211. (Prepared by the Southern California-RAND Evidence-based Practice Center under Contract No. 290-2007-10062-I.) AHRQ publication no. 13-E001-EF. Rockville, MD: Agency for Healthcare Research and Quality. <www.ahrq.gov/research/findings/evidence-based-reports/ptsafetyuptp.html>.

Sikula, N., Mancillas, R., Linkov, J., & McDonagh, W. (2015). Risk management is not enough: A conceptual model for resilience and adaptation-based vulnerability assessments. *Environment Systems and Decisions, 35*(2), 219–228.

Sterman, J. D. (2001). System dynamics modeling: Tools for learning in a complex world. *California Management Review, 43*(4), 8–25.

Swoboda, S. M., Earsing, K., Strauss, K., Lane, S., & Lipsett, P. A. (2004). Electronic monitoring and voice prompts improve hand hygiene and decrease nosocomial infections in an intermediate care unit. *Critical Care Medicine, 32*(2), 358–363.

The American National Standards Institute (ANSI) and The American Society of Safety Engineers (ASSE). (2016). *Prevention through design: Guidelines for addressing occupational hazards and risks in design and redesign processes.* Park Ridge, IL: American Society of Safety Engineers, ANSI/ASSE Z590.3-2011 (R2016).

The American National Standards Institute (ANSI) and The American Society of Safety Engineers (ASSE). (2017). *Occupational health and safety management systems.* Park Ridge, IL: American Society of Safety Engineers, ANSI/ASSE Z10-2012 (R2017).

The Telegraph. (July 7, 2009). *Heavy ambulances banned from Clifton Suspension Bridge.* Retrieved from <https://www.telegraph.co.uk/news/newstopics/howaboutthat/5766901/Heavy-ambulances-banned-from-Clifton-Suspension-Bridge.html>.

Wilensky, U., & Rand, W. (2015). *An introduction to agent-based modeling: modeling natural, social, and engineered complex systems with NetLogo.* Cambridge, MA: MIT Press.

Woods, D. D. (2015). Four concepts for resilience and the implications for the future of resilience engineering. *Reliability Engineering & System Safety, 141*, 5–9.

Yu, K., & Li, H. (2016). Mechanism of persuasive experience — A new design and evaluation framework of persuasive systems. In A. Marcus (Ed.), *Design, user experience and usability: Novel user experiences* (pp. 132–143). Cham, Switzerland: Springer International Publishing, LNCS 9747.

Zhang, S., Kong, X., Lamb, K. V., & Wu, Y. (2019). High nursing workload is a main associated factor of poor hand hygiene adherence in Beijing, China: An observational study. *International Journal of Nursing Practice*, 25, e12720. Available from https://doi.org/10.1111/ijn.12720.

Further reading

Blanchard, B., & Fabrycky, W. J. (2011). *Systems engineering and analysis. Prentice Hall international series in industrial and systems engineering* (5th ed.). Boston, MA: Prentice Hall.

Chapter 10

Designing for collaborative work

Rachel E. Mason[1,2] and Ashley M. Hughes[2]

[1]*Department of Epidemiology and Biostatistics, School of Public Health, University of Illinois at Chicago, Chicago, IL, United States,* [2]*Department of Biomedical and Health Information Sciences, College of Applied Health Sciences, University of Illinois at Chicago, Chicago, IL, United States*

Introduction

Every system is perfectly designed to get the results it gets.

Paul Batalden, MD (Carr, 2008).

Dr. Batalden's quote serves as a reminder that each system's efficiency and capacities produce results. Considering this quote in context, health-care systems currently produce long wait times (Gorey, 2009), unnecessary testing (Flamm, Fritsch, Seer, Panisch, & Sönnichsen, 2011; Kwok & Jones, 2005), overmedication (Dhalla, Persaud, & Juurlink, 2011; Kolodny et al., 2015), and misdiagnoses (Graber, 2013) by design. Failures in coordination of patient care result in the loss of health information (McDonald, 2007) and introduce risk for serious patient harm (Zwaan, Thijs, Wagner, van der Wal, & Timmermans, 2009). Poor outcomes, inefficiencies, and lapses in successful information exchange have been linked to suboptimal execution of team-based skills, including lack of leadership, miscommunication(s), and coordination failures (Joint Commission, 2014). Bolstering aspects of teamwork for health-care teams may move system level changes toward high reliability (Baker, Day, & Salas, 2006), which bear tremendous potential to impact human lives.

Provision of safe and efficient care requires more than a set of clinical experts caring for the same patient; rather, it requires expert teams who exhibit expert levels of knowledge, skills, and attitudes (KSAs) necessary for two or more people to work together dynamically to accomplish shared goals, otherwise known as teamwork. The science of teamwork demonstrates underpinning factors which yield successful team adaptation (Gregory et al., 2019), including timely redistribution of workload to key team members,

Design for Health. DOI: https://doi.org/10.1016/B978-0-12-816427-3.00010-5
183

provision of backup behavior to a struggling teammate, and engagement in creative problem solving (Hoegl & Parboteeah, 2007; Salas, Sims, & Burke, 2005). Evidence further highlights the link between demonstration of proficient teamwork and improvements in clinical performance (e.g., timely administration of an antibiotic in surgical settings) (Hughes et al., 2016), as well as enhanced care quality (Hysong et al., 2019; Leonard, Graham, & Bonacum, 2004). Despite the growing awareness of teamwork's importance in the health-care arena, less attention is paid to the conditions which facilitate and support optimal teamwork (Salas, Shuffler, Thayer, Bedwell, & Lazzara, 2015). To this end, we offer empirical evidence to inform the design of sociotechnical systems (STSs) such that organizational health-care systems can reap the benefits of collaborative practice.

Teams are affected by a number of sociotechnical and environment factors which can inhibit or facilitate their success. Historically, teamwork is characterized by the nature of the tasks, timing (LePine, Piccolo, Jackson, Mathieu, & Saul, 2008; Marks, Mathieu, & Zaccaro, 2001; Morgeson, DeRue, & Karam, 2010), and the overall context in which they operate (Holden et al., 2013; Salas et al., 2015)—including but not limited to the organizational culture (e.g., policy and procedures), physical environment, team structure, and time demands. These contextual factors appear within well-validated STSs models [e.g., Systems Engineering Initiative for Patient Safety (SEIPS) STS] which illustrate how multilevel input factors (organizational conditions, team conditions, etc., as mentioned above) influence processes of care and, ultimately, outcomes, including provider- (e.g., injury on-the-job; burnout; Patterson et al., 2016), as well as patient-related outcomes (e.g., quality of care; near misses). Changes to these inputs influence the explanatory mechanisms which influence outcomes for teams—that is, the KSAs drivers of teamwork (Salas, Rosen, Burke, & Goodwin, 2009). We use the following sections to highlight principles which are likely to foster optimal teamwork and, with it, collaborative practice.

Sociotechnical system functions and inputs

STSs contain dynamic, hierarchical, and interactive processes by which work is performed. This involves a set of input(s), throughput(s), and output(s). Similarly, groups and teams research focuses on *why* some groups are more effective than others (Ilgen, Hollenback, Johnson, & Jundt, 2005), involving an examination of input(s), throughput(s), and outputs of team performance. Examining care processes in health-care teams, system-level components of an organization, or STS contributes to the prevention of medical errors, incidents, and adverse events. These components include the internal (i.e., policies and procedures, organizational culture) and external environments (i.e., political infrastructure, geographical location), organization (i.e., social norms), tasks (i.e., care activities), tools and technologies (i.e., artifacts involved in conducting work), and person(s) (i.e., individuals and team[s] involved in patient care activities) (see Table 10.1) (Carayon, 2012; Dekker, Hancock, & Wilkin, 2013; Hollnagel, Woods, & Leveson, 2006; Russ, et al., 2013; Wilson, 2013). Next, we highlight some of the key features of STSs in relation to their pertinence to team process, explaining the science which drives our design guidelines.

Work environment

Health-care teams operate in uniquely stressful conditions, which warrant consideration when examining or seeking to improve their function. Namely, health-care teams are characterized by team member fluidity either through shift changes or turnover (Andreatta, 2010). Scheduling norms and organizational policies which attest to the work environment's culture can influence team process in a number of ways. These factors often result in rotation(s) in leadership (Wildman et al., 2012), which may result in confusion over roles and responsibilities, creating lapses in execution of a critical team task (e.g., timely administration of a medication). For example, nurses and certified nursing assistants (CNAs) often work on a rotating shift schedule, meaning the people on a team constantly shift between and within shifts of an individual worker; important information exchanges (i.e., handoffs) must be continuously supported by the policies, protocols, and norms of an organization for exchanges to avoid loss of critical health information and to mitigate the potential for direct patient harm (Keebler et al., 2016). The criticality of the work environment, including organizational culture and policies, is necessary to foster the enactment of essential teamwork behaviors.

Physical environment

Team function is readily influenced by environmental design characteristics which can produce negative outcomes. For instance, disruptions in team workflow can stem from the physical layout of the operating room, such as the positioning of equipment within the room to optimize team members' task flow (Catchpole et al., 2007; Cohen et al., 2016; Palmer et al., 2013; Wiegmann, ElBardissi, Dearani, Daly, & Sundt, 2007). Further, launching a team approach to outpatient care is more effective when physical layout accommodates face-to-face interaction with team members (Lyson et al., 2019). Taken together, there is a need to examine environmental design to enhance teamwork at the point of care.

Team-level structure

Another consideration for conditions impacting teams is in regard to the distribution of expertise within the team composition. High-skill differentials

TABLE 10.1 Inputs from case scenario.

	External environment	Internal environment	Physical environment	Organization	Person(s)	Tools/technologies
Case excerpt	Not much is known or provided about the environment external to the hospital in this case	Training hospital will have access to residents and interns who may be assigned as members of the code team; availability of resuscitation services	Different wing of the hospital	Did not have a culture or policy in place to regularly check equipment such as crash carts; mock codes for nonroutine events (such as codes in psychiatric in patient) should be made routine	Senior medical resident, intern unfamiliar with layout of the hospital, lack of involvement/ communication between psychiatric care teams	Do-not-resusciate order was not properly entered or readily available information within the health information technology(ies) available; leads for proper equipment were unavailable

between members is a hallmark trait of health-care teams which may impact function (Hollenbeck, Beersma, & Schouten, 2012; e.g., physician has considerably more education and expertise than a clerk, yet they are considered team members by Patient-Centered Medical Home standards). As they must coordinate to accomplish patient-oriented care tasks, the degree to which team members depend upon one another is often high (Wildman et al., 2012). For example, within test results management settings, the nurse administers the test, the CNA packages the test to send to the lab, the lab technician tests the specimen and sends it back to the office, the clerk alerts the physician that the result has arrived, and the physician alerts the patient of the result.

Tools and technologies

In today's health-care setting, clinical and nonclinical members no longer have to work face to face. Advances in medical research yield an increase in specialization, while health informatics, mobile health, and medical devices expand access to and for patients. For instance, patients are able to connect with health providers remotely via telehealth appointments (e.g., telemedicine being used to connect patients to specialists who are hundreds of miles apart), monitor blood glucose levels via mobile health apps, or undergo surgery through the use of tele-robotic assisted surgical devices (Tan et al., 2016; Weinberg, Rao, & Escobar, 2011). Incompatibility between technologies leveraged to perform patient care-related work and teamwork needs can impede the team's ability to realize patient care goals. Thus, tools which support team-based tasks and associated teamwork needs should be designed or selected. Electronic health records (EHRs) offer one example of a tool-realizing potential for supporting teamwork. Despite rapid uptake rates nationwide, EHRs currently fail to satisfy demands for care coordination. Timely and secure exchange of health information across systems (Office of the National Coordinator for Health Information Technologies, 2018), built-in functions to support team-based tasks (e.g., test results management; Smith, Hughes, et al., 2018), interface usability (Howe, Adams, Hettinger, & Ratwani, 2018), and readily interpretable interprofessional team notes (Boyd et al., 2018) are all areas in which current EHRs are deficient in supporting collaborative practice. Aligning teamwork needs and the capabilities of the tools used to perform work is necessary to eliminate workarounds and potential for failures in execution of patient care tasks.

Team adaptability

The "perfect" medical team is not the one that makes no errors, but it is the team that learns from those errors (Gregory et al., 2019). Overall, teams have the ability to adapt, produce, and creatively solve problems in a way that is unmatched by a single individual (e.g., Gladstein, 1984; Hackman, 1987; Sundstrom, DeMeuse, & Futrell, 1990), making them a necessity in today's arena of complex and chronic care. Expert teams display the requisite KSAs to work well together to accomplish shared goals. These highly skilled teams are intentionally developed. Fortunately, teamwork can be fostered under proper conditions and with the appropriate team-development tools (e.g., Gladstein, 1984; Hackman, 1987; McGrath, 1964). We build upon existing work by considering team adaptation as the goal in designing STSs for collaboration-based work.

Design guidelines

Designing for collaborative practice employs use of evidence-based design guidelines. Stemming from the evidence in our introduction, we advocate employing the following design guidelines in conjunction with the findings from a thorough needs analysis. Needs analysis uncovers underlying information or cognitive processes that are required to perform a job or task. Through this process, training or tools can be developed to better meet end user needs (Arthur Jr, Bennett Jr, Edens, & Bell, 2003). By coupling the guidelines with a needs analysis, practitioners are supported in executing guidelines to the exact team- and task-work needs for patients, their care, and optimal function in the health-care team.

Create a stable infrastructure for collaborative practice

Minding the scheduling of teammates, formation of team norms, and a physical environment that will support collaborative efforts is imperative to the team's success. Arranging the physical layout of the room to foster collaborative practice means having shared spaces for individuals belonging to a particular team. An illustrative example comes from implementation practices for the Patient-Centered Medical Home model. This team-based approach for outpatient care is more effective when the physical layout accommodates the need for frequent face-to-face communication and shared spaces emphasizing a team perspective. The antithesis of this would be that each professional role on a team (e.g., nurses) has their own separate space, including lounge area, separate area for charting patient information, and station. Creating shared space emphasizes cross-talk amongst individuals based on the interprofessional nature of the team's collaborative work rather than on the professional role of the individual(s).

Part of this structure to build a team perspective is the creation of team-level conditions to foster development and execution of optimal team KSAs. This is for the benefit of the patient, as well as members of the care team. Team familiarity, that is, the extent to which team members know one another, is a significant predictor of injury on the job (Patterson et al., 2016).

Creating regularity within the team can enable the team to form norms, improve upon process, and exhibit emergent states critical to performance, such as cohesion and trust. Health-care teams are, by definition, multiprofessional and often interdisciplinary; therefore, creating opportunities for increased exposure in the design of work space and interaction is key.

Embed tools to foster effective team process and minimize work arounds

Consider team-level needs, including: the information needed for each role, team processes involved in team-based tasks, and tools/technologies which best fit into team workflow. This should occur prior to selection of a team-based intervention. Computer-supported cooperative work principles, distributed cognition, team task analysis, and workflow evaluations can all assist in identification and design of tools to support team process. By embedding and sharing team tools across professions and disciplines, a team orientation can be supported.

Create norms, expectations, and space for teamwork: create a culture of collaboration

In order for collaborative practice to exist within the organization's expectations, the organization must reinforce expectations for clinicians and staff to exhibit teamwork. Part of this means that the organization should conduct evaluations. A proper evaluation will consist of team process-based measures (e.g., closed loop communication), as well as team outcomes (e.g., timely execution of a team-based task). Some examples of commonly used team outcomes include team performance, efficiency, cost, quality, and quantity (Moreland, Argote, & Krishnan, 1996).

Since the Institute of Medicine's landmark report on medical errors (Kohn, Corrigan, & Donaldson, 1999), patient safety has emerged as a salient concern nationwide. *What* and *how* to evaluate should be determined up front as part of a multilevel needs analysis before implementing any new patient safety initiative. However, evaluation should be thought of at the forefront and will consist of metrics which serve as "standards by which the value of the program can be judged" (Goldstein & Ford, 2002).

Develop teams by training and cross training for roles and responsibilities

Team training can be effective at improving teamwork (Salas et al., 2008) and patient care (Hughes et al., 2016). Several off-the-shelf teamwork training tools exist which can assist with development of team-based competencies. For instance, Team Strategies and Tools to Enhance Performance and

Patient Safety (TeamSTEPPS) is an evidence-based, practical team-training strategy toolkit put forth by the United States Department of Defense, Agency for Healthcare Research and Quality (AHRQ), and leading members of the scientific community (Howard, Gaba, Fish, Yang, & Sarnquist, 1992). Modules cover critical domains for teamwork development (as well as evaluations; see team performance questionnaire and team attitudes questionnaire) and provide guidance on change management and support for teamwork on the job. TeamSTEPPS is not the only team training tool available; we recommend selecting and contextualizing a program based on the results of a thorough needs analysis.

In the next section, we have leveraged a series of case studies to illustrate these principles in action.

Case studies—problem breakdown and design solutions

Alter work system support structures

> *Within psychiatric services at a training hospital, a code blue is called for an elderly patient with a history of coronary artery disease, hypertension, and schizophrenia. A code team (comprising a senior medical resident, intern, anesthesia resident, anesthesia attending, and critical care nurse) was alerted to respond to the scene. However, mass confusion erupted as the senior resident and intern did not know how to get to psychiatric inpatient services. Upon arrival, the team finds that their equipment is incompatible with the leads on the patient. The team sent a nurse to obtain compatible stickers for the patient, continuing cardiopulmonary resuscitation (CPR). At this point, a nurse located in the inpatient unit recognizes the patient and informs the team that the patient is a 'no code.' In fact, the patient did not wish to be resuscitated.*

Adapted from "Code Blue—Where To?" (Franklin, 2007).

Beyond systems level policies and procedures, supports for individuals and teams must be situated effectively within the physical space in which teams work. The vignette illustrates misapplication and need for three of our four design principles: *create a stable infrastructure for collaborative practice, embed tools to foster effective team process and minimize workarounds,* and *train and develop teams.* In this case, the physical design of the hospital and lack of training precluded the team's understanding and ability to respond in a timely way to the needs of an urgent patient. The team's lack of knowledge regarding the location of where they were responding to and their incompatible equipment created time intensive delays, which in turn could have affected a patient's outcome, if the patient had wanted to be resuscitated. Specifically, this case speaks to the importance of procedure adherence regarding the coding status. Pertinent information about the patient was not displayed in a way that helped facilitate team process. Rather, the incompatible stickers and the lack of a signifier for the do-not-resuscitate (DNR) order detracted from the team's ability to respond in an appropriate manner. The team should have first determined the coding status before beginning CPR. Individual patient needs demand attention to ensure effective and appropriate care.

How to situate effectively: identify coordination demands and process needs

Job and team task analysis can reveal the relevant needs of collaborative health-care teams such that design guidelines can most appropriately be embedded within organizational structures and norms, including their demands for coordination. Critical incident (CI) style interviews describe an approach (Flanagan, 1954); cognitive walk-throughs and/or role-specific inquiry can assist in determining information needs of specific team members. Observations which are organized ethnographically to observe specific aspects of team performance, STSs, or collaborative efforts also provide insight into team function. Surveys are also useful in determining team-task analysis. Then, analyses are based on those observations to determine which team-related KSAs are required to perform those tasks. While task analysis specifies the required job operations, KSAs further delve into the human capacities necessary to perform those tasks. It also encompasses which KSAs are difficult to learn (e.g., information exchange and shared mental models). Identifying the team KSAs necessary to performing team-based tasks and successfully accomplishing collaborative work is imperative.

Collaborative practice—beyond patient outcomes

Ana is a second-year resident in a demanding internal medicine residency program. She is generally regarded as one of the most talented residents and has just been elected to the chief resident position for the next year. For several months, however, she has been feeling a significant amount of burnout. Ana's mood has become low, her energy level has dropped, and she is having difficulty getting out of bed in the morning. She is in the middle of a very demanding intensive care unit (ICU) rotation. At first, she thinks that it might just be sleep deprivation causing the problem. But she continues to feel increasingly unwell both physically and emotionally.

Ana is afraid to tell anyone how she feels because she thinks that people in the program will start to regard her as a "weak" resident if she complains. The competitive atmosphere makes her believe that the other residents are working just as hard and aren't having any problems. She does not even discuss the situation with her family at home because she does not want to disappoint them. She is feeling completely trapped and wonders why she went into the medical field in the first place; she would do anything at this point to escape it.

Adapted from "Dealing with Burnout" (Ellis, n.d.).

Resident Ana is struggling, feeling isolated in a work environment which offers little tolerance for error, and provides little support. This unfortunate case helps illustrate our design guideline, *Create norms, expectations, and space for teamwork: create a culture of collaboration.* Improving collaborative practice is not limited to improving outcomes for patients; provider well-being is a critical outcome that can be improved as systems shift toward creating a collaborative climate. Cole (2019) notes that providers are faced with increasing dissatisfaction, depression, and burnout. This in turn yields decreased productivity, rapid physician turnover, and, of course, compromises in patient safety (Cole, 2019). Structuring the process of teamwork is paramount to improving provider outcomes, as teamwork is a job resource, directly affecting individuals at work. The work environment needs to treat teams and their associated members as complex, multilevel systems that function across time, tasks, and contexts (Ilgen, Hollenbeck, Johnson, & Jundt, 2005); this should further include a feedback loop to properly contextualize the changes that occur throughout the existence of the team. These support structures pose demonstrable benefits. Employees who are emotionally committed to an organization demonstrate heightened job performance, reduced absenteeism, and a higher job retention rate (Mathieu & Zajac, 1990; Mowday, Porter, & Steers, 1982) in nonhealth-care settings. In the context of this vignette, Ana ideally would have felt comfortable reaching out for support from not only her fellow colleagues and family but also from her supervisors. Improvements in teamwork are associated with increased feelings of job satisfaction and reduced turnover in clinical staff (Manser, 2009). With identified needs in hand, potential solutions can be developed in conjunction with engaged stakeholders, including members of top leadership.

How do we create culture change for teamwork?

The question of how to initiate and sustain collaborative practice as a key component of organizational culture may lie in perceived organizational support (POS). POS refers to "the extent to which the organization values [employees'] contributions and cares about their well-being" (Eisenberger, Huntington, Hutchison, & Sowa, 1986). According to organizational support literature, high POS improves work attitudes and cultivates effective work behavior (Eisenberger et al., 1986; Howes, Cropanzano, Grandey, & Mohler, 2000). This process is facilitated through social exchange (such as collaborative work), from the organization to the individual employee. Workers may examine actions of their employers and weigh them against potential unfavorable actions (Eisenberger, Cummings, Armeli, & Lynch, 1997). In this context, if the organization perceivably protects the interests of their workers, employees conclude that they are supported. This can be reciprocated by employees becoming harder working and more committed to the organization (Eisenberger et al., 1986).

Perceived team support refers to the extent to which teams perceive that management provides them with all the "tools" that they need to succeed (Pearce & Herbik, 2004). This construct is similar to POS (Eisenberger, Fasolo, & Davis-LaMastro, 1990) but is distinct in that it is measured at the team level. This concept includes resources, training, and a management system that enables the team to perform (Pearce & Herbik, 2004). Through the development of collaborative team culture, clinicians will more effectively and safely be able to take care of their patients. Truly, this process encompasses a thorough examination of practices within the organization; while this can be altered to speak directly to organizational level interventions alone (e.g., policy change), the culture for teamwork and collaboration should be felt by employees at all levels of the organization.

Team process in the care arena

A middle-aged man was admitted to the medical service of a teaching hospital with suspected vasculitis. When the initial diagnostic studies failed to provide a definitive diagnosis, the team decided to treat the patient empirically with high-dose steroids.

When discussing the patient on morning rounds, the senior resident instructed the intern quite clearly to "give the patient one gram of steroids." After rounds (and some quick math), the intern ordered: "Prednisone 20 mg tabs 50 pills PO x 1 now."

After receiving the written order, the pharmacist contacted the intern to clarify the order. She suggested to the intern that the one gram of steroids probably was supposed to be given in an intravenous form. The busy and harried intern stated firmly that he wished to give the patient fifty 20-mg pills. When the pharmacist continued questioning the order and gently suggested the intern may want to contact his senior resident for clarification, the intern refused and replied, "You can give it with a tablespoon of Maalox." The patient was brought fifty 20-mg pills of prednisone and became angry and frustrated as he swallowed pill after pill. He developed mild nausea and heartburn while taking the prednisone.

Upon review of the medication record the following day, the senior resident found the error. The oral prednisone was stopped, and the patient was correctly given a gram of intravenous methylprednisolone (Solu-Medrol). He eventually recovered from his vasculitis and was discharged in a stable condition.

Adapted from "One Dose, Fifty Pills" (Smith, 2005).

The vignette above describes an event in which care quality suffers rather than a mistake which compromises patient safety. The vignette illustrates the need(s) for two of our design guidelines: *create norms, expectations, and space for teamwork: create a culture of collaboration* and *develop teams by training and cross training for roles and responsibilities.*

Fortunately, the event described above features a mistake made by an intern which resulted in momentary patient discomfort rather than severe patient harm. However, it features a missed opportunity to monitor progress towards goal(s) on the part of the senior medical resident and to assert mutual support by challenging the order more than once by the pharmacist.

How to support team process

In the context of this vignette, there were no official administrative repercussions for this particular lack of effective communication between team members. Not holding the intern accountable for his prescribing behaviors means that these behaviors were not corrected and that teamwork, as a means of accomplishing shared tasks, was not reinforced. Considering that system level change moves slowly, it is critical to engage top leaders and change agents within each unit, forming an interprofessional, multidisciplinary coalition for change team. This team can act as a liaison between members of top management and members of frontline care staff to convey messages of change and to stimulate involvement. One mechanism by which change can be continually achieved is through developing implementation and evaluation plan(s) for intervention(s) of interest (e.g., AHRQ quality improvement toolkit).

How do we determine important teamwork processes in care? Develop teams

First, team training should impart the KSAs necessary for teams to work together effectively. This principle applies not just to in-hospital teams but to interprofessional teams as well. Team-development interventions (i.e., strategies which seek to stimulate optimal team-based function; e.g., team training; Shuffler, DiazGranados, & Salas, 2011) have been met with encouraging evidence as to their effectiveness at improving team-related KSAs (Salas, DiazGranados et al., 2008; Shuffler et al., 2011), as well as patient care (Hughes et al., 2016; Marlow et al., 2017). Yet, evidence suggests that teams can only do as much as their work condition(s) allow (Burke et al., 2006; Salas et al., 2015). This means that the case study above illustrates the importance of mutual support; however, it also illustrates that when there is a lack of repercussions or oversight for the failure or improper enactment of team-based skills, patient care quality can suffer as a result. In the case illustrated above, the patient's situation was remedied when the senior resident reviewed patient chart information.

Conclusion

Teams are integral in facilitating health-care and, as discussed in the chapter, their outcomes are influenced by their design. Technological and medical advances pose the promise of enhancing, yet further complicating, healthcare impacts. The evidence is compelling that optimizing team function yields improved patient safety outcomes (Hughes et al., 2016; Neily et al., 2010); we advocate further testing of these empirically grounded design guidelines in future work.

We presented several frameworks, models, theories, and case studies that informed the selection of evidence-based guidance. Salient frameworks in teamwork literature have been noted (e.g., SEIPS, STS, TeamSTEPPS), including key features which further perceived team support, organizational commitment, and organizational identification for exhibiting optimal teamwork. The design guidelines stemming from the literature at large serve as the foundational building blocks for more advanced team science interventions.

Future work should report successful and comprehensive systems change initiatives and report lessons learned on the journey to improving quality and safety of patient care.

References

Andreatta, P. B. (2010). A typology for health care teams. *Health Care Management Review, 35* (4), 345–354.

Arthur, W., Jr, Bennett Jr, W., Edens, P. S., & Bell, S. T. (2003). Effectiveness of training in organizations: A meta-analysis of design and evaluation features. *Journal of Applied Psychology, 88*(2), 234.

Baker, D. P., Day, R., & Salas, E. (2006). Teamwork as an essential component of high-reliability organizations. *Health Services Research, 41*(2), 1576–1598.

Boyd, A. D., Lopez, K. D., Lugaresi, C., Macieira, T., Sousa, V., Acharya, S., ... Burton, M. (2018). Physician nurse care: A new use of UMLS to measure professional contribution: Are we talking about the same patient a new graph matching algorithm? *International Journal of Medical Informatics, 113*, 63–71.

Burke, C. S., Stagl, K. C., Klein, C., Goodwin, G. F., Salas, E., & Halpin, S. M. (2006). What type of leadership behaviors are functional in teams? A meta-analysis. *The Leadership Quarterly, 17*(3), 288–307.

Carayon, P. (2012). Sociotechnical systems approach to healthcare quality and patient safety. *Work, 41*(1), 3850.

Carr, S. (2008). *A Quotation with a life of its own. Patient Safety and Quality Healthcare.* Retrievedfrom: <https://www.psqh.com/analysis/editor-s-notebook-a-quotation-with-a-life-of-its-own/>.

Catchpole, K. R., Giddings, A. E. B., Wilkinson, M., Hirst, G., Dale, T., & de Leval, M. R. (2007). Improving patient safety by identifying latent failures in successful operations. *Surgery, 142*(1), 102–110.

Cohen, T. N., Cabrera, J. S., Sisk, O. D., Welsh, K. L., Abernathy, J. H., Reeves, S. T., ... Boquet, A. J. (2016). Identifying workflow disruptions in the cardiovascular operating room. *Anesthesia, 71*(8), 948–954.

Cole, S. P. (2019). Burnout prevention and resilience training for critical care trainees. *International Anesthesiology Clinics, 57*(2), 118–131.

Dekker, S. W., Hancock, P. A., & Wilkin, P. (2013). Ergonomics and sustainability: Towards an embrace of complexity and emergence. *Ergonomics, 56*(3), 357–364.

Dhalla, I. A., Persaud, N., & Juurlink, D. N. (2011). Facing up to the prescription opioid crisis. *British Medical Journal, 343*, d5142.

Ellis, K. (n.d.). Dealing with burnout. *IHI Open School*. Retrieved from <http://www.ihi.org/education/IHIOpenSchool/resources/Pages/CaseStudies/DealingWithBurnout.aspx>.

Eisenberger, R., Cummings, J., Armeli, S., & Lynch, P. (1997). Perceived organizational support, discretionary treatment, and job satisfaction. *Journal of Applied Psychology, 82*(5), 812.

Eisenberger, R., Fasolo, P., & Davis-LaMastro, V. (1990). Perceived organizational support and employee diligence, commitment, and innovation. *Journal of Applied Psychology, 75*(1), 51–59.

Eisenberger, R., Huntington, R., Hutchison, S., & Sowa, D. (1986). Perceived organizational support. *Journal of Applied Psychology, 71*(3), 500–507.

Flamm, M., Fritsch, G., Seer, J., Panisch, S., & Sönnichsen, A. C. (2011). Non-adherence to guidelines for preoperative testing in a secondary care hospital in Austria: The economic impact of unnecessary and double testing. *European Journal of Anaesthesiology, 28*(12), 867–873.

Flanagan, J. C. (1954). The critical incident technique. *Psychological Bulletin, 51*(4), 327.

Franklin, B. D. (2007). Code blue-where to? *AHRQ WebM&M*. Retrieved from <http://www.webmm.ahrq.gov/case.aspx?caseID = 162>.

Gladstein, D. L. (1984). Groups in context: A model of task group effectiveness. *Administrative Science Quarterly, 29*(4), 499–517.

Goldstein, I. L., & Ford, J. K. (2002). *Training in organizations: Needs assessment, development, and evaluation*. Boston, MA: Wadsworth/Thomson Learning.

Gorey, K. M. (2009). Breast cancer survival in Canada and the USA: Meta-analytic evidence of a Canadian advantage in low-income areas. *International Journal of Epidemiology, 38*(6), 1543–1551.

Graber, M. L. (2013). The incidence of diagnostic error in medicine. *British Medical Journal of Quality and Safety, 22*(Suppl 2), ii21–ii27.

Gregory, M. E., Hughes, A. M., Benishek, L. E., Sonesh, S. C., Lazzara, E. H., Woodard, L. D., Salas, E., 2019. Toward the development of the perfect medical team: Critical components for adaptation. *Journal of Patient Safety*. Published ahead of print. Available from: https://doi.org/10.1097/PTS.0000000000000598.

Hackman, J. R. (1987). The design of work teams. In J. Lorsch (Ed.), *Handbook of organizational behavior* (pp. 315–342). Englewood Cliffs, NJ: Prentice Hall.

Hoegl, M., & Parboteeah, K. P. (2007). Creativity in innovative projects: How teamwork matters. *Journal of Engineering and Technology Management, 24*(1–2), 148–166.

Holden, R. J., Carayon, P., Gurses, A. P., Hoonakker, P., Hundt, A. S., Ozok, A. A., & Rivera-Rodriguez, A. J. (2013). SEIPS 2.0: A human factors framework for studying and improving the work of healthcare professionals and patients. *Ergonomics, 56*(11), 1669–1686.

Hollenbeck, J. R., Beersma, B., & Schouten, M. E. (2012). Beyond team types and taxonomies: A dimensional scaling conceptualization for team description. *Academy of Management Review, 37*(1), 82–106.

Hollnagel, E., Woods, D. D., & Leveson, N. (2006). *Resilience engineering: Concepts and precepts*. Burlington, VT: Ashgate Publishing.

Howard, S. K., Gaba, D. M., Fish, K. J., Yang, G., & Sarnquist, F. H. (1992). Anesthesia crisis resource management training: Teaching anesthesiologists to handle critical incidents. *Aviation, Space, and Environmental Medicine, 63*(9), 763–770.

Howe, J. L., Adams, K. T., Hettinger, A. Z., & Ratwani, R. M. (2018). Electronic health record usability issues and potential contribution to patient harm. *JAMA, 319*(12), 1276–1278.

Howes, J. C., Cropanzano, R., Grandey, A. A., & Mohler, C. J. (2000). Who is supporting whom? Quality team effectiveness and perceived organizational support. *Journal of Quality Management, 5*(2), 207–223.

Hughes, A. M., Gregory, M. E., Joseph, D. L., Sonesh, S. C., Marlow, S. L., Lacerenza, C. N., ... Salas, E. (2016). Saving lives: A meta-analysis of team training in healthcare. *Journal of Applied Psychology, 101*(9), 1266–1304.

Hysong, S. J., Amspoker, A. B., Hughes, A. M., Woodard, L., Oswald, F. L., Petersen, L. A., & Lester, H. F. (2019). Impact of team configuration and team stability on primary care quality. *Implementation Science, 14*(1), 22.

Ilgen, D. R., Hollenbeck, J. R., Johnson, M., & Jundt, D. (2005). Teams in organizations: From input-process-output models to IMOI models. *Annual Review of Psychology, 56*, 517–543.

Joint Commission. (2014). Specifications manual for national hospital inpatient quality measures. *Version, 3*, 135–136.

Keebler, J. R., Lazzara, E. H., Patzer, B. S., Palmer, E. M., Plummer, J. P., Smith, D. C., & Riss, R. (2016). Meta-analyses of the effects of standardized handoff protocols on patient, provider, and organizational outcomes. *Human Factors, 58*(8), 1187–1205.

Kohn, L., Corrigan, J., & Donaldson, M. (1999). *To err is human. Committee on quality of health care in America*. Washington, DC: Institute of Medicine.

Kolodny, A., Courtwright, D. T., Hwang, C. S., Kreiner, P., Eadie, J. L., Clark, T. W., & Alexander, G. C. (2015). The prescription opioid and heroin crisis: A public health approach to an epidemic of addiction. *Annual Review of Public Health, 36*, 559–574.

Kwok, J., & Jones, B. (2005). Unnecessary repeat requesting of tests: An audit in a government hospital immunology laboratory. *Journal of Clinical Pathology, 58*(5), 457–462.

Leonard, M., Graham, S., & Bonacum, D. (2004). The human factor: The critical importance of effective teamwork and communication in providing safe care. *British Medical Journal Quality & Safety, 13*(suppl 1), i85–i90.

LePine, J. A., Piccolo, R. F., Jackson, C. L., Mathieu, J. E., & Saul, J. R. (2008). A meta-analysis of teamwork processes: Tests of a multidimensional model and relationships with team effectiveness criteria. *Personnel Psychology, 61*(2), 273–307.

Lyson, H. C., Ackerman, S., Lyles, C., Schillinger, D., Williams, P., Gourley, G., ... Sarkar, U. (2019). Redesigning primary care in the safety net: A qualitative analysis of team-based care implementation. *Healthcare, 7*(1), 22–29.

Manser, T. (2009). Teamwork and patient safety in dynamic domains of healthcare: A review of the literature. *Acta Anaesthesiologica Scandinavica, 53*, 143–151. Available from https://doi.org/10.1111/j.1399-6576.2008.01717.x.

Marks, M. A., Mathieu, J. E., & Zaccaro, S. J. (2001). A temporally based framework and taxonomy of team processes. *Academy of Management Review, 26*(3), 356–376.

Marlow, S. L., Hughes, A. M., Sonesh, S. C., Gregory, M. E., Lacerenza, C. N., Benishek, L. E., ... Salas, E. (2017). A comprehensive review of team training in healthcare: Ten questions. *Journal of the Joint Commission, 43*(4), 197–204.

Mathieu, J. E., & Zajac, D. M. (1990). A review and meta-analysis of the antecedents, correlates, and consequences of organizational commitment. *Psychological Bulletin, 108*(2), 171.

McDonald, S. (2007). Management of the third stage of labor. *The Journal of Midwifery & Women's Health, 52*(3), 254–261.

McGrath, J. E. (1964). Toward a "theory of method" for research on organizations. In W. W. Cooper (Ed.), *New perspectives in organization research.* New York: Wiley.

Moreland, R. L., Argote, L., & Krishnan, R. (1996). Socially shared cognition at work: Transactive memory and group performance. In J. L. Nye, & A. M. Brower (Eds.), *What's social about social cognition? Research on socially shared cognition in small groups* (pp. 57–84). Thousand Oaks, CA: Sage Publications, Inc.

Morgeson, F. P., DeRue, D. S., & Karam, E. P. (2010). Leadership in teams: A functional approach to understanding leadership structures and processes. *Journal of Management, 36* (1), 5–39.

Mowday, R. T., Porter, L. W., & Steers, R. M. (1982). *Employee-organization linkage. The psychology of commitment absenteeism, and turn over.* London; Norwood, NJ.: Academic Press Inc.; Ablex Publishing.

Neily, J., Mills, P. D., Young-Xu, Y., Carney, B. T., West, P., Berger, D. H., ... Bagian, J. P. (2010). Association between implementation of a medical team training program and surgical mortality. *Journal of the American Medical Association, 304*(15), 1693–1700.

Palmer, G., Abernathy, J. H., Swinton, G., Allison, D., Greenstein, J., Shappell, S., & Reeves, S. T. (2013). Realizing improved patient care through human-centered operating room design and human factors methodology for observing flow disruptions in the cardiothoracic operating room. *The Journal of the American Society of Anesthesiologists, 119*(5), 1066–1077.

Patterson, P. D., Weaver, M. D., Landsittel, D., Krackhardt, D., Hostler, D., Vena, J., ... Yealy, D. M. (2016). Association between Emergency Medical Services co-worker familiarity and workplace injury. *Journal of Emergency Medicine, 33*(4), 280–285.

Pearce, C. L., & Herbik, P. A. (2004). Citizenship behavior at the team level of analysis: The effects of team leadership, team commitment, perceived team support, and team size. *The Journal of Social Psychology, 144*(3), 293–310.

Russ, A. L., Fairbanks, R. J., Karsh, B. T., Militello, L. G., Saleem, J. J., & Wears, R. L. (2013). The science of human factors: Separating fact from fiction. *British Medical Journal of Quality and Safety, 22*(10), 802–808.

Salas, E., DiazGranados, D., Klein, C., Burke, C. S., Stagl, K. C., Goodwin, G. F., & Halpin, S. M. (2008). Does team training improve team performance? A meta-analysis. *Human Factors, 50*(6), 903–933.

Salas, E., Rosen, M. A., Burke, C. S., & Goodwin, G. F. (2009). The wisdom of collectives in organizations: An update of the teamwork competencies. In E. Salas, G. F. Goodwin, & C. S. Burke (Eds.), *Team effectiveness in complex organizations: Cross-disciplinary perspectives and approaches* (pp. 39–79). New York: Taylor & Francis Group.

Salas, E., Shuffler, M. L., Thayer, A. L., Bedwell, W. L., & Lazzara, E. H. (2015). Understanding and improving teamwork in organizations: A scientifically based practical guide. *Human Resource Management, 54*(4), 599–622.

Salas, E., Sims, D. E., & Burke, C. S. (2005). Is there a "big five" in teamwork? *Small Group Research, 36*(5), 555–599.

Shuffler, M. L., DiazGranados, D., & Salas, E. (2011). There's a science for that: Team development interventions in organizations. *Current Directions in Psychological Science, 20*(6), 365–372.

Smith, L. (2005). One Dose, Fifty Pills. *AHRQ WebM&M*. Retrieved from <http://www.webmm.ahrq.gov/case.aspx?caseID = 109>.

Smith, M. W., Hughes, A. M., Brown, C., Russo, E., Giardina, T. D., Mehta, P., & Singh, H. (2018). Test results management and distributed cognition in electronic health record−enabled primary care. *Health Informatics Journal*. Available from https://doi.org/1460458218779114.

Sundstrom, E., DeMeuse, K. P., & Futrell, D. (1990). Work teams: Applications and effectiveness. *American Psychologist., 45*, 120–133.

Tan, W. S., Khetrapal, P., Tan, W. P., Rodney, S., Chau, M., & Kelly, J. D. (2016). Robotic assisted radical cystectomy with extracorporeal urinary diversion does not show a benefit over open radical cystectomy: A systematic review and meta-analysis of randomised controlled trials. *PLoS One, 11*(11), e0166221.

The Office of the National Coordinator for Health Information Technology. (2018). *Strategy on reducing regulatory and administrative burden relating to the use of Health IT and EHRs: Draft for public comment*. Retrieved from <https://www.healthit.gov/sites/default/files/webform/reducing_burden_report/draft-strategy-on-reducing-regulatory-and-administrative-burden-relating---rkb-comments.pdf>.

Weinberg, L., Rao, S., & Escobar, P. F. (2011). Robotic surgery in gynecology: An updated systematic review. *Obstetrics and Gynecology International*. Available from https://doi.org/10.1155/2011/852061.

Wiegmann, D. A., ElBardissi, A. W., Dearani, J. A., Daly, R. C., & Sundt, T. M., III (2007). Disruptions in surgical flow and their relationship to surgical errors: An exploratory investigation. *Surgery, 142*(5), 658–665.

Wildman, J. L., Thayer, A. L., Rosen, M. A., Salas, E., Mathieu, J. E., & Rayne, S. R. (2012). Task types and team-level attributes: Synthesis of team classification literature. *Human Resource Development Review, 11*(1), 97–129.

Wilson, J. R. (2013). Fundamentals of systems ergonomics/human factors. *Applied Ergonomics, 45*(1), 5–13.

Zwaan, L., Thijs, A., Wagner, C., van der Wal, G., & Timmermans, D. R. (2009). Design of a study on suboptimal cognitive acts in the diagnostic process, the effect on patient outcomes and the influence of workload, fatigue and experience of physician. *BMC Health Services Research, 9*(1), 65.

Further reading

Agency for Healthcare Research and Quality. (n.d.). *QI toolkit*. Retrieved from: <https://www.ahrq.gov/professionals/systems/hospital/qitoolkit/index.html> Accessed 08.14.18.

Agency for Healthcare Research and Quality. (n.d.). *Quality indicators*. Retrieved from: <http://www.qualityindicators.ahrq.gov/> Accessed 08.14.18.

Aligning, Improving Key Measures Net Texas Healthcare Organization Baldrige Honor. (n.d.). Retrieved from: <http://asq.org/knowledge-center/case-studies-aligning-key-measures-st-davids-baldrige.html> Accessed 08.14.18.

Carayon, P., Hundt, A. S., Karsh, B. T., Gurses, A. P., Alvarado, C. J., Smith, M., & Brennan, P. F. (2006). Work system design for patient safety: The SEIPS model. *BMJ Quality & Safety, 15*(suppl 1), i50–i58.

Cromwell, S. E., & Kolb, J. A. (2004). An examination of work-environment support factors affecting transfer of supervisory skills training to the workplace. *Human Resource Development Quarterly, 15*(4), 449–471.

Edmondson, A. (1999). Psychological safety and learning behavior in work teams. *Administrative Science Quarterly, 44*(2), 350–383.

Gaba, D. M., Howard, S. K., & Small, S. D. (1995). Situation awareness in anesthesiology. *Human Factors, 37*(1), 20–31.

Glucose Roller Coaster. (n.d.) Retrieved from: <http://www.ihi.org/education/IHIOpenSchool/resources/Pages/Activities/AHRQCaseStudyGlucoseRollerCoaster.aspx> Accessed 08.14.18.

HealthGrades 2011 Healthcare Consumerism and Hospital Quality in America Report. (2011). Retrieved from: <http://hg-article-center.s3-website-us-east-1.amazonaws.com/7b/de/dc25d2c94d25ad88c9e1688c9adc/HealthcareConsumerismHospitalQualityReport2011.pdf> Accessed 08.14.18.

Kirkpatrick, D. L. (1976). Evaluation of training. In R. L. Craig (Ed.), *Training and development handbook: A guide to human resource development.* New York: McGraw Hill.

Kirkpatrick, D. L. (1994). *Evaluating training programs: The four levels.* San Francisco, CA: Berrett-Koehler.

Kozlowski, S. W., & Ilgen, D. R. (2006). Enhancing the effectiveness of work groups and teams. *Psychological Science in the Public Interest, 7*(3), 77–124.

Lim, D. H., & Morris, M. L. (2006). Influence of trainee characteristics, instructional satisfaction, and organizational climate on perceived learning and training transfer. *Human Resource Development Quarterly, 17*(1), 85–115.

Reason, J. (2000). Human error: Models and management. *British Medical Journal, 320*(7237), 768–770.

Salas, E., Tannenbaum, S. I., Kraiger, K., & Smith-Jentsch, K. A. (2012). The science of training and development in organizations: What matters in practice. *Psychological Science in the Public Interest, 13*(2), 74–101.

Vincent, C., Taylor-Adams, S., & Stanhope, N. (1998). Framework for analysing risk and safety in clinical medicine. *British Medical Journal, 316*(7138), 1154.

Chapter 11

Design for stress, fatigue, and workload management

Joseph K. Nuamah and Ranjana K. Mehta
Industrial & Systems Engineering, Texas A&M University, College Station, TX, United States

Introduction

Improving the quality of working life for healthcare workers and the quality and safety of patients remains one of the most challenging issues in health care. Meeting these challenges requires in-depth understanding of the mismatch between the various work stressors and individual capabilities that could lead to increased workload, stress, burnout, and fatigue in healthcare workers. Under overloaded conditions, healthcare workers are vulnerable to making errors that adversely impact patient safety. For example, each year, approximately 1.3 million patients are injured because of errors during their hospitalization (Leape, 2018), and more than 100,000 deaths due to preventable adverse events occur (Institute of Medicine, 2000). Evidence suggests that worker states of intensified workload, fatigue, and stress may contribute to the human error component of these medical errors (Krueger, 2018).

In order to design or recommend solutions and technologies to manage these critical challenges, it is first imperative that we understand the various causes and consequences of operator states of workload, stress, and fatigue in healthcare workers. In order to provide our assessment of current trends in operator states, a scoping review was conducted on physicians/surgeons, nurses, and home caregivers. This chapter provides a short overview of current definitions of workload, stress, and fatigue, etiology and theoretical foundations, and measurement and management techniques in healthcare application, with these specific populations of healthcare workers in mind. Design guidelines are presented followed by their potential applications in a relevant healthcare case study.

Workload

Workload reflects the margin between the amount of physical and/or cognitive effort required to complete a task and the resources (e.g., time) available

Design for Health. DOI: https://doi.org/10.1016/B978-0-12-816427-3.00011-7

201

to use for that task (Rosen et al., 2018), and can be viewed as a ratio of demand to available resources (Xie & Salvendy, 2000).

Nurses

Traditionally, the definition of nursing workload has been associated with nurse-to-patient ratios (Pearson et al., 2006; Unruh & Fottler, 2006). However, nurse-to-patient ratios may not be a good representation of workload (Carayon & Alvarado, 2007) as there are other levels at which demand and resources interact to produce workload (Holden et al., 2011). *We define nursing workload as the physical and/or cognitive requirements associated with carrying out nursing activities.* Upenieks, Kotlerman, Akhavan, Esser, and Ngo (2007) categorized nursing activities into those that directly benefit the patient (e.g., wound management and giving medications), activities that are necessary but do not directly benefit the patient (e.g., administrative paper work and chart documentation), and activities that are neither necessary nor benefit the patient (e.g., personal break and waiting delay). Holden et al. (2011) conceptualized a three-level framework of nursing workload based in human factors: unit-level (tasks requiring a group of nurses during a specific shift—nurse-to-patient staffing ratios), job-level (general amount of work to be done, difficulty of the work, and amount of concentration or attention required), and task-level (demands and resources for a specific nursing task, e.g., medication administration). Task-level is embedded in job-level, which in turn is embedded in unit-level workload.

Carayon and Alvarado (2007) described various dimensions of nursing workload including amount of physical work (physical workload), information overload (cognitive workload), dealing with emotional issues such as patient death and family demands (emotional workload), and changes in workload (workload variability). Physical workload relates to patient handling activities (moving, lifting, and bathing patients), working in awkward postures, stooping, and walking to and from another area of a unit or hospital for supplies or equipment needed for a task (Carayon & Alvarado, 2007; Davis & Kotowski, 2015). Cognitive workload relates to processing patient information, clinical reasoning, and decision-making. In addition to interruptions that may disrupt nurses' ability to identify and assess patient needs (Potter et al., 2005), nurses perform planned (e.g., morning reports for assigned patients) and unplanned (e.g., stable patients suddenly becoming unstable) cognitive adjustments across patients throughout an assigned period of care (Carayon & Alvarado, 2007; Kim, Lee, Kim, Park, & Kang, 2018; Potter et al., 2005). Emotional workload, especially on intensive care unit nurses, may arise as a result of patient acuity and severity, end-of-life care, dealing with angry families of patients, and verbal and physical assaults by patients and their families (Carayon & Alvarado, 2007). Workload variability refers to changes in workload during a period of time (e.g., day shift vs night shift, and code situation vs no code situation; Carayon & Alvarado, 2007).

Physicians

Physician workload, defined as "the total number of hours worked per week in the practice by general practitioners per 1000 patients" (Wensing, van den Hombergh, Akkermans, van Doremalen, & Grol, 2006) and patient encounters performed per shift (Michtalik, Yeh, Pronovost, & Brotman, 2013), is associated with relative value units (RVUs) and workflow interruptions (Weigl, Müller, Vincent, Angerer, & Sevdalis, 2012). RVUs are used to quantify the different services that physicians provide (Mitchell, McBride, & Jarocki, 2017). Frequent workflow interruptions have been shown to increase physician workload (Weigl et al., 2012). Oftentimes, physicians perform complex tasks that demand undivided attention. An interruption leads to suspension of the focal task to perform an unplanned task, thereby hindering work performance and causing attention resources to be assigned to the unplanned task (Weigl et al., 2012; Westbrook, Woods, Rob, Dunsmuir, & Day, 2010). Michtalik et al. (2013) developed a model for factors (i.e., physician, hospital, team, and patient) that may affect physician workload (see Fig. 11.1).

Surgeons

Surgeons encounter physical and mental workloads during surgical operations (Park, Lee, Seagull, Meenaghan, & Dexter, 2010; Rieger et al., 2015; Wallston et al., 2014; Zhang et al., 2017). They need to be extremely skillful with their hands and require high levels of mental concentration that can be considered mild-to-moderate physical demands (Szeto et al., 2009). Physical workload results from extended periods of muscle tension and awkward postures (Zhang et al., 2017), ward rounds, surgical meetings, patient consultations, and report writing (Szeto et al., 2009). Meanwhile, mental workload results from high level of mental concentration, introduction of new technologies, new surgical methods (Rieger et al., 2015), and intraoperative disruptions (Blikkendaal et al., 2017; Weigl, Antoniadis, Chiapponi, Bruns, & Sevdalis, 2015; Wilson et al., 2011), defined as "deviations from the natural progression of an operation" (Wiegmann, ElBardissi, Dearani, Daly, & Sundt, 2007).

Caregivers

Caregiver workload may be defined as the activities in which caregivers engage and the responsibilities which they accept in order to promote the physical and mental well-being of their dependents (Pearlin, Mullan, Semple,

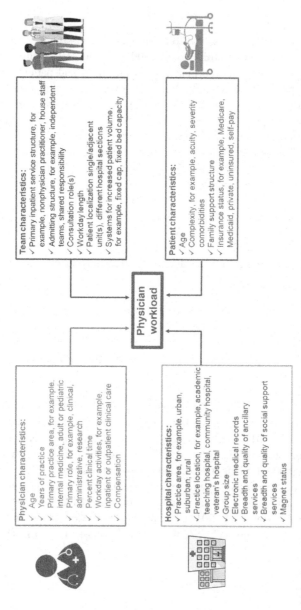

Physician characteristics:
√ Age
√ Years of practice
√ Primary practice area, for example, internal medicine, adult or pediatric
√ Primary role, for example, clinical, administrative, research
√ Percent clinical time
√ Workday activities, for example, inpatient or outpatient clinical care
√ Compensation

Team characteristics:
√ Primary inpatient service structure, for example, nonphysician practitioner, house staff
√ Admitting structure, for example, independent teams, shared responsibility
√ Consultation role(s)
√ Workday length
√ Patient localization single/adjacent unit(s), different hospital sections
√ Systems for increased patient volume, for example, fixed cap, fixed bed capacity

Hospital characteristics:
√ Practice area, for example, urban, suburban, rural
√ Practice location, for example, academic teaching hospital, community hospital, veteran's hospital
√ Group size
√ Electronic medical records
√ Breadth and quality of ancillary services
√ Breadth and quality of social support services
√ Magnet status

Patient characteristics:
√ Age
√ Complexity, for example, acuity, severity comorbidities
√ Family support structure
√ Insurance status, for example, Medicare, Medicaid, private, uninsured, self-pay

Physician workload

FIGURE 11.1 Select factors that affect physician workload. *Adapted from Michtalik, H.J., Yeh, H.-C., Pronovost, P.J., & Brotman, D.J. (2013). Impact of attending physician workload on patient care: A survey of hospitalists. JAMA Internal Medicine, 173(5), 375–377.*

& Skaff, 1990) and is therefore associated with the care receiver's demand for care (van Groenou & De Boer, 2016). Task-oriented demands include activities of daily living (e.g., bathing/showering, dressing, feeding, and functional mobility) and instrumental activities of daily living (e.g., home management, grocery shopping, meal preparation, and community mobility) (Darragh et al., 2015; Llanque, Savage, Rosenburg, & Caserta, 2016). Caregivers' beliefs about the caregiving role and care recipients' functional abilities determine caregiver workload (Friedemann, Newman, Buckwalter, & Montgomery, 2014). Physically demanding caregiving activities include transfers (toilet, in and out of bed, out of/up from chair, wheel chair), falls (picking up from, catching during), bathing, toilet hygiene, stairs, repositioning, dressing, home management, wound care, personal hygiene, and grooming (Darragh et al., 2015).

Workload measurements

Workload may be described in terms of what is required of an individual or in terms of the demand the system places on an individual. It is measured using subjective (self-report or observer-ratings), performance-based, and physiological techniques (Borghini, Astolfi, Vecchiato, Mattia, & Babiloni, 2014; Orlandi & Brooks, 2018). Subjective measures reflect the healthcare worker's perceived workload and include unidimensional scales (e.g., Modified Cooper–Harper Scale and Overall Workload Scale) and multidimensional scales (e.g., NASA-Task Load Index and Subjective Workload Assessment Technique) (Anthony & Biers, 1997; Mansikka, Virtanen, & Harris, 2018). Primary and secondary task performance measures are used to measure workload based on the assumption that humans have limited resources, and performance decreases when tasks that demand the same resource structure are time-shared (Hsu et al., 2018; Yeh & Wickens, 1988). Performance in secondary task can be used to determine if there is any spare mental capacity left. Secondary task measures reflect residual attention or capacity (Kim et al., 2018; Yeh & Wickens, 1988). Physiological approaches to measuring workload include cardiac activity, respiratory, dermal, ocular, and brain activity. Cardiac measures include heart rate, heart rate variability, and blood pressure (Fallahi, Motamedzade, Heidarimoghadam, Soltanian, & Miyake, 2016). Respiratory measures include respiration rate, airflow, and respiration volume (Grassmann, Vlemincx, von Leupoldt, Mittelstädt, & Van den Bergh, 2016; Zhang et al., 2017). Skin conductance level has been shown to increase with increasing workload (Fairclough & Venables, 2006; Miyake et al., 2009). Ocular measures include eye blink rate and pupil diameter (Gao, Wang, Song, Li, & Dong, 2013). Brain activity measures include electroencephalography (EEG) and functional near-infrared spectroscopy (fNIRS; Mazur et al., 2016). Fig. 11.2 describes workload assessment methods.

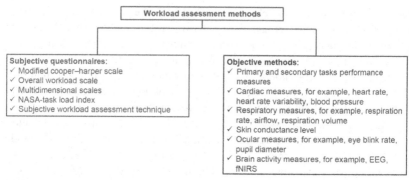

FIGURE 11.2   Workload assessment methods.

Stress

Stress is defined as changes in physical and emotional responses that occur due to conflicts between job demands placed on the employee and the amount of control s/he has over meeting these demands (Karasek, 1979). It relates to a healthcare worker's perception of the demands (stressors) and of his/her capability to meet those demands (McVicar, 2003). Generally, stress is the response of the healthcare worker to physical and/or psychological environmental demands or stressors (Jones et al., 2015; Kavushansky, Ben-Shachar, Richter-Levin, & Klein, 2009). Stress response is mediated by the sympatho−adrenal−medullary (SAM) and the hypothalamo−pituitary−adrenal axes (Jayasinghe et al., 2016). Activation of the SAM axis leads to secretion of adrenaline and noradrenaline and an increase in cardiovascular system activities such as increased heart rate, vascular tone, blood pressure, and breathing frequency (De Kloet, Joëls, & Holsboer, 2005). Stress causes the hypothalamus to release the corticotropin-releasing hormone (CRH) into the bloodstream. CRH acts on the pituitary gland, causing it to secrete a substance called adrenocorticotropic hormone (ACTH). ACTH binds to the adrenal cortex, the outer layer of the adrenal glands, and stimulates them to secrete cortisol (Chrousos, 2009; Ulrich-Lai & Herman, 2009).

A distinct adverse psychological condition that healthcare workers experience is burnout. Prolonged high stress results in burnout, a cumulative negative reaction to continuous occupational stressors relating to the mismatch between nurses and their designated jobs (Maslach, 2003), which in turn affects job satisfaction, performance, and quality of care (Guo et al., 2018; Portoghese, Galletta, Coppola, Finco, & Campagna, 2014).

Nurses

Major stressors that impact work satisfaction for staff nurses include workload (McGowan, 2001), relation with other clinical staff (Bahadori et al.,

2014), leadership and management style (Bahadori et al., 2014), coping with emotional need of patients and their families (Espinosa, Young, Symes, Haile, & Walsh, 2010; McVicar, 2003), shift working (Dehais et al., 2018), and lack of compensation (McGowan, 2001).

Physicians

Workplace factors that increase stress in physicians include excessive workload (Virtanen et al., 2008; West, Dyrbye, & Shanafelt, 2018), long work hours (Martin, 2002), delayed gratification (Dimou, Eckelbarger, & Riall, 2016), sleep deprivation, and work conflicts (Richter, Kostova, Baur, & Wegner, 2014). Stress has been found to contribute to physician burnout (Dimou et al., 2016; West et al., 2018), which leads to lower care quality (Dewa, Loong, Bonato, & Trojanowski, 2017), medical errors (Fahrenkopf et al., 2008), lower patient satisfaction (Shanafelt et al., 2009), reduced physician productivity (Dewa et al., 2017), increased physician turnover (Dyrbye et al., 2013), physician depression, and suicidal ideation (Stehman, Testo, Gershaw, & Kellogg, 2019).

Surgeons

Surgery is a stressful task (Arora et al., 2009). Stressors for surgeons include increased workload (Rieger et al., 2015), time pressures (Wetzel et al., 2006), distractions (Blikkendaal et al., 2017), and intraoperative stressors (Arora et al., 2009). Intraoperative stressors include emergency cases, surgical complications (e.g., surgical error and unexpected bleeding), advanced tasks (e.g., complex procedure and multitasking), equipment problems (e.g., missing equipment, equipment failure, and unfamiliar equipment), team work problems (e.g., incompetent staff, inexperienced staff, and language problems), distractions (e.g., bleeps, phone calls, and talking noises), and personal factors (e.g., physical discomfort, tiredness, and hunger; Arora et al., 2009).

Caregivers

Stress may be defined as the relationship between the person and the environment, which the person appraises as taxing or exceeding his or her resources (Lazarus & Folkman, 1987, p. 21). We define caregiver stress as "a response to financial, physical, and/or psychological demands and relationship challenges associated with caregiving." Caregiving stress can lead to burnout, which in turn results in compassion fatigue—disengagement of caregivers from their patients (Burtson & Stichler, 2010; Coetzee & Laschinger, 2018).

Stress measurements

Subjective questionnaires used to measure stress include Nursing Stress Scale (Gray-Toft & Anderson, 1981), Nurse Stress Checklist (Benoliel, McCorkle, Georgiadou, Denton, & Spitzer, 1990), Nurse Stress Index (Harris, 1989), Daily Stress Inventory (Brantley, Waggoner, Jones, & Rappaport, 1987), Positive Affect and Negative Affect Schedule (Watson, Clark, & Tellegen, 1988), Perceived Stress Scale (Cohen, Kamarck, & Mermelstein, 1983), Maslach Burnout Inventory (Maslach, Jackson, Leiter, Schaufeli, & Schwab, 1986), Effort–Reward Imbalance Questionnaire (Siegrist et al., 2004), and Trier Social Stress Test (Kirschbaum, Pirke, & Hellhammer, 1993). Objective methods for assessing stress include heart rate and heart rate variability (Jones et al., 2015; Rieger et al., 2015), electrodermal activity (Betti et al., 2018; Posada-Quintero, Florian, Orjuela-Cañón, & Chon, 2018), salivary cortisol (Arora et al., 2009; Bedini et al., 2017), EEG (Betti et al., 2018), and fNIRS (Al-Shargie et al., 2016; Rosenbaum et al., 2018). Fig. 11.3 describes stress assessment methods.

Fatigue

Fatigue is multidimensional (e.g., physical and mental) and multilevel (e.g., acute, chronic, passive, and active), with several definitions in the healthcare literature (Aaronson, Pallikkathayil, & Crighton, 2003; Barker & Nussbaum, 2011; Desmond & Hancock, 2001; Hancock & Verwey, 1997; Shen, Barbera, & Shapiro, 2006). We choose the definition of fatigue from Barker and Nussbaum (2011, p. 816) as a "multi-causal, multidimensional, non-specific and subjective phenomenon, which results from prolonged activity and psychological, socioeconomic and environmental factors that affect both the mind and the body." In general, fatigue is a complex state characterized by a lack of alertness and reduced mental and physical performance.

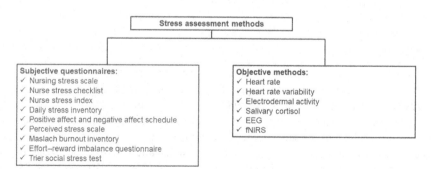

FIGURE 11.3   Stress assessment methods.

Nurses

There is no unified, tailored definition of nurse fatigue in the nursing literature. Whereas some prior studies (e.g., Barker Steege & Nussbaum, 2013; Barker & Nussbaum, 2011; Coetzee & Klopper, 2010) have categorized nurse fatigue into multiple dimensions such as physical fatigue, mental fatigue, total fatigue, emotional fatigue, and compassion fatigue, others (e.g., Barker & Pasupathy, 2010; Trinkoff et al., 2011) have described nurse fatigue in terms of acute and chronic fatigue states. Factors that contribute to physical and mental fatigue in nurses include work content demands (e.g., physical, mental, and time/multiple task demands), practice environment (e.g., psychosocial factors, physical environment, work organization, and technology), nurse capacity (physical, mental, and emotional), and patient/family factors (Steege, Drake, Olivas, & Mazza, 2015).

Physicians and caregivers

Physician fatigue relates to the physical and mental exhaustion generated by time-on-duty. Fatigue has been associated with impaired physician performance, negative physician health outcomes, and increased patient risk (Gates et al., 2018; Govindarajan et al., 2015). We define caregiver fatigue as "a state that arises as a result of prolonged exposure to task-oriented demands and stressors that may inhibit with the caregiver's cognitive and physical abilities to carry out caregiving tasks."

Fatigue measurements

Subjective fatigue assessment questionnaires include the Fatigue Questionnaire (Pawlikowska et al., 1994), Fatigue Impact Scale (Fisk et al., 1994), Fatigue Severity Scale (Krupp, LaRocca, Muir-Nash, & Steinberg, 1989), Fatigue Assessment Scale (Michielsen, De Vries, Van Heck, Van de Vijver, & Sijtsma, 2004), Short Form-36 Vitality Subscale of the Short Form Health Survey (Ware & Sherbourne, 1992), and Visual Analogue Scale for Fatigue (Lee, Hicks, & Nino-Murcia, 1991). Performance-based measures of fatigue include psychomotor vigilance task (Dinges & Powell, 1985) and prescribing errors (Westbrook, Raban, Walter, & Douglas, 2018). Physiological measures of fatigue include heart rate and heart rate variability (Heemskerk et al., 2014; Holdsworth & Evens, 2017; Oriyama, Miyakoshi, & Kobayashi, 2013), electrooculogram (Diaz-Piedra et al., 2016; Hirvonen et al., 2010), EEG (Guru et al., 2015; Kahol, Smith, Brandenberger, Ashby, & Ferrara, 2011), and fNIRS (Singh et al., 2018). Subjective and objective methods exist to assess fatigue. Fig. 11.4 describes some of these fatigue assessment methods.

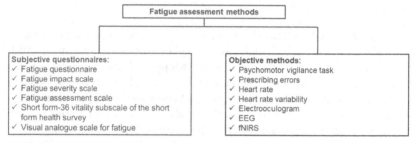

FIGURE 11.4   Fatigue assessment methods.

Recommendations for workload, stress, and fatigue management

Workload and fatigue management

Here, we seek to balance required resources with available resources and to emphasize sufficient rest and recovery post work shifts. In this section, we will discuss staffing, shift work, patient handling, and electronic health records (EHRs) as they relate to workload management.

- To deliver good-quality service to patients, there must be a good balance between patient needs and nursing and/or physician staff size and expertise. When the workplace is understaffed, workload can be reduced by providing technical support, improving communication, and enhancing workplace ergonomics.
- Enhanced patient interactions, job trainings, and periodic performance feedbacks can help healthcare workers to manage high workload.
- Fatigue resulting from shift work affects worker selective attention and vigilance; therefore, tasks, tools, and trainings should be designed to compensate for compromised capabilities.
- Shift pattern (e.g., day, night, and rotating), shift length, and number of consecutive days at work should be considered when designing shift work for healthcare workers.
- Low back pain etiology involves both physical and psychosocial risk factors. Healthcare workers, especially nurses, are exposed to patient manual handling, which leads to loads on the lumbar spine (Kurowski, Buchholz, ProCare Research Team, & Punnett, 2014). Strategies for better designs of patient transport and handling require considerations of the healthcare workers' psychosocial exposures. Improved techniques, trainings, and ergonomically designed patient transport equipment can facilitate safe patient handling.
- Clinicians experience increased workload when they work in the EHRs (Arndt et al., 2017). Designers of EHR platforms should seek healthcare workers' insights to improve usefulness, learnability, and usability. Better designs have the potential to reduce cognitive load.

Stress management

Stress management, whether at the individual or organization level, seeks to remove sources of stress, reduce the severity and duration of stress once it has occurred (Holman, Johnson, & O'Connor, 2018). It rehabilitates or maximizes the functioning for healthcare workers experiencing or suffering ill-health due to stress (Holman et al., 2018).

- At the organizational level, work redesign (e.g., distribution of work and role, and workflow optimization), changes in working time and schedules, change in management style (e.g., more participation in making decisions and more recognition for good job performance), and management training (e.g., mentoring) may be implemented to remove the causes of stress at the workplace (Anger et al., 2015).
- Peer support groups that enable healthcare workers to discuss the difficulties they face and training in communication skills and conflict management can reduce the severity and/or duration of stress itself.
- Vocational rehabilitation or, in the worst case, outplacement services may be offered for healthcare workers who are already experiencing or suffering ill-health due to stress.
- Techniques available to equip healthcare workers to manage stress at the individual level include relaxation, cognitive behavioral therapy, mindfulness training, and coping skills training. Relaxation techniques counter stress directly through muscle, breathing, and mental (meditation) relaxation exercises. Cognitive behavioral therapy encourages healthcare workers to develop new behavioral responses to stressful events, so they can respond to them in a more effective way. Mindfulness training seeks to promote a state of attention centered on the present moment, thus fostering response-focused emotion regulation strategies (Kuyken et al., 2010).

Heuristics to design for workload, stress, and fatigue

Reducing workload, stress, and fatigue is the shared responsibility of individual healthcare professionals and healthcare organizations (Dyrbye, Johnson, Johnson, Satele, & Shanafelt, 2018; Dyrbye et al., 2018; Shanafelt & Noseworthy, 2017). In Table 11.1, we present a set of rules and advices about good design solutions based on theory and practical experiences. They have been categorized into organizational design, healthcare tool/technology design, task design, and environmental design. It is essential that issues of workload, stress, and fatigue are first acknowledged, after which they can be assessed using a combination of subjective and objective measures. Results should be benchmarked with national benchmark data.

TABLE 11.1 Design heuristics to address workload, stress, and fatigue challenges in health care.

Category	Design heuristic
Organizational design	Provide opportunities for professional development and involvement in leadership
	Acknowledge and/or reward staff for accomplishments
	Make use of adequate health professionals
	Provide development and education opportunities to build capacity and enhance professional competencies
	Implement team huddles to promote team work and communication (Provost, Lanham, Leykum, McDaniel, & Pugh, 2015)
	Encourage engagement and open communication
	Make wellness a priority. Emphasize and promote wellness of healthcare professionals. Incorporate wellness initiatives at the workplace
	Organize mindfulness training and stress management workshops
	Promote self-awareness and reflection so that healthcare professional can identify what they value and connect with what is most meaningful in their work (Shanafelt, 2009)
	Explore strategic napping as part of a comprehensive strategy aimed at decreasing fatigue in shift workers (Ruggiero, Redeker, Fiedler, Avi-Itzhak, & Fischetti, 2012)
	Ensure appropriate mix of professional staff (efficient team structure)
Job design	Allow for more job control and flexibility, for example, provide flexible scheduling choices and part-time work options
	Assign work reasonably such that health professionals are not functioning beyond individual productivity capacity
	Match work to the talents and interests of individuals
	Focus on improving efficiency and reducing clerical burden. Use EHR event logs to identify areas of EHR-related work that could be delegated (Arndt et al., 2017)
	Ensure balance between patient needs and caregiver staff size and expertise
	Reduce unnecessary workflow interruptions and distractions to allow healthcare professionals to efficiently and effectively manage their work (Weigl et al., 2012)
	Explore strategic napping as part of a comprehensive strategy aimed at decreasing fatigue in shift workers (Ruggiero et al., 2012)

(Continued)

TABLE 11.1 (Continued)

Category	Design heuristic
Healthcare tool/ technology design	Provide appropriate tools (e.g., checklists), equipment, and technology (e.g., EHR, appointment system, and ordering systems) to carry out work
	Focus on improving efficiency and reducing clerical burden. Use EHR event logs to identify areas of EHR-related work that could be delegated (Arndt et al., 2017)
	Clinicians use task switching and multitasking to handle workload demands (Walter, Li, Dunsmuir, & Westbrook, 2014). Use multimodal displays to support time-sharing and attention management
Environmental design	Noise-induced stress is associated with higher levels of fatigue and burnout (Chaudhury, Chaudhury, & Mahmood, 2007). Reduce sources of noise
	Physical layout of workstations affects workload (Chaudhury et al., 2007). Workstations should be ergonomically designed. Furniture and equipment should be suitable, available, and well maintained
	Ensure adequate ventilation and its maintenance (Zimring, Joseph, & Choudhary, 2004)

EHR, Electronic health record.

Case study

We present a case study, obtained from the Institute for Healthcare Improvement (n.d.), that described how burnout impacted a healthcare worker's responses and job performances, resulting in a potentially adverse medical event that jeopardized patient safety. We chose this specific case study as it targets collective challenges on workload, stress, and fatigue. Fig. 11.5 describes the persona used in the case study and the description of the case. Fig. 11.6 provides the collective causes of Ana's burnout that potentially impacted her psychological health and cognitive performance.

Table 11.2 provides specific recommendations for work task (re)design and stress management—both self and company initiated.

Advances in workload, stress, fatigue monitoring, and management

Advances in wearable sensors, information and communication technologies, and artificial intelligence, have allowed for the ability to passively and

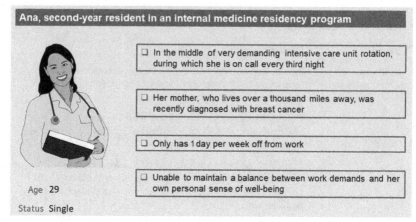

Ana, second-year resident in an internal medicine residency program

☐ In the middle of very demanding intensive care unit rotation, during which she is on call every third night

☐ Her mother, who lives over a thousand miles away, was recently diagnosed with breast cancer

☐ Only has 1 day per week off from work

☐ Unable to maintain a balance between work demands and her own personal sense of well-being

Age 29

Status Single

FIGURE 11.5   Ana's persona. *Adapted from the* Institute for Healthcare Improvement. Dealing with burnout. *(n.d.).   Available   from   <http://www.ihi.org:80/education/IHIOpenSchool/ resources/Pages/CaseStudies/DealingWithBurnout.aspx> Retrieved 09.04.19.*

noninvasively acquire, transmit, and process health data (Andreu-Perez, Leff, Ip, & Yang, 2015; Fallahzadeh, Ma, & Ghasemzadeh, 2017). This has shown promise in remote patient monitoring (RPM) and mobile medical diagnostic devices. RPM—the use of wearable devices to acquire and transmit health-related data for patient self-monitoring and/or clinician assessment (Noah et al., 2018)—has enabled traditional health monitoring to move beyond conventional clinical settings, thereby breaking temporal and geographic barriers (see Fig. 11.7). Disease states that have been monitored include acute coronary syndrome with wireless electrocardiography (ECG; Lee et al., 2013); cardiac arrhythmia using internet-based ECG monitoring device (Tan, Ho, Ching, & Teo, 2010); chronic obstructive pulmonary disease (COPD) using pulse oximeter and a wrist band that measured heart rate, physical activity, and temperature (Pedone, Chiurco, Scarlata, & Incalzi, 2013); stroke using accelerometer with feedback from data (Dorsch, Thomas, Xu, Kaiser, & Dobkin, 2015); obesity using a multisensor device worn on upper arm (Jakicic et al., 2016); chronic back pain using motion-sensor movement device with feedback (Kent, Laird, & Haines, 2015); and asthma using spirometer with mobile application (Ryan et al., 2012).

Patient-focused mobile diagnostic devices use noninvasive sensors to collect patient data. They synthesize the data with artificial intelligence−based diagnostic engines to make quick and accurate assessments. Recently, Final Frontier Medical Devices (Paoli, PA) won the Qualcom Tricorder XPRICE with DxtER, a mobile diagnostic device that weighs less than five pounds and can interpret a set of 13 health conditions and continuously monitor five vital health metrics: blood pressure, heart rate variability, respiratory rate,

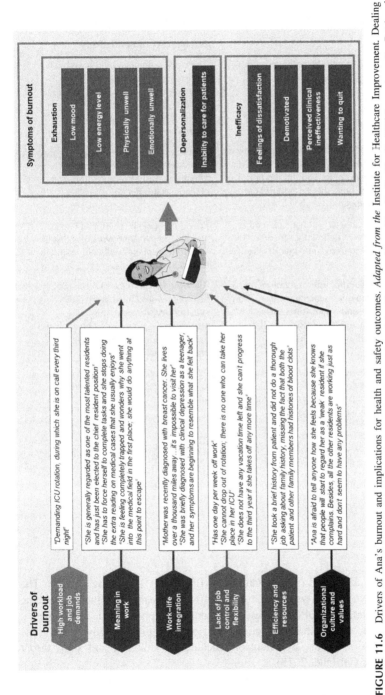

Drivers of burnout

High workload and job demands
"Demanding ICU rotation, during which she is on call every third night"

Meaning in work
"She is generally regarded as one of the most talented residents and has just been elected to the chief resident position"
"She has to force herself to complete tasks and she stops doing the extra reading on medical cases that she usually enjoys"
"She is feeling completely trapped and wonders why she went into the medical field in the first place; she would do anything at this point to escape"

Work–life integration
"Mother was recently diagnosed with breast cancer. She lives over a thousand miles away…it's impossible to visit her"
"She was briefly diagnosed with clinical depression as a teenager, and her symptoms are beginning to resemble what she felt back"

Lack of job control and flexibility
"Has one day per week off work"
"She cannot drop out of rotation; there is no one who can take her place in her ICU"
"She does not have any vacation time left and she can't progress to the third year if she takes off any more time"

Efficiency and resources
"She took a brief history from patient and did not do a thorough job asking about family history, missing the fact that both the patient and other family members had histories of blood clots"

Organizational culture and values
"Ana is afraid to tell anyone how she feels because she knows that people will start to regard her as a 'weak' resident if she complains. Besides, all the other residents are working just as hard and don't seem to have any problems"

Symptoms of burnout

Exhaustion
Low mood
Low energy level
Physically unwell
Emotionally unwell

Depersonalization
Inability to care for patients

Inefficacy
Feelings of dissatisfaction
Demotivated
Perceived clinical ineffectiveness
Wanting to quit

FIGURE 11.6 Drivers of Ana's burnout and implications for health and safety outcomes. *Adapted from the* Institute for Healthcare Improvement. Dealing with burnout. *(n.d.). Available from* <http://www.ihi.org:80/education/IHIOpenSchool/resources/Pages/CaseStudies/DealingWithBurnout.aspx> *Retrieved 09.04.19.*

TABLE 11.2 Design recommendations to mitigate drivers of burnout.

Cause(s)	Design recommendations
Ana worked in an inherently stressful environment typical of ICUs	The work schedule could have been redesigned to promote breaks, decreasing fatigue. Planned napping could be used as part of a comprehensive strategy aimed at decreasing fatigue among healthcare professional working shift work
She was demotivated, lost purpose in the work she was doing, and did not find it fulfilling. In short, she did not find her work meaningful	Mindfulness training may help increase attention, awareness, intention, and promote self-reflection
Ana was unable to visit her sick mother because of very tight work schedule, resulting in an unbalanced work–life integration	Providing flexible scheduling choices and having part-time work and flexible scheduling policies will help maintain this balance
She could not drop out of rotation, and there was no one to take her place. Even if she had found a substitute, she still could not take time off since she had exhausted all her vacation time	Allowing for more job control and flexibility would have averted this situation. While ideal, this recommendation needs to be analyzed based on trade-offs associated with organizational resources
Ana failed to ask the patient about family history. This error could be either a slip (caused by lapses in concentration and/or fatigue) or a mistake (caused by insufficient training)	By standardizing the list of steps to be followed, checklists can be used to minimize the risk of slips
Ana was unwilling to ask for time off or talk to the other residents. This reflects the workplace culture, which seemed to value self-denial and self-sacrifice	The workplace lacked wellness initiatives. There is the need to incorporate wellness initiatives in the medical residency program

ICU, Intensive care unit.

body temperature, and oxygen saturation (Basil Leaf Technologies, n.d.). The 13 health conditions were made up of 10 core health conditions—anemia, atrial fibrillation, COPD, diabetes, leukocytosis, pneumonia, otitis media, sleep apnea, urinary tract infection—and at least three elective conditions including HIV screen, hypertension, melanoma, shingles, and strep throat (Gartland & Gartland, 2018).

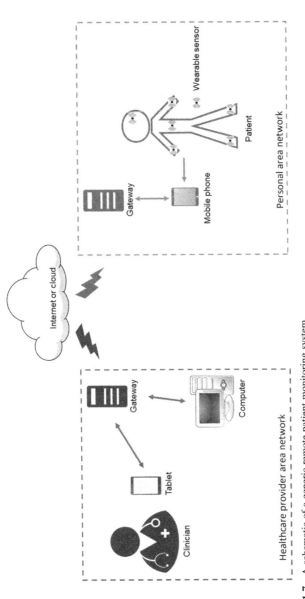

FIGURE 11.7 A schematic of a generic remote patient monitoring system.

Conclusion

Designing for stress, fatigue, and workload management with the aim to optimize performance of healthcare workers requires deeper understanding of underlying mechanisms. Workload reflects the margin between the amount of effort required to complete a task and the resources available to use for that task. Stress is a response to financial, physical, and/or psychological demands and relationship challenges associated with work. Fatigue is a complex state characterized by a lack of alertness and reduced mental and physical performance. These constructs have been primarily measured retrospectively, with many data collection methods inappropriate for the naturalistic healthcare environment. Future research should take advantage of advancements in wearable sensor technology to examine stress, fatigue, and workload in healthcare workers. Sustained stress, workload, and fatigue have deleterious impact on both the performance and the health of healthcare professionals, as well as the health and safety of patients. Designing of human–machine systems in this environment, such as EHR design, can substantially reduce stressors that overload and confuse workers. Organizational culture, work tasks, communications, feedback systems, trainings, and built environments play crucial roles in whether healthcare professionals remain stressed, overloaded, and/or fatigued. Addressing issues of high workload, sustained stress, and fatigue is the shared responsibility of both the individual healthcare worker and the organization in which s/he works and thus needs a systems perspective to mitigate adverse outcomes.

References

Aaronson, L. S., Pallikkathayil, L., & Crighton, F. (2003). A qualitative investigation of fatigue among healthy working adults. *Western Journal of Nursing Research*, 25(4), 419–433.

Al-Shargie, F., Kiguchi, M., Badruddin, N., Dass, S. C., Hani, A. F. M., & Tang, T. B. (2016). Mental stress assessment using simultaneous measurement of EEG and fNIRS. *Biomedical Optics Express*, 7(10), 3882–3898.

Andreu-Perez, J., Leff, D. R., Ip, H. M., & Yang, G. Z. (2015). From wearable sensors to smart implants—Toward pervasive and personalized healthcare. *IEEE Transactions on Biomedical Engineering*, 62(12), 2750–2762.

Anger, W. K., Elliot, D. L., Bodner, T., Olson, R., Rohlman, D. S., Truxillo, D. M., ... Montgomery, D. (2015). Effectiveness of total worker health interventions. *Journal of Occupational Health Psychology*, 20(2), 226.

Anthony, C. R., & Biers, D. W. (1997). Unidimensional versus multidimensional workload scales and the effect of number of rating scale categories. *Proceedings of the Human Factors and Ergonomics Society Annual Meeting*, 41, 1084–1088.

Arndt, B. G., Beasley, J. W., Watkinson, M. D., Temte, J. L., Tuan, W. J., Sinsky, C. A., & Gilchrist, V. J. (2017). Tethered to the EHR: Primary care physician workload assessment using EHR event log data and time-motion observations. *The Annals of Family Medicine*, 15(5), 419–426.

Arora, S., Sevdalis, N., Nestel, D., Tierney, T., Woloshynowych, M., & Kneebone, R. (2009). Managing intraoperative stress: What do surgeons want from a crisis training program? *The American Journal of Surgery*, 197(4), 537–543.

Bahadori, M., Ravangard, R., Raadabadi, M., Mosavi, S. M., Fesharaki, M. G., & Mehrabian, F. (2014). Factors affecting intensive care units nursing workload. *Iranian Red Crescent Medical Journal*, *16*(8), e20072. Available from https://doi.org/10.5812/ircmj.20072.

Barker Steege, L. M., & Nussbaum, M. A. (2013). Dimensions of fatigue as predictors of performance: A structural equation modeling approach among registered nurses. *IIE Transactions on Occupational Ergonomics and Human Factors*, *1*(1), 16−30.

Barker, L. M., & Nussbaum, M. A. (2011). The effects of fatigue on performance in simulated nursing work. *Ergonomics*, *54*(9), 815−829.

Barker, L. M., & Pasupathy, K. S. (2010). Identification of relationships between work system parameters and fatigue in registered nurses: A data mining approach. *Proceedings of the Human Factors and Ergonomics Society Annual Meeting*, *54*(4), 364−368.

Basil Leaf Technologies. *News blog.* (n.d.). Available from <http://www.basilleaftech.com/blog-1/> Retrieved 15.12.18.

Bedini, S., Braun, F., Weibel, L., Aussedat, M., Pereira, B., & Dutheil, F. (2017). Stress and salivary cortisol in emergency medical dispatchers: A randomized shifts control trial. *PLoS One*, *12*(5), e0177094. Available from https://doi.org/10.1371/journal.pone.0177094.

Benoliel, J. Q., McCorkle, R., Georgiadou, F., Denton, T., & Spitzer, A. (1990). Measurement of stress in clinical nursing. *Cancer Nursing*, *13*(4), 221−228.

Betti, S., Lova, R. M., Rovini, E., Acerbi, G., Santarelli, L., Cabiati, M., . . . Cavallo, F. (2018). Evaluation of an integrated system of wearable physiological sensors for stress monitoring in working environments by using biological markers. *IEEE Transactions on Biomedical Engineering*, *65*(8), 1748−1758.

Blikkendaal, M. D., Driessen, S. R., Rodrigues, S. P., Rhemrev, J. P., Smeets, M. J., Dankelman, J., . . . Jansen, F. W. (2017). Surgical flow disturbances in dedicated minimally invasive surgery suites: An observational study to assess its supposed superiority over conventional suites. *Surgical Endoscopy*, *31*(1), 288−298.

Borghini, G., Astolfi, L., Vecchiato, G., Mattia, D., & Babiloni, F. (2014). Measuring neurophysiological signals in aircraft pilots and car drivers for the assessment of mental workload, fatigue and drowsiness. *Neuroscience & Biobehavioral Reviews*, *44*, 58−75.

Brantley, P. J., Waggoner, C. D., Jones, G. N., & Rappaport, N. B. (1987). A daily stress inventory: Development, reliability, and validity. *Journal of Behavioral Medicine*, *10*(1), 61−73.

Burtson, P. L., & Stichler, J. F. (2010). Nursing work environment and nurse caring: Relationship among motivational factors. *Journal of Advanced Nursing*, *66*(8), 1819−1831.

Carayon, P., & Alvarado, C. J. (2007). Workload and patient safety among critical care nurses. *Critical Care Nursing Clinics of North America*, *19*(2), 121−129.

Chaudhury, H., Chaudhury, H., & Mahmood, A. (2007). *The effect of environmental design on reducing nursing and medication errors in acute care settings*. Coalition for Health Environments Research and The Center for Health Design. https://www.healthdesign.org/chd/research/effect-environmental-design-reducing-nursing-and-medication-errors-acute-care-settings.

Chrousos, G. P. (2009). Stress and disorders of the stress system. *Nature Reviews Endocrinology*, *5*(7), 374.

Coetzee, S. K., & Klopper, H. C. (2010). Compassion fatigue within nursing practice: A concept analysis. *Nursing & Health Sciences*, *12*(2), 235−243.

Coetzee, S. K., & Laschinger, H. K. (2018). Toward a comprehensive, theoretical model of compassion fatigue: An integrative literature review. *Nursing & Health Sciences*, *20*(1), 4−15.

Cohen, S., Kamarck, T., & Mermelstein, R. (1983). A global measure of perceived stress. *Journal of Health and Social Behavior*, 385−396.

Darragh, A. R., Sommerich, C. M., Lavender, S. A., Tanner, K. J., Vogel, K., & Campo, M. (2015). Musculoskeletal discomfort, physical demand, and caregiving activities in informal caregivers. *Journal of Applied Gerontology, 34*(6), 734–760.

Davis, K. G., & Kotowski, S. E. (2015). Prevalence of musculoskeletal disorders for nurses in hospitals, long-term care facilities, and home health care: A comprehensive review. *Human Factors, 57*(5), 754–792.

Dehais, F., Dupres, A., Flumeri, G. D., Verdiere, K., Borghini, G., Babiloni, F., & Roy, R. (2018). *Monitoring pilot's cognitive fatigue with engagement features in simulated and actual flight conditions using an hybrid fNIRS-EEG passive BCI. 2018 IEEE international conference on systems, man, and cybernetics (SMC)* (pp. 544–549). Available from https://doi.org/10.1109/SMC.2018.00102.

De Kloet, E. R., Joëls, M., & Holsboer, F. (2005). Stress and the brain: From adaptation to disease. *Nature Reviews Neuroscience, 6*(6), 463.

Desmond, P. A., & Hancock, P. A. (2001). Active and passive fatigue states. In P. A. Hancock, & P. A. Desmond (Eds.), *Human factors in transportation. Stress, workload, and fatigue* (pp. 455–465). Mahwah, NJ: Lawrence Erlbaum Associates Publishers.

Dewa, C. S., Loong, D., Bonato, S., & Trojanowski, L. (2017). The relationship between physician burnout and quality of healthcare in terms of safety and acceptability: A systematic review. *BMJ Open, 7*(6), e015141.

Diaz-Piedra, C., Rieiro, H., Suárez, J., Rios-Tejada, F., Catena, A., & Di Stasi, L. L. (2016). Fatigue in the military: Towards a fatigue detection test based on the saccadic velocity. *Physiological Measurement, 37*(9), N62.

Dimou, F. M., Eckelbarger, D., & Riall, T. S. (2016). Surgeon burnout: A systematic review. *Journal of the American College of Surgeons, 222*(6), 1230.

Dinges, D. F., & Powell, J. W. (1985). Microcomputer analyses of performance on a portable, simple visual RT task during sustained operations. *Behavior Research Methods, Instruments, & Computers, 17*(6), 652–655.

Dorsch, A. K., Thomas, S., Xu, X., Kaiser, W., & Dobkin, B. H. (2015). SIRRACT: An international randomized clinical trial of activity feedback during inpatient stroke rehabilitation enabled by wireless sensing. *Neurorehabilitation and Neural Repair, 29*(5), 407–415.

Dyrbye, L. N., Varkey, P., Boone, S. L., Satele, D. V., Sloan, J. A., & Shanafelt, T. D. (2013). *Physician satisfaction and burnout at different career stages, . Mayo Clinic Proceedings* (88, pp. 1358–1367). Elsevier, No. 12.

Espinosa, L., Young, A., Symes, L., Haile, B., & Walsh, T. (2010). ICU nurses' experiences in providing terminal care. *Critical Care Nursing Quarterly, 33*(3), 273–281.

Fahrenkopf, A. M., Sectish, T. C., Barger, L. K., Sharek, P. J., Lewin, D., Chiang, V. W., ... Landrigan, C. P. (2008). Rates of medication errors among depressed and burnt out residents: Prospective cohort study. *British Medical Journal, 336*(7642), 488–491.

Fairclough, S. H., & Venables, L. (2006). Prediction of subjective states from psychophysiology: A multivariate approach. *Biological Psychology, 71*(1), 100–110.

Fallahi, M., Motamedzade, M., Heidarimoghadam, R., Soltanian, A. R., & Miyake, S. (2016). Effects of mental workload on physiological and subjective responses during traffic density monitoring: A field study. *Applied Ergonomics, 52*, 95–103.

Fallahzadeh, R., Ma, Y., & Ghasemzadeh, H. (2017). Context-aware system design for remote health monitoring: An application to continuous edema assessment. *IEEE Transactions on Mobile Computing, 16*(8), 2159–2173.

Fisk, J. D., Ritvo, P. G., Ross, L., Haase, D. A., Marrie, T. J., & Schlech, W. F. (1994). Measuring the functional impact of fatigue: Initial validation of the fatigue impact scale. *Clinical Infectious Diseases, 18*(Supplement_1), S79−S83.

Friedemann, M.-L., Newman, F. L., Buckwalter, K. C., & Montgomery, R. J. (2014). Resource need and use of multiethnic caregivers of elders in their homes. *Journal of Advanced Nursing, 70*(3), 662−673.

Gao, Q., Wang, Y., Song, F., Li, Z., & Dong, X. (2013). Mental workload measurement for emergency operating procedures in digital nuclear power plants. *Ergonomics, 56*(7), 1070−1085.

Gartland, K. M., & Gartland, J. S. (2018). Opportunities in biotechnology. *Journal of Biotechnology, 282*, 38−45.

Gates, M., Wingert, A., Featherstone, R., Samuels, C., Simon, C., & Dyson, M. P. (2018). Impact of fatigue and insufficient sleep on physician and patient outcomes: A systematic review. *BMJ Open, 8*(9), e021967. Available from https://doi.org/10.1136/bmjopen-2018-021967.

Govindarajan, A., Urbach, D. R., Kumar, M., Li, Q., Murray, B. J., Juurlink, D., ... Baxter, N. N. (2015). Outcomes of daytime procedures performed by attending surgeons after night work. *New England Journal of Medicine, 373*(9), 845−853.

Grassmann, M., Vlemincx, E., von Leupoldt, A., Mittelstädt, J. M., & Van den Bergh, O. (2016). Respiratory changes in response to cognitive load: A systematic review. *Neural Plasticity, 2016*, Article ID 8146809. Available from https://doi.org/10.1155/2016/8146809.

Gray-Toft, P., & Anderson, J. G. (1981). The nursing stress scale: Development of an instrument. *Journal of Behavioral Assessment, 3*(1), 11−23.

Guo, Y., Luo, Y., Lam, L., Cross, W., Plummer, V., & Zhang, J. (2018). Burnout and its association with resilience in nurses: A cross-sectional study. *Journal of Clinical Nursing, 27*(1−2), 441−449.

Guru, K. A., Shafiei, S. B., Khan, A., Hussein, A. A., Sharif, M., & Esfahani, E. T. (2015). Understanding cognitive performance during robot-assisted surgery. *Urology, 86*(4), 751−757.

Hancock, P. A., & Verwey, W. B. (1997). Fatigue, workload and adaptive driver systems. *Accident Analysis & Prevention, 29*(4), 495−506.

Harris, P. E. (1989). The nurse stress index. *Work & Stress, 3*(4), 335−346.

Heemskerk, J., Zandbergen, H. R., Keet, S. W., Martijnse, I., Van Montfort, G., Peters, R. J., ... Bouvy, N. D. (2014). Relax, it's just laparoscopy! A prospective randomized trial on heart rate variability of the surgeon in robot-assisted versus conventional laparoscopic cholecystectomy. *Digestive Surgery, 31*(3), 225−232.

Hirvonen, K., Puttonen, S., Gould, K., Korpela, J., Koefoed, V. F., & Müller, K. (2010). Improving the saccade peak velocity measurement for detecting fatigue. *Journal of Neuroscience Methods, 187*(2), 199−206.

Holden, R. J., Scanlon, M. C., Patel, N. R., Kaushal, R., Escoto, K. H., Brown, R. L., ... Murkowski, K. (2011). A human factors framework and study of the effect of nursing workload on patient safety and employee quality of working life. *BMJ Quality & Safety, 20*(1), 15−24.

Holdsworth, L., & Evens, T. (2017). Is heart rate variability a useful marker of stress and fatigue in emergency and pre-hospital clinicians?—A systematic review. *Resuscitation, 118*, e95. Available from https://doi.org/10.1016/j.resuscitation.2017.11.011.

Holman, D., Johnson, S., & O'Connor, E. (2018). *Stress management interventions: Improving subjective psychological well-being in the workplace. Handbook of wellbeing.* Salt Lake City, UT: DEF Publishers. DOI: https://nobascholar.com/chapters/44/download.pdf.

Hsu, C.-F., Propp, L., Panetta, L., Martin, S., Dentakos, S., Toplak, M. E., & Eastwood, J. D. (2018). Mental effort and discomfort: Testing the peak-end effect during a cognitively demanding task. *PLoS One, 13*(2), e0191479. Available from https://dx.doi.org/10.1371%2Fjournal.pone.0191479.

Institute for Healthcare Improvement. *Dealing with burnout.* (n.d.). Available from <http://www.ihi.org:80/education/IHIOpenSchool/resources/Pages/CaseStudies/DealingWithBurnout.aspx> Retrieved 09.04.19.

Institute of Medicine. (2000). Shaping the future for health. In L. T. Kohn, J. Corrigan, & M. S. Donaldson (Eds.), *To err is human: Building a safer health system.* Washington, DC: National Academy Press.

Jakicic, J. M., Davis, K. K., Rogers, R. J., King, W. C., Marcus, M. D., Helsel, D., ... Belle, S. H. (2016). Effect of wearable technology combined with a lifestyle intervention on long-term weight loss: The IDEA randomized clinical trial. *JAMA, 316*(11), 1161−1171.

Jayasinghe, S. U., Lambert, G. W., Torres, S. J., Fraser, S. F., Eikelis, N., & Turner, A. I. (2016). Hypothalamo-pituitary adrenal axis and sympatho-adrenal medullary system responses to psychological stress were not attenuated in women with elevated physical fitness levels. *Endocrine, 51*(2), 369−379.

Jones, K. I., Amawi, F., Bhalla, A., Peacock, O., Williams, J. P., & Lund, J. N. (2015). Assessing surgeon stress when operating using heart rate variability and the State Trait Anxiety Inventory: Will surgery be the death of us? *Colorectal Disease, 17*(4), 335−341.

Kahol, K., Smith, M., Brandenberger, J., Ashby, A., & Ferrara, J. J. (2011). Impact of fatigue on neurophysiologic measures of surgical residents. *Journal of the American College of Surgeons, 213*(1), 29−34.

Karasek, R. A., Jr (1979). Job demands, job decision latitude, and mental strain: Implications for job redesign. *Administrative Science Quarterly, 24*(2), 285−308.

Kavushansky, A., Ben-Shachar, D., Richter-Levin, G., & Klein, E. (2009). Physical stress differs from psychosocial stress in the pattern and time-course of behavioral responses, serum corticosterone and expression of plasticity-related genes in the rat. *Stress, 12*(5), 412−425.

Kent, P., Laird, R., & Haines, T. (2015). The effect of changing movement and posture using motion-sensor biofeedback, versus guidelines-based care, on the clinical outcomes of people with sub-acute or chronic low back pain-a multicentre, cluster-randomised, placebo-controlled, pilot trial. *BMC Musculoskeletal Disorders, 16*(1), 131.

Kim, C., Lee, J., Kim, R., Park, Y., & Kang, J. (2018). DeepNAP: Deep neural anomaly pre-detection in a semiconductor fab. *Information Sciences, 457−458*, 1−11. Available from https://doi.org/10.1016/j.ins.2018.05.020.

Kirschbaum, C., Pirke, K. M., & Hellhammer, D. H. (1993). The 'Trier Social Stress Test'—A tool for investigating psychobiological stress responses in a laboratory setting. *Neuropsychobiology, 28*(1−2), 76−81.

Krueger, G. P. (2018). A Fatigue, performance, and medical error. In M. S. Bogner (Ed.), *Human error in medicine* (pp. 311−326). Boca Raton, FL: CRC Press.

Krupp, L. B., LaRocca, N. G., Muir-Nash, J., & Steinberg, A. D. (1989). The fatigue severity scale: Application to patients with multiple sclerosis and systemic lupus erythematosus. *Archives of Neurology, 46*(10), 1121−1123.

Kurowski, A., Buchholz, B., ProCare Research Team., & Punnett, L. (2014). A physical workload index to evaluate a safe resident handling program for nursing home personnel. *Human Factors, 56*(4), 669−683.

Kuyken, W., Watkins, E., Holden, E., White, K., Taylor, R. S., Byford, S., ... Dalgleish, T. (2010). How does mindfulness-based cognitive therapy work? *Behaviour Research and Therapy, 48*(11), 1105−1112.

Lazarus, R. S., & Folkman, S. (1987). Transactional theory and research on emotions and coping. *European Journal of Personality*, *1*(3), 141−169.

Leape, L. L. (2018). The preventability of medical injury. In M. S. Bogner (Ed.), *Human error in medicine* (pp. 13−25). Boca Raton, FL: CRC Press.

Lee, K. A., Hicks, G., & Nino-Murcia, G. (1991). Validity and reliability of a scale to assess fatigue. *Psychiatry Research*, *36*(3), 291−298.

Lee, Y., Lee, J., Seo, H., Kim, K., Min, D., Lee, J., & Choi, J. (2013). Effects of home-based exercise training with wireless monitoring on the left ventricular function of acute coronary syndrome patients. *Journal of Physical Therapy Science*, *25*(5), 631−633.

Llanque, S., Savage, L., Rosenburg, N., & Caserta, M. (2016). Concept analysis: Alzheimer's caregiver stress. *Nursing Forum*, *51*, 21−31.

Mansikka, H., Virtanen, K., & Harris, D. (2018). Comparison of NASA-TLX scale, modified Cooper−Harper scale and mean inter-beat interval as measures of pilot mental workload during simulated flight tasks. *Ergonomics*, 1−9.

Martin, S. (2002). More hours, more tired, more to do: Results from the CMA's 2002 Physician Resource Questionnaire. *Canadian Medical Association Journal*, *167*(5), 2002, 521-522.

Maslach, C. (2003). Job burnout: New directions in research and intervention. *Current Directions in Psychological Science*, *12*(5), 189−192.

Maslach, C., Jackson, S. E., Leiter, M. P., Schaufeli, W. B., & Schwab, R. L. (1986). *Maslach burnout inventory* (Vol. 21, pp. 3463−3464). Palo Alto, CA: Consulting Psychologists Press.

Mazur, L. M., Mosaly, P. R., Moore, C., Comitz, E., Yu, F., Falchook, A. D., ... Chera, B. S. (2016). Toward a better understanding of task demands, workload, and performance during physician-computer interactions. *Journal of the American Medical Informatics Association*, *23*(6), 1113−1120.

McGowan, B. (2001). Self-reported stress and its effects on nurses. *Nursing Standard (through 2013)*, *15*(42), 33.

McVicar, A. (2003). Workplace stress in nursing: A literature review. *Journal of Advanced Nursing*, *44*(6), 633−642.

Michielsen, H. J., De Vries, J., Van Heck, G. L., Van de Vijver, F. J., & Sijtsma, K. (2004). Examination of the dimensionality of fatigue. *European Journal of Psychological Assessment*, *20*(1), 39−48.

Michtalik, H. J., Yeh, H.-C., Pronovost, P. J., & Brotman, D. J. (2013). Impact of attending physician workload on patient care: A survey of hospitalists. *JAMA Internal Medicine*, *173*(5), 375−377.

Mitchell, R., McBride, M., & Jarocki, J. (2017). Linkography abstraction refinement and cyber security. In: 2017 IEEE conference on communications and network security (CNS) (pp. 595−601). https://doi.org/10.1109/CNS.2017.8228675.

Miyake, S., Yamada, S., Shoji, T., Takae, Y., Kuge, N., & Yamamura, T. (2009). Physiological responses to workload change. A test/retest examination. *Applied Ergonomics*, *40*(6), 987−996.

Noah, B., Keller, M. S., Mosadeghi, S., Stein, L., Johl, S., Delshad, S., ... Spiegel, B. M. (2018). Impact of remote patient monitoring on clinical outcomes: An updated meta-analysis of randomized controlled trials. *NPJ Digital Medicine*, *1*(1), 20172.

Oriyama, S., Miyakoshi, Y., & Kobayashi, T. (2013). Effects of two 15-min naps on the subjective sleepiness, fatigue and heart rate variability of night shift nurses. *Industrial Health*, *52*, 25−35.

Orlandi, L., & Brooks, B. (2018). Measuring mental workload and physiological reactions in marine pilots: Building bridges towards redlines of performance. *Applied Ergonomics*, *69*, 74−92.

Park, A., Lee, G., Seagull, F. J., Meenaghan, N., & Dexter, D. (2010). Patients benefit while surgeons suffer: An impending epidemic. *Journal of the American College of Surgeons, 210*(3), 306−313.

Pawlikowska, T., Chalder, T., Hirsch, S. R., Wallace, P., Wright, D. J. M., & Wessely, S. C. (1994). Population based study of fatigue and psychological distress. *British Medical Journal, 308*(6931), 763−766.

Pearlin, L. I., Mullan, J. T., Semple, S. J., & Skaff, M. M. (1990). Caregiving and the stress process: An overview of concepts and their measures. *The Gerontologist, 30*(5), 583−594.

Pearson, A., Pallas, L. O., Thomson, D., Doucette, E., Tucker, D., Wiechula, R., ... Jordan, Z. (2006). Systematic review of evidence on the impact of nursing workload and staffing on establishing healthy work environments. *International Journal of Evidence-Based Healthcare, 4*(4), 337−384.

Pedone, C., Chiurco, D., Scarlata, S., & Incalzi, R. A. (2013). Efficacy of multiparametric telemonitoring on respiratory outcomes in elderly people with COPD: A randomized controlled trial. *BMC Health Services Research, 13*(1), 82.

Portoghese, I., Galletta, M., Coppola, R. C., Finco, G., & Campagna, M. (2014). Burnout and workload among health care workers: The moderating role of job control. *Safety and Health at Work, 5*(3), 152−157.

Posada-Quintero, H. F., Florian, J. P., Orjuela-Cañón, A. D., & Chon, K. H. (2018). Electrodermal activity is sensitive to cognitive stress under water. *Frontiers in Physiology, 8*, 1128.

Potter, P., Wolf, L., Boxerman, S., Grayson, D., Sledge, J., Dunagan, C., & Evanoff, B. (2005). Understanding the cognitive work of nursing in the acute care environment. *Journal of Nursing Administration, 35*(7), 327−335.

Provost, S. M., Lanham, H. J., Leykum, L. K., McDaniel, R. R., Jr, & Pugh, J. (2015). Health care huddles: Managing complexity to achieve high reliability. *Health Care Management Review, 40*(1), 2−12.

Richter, A., Kostova, P., Baur, X., & Wegner, R. (2014). Less work: More burnout? A comparison of working conditions and the risk of burnout by German physicians before and after the implementation of the EU Working Time Directive. *International Archives of Occupational and Environmental Health, 87*(2), 205−215.

Rieger, A., Fenger, S., Neubert, S., Weippert, M., Kreuzfeld, S., & Stoll, R. (2015). Psychophysical workload in the operating room: Primary surgeon versus assistant. *Surgical Endoscopy, 29*(7), 1990−1998.

Rosen, M. A., Dietz, A. S., Lee, N., Wang, I.-J., Markowitz, J., Wyskiel, R. M., ... Gurses, A. P. (2018). Sensor-based measurement of critical care nursing workload: Unobtrusive measures of nursing activity complement traditional task and patient level indicators of workload to predict perceived exertion. *PLoS One, 13*(10), e0204819. Available from https://doi.org/10.1371/journal.pone.0204819.

Rosenbaum, D., Hilsendegen, P., Thomas, M., Haeussinger, F. B., Metzger, F. G., Nuerk, H. C., ... Ehlis, A. C. (2018). Cortical hemodynamic changes during the Trier social stress test: An fNIRS study. *NeuroImage, 171*, 107−115.

Ruggiero, J. S., Redeker, N. S., Fiedler, N., Avi-Itzhak, T., & Fischetti, N. (2012). Sleep and psychomotor vigilance in female shiftworkers. *Biological Research for Nursing, 14*(3), 225−235.

Ryan, D., Price, D., Musgrave, S. D., Malhotra, S., Lee, A. J., Ayansina, D., ... Pinnock, H. (2012). Clinical and cost effectiveness of mobile phone supported self monitoring of asthma: Multicentre randomised controlled trial. *British Medical Journal, 344*, e1756.

Shanafelt, T. D. (2009). Enhancing meaning in work: A prescription for preventing physician burnout and promoting patient-centered care. *JAMA, 302*(12), 1338−1340.

Shanafelt, T. D., Balch, C. M., Bechamps, G. J., Russell, T., Dyrbye, L., Satele, D., . . . Freischlag, J. A. (2009). Burnout and career satisfaction among American surgeons. *Annals of Surgery*, *250*(3), 463–471.

Shen, J., Barbera, J., & Shapiro, C. M. (2006). Distinguishing sleepiness and fatigue: Focus on definition and measurement. *Sleep Medicine Reviews*, *10*(1), 63–76.

Siegrist, J., Starke, D., Chandola, T., Godin, I., Marmot, M., Niedhammer, I., & Peter, R. (2004). The measurement of effort–reward imbalance at work: European comparisons. *Social Science & Medicine*, *58*(8), 1483–1499.

Singh, H., Modi, H. N., Ranjan, S., Dilley, J. W., Airantzis, D., Yang, G. Z., . . . Leff, D. R. (2018). Robotic surgery improves technical performance and enhances prefrontal activation during high temporal demand. *Annals of Biomedical Engineering*, *46*(10), 1621–1636.

Steege, L. M., Drake, D. A., Olivas, M., & Mazza, G. (2015). Evaluation of physically and mentally fatiguing tasks and sources of fatigue as reported by registered nurses. *Journal of Nursing Management*, *23*(2), 179–189.

Stehman, C. R., Testo, Z., Gershaw, R. S., & Kellogg, A. R. (2019). Burnout, drop out, suicide: Physician loss in emergency medicine, part I. *Western Journal of Emergency Medicine: Integrating Emergency Care with Population Health*, *20*, 485–494.

Szeto, G. P., Ho, P., Ting, A. C., Poon, J. T., Cheng, S. W., & Tsang, R. C. (2009). Work-related musculoskeletal symptoms in surgeons. *Journal of Occupational Rehabilitation*, *19*(2), 175–184.

Tan, B. Y., Ho, K. L., Ching, C. K., & Teo, W. S. (2010). Novel electrogram device with web-based service centre for ambulatory ECG monitoring. *Singapore Medical Journal*, *51*(7), 565.

Trinkoff, A. M., Storr, C. L., Johantgen, M., Liang, Y., Han, K., & Gurses, A. P. (2011). Linking nursing work environment and patient outcomes. *Journal of Nursing Regulation*, *2* (1), 10–16.

Ulrich-Lai, Y. M., & Herman, J. P. (2009). Neural regulation of endocrine and autonomic stress responses. *Nature Reviews Neuroscience*, *10*(6), 397.

Unruh, L. Y., & Fottler, M. D. (2006). Patient turnover and nursing staff adequacy. *Health Services Research*, *41*(2), 599–612.

Upenieks, V. V., Kotlerman, J., Akhavan, J., Esser, J., & Ngo, M. J. (2007). Assessing nursing staffing ratios: Variability in workload intensity. *Policy, Politics, & Nursing Practice*, *8*(1), 7–19.

van Groenou, M. I. B., & De Boer, A. (2016). Providing informal care in a changing society. *European Journal of Ageing*, *13*(3), 271–279.

Virtanen, P., Oksanen, T., Kivimäki, M., Virtanen, M., Pentti, J., & Vahtera, J. (2008). Work stress and health in primary health care physicians and hospital physicians. *Occupational and Environmental Medicine*, *65*(5), 364–366.

Wallston, K. A., Slagle, J. M., Speroff, T., Nwosu, S., Crimin, K., Feurer, I. D., . . . Weinger, M. B. (2014). Operating room clinicians' ratings of workload: A vignette simulation study. *Journal of Patient Safety*, *10*(2), 95–100.

Walter, S. R., Li, L., Dunsmuir, W. T., & Westbrook, J. I. (2014). Managing competing demands through task-switching and multitasking: A multi-setting observational study of 200 clinicians over 1000 hours. *BMJ Quality & Safety*, *23*(3), 231–241.

Ware, J. E., Jr., & Sherbourne, C. D. (1992). The MOS 36-item short-form health survey (SF-36). I. Conceptual framework and item selection. *Medical Care*, *30*, 473–483.

Watson, D., Clark, L. A., & Tellegen, A. (1988). Development and validation of brief measures of positive and negative affect: The PANAS scales. *Journal of Personality and Social Psychology*, *54*(6), 1063.

Weigl, M., Antoniadis, S., Chiapponi, C., Bruns, C., & Sevdalis, N. (2015). The impact of intra-operative interruptions on surgeons' perceived workload: An observational study in elective general and orthopedic surgery. *Surgical Endoscopy, 29*(1), 145–153.

Weigl, M., Müller, A., Vincent, C., Angerer, P., & Sevdalis, N. (2012). The association of workflow interruptions and hospital doctors' workload: A prospective observational study. *BMJ Quality & Safety, 21*(5), 399–407.

Wensing, M., van den Hombergh, P., Akkermans, R., van Doremalen, J., & Grol, R. (2006). Physician workload in primary care: What is the optimal size of practices?: A cross-sectional study. *Health Policy, 77*(3), 260–267.

West, C. P., Dyrbye, L. N., & Shanafelt, T. D. (2018). Physician burnout: Contributors, consequences and solutions. *Journal of Internal Medicine, 283*(6), 516–529.

Westbrook, J. I., Raban, M. Z., Walter, S. R., & Douglas, H. (2018). Task errors by emergency physicians are associated with interruptions, multitasking, fatigue and working memory capacity: A prospective, direct observation study. *BMJ Quality & Safety, 27*(8), 655–663.

Westbrook, J. I., Woods, A., Rob, M. I., Dunsmuir, W. T., & Day, R. O. (2010). Association of interruptions with an increased risk and severity of medication administration errors. *Archives of Internal Medicine, 170*(8), 683–690.

Wetzel, C. M., Kneebone, R. L., Woloshynowych, M., Nestel, D., Moorthy, K., Kidd, J., & Darzi, A. (2006). The effects of stress on surgical performance. *The American Journal of Surgery, 191*(1), 5–10.

Wiegmann, D. A., ElBardissi, A. W., Dearani, J. A., Daly, R. C., & Sundt, T. M., III (2007). Disruptions in surgical flow and their relationship to surgical errors: An exploratory investigation. *Surgery, 142*(5), 658–665.

Wilson, M. R., Poolton, J. M., Malhotra, N., Ngo, K., Bright, E., & Masters, R. S. (2011). Development and validation of a surgical workload measure: The surgery task load index (SURG-TLX). *World Journal of Surgery, 35*(9), 1961.

Xie, B., & Salvendy, G. (2000). Review and reappraisal of modelling and predicting mental workload in single- and multi-task environments. *Work & Stress, 14*(1), 74–99.

Yeh, Y.-Y., & Wickens, C. D. (1988). Dissociation of performance and subjective measures of workload. *Human Factors, 30*(1), 111–120.

Zhang, T., Wang, X., Li, Z., Guo, F., Ma, Y., & Chen, W. (2017). A survey of network anomaly visualization. *Science China Information Sciences, 60*(12), 121101. Available from https://doi.org/10.1007/s11432-016-0428-2.

Zimring, C., Joseph, A., & Choudhary, R. (2004). *The role of the physical environment in the hospital of the 21st century: A once-in-a-lifetime opportunity.* Concord, CA: The Center for Health Design.

Chapter 12

Design for cognitive support

L.C. Schubel[1], N. Muthu[2], D.J. Karavite[2], R. Arnold[3] and K.M. Miller[1]
[1]National Center for Human Factors in Healthcare, MedStar Health, Washington, DC, United States, [2]Department of Biomedical and Health Informatics, Children's Hospital of Philadelphia, Philadelphia, PA, United States, [3]Drexel University College of Medicine, Philadelphia, PA, United States

Introduction

Clinical settings are complex and fast paced. With an unpredictable variety of clinical cases and a sometimes-overwhelming volume of patients, the health-care system is a multifaceted and highly demanding environment and can be extremely conducive to errors. In medicine, errors do not occur in a vacuum, and a simple blunder can lead to severe patient harm. For example, a doctor prescribing a pain medication to a patient could mistakenly prescribe the individual 100 mg when 10 mg was the intended dose, or a nurse might not take the time for thorough handwashing before examining a wound, putting the patient at risk for a health-care-associated infection. Both cases could lead to an extended, costly, and otherwise avoidable hospital stay. Mistakes such as these can have serious and detrimental effects for patients and their providers.

Health-care literature has identified that adverse events—defined for our purposes as *an unintentional injury or complication caused by health-care management that leads to a longer patient stay, disability, or death*—occur in an immense number of hospitalizations. Large, international reviews of patient safety events estimate their occurrence to fall somewhere between 4% and 17% of hospitalizations, with one to two-thirds being preventable (Baker et al., 2004; Bates, O'Neil, Petersen, Lee, & Brennan, 1995; Kohn, Corrigan, & Donaldson, 1999; Sari et al., 2007; Thomas et al., 2000; Vincent, Neale, & Woloshynowych, 2001; Wilson, Runciman, Gibberd, Harrison, & Hamilton, 1996). Adverse events in hospitals affect nearly 1 out of every 10 patients, annually resulting in more fatalities than breast cancer or AIDS (Kohn et al., 1999). The financial impact of adverse events is detrimental to the health-care system as well. It is projected that adverse safety events in the United States

Design for Health. DOI: https://doi.org/10.1016/B978-0-12-816427-3.00012-9

227

and Western Europe will drive an estimated health-care cost burden of \$383.7 billion by 2022 (Frost & Sullivan, 2018).

Understanding the underlying cognitive processes of clinicians can help to enable innovative strategies within human factors engineering (HFE) and ultimately reduce the rate of adverse events. In fact, close to 75% of diagnostic errors have an identifiable underlying cognitive component at fault (Schiff et al., 2009). By acknowledging human limitations and system vulnerabilities, HFE can minimize and mitigate human limitations to optimize system performance (Carayon et al., 2014). Health-care systems can be made safer by recognizing the potential for error and developing systems and strategies to minimize their occurrence and effects.

In this chapter, there are three areas outlined in which health-care workers can most benefit from HFE solutions: perception and attention, working memory, and decision-making. By first understanding the cognitive basis of each of these, we can then consider innovative HFE solutions for ensuring optimal care.

Perception and attention

At any moment, one can sense familiar objects in their environment. In a hospital, a clinician may feel the smooth fabric of scrubs against their skin or hear the steady clack of a keyboard as a provider types notes into a patient's medical record. Sensations such as these make up the conscious experience and allow individuals to interact with their environment. Sensory memory assists in processing incoming information—auditory, tactile, olfactory, visual, and so on—for a brief period. One of the main purposes of sensory memory is to filter incoming stimuli and process only that which is most relevant.

Perception refers to the *organization, experience, identification, and interpretation of sensory information to facilitate one's representation of their environment*. It is what helps humans interpret the stimuli around them and form inferences about the world. Perception is also responsible for "tuning out" relatively constant, unchanging, and irrelevant stimuli. This phenomenon is known as selective attention, or the "cocktail effect," referring to the way a listener can focus on a single speaker in a wide variety of environments, such as a noisy restaurant (Arons, 1992).

Heuristics are simple and efficient rules used to form judgments and make decisions. They often act as mental "shortcuts," permitting individuals to quickly process information and make decisions. Though heuristics are typically effective and reliable, they can be distorted under some circumstances and lead to errors in thinking and interpreting information. Such errors are known as cognitive biases and can lead to grave mistakes. Though there are a wide variety of biases, the following are three that can have a significant and lasting impact on patient safety:

1. *Anchoring bias*, also known as the relativity trap, is the tendency to rely too heavily, or "anchor," on an initial piece of information offered prior to making a decision. This bias may occur when physicians inadequately adjust their initial clinical impression of a patient, even as differing diagnostic information becomes available (Wilson, Houston, Etling, & Brekke, 1996).

2. *Attentional narrowing* refers to the state in which operators, involuntarily and unconsciously, neglect to process a subset of potentially critical information that occurs outside of the narrow band of information they are currently processing (Prinet, Mize, & Sarter, 2016). For example, an emergency medical technician rushing to transport a patient to the hospital may focus attention on the road ahead and thus neglect events taking place on the side, such as a distracted pedestrian wandering into a crosswalk.

3. *Hindsight bias* is the tendency for an individual considering a past event to overestimate his or her ability to have predicted its occurrence. For example, a patient who presents to the emergency room with a variety of odd symptoms may leave the care team puzzled. After the disease is identified by the physician, the rest of the care team claims that they, too, recognized the diagnostic pattern. This misperception may thus obstruct the care team from acknowledging a knowledge gap, or it may delay their retraining to better identify the next puzzling case.

Working memory

After stimuli enter sensory memory, they are either deleted from the system or forwarded to one's working memory. Working memory refers to the temporary storage, multicomponent memory system that underlies human thought processes. It provides an interface between perception and long-term memory and is critical to tasks, such as reading, problem-solving, and learning (Baddeley, 2003).

Working memory relates to what we are thinking or doing at any given moment. In working memory, meaning is assigned to stimuli and individual pieces of information are linked into larger units, similar to identifying a disease based on its symptoms. A major limit on information processing in working memory is the number of units that can be processed and held in working memory at any one time. Originally, the number seven, plus or minus two, was proposed (Miller, 1956), but more recent research suggests that the number may be closer to five plus or minus two (Schweickert & Boruff, 1986; Shiffrin & Nosofsky, 1994). Because of the high variability in working memory capacity for individuals (for some it may be three, for others nine), it is vital to call attention to only the most critical pieces of information. If a health-care provider can only process three units of information at a time, it is crucial to identify and prioritize the most important three.

Several useful terms have been developed to describe efficient cognitive processing in working memory. One is *limited attentional resources*, referring to the highly limited nature of information processing (Anderson & Craik, 2000; Neath, 1998). Individuals experience severe limitations in how much mental activity they can engage in due to limited cognitive resources (Kane & Engle, 2002). Often, differences between one learner and another are not due to the amount of resources, but rather how efficiently those resources are used.

Working memory underlies many cognitive components vital to learning, reasoning, and comprehension. Especially relevant to the clinical setting are vigilance and interruptions.

Vigilance

Vigilance refers to the ability to concentrate on or attend to a situation for an extended period of time. The goal is usually the detection of "something"— or, in more technical terms, a sensory event or signal. During extended search sessions, however, the ability to consistently detect a signal decreases dramatically due to a depletion of cognitive resources (Mackworth, 1948). This is known as the vigilance decrement. The vigilance decrement typically occurs within the first 15 minutes of a viewer's search, but in a stressful or demanding environment, it can occur in as early as 5 minutes (Helton, Dember, Warm, & Matthews, 1999; Teichner, 1974).

Vigilance is relevant to all health-care fields that involve visual search components, but it also extends to any aspect of the field that requires complex monitoring or sustained attention—including radiology (Pinto et al., 2012), anesthesiology (Weinger, Smith, Ehrenwerth, & Eisenkraft, 1993), and many other specialties (Cina et al., 2006; Mortimer, 2002; Scott, Rogers, Hwang, & Zhang, 2006). Luckily, there is evidence to suggest that the vigilance decrement can be combated through frequent breaks and variation in workload, intended to keep searchers alert and provide an array of diverse cognitive activities (Alves & Kelsey, 2010; Ariga & Lleras, 2011). Vigilance can also be supported through human factors design. In the clinical setting, workers are more likely to commit errors when they are mismatched to the task or when the system is inadequately designed to support the needs of the user (Cooper, Newbower, Long, & McPeek, 2002; Weinger et al., 1993). Thus, to ease cognitive load and reduce errors as a result of the vigilance decrement, system design should facilitate the cognitive processes that are required to perform the task (Karsh, Holden, Alper, & Or, 2006).

Interruptions

Interruptions refer to situations in which a clinician ceases an initial task to attend to an external stimulus. Oftentimes, health-care workers are expected to perform tasks that require their undivided attention; however, clinicians are frequently interrupted, which can distract their attention and add to the complexity of their work. Research suggests that interruptions contribute frequently to medication errors, detract from a clinician's ability to follow best practice protocols, and can delay patient-centered care (Brixey et al., 2005; Cheung et al., 2017; Gorini & Pravettoni, 2013; Rivera-Rodriguez & Karsh, 2010; Westbrook, Woods, Rob, Dunsmuir, & Day, 2010).

Interruptions make demands on working memory by requiring individuals to process information unrelated to their primary task, increasing cognitive load (Sweller, 1988). When a disruption occurs, it causes a shift in attention, precipitating a decay in memory of the primary task to accommodate the processes required to deal with the interrupting task. Interruptions are therefore commonly associated with poor performance immediately after an interruption signal, and for the most disruptive interruptions, the primary task is never resumed (Hodgetts & Jones, 2006; Mark, Gonzalez, & Harris, 2005; McFarlane, 2002). Fortunately, there are many HFE interventions that may alleviate the burden brought on through interruptions. For example, awareness displays, which are used to reveal information regarding the state of a worker, are designed to encourage communication while minimizing disruptions (Dabbish & Kraut, 2004). Awareness displays can range from away messages to video displays of the individual, and all are intended to coordinate interaction in a way that mitigates the harmful effects of an interruption. Other examples include a motion light that can serve as a busy indicator during the execution of a complex task, informing coworkers and patients not to interrupt the task at hand. Participants in one study commented that the varying numbers of tactile "buzzes" on a cell phone or modified beeper device (e.g., two buzzes vs four buzzes) and the amplitude of tactile cues were effective ways to indicate the urgency of a message (Sarter, 2005).

Decision-making

To aid with decisions, humans commonly use heuristics or practical problem-solving methods. Mentioned previously, heuristics simplify complicated decisions to simple judgment-based processes. For the purpose of this section, there are two heuristics important to note that are critical to clinical care:

1. *The representativeness heuristic:* This heuristic claims that representativeness is more likely to affect a judgment than probability (Kahneman & Tversky, 1973). In an experiment led by Brannon and Carson (2003), nurses were given two fictitious scenarios of patients with symptoms suggestive of either a heart attack or a stroke and asked to provide a diagnosis. The heart attack case sometimes included the additional information that the patient had recently lost his job, and the stroke scenario

sometimes included the information that the patient smelled of alcohol. The additional information had a significant effect on the diagnosis and made it less likely that the nurses would attribute the symptoms to a serious physical cause.

2. *The availability heuristic:* Easily retrieved examples, or thoughts that readily come to mind, influence the decision maker to overestimate the incidence of a similar happening or situation, such as a doctor who sees a patient with a case of a rare tumor being more likely to call upon that diagnosis the next time she sees a patient with similar symptoms (Poses & Anthony, 1991). Ironically, this directly contradicts well-known adages in health-care, such as the saying, "When you hear hoof beats, think of horses, not zebras," aiming to rein in a broad differential diagnosis, particularly that of an unlikely etiology. While the saying may hold up in many instances, it is vital to consider all options and possibilities so as to never be surprised when your horse turns out to be a zebra.

Clinical decision support (CDS) is one way in which health-care organizations are seeking to enhance the decision-making process. CDS can be utilized in an electronic health record (EHR), electronic device, or even written documents, and it provides clinicians time-sensitive, patient-specific information in order to facilitate safe and effective patient care. CDS can provide assessments specific to a patient, offer recommended order sets for common disorders, alert providers to potential concerns, catch false information entered into a medical record, and offer a variety of other medical interventions. Since its implementation, CDS has improved the adherence to recommended care standards, and evidence suggests that CDS is more likely to result in lasting improvements in clinical practice (Bero et al., 1998; Oxman, Thomson, Davis, & Haynes, 1995; Shiffman, Liaw, Brandt, & Corb, 1999).

Design guidelines

The following HFE strategies can help clinicians combat human error attributed to perception and attention:

- Learning to recognize cognitive errors and biases increases one's ability to create active change, enabling clinicians to intentionally change their emotions and behaviors.
- Providing contrast is a crucial component of clear and correct perception. Poor contrast, such as light lettering on a light background or dark lettering on a dark background, can create confusion and lead to errors. Using high contrast for displays, labeling, and handwriting can reveal significant improvement.
- Ensuring discriminability, how well items can be differentiated, is vitally important. The existence of confusingly similar drug names is one of the most common causes of medication error and is of concern worldwide

(Davis, 1999; Lambert, 1997). Whenever possible, facilities should eliminate "look-alike" and "sound-alike" drugs or develop systems processes to combat confusion. Process solutions include utilizing computerized physician order entry when available, or developing protocols that require clinicians to check the purpose of the medication on the prescription, and an active diagnosis that matches that purpose, prior to administering the medication.

HFE strategies can also address risk of human error due to working memory limitations:

- Strategies to support working memory include chunking and allowing for frequent offloading of working memory after rehearsal. Chunking is a strategy involving splitting concepts into small pieces or "chunks" of information for retention (e.g., it is easier to remember 123, 456 rather than 1, 2, 3, 4, 5, and 6) (Miller, 1956). A second technique is supporting memory or perceptual judgments through technology recognition rather than recall (Horsky, Kaufman, Oppenheim, & Patel, 2003), for example, an EHR displaying test results alongside the screen for sending a message to the patient about those test results (Nielsen, 1994).
- General techniques to maximize vigilance detection include shorter vigilance periods with frequent rest breaks, strategic use of caffeine, and enhanced signal visibility (Alves & Kelsey, 2010; Ariga & Lleras, 2011; Young, Robinson, & Alberts, 2009). Well-designed alarms that differentiate between a routine alert and a potential emergency also decrease the need for continuous vigilance (e.g., a disconnected ventilator needing an immediate response vs an alarm notifying a nurse that an intravenous infusion needs to be adjusted) (Barnsteiner, 2011; Weinger et al., 1993).
- Strategies for interruptions in the clinical setting include establishing a no-interruption or "quiet" zone (OR Manager, 2013), creating checklists to working memory support (Reason, 1990), and utilizing awareness displays (Dabbish & Kraut, 2004).

Clinical decision-making benefits from the following HFE strategies:

- Decision support techniques and technologies should account for a diagnosis' occurrence, likelihood, and case-specific factors with the intention of guarding against the effects of anchoring, priming, recency bias, or availability heuristics. If a provider is inclined to diagnose a second case of adolescent congestive heart failure that week, technologies should evaluate the probabilistic likelihood of the occurrence against the potential of distorted influence from the availability heuristic (Kahneman & Tversky, 1973).
- Cognitive support technologies and clinician education should account for and train medical personnel to police for unconscious stereotyping by race, ethnicity, or gender. Literature has documented variable prescribing

practices as they relate to patients' demographics (Groenewald, Rabbitts, Hansen, & Palermo, 2018; Smith, Dolk, Smieszek, Robotham, & Pouwels, 2018). Physicians and their support should thus counterintuitively seek reasons to challenge initial decisions to ensure optimal patient care.

• If a practice offers CDS systems, clinicians should pay special attention to alerts and take advantage of existing datasets and protocols. Well-designed CDS tools are intended to facilitate the care process from diagnosis to treatment protocols and can even alert clinicians when incorrect and impractical information is entered into a patient's chart (such as a 2 m tall toddler).

Case study

Our case study describes the optimization of CDS for sepsis. Sepsis is a life-threatening condition caused by an overreaction of the body's immune system to an infection, resulting in dysfunction of vital organ systems. Sepsis affects more than a million Americans every year (Singer et al., 2016), and it represents a rapidly growing problem in terms of the number of patients afflicted by the condition and the varying complexity of their cases. Patients who develop sepsis have an increased risk of complications and death and face longer courses of treatment, long-term cognitive impairment, and functional disability (Iwashyna, Ely, Smith, & Langa, 2010). Sepsis is present on admission or develops in approximately 1 of every 23 hospital admissions and accounts for nearly half of all hospital deaths (Elixhauser, Friedman, & Stranges, 2006; Liu et al., 2014). Early recognition and intervention in sepsis is proven to reduce mortality; thus failure to diagnose sepsis early in a patient's presentation may result in significant adverse outcomes (Kumar et al., 2006; Rivers et al., 2001). Early diagnostic and therapeutic response to sepsis can impact the patients' trajectory of health significantly (Linder et al., 2014).

Central to the successful control of sepsis-associated infection is the ability to rapidly diagnose and treat the disease which requires cognitive support to ensure attention and early recognition, reduced reliance on memory and vigilance, and optimized decision-making. Decision support tools to aid in sepsis clinical decision-making are available including screening, diagnostic, and prognostic tools, but these have not always been to the advantage of the clinician (Chapman, Char, & Aubin, 2002). Mixed models addressing alerts for sepsis, integrating organ failure assessment scores and general severity scores, have been published but have not gained widespread acceptance (Levy et al., 2003; Timsit et al., 2001). Early alert systems commonly use a "one-size-fits-all" approach derived from empirical studies to initiate clinical interventions if the physiological measures exceed certain clinical thresholds. Reports of clinician perception of sepsis CDS efficacy have been mixed, and, most importantly, implementations typically have not had the desired positive impact on patient outcomes, such as reduced sepsis-attributable mortality (Guidi et al., 2015; Moja et al., 2014).

A clinical decision support primer

Reviewing in full a patient's medical record stresses the capacity of both the visual and cognitive systems to process multiple stimuli at a given time. Essentially, sorting through an avalanche of raw data creates information scatter and overload problems (Woods, 1995). With respect to cognitive support for attention and perception, attentional mechanisms are required to select relevant information from among the vast display of information competing for visual processing. CDSs, features within the EHR, are increasingly recognized as valuable tools for providing cognitive support, reducing adverse events, and improving patient safety (Garg et al., 2005). CDS is defined as "providing clinicians with clinical knowledge and patient-related information, intelligently filtered, and presented at appropriate times to enhance patient care" (Bailey et al., 2013; LaRosa et al., 2012). In the best examples, CDS systems guide clinician decision-making and actions (Field et al., 2009; Garg et al., 2005), prevent errors (Ammenwerth, Schnell-Inderst, Machan, & Siebert, 2008; Wolfstadt et al., 2008), improve quality (Field et al., 2009; Kawamoto, Houlihan, Balas, & Lobach, 2005), reduce costs (Fischer et al., 2008), save time (Murphy, 2014), and promote the use of evidence-based recommendations (Eslami, Abu-Hanna, & De Keizer, 2007).

CDS systems are designed to assist the clinical user but often generate too many alerts, produce unwelcome distractions, or miss the opportunity to catch a patient harm event (Cash, 2009). The potential solution that CDS represents is limited by problems associated with improper interface design, implementation, and local customization. Despite an emphasis on EHR usability, little progress has been made to protect end users from inadequately designed workflows and unnecessary interruptions (Kellogg, Wang, Fairbanks, & Ratwani, 2016; Ratwani, Benda, Hettinger, & Fairbanks, 2015; Ratwani, Wang, Fong, & Cooper, 2016). Computerized systems that help clinicians make decisions fail two-thirds of the time (Hussey et al., 2015). High rates of alert overrides have been widely acknowledged as a deterrent to acceptance and appropriate use of CDS (Isaac et al., 2009; Ko et al., 2007; Payne, Nichol, Hoey, & Savarino, 2002; Shah et al., 2006; Strom et al., 2010; Van Der Sijs, Aarts, Van Gelder, Berg, & Vulto, 2008; Van Der Sijs, Aarts, Vulto, & Berg, 2006). Alert overload is detrimental to clinician performance, not only because it can lead to errors by overriding true positive alerts but also because the false alerts consume clinicians' time and mental energy.

A useful framework for achieving success in CDS design, development, and implementation is the "CDS Five Rights" approach (Campbell, 2013). The CDS Five Rights model states that we can achieve CDS-supported improvements in desired health-care outcomes if we communicate (1) the *right information*: evidence-based, suitable to guide action, pertinent to the circumstance; (2) to the *right person:* considering all members of the care team, including clinicians, patients, and their caretakers; (3) in the *right CDS intervention format*: such as an alert, order set, or reference information to answer a clinical question; (4) through the *right channel*: for example, a clinical information system (CIS), such as the EHR, a personal health record, or a more general channel, such as the Internet or a mobile device; and (5) at the *right time in workflow*: for example, at time of decision/action/need. For this case study, we focus on right data (right information, specifically choosing to alert with CDS, leveraging signal detection theory [SDT] and threshold selection) and right design (the design process with considerations of the right information leveraging user-centered design and right time in the workflow leveraging usability and workflow analysis).

Choosing to alert: right data

Many hospital systems use an outdated definition of sepsis defined by the presence of the systemic inflammatory response syndrome (SIRS) with a presumed source of infection, though it is known that sepsis can be present in the absence of these findings (Bone et al., 2009; McQuillan et al., 1998). Algorithms using newly developed criteria which can accurately predict which patients with sepsis will experience in-hospital mortality course may significantly improve outcomes (Howell et al., 2011). Sepsis early alert systems have demonstrated increased compliance with sepsis resuscitation and management bundle elements (LaRosa et al., 2012); however, they are multidimensional, complex, and require in-depth and interdisciplinary approaches to understand their impact. Little information exists in current medical literature to suggest which sepsis screening tool is optimal (Seymour et al., 2016). A health system's decision regarding which prediction score to use is often based on expert opinion and the comparison of prognostic and diagnostic value using meta-analysis—which compares different scores as applied to different populations. The results of these studies should be interpreted with caution. Every health system is unique and any alert needs to be validated and fine-tuned for the appropriate use in the given health-care setting.

SDT is a framework for thinking about alert/alarm criteria. There is always a relationship between true "signal" and "noise" and the trade-offs inherent in choosing the alerting criteria (sometimes, but not always, viewed as a simple threshold—e.g., sepsis trigger alert). SDT is an adaptation of statistical decision theory (Swets, 2014). The theory models the performance of a discrimination task in the presence of uncertainty, as in the diagnosis of

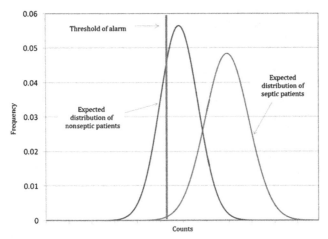

FIGURE 12.1 Hypothetical signal detection model for sepsis includes a combination of signal and noise.

sepsis. An observer is exposed to two types of stimulus, signal and noise. The task is to distinguish between the two, and to respond only to the signal. That is to say, the observer's ability and likelihood to detect some stimulus is affected by the intensity of the stimulation (e.g., how loud a noise is) and the observer's physical and psychological state (e.g., level of alertness). Fig. 12.1 shows a hypothetical signal detection model for sepsis, illustrating that the threshold of alarm, as determined by unique criteria, will be a combination of both signal (expected distribution of septic patients on the right) and noise (expected distribution of nonseptic patients on the left).

Using this model, we imagine the role of the observer is performed by the sepsis detection tool. The complex algorithms used in early detection create the stimulus and the noise. The challenge is for the tool to accurately detect sepsis in this environment. Based on the signal response, there are four possible outcomes, reflecting how sensitive the alerting criteria can be. When the sepsis tool correctly identifies a septic patient, this hit is an indication of sensitivity, specificity, and strong positive predictive value. The true positive alarm indicates that there is a significant patient safety risk, and the provider should take action. A false alarm indicates a lack of sensitivity and specificity and poor positive predictive value. The false-positive alarm may create a risk to patient safety because providers may take action when no corrective action is necessary (Fig. 12.2), but a flood of false-negative alarms can also be a factor in alert desensitization. In systems utilizing outdated sepsis definitions based on the SIRS criteria, false positives are common events. In one study looking at 3147 adult patient stays in 198 European intensive care units, a staggering 93% of patients triggered at least 2 SIRS criteria (Sprung et al., 2006).

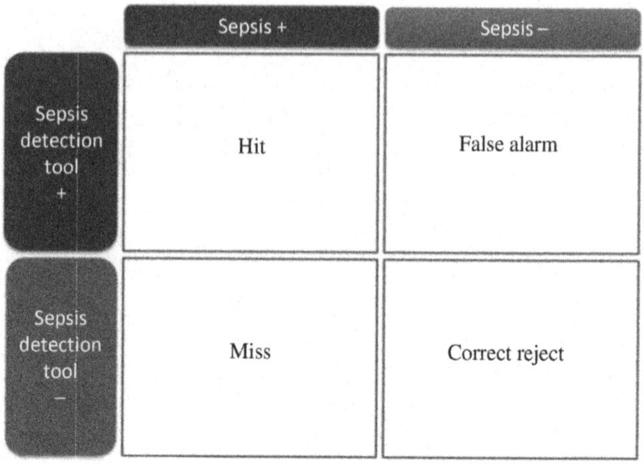

	Sepsis +	Sepsis −
Sepsis detection tool +	Hit	False alarm
Sepsis detection tool −	Miss	Correct reject

FIGURE 12.2 Assessment of signal response demonstrated by presence of disease and detection.

Efficient alert design depends on high positive predictive value. A strong, accurate signal paired with effective presentation of the alert, including how and what is displayed, may offer better cognitive support during busy patient encounters and may help providers extract information quickly. Once a strong signal is established, the expected response should be prompt and appropriate, demonstrating improved communication and trust in CDS. Alternatively, poorly designed alerts that do not accurately convey severity or time sensitivity may cause providers to prematurely dismiss alerts, or act inappropriately, resulting in inefficient use of limited resources. False-positive alerts result in delayed or inappropriate response including unnecessary treatment and misappropriation of resources as a result of distraction, interference, and alert fatigue. The problem of alert desensitization is multi-faceted and related to high false alert rate, poor positive predictive value, lack of alert standardization, and the number of alarm-producing medical devices in hospitals today. Excessive false alarms occur frequently and contribute to alert desensitization, mistrust, and lack of caregiver response (Atzema, Schull, Borgundvaag, Slaughter, & Lee, 2006; Chambrin et al., 1999; Drews, Musters, Markham, & Samore, 2007; Lawless, 1994; Schmid et al., 2011; Siebig et al., 2010; Tsien & Fackler, 1997). The periods where alarms are densest are also likely to be those time periods of the highest cognitive load and task criticality for providers (Woods, 1995). It is precisely during these periods of high workload that technological artifacts are supposed to provide assistance. But this is the time period where nuisance alarms will occur, where poorly designed alerts will distract and disrupt other tasks, where diagnostic search is most difficult, and where there is the need to act to prioritize information-processing tasks.

Current alerts reflect the clinical proclivity to favor sensitivity (false positives for the comfort of not missing a true case) over specificity (fewer false positives, which carries the anxiety of missing a case via false negative). In designing the right data, health-care systems need to consider elements of signal detection, the overall goal of the CDS tool (e.g., diagnostic or prognostic), and availability of trigger elements within the CDS logic, assessing the real-world clinical consequences of the sensitivity—specificity balance without an inherent bias.

Designing the alert: right design

There are serious shortcomings in the existing system for alerting providers to a deteriorating patient in a meaningful way. A central unresolved challenge is timely and consistent implementation of evidence-based diagnostic and therapeutic sepsis guidelines. Despite advances in CDS technology, low adoption rates prevail, and providers still lack responsiveness in recognizing and treating septic patients. Provider adoption and utilization of CDS extends beyond the right data (statistical validity of the rule engine) to usability issues, such as optimal display of critical information and most advantageous timing in the patient encounter for alert "triggers" (e.g., at presentation of chief complaint, at assessment/diagnosis, or at ordering); right design also helps avoid alert fatigue and achieve high synchronization of CDS alerting logic with established protocols and clinician workflow decision points (Press et al., 2015).

Interpretation in the usual care model ("hunting and gathering" in the EHR) can be difficult. EHR displays often are incompatible with clinicians' workflow and unnecessarily fragment patient information (Stanton, 1996). Providers have to first identify which data are linked and then determine the meaning behind the sequence, linking information embedded in other information. Information is often spread across multiple tabs and locations that require piecemeal information search and acquisition. This confounds the ability to detect evolving changes and/or to form a holistic view of a patient's state, leading to care inefficiencies and frustrated clinicians (Anders et al., 2012; Koch et al., 2012). In this environment of information scatter and error-prone decision-making, well-designed alerts can call attention to salient information. The design of alerts must improve the process of information display, reducing cognitive load on the working memory of the provider and improving the usual process that is often characterized by fragmented, nondirected information gathering. This requires the multiphase and iterative cognitive engineering approach to system design (Hettinger, Roth, & Bisantz, 2017).

In the initial knowledge elicitation and capture phase, a multimodal approach using methods, such as artifact analysis and semistructured interviews, can map current information flow and processes and constraints of the clinical problem. Specific work domain demands relevant for alerting, such as time pressure, competing clinical goals, and ambiguous design of existing alerts, may be identified that reduce a user's opportunity to detect signals in the face of workplace "noise" and lead to inadvertent confirmation bias. Clinical, problem-specific constraints will also be identified that should inform elements of the five rights, such as the right time in the workflow. For example, in sepsis, one of the primary constraints is the one identified by Machiavelli in the 16th century: If a provider waits to act until fully certain that the patient has sepsis, it may be too late to save the patient (Machiavelli, 1995).

From a knowledge capture and analysis phase, the process proceeds to alert design. Effective presentation of an alert, including how and what is displayed, may offer better cognitive support during busy patient encounters and help providers extract information quickly (LaRosa et al., 2012). However, there is little consensus on how alerts should be generated and displayed (Miller et al., 2017). Specifically, there is a lack of knowledge regarding the most effective ways to differentiate alerts, highlighting important pieces of information without adding noise, to create a universal standard (Miller, Waitman, Chen, & Rosenbloom, 2005). While underlying models and algorithms of CDS have been intensively studied, there remains a lack of evidence-based guidelines in terms of functional and design requirements of the system.

In the absence of evidence-based guidelines specific to EHR alerting, effective alert design can be informed by several guidelines for design, implementation, and reengineering that help providers take the correct action at the correct time in response to recognition of the patient's condition. Hollifield and Habibi (2006) proposed the following six guidelines for alert development: (1) alerts are properly chosen and implemented; (2) alerts are relevant, clear, and easy to understand; (3) operators can rapidly assess the relative importance of alerts; (4) operators can process alert information during high-frequency events; (5) alert management is based on priority determination; and (6) alert management enhances the operator's ability to make a judgment based on experience and skill. Easterby (1984) suggests seven psychological processes to be considered in display design which determine the limits of display formats (Table 12.1) (Easterby, 1984). Stanton and Stammers (1998) place importance on alert prioritization and organization, which impact early detection of critical alerts. Information must be presented so it is compatible with human capabilities and limitations, so that the system remains usable for the provider in all situations (Shneiderman, 2010). Designs should consider aspects of display design in relation to multiple provider psychological processes which illustrate the different nature of enhanced visual display models.

Because usability factors are a major obstacle to health IT adoption, and a common criticism of CDS systems is their poor usability, the last phase of

TABLE 12.1 Psychological processes and implications for design of visual alarms.

Psychological process	Implications for design of visual displays
Detection	Determining the presence of an alarm
Discrimination	Defining the differences between one alarm and another
Identification	Attributing a name of meaning to an alarm
Classification	Grouping the alarms with a similar purpose of function
Recognition	Knowing what an alarm purports to mean
Scaling	Assigning values to alarms
Ordering and sequencing	Determining the relative order and priority of alarms

the cognitive engineering process of iterative testing and refinement, including formal usability testing, has begun to be considered critical to the EHR and associated CDS adoption and implementation life cycle (Schumacher & Lowry, 2010; Shibl, Lawley, & Debuse, 2013; Yuan, Finley, Long, Mills, & Johnson, 2013). Usability testing is a critical step in informing and defining the standard of care for the health-care system, promoting safe, high-quality care for patients. It provides the opportunity to assess user behavior, interaction, and performance data to measure how the design of medical devices, equipment, practices, and protocols affects performance, quality, and patient safety. A lack of usability testing prior to use can result in poor integration within an established workflow. Therefore studies have begun to focus on usability testing of risk prediction CDS tools directly in workflow-sensitive settings, such as emergency departments and ICUs.

Early stage (formative) usability testing is designed to obtain qualitative reactions to user interface concepts and designs to achieve better understanding of real-world provider decision-making processes and how best to provide meaningful bedside assistance required to achieve the CDS benefits of improved protocol compliance and outcomes. This ideally is followed by preimplementation testing in a production environment, or an environment as close to production as possible, as development environments in EHRs have been known to hide issues in alert design that are found in a production environment (Wright, Aaron, & Sittig, 2016). This last iteration of preimplementation testing in the production environment can ensure the alert functions as expected, including the overall volume of alerting and display of the alert to the right users. Lastly, a period of postimplementation surveillance has been shown to allow for further alert refinement that can reduce inappropriate alerting and increase provider adoption (Yoshida, Fei, Bavuso, Lagor, & Maviglia, 2018).

Conclusion

As health-care environments become increasingly complex, it is critical to recognize where clinicians would benefit from cognitive support. HFE considers the capabilities and limitations of users with the goal of promoting high-quality care for patients by preventing human error. This chapter outlined specific cognitive challenges for clinicians with the goal of optimizing performance, informing design, and creating work environments that are conducive to quality performance and patient safety.

CDS, when implemented correctly, is one form of support. CDS can be utilized across a variety of conditions and circumstances to promote optimal care. It has ultimately improved adherence to recommended care standards and may result in lasting improvements in the clinical setting (Bero et al., 1998; Oxman et al., 1995; Shiffman et al., 1999). However, the accuracy and acceptance of CDS can be limited by numerous factors, including poor usability and too many false-positive alerts. Using sepsis as a lens through which we view CDS usability allows us to analyze the current effectiveness of alerts and design, and to correct systems for further optimization. In the case study outlined, we focused on two specific aspects: choosing when to alert with CDS (ensuring that the CDS is triggered from the right data) and the design process with considerations of the correct information and appropriate time in the workflow (right design).

When implementing CDS, there are a few factors imperative to consider to ensure actionable support. First, presentation of alerts must be carefully designed. Alerts must be differentiated according to subject matter, highlighting important information without adding noise. Effective alert presentation may offer better cognitive support during patient encounters and may help providers extract information quickly. Following recommended HFE principles, alerts should call attention to important matters while informing and guiding the provider (Engineering Equipment & Materials Users' Association, 1999). Second, CDS must be designed and implemented specifically to each health-care system's workflow. Critical to effective implementation, CDS must provide clinicians the right information at the right time. As each health-care system varies widely in staff, structure, and administration, CDS should be modified to work within the constraints of each system.

There is growing evidence that health information technology interventions ultimately improve patient outcomes through early diagnosis and recommendations of evidence-based protocols (Chaudhry et al., 2006). Although there are still improvements to be made, the future of cognitive support is promising due to rapid advancements in technology and a growing body of knowledge of HFE principles.

References

Alves, E. E., & Kelsey, C. M. (2010). Combating vigilance decrement in a single-operator radar platform. *Ergonomics in Design, 18*(2), 6–9.

Ammenwerth, E., Schnell-Inderst, P., Machan, C., & Siebert, U. (2008). The effect of electronic prescribing on medication errors and adverse drug events: A systematic review. *Journal of the American Medical Informatics Association, 15*(5), 585–600.

An, N. I. Z. (2013). Adopting a 'no interruption zone' for patient safety. *OR Manager, 29*(2).

Anders, S., Albert, R., Miller, A., Weinger, M. B., Doig, A. K., Behrens, M., & Agutter, J. (2012). Evaluation of an integrated graphical display to promote acute change detection in ICU patients. *International Journal of Medical Informatics, 81*(12), 842–851.

Anderson, N. D., & Craik, F. I. (2000). *Memory in the aging brain. The Oxford handbook of memory* (pp. 411–425). New York: Oxford University Press.

Ariga, A., & Lleras, A. (2011). Brief and rare mental "breaks" keep you focused: Deactivation and reactivation of task goals preempt vigilance decrements. *Cognition, 118*(3), 439–443.

Arons, B. (1992). A review of the cocktail party effect. *Journal of the American Voice I/O Society, 12*(7), 35–50.

Atzema, C., Schull, M. J., Borgundvaag, B., Slaughter, G. R., & Lee, C. K. (2006). ALARMED: Adverse events in low-risk patients with chest pain receiving continuous electrocardiographic monitoring in the emergency department. A pilot study. *The American Journal of Emergency Medicine, 24*(1), 62–67.

Baddeley, A. (2003). Working memory: Looking back and looking forward. *Nature Reviews Neuroscience, 4*(10), 829.

Bailey, T. C., Chen, Y., Mao, Y., Lu, C., Hackmann, G., Micek, S. T., . . . Kollef, M. H. (2013). A trial of a real-time alert for clinical deterioration in Patients hospitalized on general medical wards. *Journal of Hospital Medicine, 8*(5), 236–242.

Baker, G. R., Norton, P. G., Flintoft, V., Blais, R., Brown, A., Cox, J., . . . O'Beirne, M. (2004). The Canadian Adverse Events Study: The incidence of adverse events among hospital patients in Canada. *Canadian Medical Association Journal, 170*(11), 1678–1686.

Barnsteiner, J. (2011). Teaching the culture of safety. *The Online Journal of Issues in Nursing, 16*(3). https://doi.org/10.3912/OJIN.Vol16No03Man05.

Bates, D. W., O'Neil, A. C., Petersen, L. A., Lee, T. H., & Brennan, T. A. (1995). Evaluation of screening criteria for adverse events in medical patients. *Medical Care, 33*, 452–462.

Bero, L. A., Grilli, R., Grimshaw, J. M., Harvey, E., Oxman, A. D., & Thomson, M. A. (1998). Closing the gap between research and practice: An overview of systematic reviews of interventions to promote the implementation of research findings. The Cochrane Effective Practice and Organization of Care Review Group. *British Medical Journal (Clinical Research ed.), 317*(7156), 465–468.

Bone, R. C., Balk, R. A., Cerra, F. B., Dellinger, R. P., Fein, A. M., Knaus, W. A., . . . Sibbald, W. J. (2009). Definitions for sepsis and organ failure and guidelines for the use of innovative therapies in sepsis. The ACCP/SCCM Consensus Conference Committee. *American College of Chest Physicians/Society of Critical Care Medicine, 136*(5 Suppl), 1992. Chest.

Brannon, L. A., & Carson, K. L. (2003). The representativeness heuristic: Influence on nurses' decision making. *Applied Nursing Research, 16*(3), 201–204.

Brixey, J. J., Robinson, D. J., Tang, Z., Johnson, T. R., Zhang, J., & Turley, J. P. (2005). Interruptions in workflow for RNs in a level one trauma center. *AMIA annual symposium proceedings, 86*, 2005.

Campbell, R. J. (2013). The five rights of clinical decision support: CDS tools helpful for meeting meaningful use. *Journal of AHIMA, 84*(10), 42–47.

Carayon, P., Wetterneck, T. B., Rivera-Rodriguez, A. J., Hundt, A. S., Hoonakker, P., Holden, R., & Gurses, A. P. (2014). Human factors systems approach to healthcare quality and patient safety. *Applied Ergonomics, 45*(1), 14–25.

Cash, J. J. (2009). Alert fatigue. *American Journal of Health-System Pharmacy*, *66*(23), 2098–2101.

Chambrin, M. C., Ravaux, P., Calvelo-Aros, D., Jaborska, A., Chopin, C., & Boniface, B. (1999). Multicentric study of monitoring alarms in the adult intensive care unit (ICU): A descriptive analysis. *Intensive Care Medicine*, *25*(12), 1360–1366.

Chapman, D. M., Char, D. M., & Aubin, C. D. (2002). Clinical decision making. In Marx J., Hockberger R., & Walls, R. (Eds.), *Rosen's emergency medicine: Concepts and clinical practice* (pp. 107–115). Elsevier.

Chaudhry, B., Wang, J., Wu, S., Maglione, M., Mojica, W., Roth, E., ... Shekelle, P. G. (2006). Systematic review: Impact of health information technology on quality, efficiency, and costs of medical care. *Annals of Internal Medicine*, *144*(10), 742–752.

Cheung, M. C., Trudeau, M. E., Mackay, H., De Mendonca, B., Eisen, A., & Singh, S. (2017). The impact of interruptions on physician workflow, productivity, and delivery of care. *Journal of Clinical Oncology*, *35*, 201.

Cina, J. L., Gandhi, T. K., Churchill, W., Fanikos, J., McCrea, M., Mitton, P., ... Poon, E. G. (2006). How many hospital pharmacy medication dispensing errors go undetected? *The Joint Commission Journal on Quality and Patient Safety*, *32*(2), 73–80.

Cooper, J. B., Newbower, R. S., Long, C. D., & McPeek, B. (2002). Preventable anesthesia mishaps: A study of human factors. *British Medical Journal Quality & Safety*, *11*(3), 277–282.

Dabbish, L., & Kraut, R. E. (2004). *Controlling interruptions: Awareness displays and social motivation for coordination. Proceedings of the 2004 ACM conference on computer supported cooperative work* (pp. 182–191). ACM.

Davis, N. M. (1999). Drug names that look and sound alike. *Hospital Pharmacy*, *34*(10), 1160–1178.

Drews, F. A., Musters, A., Markham, B., & Samore, M. H. (2007). Error producing conditions in the intensive care unit. *Proceedings of the Human Factors And Ergonomics Society Annual Meeting*, *51*(11), 702–706.

Easterby, R. (Ed.), (1984). Tasks, processes and display design. Information design (pp. 3–36). Wiley.

Elixhauser, A., Friedman, B., & Stranges, E. (2006). *Septicemia in US hospitals, 2009: Statistical brief# 122. Healthcare Cost and Utilization Project (HCUP) Statistical Briefs [Internet]*. Rockville, MD: Agency for Health Care Policy and Research (US).

Engineering Equipment and Materials Users' Association. (1999). *Alarm systems: A guide to design, management and procurement*. London: Engineering Equipment and Materials Users Association.

Eslami, S., Abu-Hanna, A., & De Keizer, N. F. (2007). Evaluation of outpatient computerized physician medication order entry systems: A systematic review. *Journal of the American Medical Informatics Association*, *14*(4), 400–406.

Field, T. S., Rochon, P., Lee, M., Gavendo, L., Baril, J. L., & Gurwitz, J. H. (2009). Computerized clinical decision support during medication ordering for long-term care residents with renal insufficiency. *Journal of the American Medical Informatics Association*, *16* (4), 480–485.

Fischer, M. A., Vogeli, C., Stedman, M., Ferris, T., Brookhart, M. A., & Weissman, J. S. (2008). Effect of electronic prescribing with formulary decision support on medication use and cost. *Archives of Internal Medicine*, *168*(22), 2433–2439.

Frost and Sullivan. (2018). Patient safety in healthcare, forecast to 2022. In: *Investment trends, growth opportunities, challenges and future perspectives*. Frost & Sullivan.

Garg, A. X., Adhikari, N. K., McDonald, H., Rosas-Arellano, M. P., Devereaux, P. J., Beyene, J., ... Haynes, R. B. (2005). Effects of computerized clinical decision support systems on practitioner performance and patient outcomes: A systematic review. *Journal of the American Medical Association, 293*(10), 1223–1238.

Gorini, A., & Pravettoni, G. (2013). Nurses' violations of a medication administration protocol in Italy: An observational study. *Clinical Nursing Studies, 1*(2), 80.

Groenewald, C. B., Rabbitts, J. A., Hansen, E. E., & Palermo, T. M. (2018). Racial differences in opioid prescribing for children in the United States. *Pain, 159*(10), 2050–2057.

Guidi, J. L., Clark, K., Upton, M. T., Faust, H., Umscheid, C. A., Lane-Fall, M. B., ... Tait, G. (2015). Clinician perception of the effectiveness of an automated early warning and response system for sepsis in an academic medical center. *Annals of the American Thoracic Society, 12*(10), 1514–1519.

Helton, W. S., Dember, W. N., Warm, J. S., & Matthews, G. (1999). Optimism, pessimism, and false failure feedback: Effects on vigilance performance. *Current Psychology, 18*(4), 311–325.

Hettinger, A. Z., Roth, E. M., & Bisantz, A. M. (2017). Cognitive engineering and health informatics: Applications and intersections. *Journal of Biomedical Informatics, 67*, 21–33.

Hodgetts, H. M., & Jones, D. M. (2006). Interruption of the tower of London task: Support for a goal-activation approach. *Journal of Experimental Psychology: General, 135*(1), 103.

Hollifield, B. R., & Habibi, E. (2006). *The alarm management handbook: A comprehensive guide: Practical and proven methods to optimize the performance of any alarm management system.* Houston, TX: PAS.

Horsky, J., Kaufman, D. R., Oppenheim, M. I., & Patel, V. L. (2003). A framework for analyzing the cognitive complexity of computer-assisted clinical ordering. *Journal of Biomedical Informatics, 36*(1–2), 4–22.

Howell, M. D., Talmor, D., Schuetz, P., Hunziker, S., Jones, A. E., & Shapiro, N. I. (2011). Proof of principle: The predisposition, infection, response, organ failure sepsis staging system. *Critical Care Medicine, 39*(2), 322–327.

Hussey, P. S., Timbie, J. W., Burgette, L. F., Wenger, N. S., Nyweide, D. J., & Kahn, K. L. (2015). Appropriateness of advanced diagnostic imaging ordering before and after implementation of clinical decision support systems. *Journal of the American Medical Association, 313*(21), 2181–2182.

Isaac, T., Weissman, J. S., Davis, R. B., Massagli, M., Cyrulik, A., Sands, D. Z., & Weingart, S. N. (2009). Overrides of medication alerts in ambulatory care. *Archives of Internal Medicine, 169*(3), 305–311.

Iwashyna, T. J., Ely, E. W., Smith, D. M., & Langa, K. M. (2010). Long-term cognitive impairment and functional disability among survivors of severe sepsis. *Journal of the American Medical Association, 304*(16), 1787–1794.

Kahneman, D., & Tversky, A. (1973). On the psychology of prediction. *Psychological Review, 80*(4), 237.

Kane, M. J., & Engle, R. W. (2002). The role of prefrontal cortex in working-memory capacity, executive attention, and general fluid intelligence: An individual-differences perspective. *Psychonomic Bulletin & Review, 9*(4), 637–671.

Karsh, B. T., Holden, R. J., Alper, S. J., & Or, C. K. L. (2006). A human factors engineering paradigm for patient safety: Designing to support the performance of the healthcare professional. *British Medical Journal Quality & Safety, 15*(Suppl 1), i59–i65.

Kawamoto, K., Houlihan, C. A., Balas, E. A., & Lobach, D. F. (2005). Improving clinical practice using clinical decision support systems: A systematic review of trials to identify features critical to success. *British Medical Journal, 330*(7494), 765.

Kellogg, K. M., Wang, E., Fairbanks, R. J., & Ratwani, R. (2016). 286 Sources of interruptions of emergency physicians: A pilot study. *Annals of Emergency Medicine, 68*(4), S111–S112.

Ko, Y., Abarca, J., Malone, D. C., Dare, D. C., Geraets, D., Houranieh, A., ... Wilhardt, M. (2007). Practitioners' views on computerized drug—Drug interaction alerts in the VA system. *Journal of the American Medical Informatics Association, 14*(1), 56–64.

Koch, S. H., Weir, C., Haar, M., Staggers, N., Agutter, J., Görges, M., & Westenskow, D. (2012). Intensive care unit nurses' information needs and recommendations for integrated displays to improve nurses' situation awareness. *Journal of the American Medical Informatics Association, 19*(4), 583–590.

Kohn, L. T., Corrigan, J. M., & Donaldson, M. S. (1999). *To err is human: building a safer health system.* Washington, DC: National Academy Press. Institute of Medicine.

Kumar, A., Roberts, D., Wood, K. E., Light, B., Parrillo, J. E., Sharma, S., ... Gurka, D. (2006). Duration of hypotension before initiation of effective antimicrobial therapy is the critical determinant of survival in human septic shock. *Critical Care Medicine, 34*(6), 1589–1596.

Lambert, B. L. (1997). Predicting look-alike and sound-alike medication errors. *American Journal of Health-System Pharmacy, 54*(10), 1161–1171.

LaRosa, J. A., Ahmad, N., Feinberg, M., Shah, M., DiBrienza, R., & Studer, S. (2012). The use of an early alert system to improve compliance with sepsis bundles and to assess impact on mortality. *Critical Care Research and Practice, 2012,* 980369.

Lawless, S. T. (1994). Crying wolf: False alarms in a pediatric intensive care unit. *Critical Care Medicine, 22*(6), 981–985.

Levy, M. M., Fink, M. P., Marshall, J. C., Abraham, E., Angus, D., Cook, D., ... Ramsay, G. (2003). 2001 SCCM/ESICM/ACCP/ATS/SIS international sepsis definitions conference. *Intensive Care Medicine, 29*(4), 530–538.

Linder, A., Guh, D., Boyd, J. H., Walley, K. R., Anis, A. H., & Russell, J. A. (2014). Long-term (10-year) mortality of younger previously healthy patients with severe sepsis/septic shock is worse than that of patients with nonseptic critical illness and of the general population. *Critical Care Medicine, 42*(10), 2211–2218.

Liu, V., Escobar, G. J., Greene, J. D., Soule, J., Whippy, A., Angus, D. C., & Iwashyna, T. J. (2014). Hospital deaths in patients with sepsis from 2 independent cohorts. *Journal of the American Medical Association, 312*(1), 90–92.

Machiavelli, N. (1995). The prince, In D. Wootton (Eds. & Trans.) Hackett Pub. Co, Indianapolis, IN.

Mackworth, N. H. (1948). The breakdown of vigilance during prolonged visual search. *Quarterly Journal of Experimental Psychology, 1*(1), 6–21.

Mark, G., Gonzalez, V. M., & Harris, J. (2005). *No task left behind?: Examining the nature of fragmented work. Proceedings of the SIGCHI conference on human factors in computing systems* (pp. 321–330). ACM.

McFarlane, D. C. (2002). Comparison of four primary methods for coordinating the interruption of people in human-computer interaction. *Human-Computer Interaction, 17*(1), 63–139.

McQuillan, P., Pilkington, S., Allan, A., Taylor, B., Short, A., Morgan, G., ... Smith, G. (1998). Confidential inquiry into quality of care before admission to intensive care. *British Medical Journal, 316*(7148), 1853–1858.

Miller, G. A. (1956). The magical number seven, plus or minus two: Some limits on our capacity for processing information. *Psychological Review, 63*(2), 81.

Miller, K., Mosby, D., Capan, M., Kowalski, R., Ratwani, R., Noaiseh, Y., ... Arnold, R. (2017). Interface, information, interaction: A narrative review of design and functional requirements for clinical decision support. *Journal of the American Medical Informatics Association, 25*(5), 585−592.

Miller, R. A., Waitman, L. R., Chen, S., & Rosenbloom, S. T. (2005). The anatomy of decision support during inpatient care provider order entry (CPOE): Empirical observations from a decade of CPOE experience at Vanderbilt. *Journal of Biomedical Informatics, 38*(6), 469−485.

Moja, L., Kwag, K. H., Lytras, T., Bertizzolo, L., Brandt, L., Pecoraro, V., . . . Iorio, A. (2014). Effectiveness of computerized decision support systems linked to electronic health records: A systematic review and meta-analysis. *American Journal of Public Health, 104*(12), e12−e22.

Mortimer, P. P. (2002). Making blood safer: Stricter vigilance and fewer transfusions are the way forward. *British Medical Journal, 2002*(325), 400−401.

Murphy, E. V. (2014). Clinical decision support: Effectiveness in improving quality processes and clinical outcomes and factors that may influence success. *The Yale Journal of Biology and Medicine, 87*(2), 187−197.

Neath, I. (1998). *Human memory: An introduction to research, data, and theory.* Thomson Brooks/Cole Publishing Co.

Nielsen, J. (1994). *10 usability heuristics for user interface design* (Vol. 1, No. 1). Nielsen Norman Group.

Oxman, A. D., Thomson, M. A., Davis, D. A., & Haynes, R. B. (1995). No magic bullets: A systematic review of 102 trials of interventions to improve professional practice. *CMAJ: Canadian Medical Association Journal, 153*(10), 1423.

Payne, T. H., Nichol, W. P., Hoey, P., & Savarino, J. (2002). *Characteristics and override rates of order checks in a practitioner order entry system. Proceedings of the AMIA Symposium* (p. 602) American Medical Informatics Association.

Pinto, A., Caranci, F., Romano, L., Carrafiello, G., Fonio, P., & Brunese, L. (2012). *Learning from errors in radiology: A comprehensive review. Seminars in Ultrasound, CT and MRI (Vol. 33, No. 4)* (pp. 379−382). WB Saunders.

Poses, R. M., & Anthony, M. (1991). Availability, wishful thinking, and physicians' diagnostic judgments for patients with suspected bacteremia. *Medical Decision Making, 11*(3), 159−168.

Press, A., McCullagh, L., Khan, S., Schachter, A., Pardo, S., & McGinn, T. (2015). Usability testing of a complex clinical decision support tool in the emergency department: Lessons learned. *JMIR Human Factors, 2*(2), e14.

Prinet, J. C., Mize, A. C., & Sarter, N. (2016). Triggering and detecting attentional narrowing in controlled environments. *Proceedings of the Human Factors and Ergonomics Society Annual Meeting, 60*(1), 298−302.

Ratwani, R. M., Benda, N. C., Hettinger, A. Z., & Fairbanks, R. J. (2015). Electronic health record vendor adherence to usability certification requirements and testing standards. *Journal of the American Medical Association, 314*(10), 1070−1071.

Ratwani, R. M., Wang, E., Fong, A., & Cooper, C. J. (2016). A human factors approach to understanding the types and sources of interruptions in radiology reading rooms. *Journal of the American College of Radiology, 13*(9), 1102−1105.

Reason, J. (1990). *Human error.* Cambridge University Press.

Rivera-Rodriguez, A. J., & Karsh, B. T. (2010). Interruptions and distractions in healthcare: Review and reappraisal. *British Medical Journal Quality & Safety,* qshc-2009.

Rivers, E., Nguyen, B., Havstad, S., Ressler, J., Muzzin, A., Knoblich, B., . . . Tomlanovich, M. (2001). Early goal-directed therapy in the treatment of severe sepsis and septic shock. *New England Journal of Medicine, 345*(19), 1368−1377.

Sari, A. B. A., Sheldon, T. A., Cracknell, A., Turnbull, A., Dobson, Y., Grant, C., ... Richardson, A. (2007). Extent, nature and consequences of adverse events: Results of a retrospective casenote review in a large NHS hospital. *British Medical Journal Quality & Safety, 16*(6), 434–439.

Sarter, N. B. (2005). Graded and multimodal interruption cueing in support of preattentive reference and attention management. *Proceedings of the Human Factors and Ergonomics Society Annual Meeting, 49*(3), 478–481.

Schiff, G. D., Hasan, O., Kim, S., Abrams, R., Cosby, K., Lambert, B. L., ... Odwazny, R. (2009). Diagnostic error in medicine: Analysis of 583 physician-reported errors. *Archives of Internal Medicine, 169*(20), 1881–1887.

Schmid, F., Goepfert, M. S., Kuhnt, D., Eichhorn, V., Diedrichs, S., Reichenspurner, H., ... Reuter, D. A. (2011). The wolf is crying in the operating room: Patient monitor and anesthesia workstation alarming patterns during cardiac surgery. *Anesthesia & Analgesia, 112*(1), 78–83.

Schumacher, R. M., & Lowry, S. Z. (2010). *NIST guide to the processes approach for improving the usability of electronic health records.* National Institute of Standards and Technology.

Schweickert, R., & Boruff, B. (1986). Short-term memory capacity: Magic number or magic spell? *Journal of Experimental Psychology: Learning, Memory, and Cognition, 12*(3), 419.

Scott, L. D., Rogers, A. E., Hwang, W. T., & Zhang, Y. (2006). Effects of critical care nurses' work hours on vigilance and patients' safety. *American Journal of Critical Care, 15*(1), 30–37.

Seymour, C. W., Liu, V. X., Iwashyna, T. J., Brunkhorst, F. M., Rea, T. D., Scherag, A., ... Deutschman, C. S. (2016). Assessment of clinical criteria for sepsis: For the Third International Consensus Definitions for Sepsis and Septic Shock (Sepsis-3). *Journal of the American Medical Association, 315*(8), 762–774.

Shah, N. R., Seger, A. C., Seger, D. L., Fiskio, J. M., Kuperman, G. J., Blumenfeld, B., ... Gandhi, T. K. (2006). Improving acceptance of computerized prescribing alerts in ambulatory care. *Journal of the American Medical Informatics Association, 13*(1), 5–11.

Shibl, R., Lawley, M., & Debuse, J. (2013). Factors influencing decision support system acceptance. *Decision Support Systems, 54*(2), 953–961.

Shiffman, R. N., Liaw, Y., Brandt, C. A., & Corb, G. J. (1999). Computer-based guideline implementation systems: A systematic review of functionality and effectiveness. *Journal of the American Medical Informatics Association, 6*(2), 104–114.

Shiffrin, R. M., & Nosofsky, R. M. (1994). Seven plus or minus two: A commentary on capacity limitations. *Psychological Review, 101*(2), 357–361.

Shneiderman, B. (2010). *Designing the user interface: Strategies for effective human-computer interaction.* Pearson Education India.

Siebig, S., Kuhls, S., Imhoff, M., Gather, U., Schölmerich, J., & Wrede, C. E. (2010). Intensive care unit alarms—how many do we need? *Critical Care Medicine, 38*(2), 451–456.

Singer, M., Deutschman, C. S., Seymour, C. W., Shankar-Hari, M., Annane, D., Bauer, M., ... Hotchkiss, R. S. (2016). The third international consensus definitions for sepsis and septic shock (Sepsis-3). *Journal of the American Medical Association, 315*(8), 801–810.

Smith, D. R., Dolk, F. C. K., Smieszek, T., Robotham, J. V., & Pouwels, K. B. (2018). Understanding the gender gap in antibiotic prescribing: A cross-sectional analysis of English primary care. *British Medical Journal Open, 8*(2), e020203.

Sprung, C. L., Sakr, Y., Vincent, J. L., Le Gall, J. R., Reinhart, K., Ranieri, V. M., ... Payen, D. (2006). An evaluation of systemic inflammatory response syndrome signs in the Sepsis Occurrence in Acutely Ill Patients (SOAP) study. *Intensive Care Medicine, 32*(3), 421–427.

Stanton, N. A. (1996). *Operator reactions to alarms fundamental similarities and situational differences. Human Factors in Nuclear Safety* (pp. 84–104). *CRC Press.*

Stanton, N. A., & Stammers, R. B. (1998). Alarm initiated activities: Matching formats to tasks. *International Journal of Cognitive Ergonomics, 2*(4).

Strom, B. L., Schinnar, R., Aberra, F., Bilker, W., Hennessy, S., Leonard, C. E., & Pifer, E. (2010). Unintended effects of a computerized physician order entry nearly hard-stop alert to prevent a drug interaction: A randomized controlled trial. *Archives of Internal Medicine, 170*(17), 1578–1583.

Sweller, J. (1988). Cognitive load during problem solving: Effects on learning. *Cognitive Science, 12*(2), 257–285.

Swets, J. A. (2014). *Signal detection theory and ROC analysis in psychology and diagnostics. Collected papers. Psychology Press.*

Teichner, W. H. (1974). The detection of a simple visual signal as a function of time of watch. *Human Factors, 16*(4), 339–352.

Thomas, E. J., Studdert, D. M., Burstin, H. R., Orav, E. J., Zeena, T., Williams, E. J., ... Brennan, T. A. (2000). Incidence and types of adverse events and negligent care in Utah and Colorado. *Medical Care,* 261–271.

Timsit, J., Fosse, J., Troche, G., De Lassence, A., Alberti, C., Garrouste-Orgeas, M., ... Cohen, Y. (2001). Accuracy of a composite score using daily SAPS II and LOD scores for predicting hospital mortality in ICU patients hospitalized for more than 72 h. *Intensive Care Medicine, 27*(6), 1012–1021.

Tsien, C. L., & Fackler, J. C. (1997). Poor prognosis for existing monitors in the intensive care unit. *Critical Care Medicine, 25*(4), 614–619.

Van Der Sijs, H., Aarts, J., Van Gelder, T., Berg, M., & Vulto, A. (2008). Turning off frequently overridden drug alerts: Limited opportunities for doing it safely. *Journal of the American Medical Informatics Association, 15*(4), 439–448.

Van Der Sijs, H., Aarts, J., Vulto, A., & Berg, M. (2006). Overriding of drug safety alerts in computerized physician order entry. *Journal of the American Medical Informatics Association, 13*(2), 138–147.

Vincent, C., Neale, G., & Woloshynowych, M. (2001). Adverse events in British hospitals: Preliminary retrospective record review. *British Medical Journal, 322*(7285), 517–519.

Weinger, M. B., Smith, N. T., Ehrenwerth, J., & Eisenkraft, J. B. (1993). *Vigilance, alarms, and integrated monitoring systems. Anesthesia equipment: Principles and applications* (pp. 350–384). Malvern, PA: Mosby Year Book.

Westbrook, J. I., Woods, A., Rob, M. I., Dunsmuir, W. T., & Day, R. O. (2010). Association of interruptions with an increased risk and severity of medication administration errors. *Archives of Internal Medicine, 170*(8), 683–690.

Wilson, R. M., Runciman, W. B., Gibberd, R. W., Harrison, B. T., & Hamilton, J. D. (1996). Quality in Australian health care study. *The Medical Journal of Australia, 164*(12), 754.

Wilson, T. D., Houston, C. E., Etling, K. M., & Brekke, N. (1996). A new look at anchoring effects: Basic anchoring and its antecedents. *Journal of Experimental Psychology: General, 125*(4), 387.

Wolfstadt, J. I., Gurwitz, J. H., Field, T. S., Lee, M., Kalkar, S., Wu, W., & Rochon, P. A. (2008). The effect of computerized physician order entry with clinical decision support on the rates of adverse drug events: A systematic review. *Journal of General Internal Medicine, 23*(4), 451–458.

Woods, D. D. (1995). The alarm problem and directed attention in dynamic fault management. *Ergonomics, 38*(11), 2371–2393.

Wright, A., Aaron, S., & Sittig, D. F. (2016). Testing electronic health records in the "production" environment: An essential step in the journey to a safe and effective health care system. *Journal of the American Medical Informatics Association, 24*(1), 188–192.

Yoshida, E., Fei, S., Bavuso, K., Lagor, C., & Maviglia, S. (2018). The value of monitoring clinical decision support interventions. *Applied Clinical Informatics, 9*(01), 163–173.

Young, M. S., Robinson, S., & Alberts, P. (2009). Students pay attention! Combating the vigilance decrement to improve learning during lectures. *Active Learning in Higher Education, 10*(1), 41–55.

Yuan, M. J., Finley, G. M., Long, J., Mills, C., & Johnson, R. K. (2013). Evaluation of user interface and workflow design of a bedside nursing clinical decision support system. *Interactive Journal of Medical Research, 2*(1), e4.

Further reading

Brook, R. H., McGlynn, E. A., & Shekelle, P. G. (2000). Defining and measuring quality of care: A perspective from US researchers. *International Journal for Quality in Health Care, 12*(4), 281–295.

McGlynn, E. A., Asch, S. M., Adams, J., Keesey, J., Hicks, J., DeCristofaro, A., & Kerr, E. A. (2003). The quality of health care delivered to adults in the United States. *New England Journal of Medicine, 348*(26), 2635–2645.

Miller, J. G. (1960). Information input overload and psychopathology. *American Journal of Psychiatry, 116*(8), 695–704.

Tomietto, M., Sartor, A., Mazzocoli, E., & Palese, A. (2012). Paradoxical effects of a hospital-based, multi-intervention programme aimed at reducing medication round interruptions. *Journal of Nursing Management, 20*(3), 335–343.

Warm, J. S., Parasuraman, R., & Matthews, G. (2008). Vigilance requires hard mental work and is stressful. *Human Factors, 50*(3), 433–441.

Williams, E. S., Konrad, T. R., Linzer, M., McMurray, J., Pathman, D. E., Gerrity, M., ... Douglas, J. (2002). Physician, practice, and patient characteristics related to primary care physician physical and mental health: Results from the Physician Worklife Study. *Health Services Research, 37*(1), 119.

Wright, P. (1974). The harassed decision maker: Time pressures, distractions, and the use of evidence. *Journal of Applied Psychology, 59*(5), 555.

Chapter 13

Design for improved workflow

Mustafa Ozkaynak[1], Blaine Reeder[1], Sun Young Park[2] and Jina Huh-Yoo[3]
[1]*College of Nursing, University of Colorado, Denver, CO, United States,* [2]*School of Information, University of Michigan School of Art and Design, Ann Arbor, MI, United States,* [3]*College of Computing and Informatics, Drexel University, Philadelphia, PA, United States*

Introduction

Workflow in health-related settings

Workflow in health-related settings has been defined in various ways, but these definitions are generally categorized into clinician- versus patient-oriented workflow. Clinician-oriented approaches focus on a collection of activities (or steps) by a single clinician or type of clinician (Ozkaynak, Reeder, et al., 2019; Ozkaynak, Wu, Hannah, Dayan, & Mistry, 2018) and capture what these individuals do. These approaches are effective in analyzing jobs or roles. Patient-oriented approaches, on the other hand, focus on the activities performed for the patient by multiple clinicians (Ozkaynak et al., 2013; Ozkaynak, Ponnala, & Werner, 2019). In either case (clinician- or patient-oriented) the building blocks of workflow include (1) tasks or activities, (2) roles (e.g., agents) who conduct these activities, and (3) the temporal organization (timing, sequence, duration) of the activities.

The concept of workflow allows for examination of various work phenomena (e.g., activities, sequence). For example, workflow can be understood by examining the clinician's interaction with the screen of the electronic health record (EHR; Saitwal, Feng, Walji, Patel, & Zhang, 2010); direct or indirect patient care activities (Ozkaynak & Brennan, 2012; Ozkaynak et al., 2015); individual jobs (Ozkaynak, Valdez, Holden, & Weiss, 2018); a specific task (e.g., medication administration; Carayon et al., 2007); documentation (Park, Lee, & Chen, 2012); handover of an artifact (Vankipuram, Kahol, Cohen, & Patel, 2011); or reconfiguration of physical layout in a clinical setting (Park & Chen, 2012). Depending on the focus of work, the scope of activities that make up workflow and time frame—for example, throughout patient stay (days), or during order entry only

Design for Health. DOI: https://doi.org/10.1016/B978-0-12-816427-3.00013-0

(minutes)—may differ. For example, activities in an operating room (where most activities are predictable and technically driven) would be different from that of an emergency department (ED, where activities are predictable and decision-making driven). Systematic approaches to understanding the delivery of activities, and how they are temporally organized, allow researchers the ability to examine how various resources come together and produce outcomes. By extension, these observations and mapping can identify and often explain desired and undesired patient and organizational outcomes.

Workflow studies can measure and compare performance outcomes, such as length of stay and documentation time, to complete an activity (Carayon et al., 2015; Wiler et al., 2016). Workflow studies have also been conducted to identify efficiency, cost, safety, and quality-related issues (Aarts, Ash, & Berg, 2007; Koppel, Wetterneck, Telles, & Karsh, 2008). Identifying these issues can inform the design and implementation of health information technologies (HIT) and other organizational interventions, such as policies, that would improve patient safety. Because of potential risks involved in the delivery of health care, safety has been the primary emphasis of workflow studies. Workflow studies can facilitate the identification of risks as well as inform the interventions that mitigate these risks (Patterson, Cook, & Render, 2002; Walker & Carayon, 2009). More specifically, workflow studies can enhance patient safety by improving the usability of EHRs (Middleton et al., 2013), systematically examining workarounds (Koppel et al., 2008), and making invisible work elements visible (Oudshoorn, 2008; Stisen, Verdezoto, Blunck, Kjærgaard, & Grønbæk, 2016).

Systematic workflow studies reveal the gaps among the perceived workflow (by clinicians or HIT users), actual workflow, and the predetermined/designed/ideal workflow (Jessee & Mion, 2013; Ozkaynak & Brennan, 2013; Sendlhofer et al., 2016). In an ideal situation the difference between these workflow representations would be minimal; however, the hectic, adaptive, and autonomous nature of health-care work (Plsek & Greenhalgh, 2001; Pype, Mertens, Helewaut, & Krystallidou, 2018) can magnify the difference. To reduce the gap among differently perceived or desired workflows, design studies can provide useful insights by better understanding and addressing user needs, augmenting individual and distributed cognition, and ensuring congruence among work system elements (e.g., tasks, environment, and tools).

Designing workflow versus designing interventions for workflow

Design studies can improve workflow in two ways: designing the overall workflow and designing interventions that would improve workflow. Designing workflow refers to (1) identifying objectives that should be achieved with work in question, (2) developing activities that would compose workflow, (3) assigning activities to appropriate roles, (4) organizing activities temporally, (5) identifying facilitators, barriers, and other needed resources, and (6) evaluating the fit of the workflow with the rest of the elements of the health system (e.g., technology, policies).

Identifying objectives (step 1) is critical, since the objectives will set the scope and relevant system boundaries. Setting boundaries appropriately ensures meaningful identification of beginning and end points of workflow and correct inputs and outputs. Activities (or steps) of workflow should be clearly identified in a balanced way to give sufficient specificity and flexibility (step 2). Activities should be goal-oriented and assigned among people and computer agents congruent with their abilities and scope of practice (step 3). These activities should also be organized in a way so that they ensure access to the right resources at the right time (step 4). Workflow designers should also identify other important building blocks such as information, artifacts, material, and tools (step 5). Workflow receives inputs from its environment and should produce outputs that are congruent with that environment, and with the organizational context in which it is embedded. Therefore the fit of the workflow should be evaluated (step 5).

Workflow can be improved by designing interventions (e.g., supportive, social, and technical infrastructures) including information technologies, physical environment (e.g., layout), task assignments, rules and policies, and training. Information technology, such as clinical decision support systems (CDSs) or provider order entry systems, can improve workflow by minimizing risk, decreasing the time needed to accomplish a task, decreasing workload on human agents, or decreasing cost (Courtney, Demiris, & Alexander, 2005; Yeow & Goh, 2015). However, it is well documented that if technology is not designed appropriately, it may worsen and disrupt the workflow (Campbell, Sittig, Ash, Guappone, & Dykstra, 2006; Harrison, Koppel, & Bar-Lev, 2007). Designing a better physical layout can also decrease workload, decrease activity time, and increase situational awareness (Hadi & Zimring, 2016; Rismanchian & Lee, 2017). Designing better organizations also involves developing congruent rules and policies with workflow. Training is an essential part of successful implementation of any organizational intervention (Bergs et al., 2015).

Health informatics, workflow, and user-centered design

Health informatics is the science and applied use of data, information, and knowledge for problem-solving and decision-making to improve human health outcomes (Kulikowski et al., 2012). User-centered design refers to an overall concept of engaging users of designed artifacts to understand their needs and preferences (Norman, 1988). One way to characterize user engagement is along the spectrum of designers' observations and understanding of users (contextual inquiry; Holtzblatt & Jones, 1993), to design artifacts or activities with input from both users and designers (codesign), and user-driven innovation (participatory design; Kushniruk & Nohr, 2016; Tang, Lim, Mansfield, McLachlan, & Quan, 2018).

In the following sections, we examine three subfields of health informatics—clinical, public health, and consumer health informatics—and how each subfield engages workflow as part of a design problem. We focus on health informatics because of the broad interdisciplinary domain in which workflow and design heavily interact. We then describe how user-centered design can enhance the workflow of the contexts covered in these subfields of health informatics.

Workflow and user-centered design in clinical informatics

Clinical informatics is the "practice of informatics in health care through medical, nursing, dental, and other forms of informatics that are applied to patients or to healthy individuals" (Kulikowski et al., 2012). Clinical informatics efforts are often undertaken in acute care settings but have also been applied in primary care, long-term care, and skilled nursing facilities, among others. Clinical informatics often focus on the use of the EHR system and, given the recent widespread adoption of EHRs in acute care settings (Henry, Pylypchuck, Searcy, & Patel, 2016), represents a major area of informatics research. Since clinical settings represent practice areas for licensed clinicians, there is a regulated scope of work, though practices vary due to facility-level and organizational factors. User-centered and participatory design approaches have long been recognized as necessary in the development of EHR systems, although they are not consistently employed. Indeed, there are many recent systematic reviews concerning usability and safety of EHRs (Ellsworth et al., 2017; Ratwani et al., 2016; Roman, Ancker, Johnson, & Senathirajah, 2017; Zahabi, Kaber, & Swangnetr, 2015). Workflow is not an unknown concept in the clinical informatics arena and is often mentioned in design efforts, even if formal workflow methodology is not employed. One recent example is of a study that connects usability and workflow focus with physicians' perceptions of EHR usability and impact on workflow in EDs (Denton et al., 2018). Another example is a study of the effect of data completeness in free-text patient directions for e-prescriptions on workflow efficiencies in ambulatory care (Yang, Ward-Charlerie, Dhavle, Rupp, & Green, 2018). More formally, Nolan et al. (2017) explicitly state that understanding workflow observations is a requirement for design efforts that result in usable EHR visualization tools. In addition, we have employed user-centered design and workflow methods in the design of a mobile clinical decision support app for urinary tract infection in long-term care (Jones et al., 2017; Ozkaynak, Reeder, et al., 2019).

Workflow and user-centered design in public health informatics

Public health informatics is defined as the "systematic application of information and computer science and technology to public health practice, research, and learning that integrates public health and information technology" (O'Carroll, 2003). Public health informatics is part of public health practice with its own set of standards, competencies, and a defined scope of work that lends itself to workflow studies. As with clinical informatics, public health informatics design efforts may document workflow activities, even if formal workflow methodology is absent. Some examples from our own research include user-centered design to support the work of public health nurses who work in maternal–child health (Reeder, Hills, Turner, & Demiris, 2014), syndromic surveillance of influenza-like illness using emergency department chief complaint data from EHRs for epidemiologists (Reeder, Revere, Olson, & Lober, 2011), and continuity of operations planning for public health administrators (Reeder & Turner, 2011; Turner, Reeder, & Wallace, 2013a). Turner, Reeder, and Ramey (2013) implemented a combined user-centered design and workflow methodology focusing on communicable disease investigations by public nurses (Turner et al., 2013). More recently, an evaluation of EHR implementation in a public health setting demonstrated the mismatch between EHR systems designed for clinical workflow and the usability needs in the public health setting, identifying the need for better tailoring (Crowley et al., 2018).

Workflow and user-centered design in consumer health informatics

Consumer health informatics focuses on the individuals who interact with health-care systems, by "putting health information into their hands, including information on their own health, such as diagnoses, lab results, personal risk factors, and prescribed drugs" (Eysenbach, 2000). The scope of this informatics subfield, however, has broadened considerably beyond information sourced in clinical settings, with the advent of mobile computing and wearable technologies (Demiris, 2012). Designing consumer health informatics is now uniquely challenged to cover daily living contexts for all people for virtually every conceivable health concern. Individuals have varying degrees of needs and preferences based on demographics (age, gender, race, ethnicity, health, technology, literacy level, educational level, and socioeconomic status).

Health conditions can range from diabetes management to chronic obstructive pulmonary disorder and irritable bowel disorder (Lai, Hsueh, Choi, & Austin, 2017). Adding even greater variability, users of consumer health informatics applications are not restricted to patients with current health conditions but to the overall population interested in proactively maintaining good health and wellness (Faiola & Holden, 2017) or to "age in place" (Reeder, Chung, et al., 2013; Reeder, Meyer, et al., 2013). Fortunately, recent efforts have been undertaken to develop frameworks for understanding patient work (Valdez, Holden, Novak, & Veinot, 2015) and workflow in the setting of everyday living (Chung, Ozkaynak, & Demiris, 2017; Ozkaynak, Jones, Weiss, Klem, & Reeder, 2016). Emerging mobile and wearable technologies are being adopted at a rapid rate. These technologies can be used to provide solutions and mechanisms to consumer health informatics applications. Design studies should therefore focus on understanding the interaction between workflow in clinical and daily living settings and technologies that support workflow across diverse settings (Ozkaynak et al., 2018).

Design guidelines

User-centered design: engaging users for improving workflow

User-centered design approaches help understand not only the user's needs and desires but also the holistic context of the user's social, technical, and cultural environments, and, as necessary, engage users as designers of the technology they will use. As part of the design process, it is crucial to identify who the target users (and their explicit and hidden needs) are, which specified tasks to design, and under which context (Barnum & Dragga, 2001). Requirements drastically change based on these factors, as do the measurements to assess whether the goal of the design has been met.

For instance, older adults may consider understanding individual data points as critical in using medical records, while clinicians may require aggregate summaries of trends over time that allow for exploration of the visualized data (Huh, Le, Reeder, Thompson, & Demiris, 2013). Patients may also need to retrieve additional background information and situate their own health status in relation to other cases, while clinicians need visual feedback that shows individual patient conditions in the current context of care (Shneiderman, Plaisant, & Hesse, 2013). Public health professionals will need integrated systems that pull together diverse data sets for surveillance and to support recommendations for new programs (Huh et al., 2013; Shneiderman et al., 2013). Capturing these contextual factors and specified needs requires multiple sets of techniques and methods that incorporate diverse perspectives.

Later we have provided examples of the user-centered design methods that can be used to improve workflow design. These methods are not a comprehensive list of user-centered design methods; rather, we argue that these are good starting points to consider for designing workflows for health-related settings. We provide definitions of each method, followed by an example case that illustrates how to get users involved in workflow designs. We then describe outcomes generated from the method.

Observations

- Definition: Observation is a method drawn from ethnography that studies people as they go about everyday work. Researchers enter the setting and earn enough trust to actively participate (participant−observer) in the community of practice that drives text adoption. This is a way to become immersed in the user experience to do user-centered design (LeCompte & Schensul, 1999). Participant observation is learning through exposure to or involvement in the day-to-day or routine activities of participants in the setting (LeCompte & Schensul, 1999). Often, this can be conducted by shadowing participants, accompanying participants through the events in a day (Ozkaynak et al., 2018; Ozkaynak, Reeder, et al., 2019).
- Examples: To improve the workflow of clinicians' documentation during the transition from papers to EHR systems, the researcher observes clinicians' documentation work process or shadow clinician participants' use of each tool (paper vs EHR) to compare for a period of time during the new EHR adoption phase.
- Outcomes: Insights and previously untapped or hidden opportunities at the potential expense of the ability to replicate and generalize.

Participant interviews

- Definition: Interview is "a process in which a researcher and participants engage in a conversation focused on questions related to a research study" (deMarrais, 2004, p. 55). The most common form of interview is the one-on-one conversation conducted (in the context, if possible) though group or collective formats to obtain data. The main purpose of an interview is to obtain a specific kind of information that the researchers want to find out, so the interview should follow a thematic protocol or it can be semistructured. This helps in understanding and identifying how people express knowledge, attitudes, perception, and belief (Ozkaynak et al., 2018; Reeder et al., 2014; Turner, Reeder, & Wallace, 2013b).
- Examples: To improve the adoption of personal health records (PHR) through the use of inpatients' bedside tablet use, the researcher conducts interviews with patients or their caregivers in inpatient settings about their experiences of bedside tablet usage.
- Outcomes: Deep knowledge and insights with small numbers, participants' experience, feelings, opinions, knowledge, sensory, or demographic data.

Focus groups

- Definition: Focus groups help assess user needs and feelings before the interface has been designed and after it has been deployed and used. Focus groups include six to nine users who together discuss new ideas and potential issues over an hour or two. A moderator maintains the focus group on the issues of interest. The conversations should be free-flowing and relatively unstructured, although the moderator should have a preplanned script with which overall structures will be determined (Le et al., 2015; Nielsen, 1993, pp. 214–217; Reeder et al., 2011, 2014; Reeder, Le, Thompson, & Demiris, 2013; Turner, Reeder, et al., 2013b).

- Examples: To understand experiences and opinions among different groups about the new EHR system deployment, researchers conduct focus groups with different stakeholders, such as physicians, nurses, administrators, patients, and caregivers. This can be done separately to reduce potential power dynamics between different stakeholders who might hinder effective group discussion.
- Outcomes: Collective answers to questions on a decision-making issue, agreement and disagreement points among stakeholders, sensemaking process among diverse stakeholders, observations of group dynamics and organizational issues, users' spontaneous reactions.

Questionnaires

- Definition: Questionnaires are instruments that collect information from respondents. Questionnaires enclose a set of open-ended and close-ended questions that can scale to a larger number of respondents. From a usability perspective, questionnaires are indirect methods because they studies users' opinions about the user interface and not the user interface itself. Accordingly, users' statements should not be taken at face value. Data about actual behavior should precede what users claimed they would do (Nielsen, 1993).
- Examples: To improve hospital care service designs and policies about patient experience, the organization conducts patient satisfaction surveys during or after patient discharge.
- Outcomes: Decision-making point on a contentious topic, significance assessment on known problems, quantitative approach to prioritizing patient experience breakdown points.

Think-aloud protocols

- Definition: One of the valuable usability engineering methods, a "think-aloud test involves having a test subject use the system while continuously thinking out loud" (Lewis, 1982). The verbalization of the users allows researchers to understand how users view and interpret the system and identify major misconceptions around the system design (Jaspers, Steen, Bos, & Geenen, 2004; Kaufman et al., 2003; Turner, Reeder, et al., 2013b).
- Examples: To improve the efficiency of EHR use on clinicians' documentation processes, the researcher conducts think-aloud protocols to

understand users' thought processes in using EHR and identifies points of breakdowns.

- Outcomes: Identification of usability problems of a specific area of EHR, users' mental models different from that of the designers.

Contextual inquiry and workflow: understanding users' tasks and activities

Contextual inquiry allows a designer to understand the hidden work structures—and hidden needs and desires—in a target audience. Contextual inquiry is appropriate for health-care settings because user needs and activities in health care heavily vary even though they provide similar service (Ozkaynak et al., 2018). Contextual inquiry refers to a set of methods that help designers gain a well-rounded understanding of the users' needs to characterize design problems, with a particular focus on tasks and activities the user performs (Holtzblatt & Jones, 1993). Contextual inquiry begins with unstructured, iterative examination of the user's frame of reference, using interviews and observations. Semistructured interviews in the beginning can help designers probe implicit (work) context and problems that interviewers may not know or anticipate before the interview (Wood, 1997). For instance the interview would begin with *grand tour* questions (Spradley, 1979), which allow users to show the designer around their physical, temporal, and conceptual space of the work domain. To prompt this grand tour, the interviewer would use *task-related* questions (e.g., *Could you discuss the major steps you go through in resolving your questions answered at the doctor's visit?*), *guided* questions (e.g., *Could you tell me the last time you visited the doctor's office?*), and *typical* questions (e.g., *Could you tell me about a typical question you might ask while visiting the doctor's office?*). Answers then inform follow-up questions, which formulate around terminologies by which users describe their experiences. The interviewers would follow up with the user-supplied words to further expand on the contexts that might inform hidden challenges, and these challenges can be developed as a seed for design implications. Other probing techniques include asking about relationships between concepts or events (e.g., patient-initiated appointments vs doctor-initiated appointments) and conflicts (e.g., preferences in asking questions to nurses vs doctors).

After the interviews have been completed the analyst performs a number of analysis methods on the interview transcripts to draw common themes (e.g., activities, coordination issues, information needs), breakdowns (activities that should be accomplished by nurses vs physicians vs technology), relationships (e.g., temporal, causal relationships between activities) among the themes, and design insights to move onto the next stage of the inquiry. Affinity diagraming, for instance, helps a group of designers to collectively make sense of the data and generates brainstorming sessions for design insights (Plain, 2007). The process begins with recording each segment of interview data on post-it notes; then the group takes turns placing the notes on the wall to share, grouping the ideas that seem related or emergent. This process will continue until the notes have all been sorted and re-sorted, and the group members agree on the emerged grouped themes. The themes then help designers and researchers prioritize and generate design insights such as how computer interface should be for best interaction and workflow support.

The interview data, combined with field observations as needed, can also be translated into models of understanding—workflow, sequence, artifact, culture, and user—for analysis. These models help the analysts visualize and systematize the observational data. The workflow model specifically helps in identifying roles and responsibilities among the stakeholders, workflow hierarchies, and communication patterns among those roles in accomplishing a specific task (Holtzblatt & Jones, 1993). Using a set of symbols, each model presents the holistic relationships among users or stakeholders (circle), task (descriptions inside the circle, which refers to the stakeholders' tasks), location (rectangle), directions of relationships (arrows that are either one way or two way), communication (rectangle on the arrow), and obstacles (thunder symbol). Fig. 13.1 provides an illustration for use of symbols in a case of antibiotic prescription in a pediatric ED. As the analyst processes the transcripts and observation notes, these units are placed on a canvas, constructing understanding of the overall workflow in the end.

Through these inquiries, we understand distinct user needs that are either individualized (Huh et al., 2016) or group-based and derived from demographic, social, or cultural commonalities shared among the group members. Inquiry also identifies relationships among culture, roles, stakeholders, and

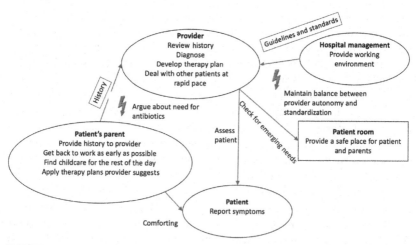

FIGURE 13.1 Antibiotic prescription in a pediatric ED.

tasks. When individuals such as patients and other consumers of health informatics applications are involved as stakeholders of technology, the workflow expands from clinical settings to home, occupational, and social environments to accommodate the diversity of activities in this larger range of settings. The challenge is how contextual inquiry examines the larger, holistic contexts of the user, prioritizing the relevant over the extraneous.

Case study: Design to support patient engagement for improved intra- and interorganizational workflow in emergency care

In the following case studies, we first discuss ED care in general as well as for two patient populations: pediatric patients with asthma and an elderly population with heart failure (HF). Both are chronic conditions which can worsen suddenly. We also explain the health technology and information system implementation in ED, which affects not only clinicians and administrative staff directly but also all patients in the ED indirectly. Through the case study we present here, we intend to highlight the significance of design for enhancing both intra and interorganizational workflows, and to emphasize the significance of engaging users into workflow design—from clinicians as well as patients.

Asthma is the most common condition for children's visits to EDs (Akinbami, Moorman, & Liu, 2011). This chronic condition sometimes requires visiting the ED in the event of worsening conditions. However, health-related activities (e.g., monitoring of symptoms and medication use) for this population spans multiple locations and may involve the pediatric patient, primary care providers, ED clinicians, school staff, family members, parents of friends, etc. All these individuals could be involved in health-related activities to various degrees.

Just as asthma is prevalent for pediatric patients, HF is one of the most common and costly reasons for hospital admission among older Americans (Jencks, Williams, & Coleman, 2009). Patients are often hospitalized after an ED visit. One strategy to reduce these hospitalizations is to identify patients at risk for admission and support the initiation of self-care activities. HF management entails cross-setting health-care activities, including numerous complex self-care activities. However, adherence to HF self-care treatment regimens is low, despite the designation of self-care as a Class I recommendation (i.e., having the highest benefit-to-risk ratio in professional guidelines; Yancy et al., 2013).

In both conditions, ED visits are common, and the workflow of ED care can significantly affect patients' health outcomes (Jang, Ozkaynak, Ayer, & Sills, 2019; Ozkaynak et al., 2015). In both cases, workflow crosses diverse clinical and daily living settings. Interorganizational workflow (i.e., chronic disease management that takes place both in clinical and daily living) faces significant challenges. For example, individuals involved in the patient's care, such as ED care provider, primary care provider, school nurse, home nurse, and informal caregivers, may need or interact with similar health-related information for conducting care activities for the patient; however, each has a different level of access to information. Design efforts should account for multiple individuals with a wide range of capabilities and access to information, as well as diverse contexts and settings where each engages with care activities to ensure effective communication and smooth transitions across these diverse care contexts.

In studying ED workflow, user-centered design and contextual inquiry can be effective qualitative approaches to characterize workflow and identify individuals' information needs that can help improve workflow in ED care (Sheehan et al., 2013). In this approach, designers can engage patients and clinicians, in their various roles, in early stages of design, to understand their experienced workflows, perceived breakdowns, and challenges in their work context in situ. Observing users situated in their actual work context is essential to gain a better understanding of the entire ED care practice by capturing various perspectives and needs of different sets of individuals who may be involved in the care activities. For example, understanding the detailed ED diagnostic process, including when and how clinicians make clinical decisions, who are involved in the diagnostic decision-making process, and what tools are used for the tasks during the ED care delivery, can inform not only the design of CDSs, but also, more importantly, how the system can be better designed to fit into the existing workflow of clinicians' care activities.

Later, we discuss the importance of workflow through the case study of emergency care, how the ED workflow is closely associated with the use of EHR systems, and how the workflow altered by the newly deployed EHR system can affect patient care in the ED as an unintended consequence.

Significance of understanding workflow in an emergency care setting

The issue of how to improve hospital workflows is one that concerns senior health-care management at every level; however, achieving workflow optimization in hospitals is daunting work. The ED is an area of hospital operations where streamlined, structured sequences of tasks and fast, secure communications are key to successful outcomes. Designing efficient and optimized workflow is critical for an ED, where critical health-care decisions are made and have profoundly positive or negative consequences for the patient. Further, an ED's workflow efficiency can affect the entire hospital's patient flow (e.g., an ED often becomes a bottleneck for timely hospital admissions).

The nature of emergency care makes it particularly worthy of studying workflow for several reasons. First, ED work is unbounded. Compared to other areas of the hospital which have specific workload plans, EDs cannot predict or control a care provider's workload or patient diagnosis and complexity. Second, the demands on emergency services are currently increasing due to an unprecedented nursing shortage; as a result, nearly all EDs are severely overcrowded (Trzeciak & Rivers, 2003). ED services are also under significant time constraints, which can cause even heavier workloads and a more challenging workflow for providers. In addition, ED work is characterized by a high level of uncertainty: ED care providers often need to make difficult decisions without background information and before critical data is available. Taken together, these factors make the ED a unique environment in which the workflow and the impact of workflow on the care practices of providers as well as patients are studied.

Redesigning clinical workflow with health information technologies implementation in the ED

With recent technological developments and government initiatives, the deployment of HIT systems has significantly affected ED work practices, including workflow, policies, clinicians, and patients. Upon HIT implementation, clinicians and hospital staff are expected to maintain and optimize their work performance with the use of the new system. However, the introduction of HIT systems, including the EHR, CDS, and computerized physician order entry, often slows down the provider's productivity and leads to unintended consequences, such as extended documentation time (Cyert & March, 1992; Poissant, Pereira, Tamblyn, & Kawasumi, 2005), increased workload (Richardson & Ash, 2008), incompatible workflow (Cyert & March, 1992; Saleem et al., 2011), and even system-induced medical errors (Han et al., 2005; Koppel et al., 2005). To alleviate these problems, clinicians often engage in various problem-solving strategies and workarounds. For example, one study found that nurses use safety alert overrides and documentation shortcuts to minimize workflow disruption in the use of the electronic medication administration system (Vogelsmeier, Halbesleben, & Scott-Cawiezell, 2008). Some providers use the copy and paste function to reduce redundancy in writing; however, on occasion, the paste may inadvertently appear in another patient's record.

Aligned with these findings, we conducted a study to show the impact and unintended consequences of a clinician's work practice in the ED after the implementation of an EHR system (Park & Chen, 2012; Park, Chen, & Rudkin, 2015). We conducted a 2-year ethnographical field study in an ED at a large teaching hospital in the United States. Our study began 4 months prior to the EHR system deployment and lasted 9 months after the deployment. We also used contextual inquiry to examine how clinicians interact with the EHR system and perform care activities. The purpose of our study was to obtain a comprehensive understanding of the immediate as well as longitudinal impact of introducing the EHR. We assessed progress at the field site at 6 months and found that the newly deployed EHR system impacted ED work practices at the individual as well as the organizational levels.

The impact at the individual level was seen in the clinician documentation: (1) roles shifted in physicians' documentation work (e.g., while the documentation workload for attending physicians decreased, resident physicians' documentation work became extensive and lengthy in the EHR); (2) physicians used paper scraps as memory aids during their bedside documentation in patient rooms; and (3) the dynamics of physical interactions shifted, due to the physicians' stationary EHR location. The ED responded at the organizational level to mitigate the resultant changes in care quality control. As a result, ED administrators decided to (1) modify electronic charts to balance out the documentation workload among physicians; (2) deploy a new rule/policy to securely manage paper scraps that might contain patients' confidential information; and (3) relocate computer stations and printers to improve physical interaction among physicians, nurses, and patients. These organizational decisions were necessary and critical to alleviate immediate problems that the new system brought to the clinicians' documentation to improve the existing workflow in the ED and to better adjust to the new system usage. Our study reflects the critical value of impacts and responses at both the individual and organizational levels, with an emphasis on the trigger and process of workflow design, for the successful implementation of a sociotechnical system in a health-care organization.

Incorporating patient's needs into the ED workflow

In the ED, patients are the other major stakeholders and the providers' counterparts. Although patients and their proxies are not currently direct users of the HIT systems, they are affected and could be users in the future as patient-generated data becomes more integrated in these HIT systems. Nevertheless, our earlier study on health-care providers' work practices shows that patients are largely left out of current system designs as well as workflow design in a hospital. Most elements considered when designing workflow (e.g., EHR systems, mobile technology, artifacts, policies, and personnel/roles) are intended to support clinical work or are based on a clinician-focused approach. Patients suffer from a severely imbalanced information environment in the ED as a result. However, as patient-generated data is more integrated in clinical systems, a patient's workflow in daily living settings can become a more central interest.

Meeting the information needs of patients is imperative to increasing their participation in and satisfaction with their own health care. Despite the necessity of providing patients with information related to their care, the design of HIT systems is often oriented toward health-care providers' needs, particularly in clinical settings. This means patients have limited or no access to health-related information and must rely heavily on their health-care providers to obtain their information. Without adequate access to information, patients suffer from a lack of awareness of the care they receive, an inability to actively participate in their own care, and inefficient patient–provider communication. This indicates a critical need to reconsider the design of information systems to incorporate patients' information needs.

Currently, a patient's need for information access is not adequately supported by the available technologies in this environment. While EHRs are designed to meet clinician-driven needs and have been widely implemented, there are few systems for patients to use while they are in the clinical setting. One widely used patient system, PHR, is designed specifically for patients to review and manage their medical records online, but the PHR is intended for use outside of the ongoing care context, mainly for access to information before, after, or in between clinical visits (Tang, Ash, Bates, Overhage, & Sands, 2006). In addition, the numerous existing mobile health applications that have also been designed to help patients search, track, and record health-related information, such as glucose levels, heart rate, and step counts, are not offered to patients in clinical or emergency care settings (Institute of Medicine Committee on Quality of Health Care in America, 2001). In the human–computer interaction and health informatics communities, few recent studies have acknowledged the need for patients to access their health information in real time during their hospital stay (e.g., information displays in patient rooms) (Bickmore, Pfeifer, & Jack, 2009; Wilcox, Lu, Lai, Feiner, & Jordan, 2010; Wilcox, Morris, Tan, & Gatewood, 2010) and on mobile phones (Vardoulakis et al., 2012). For instance, more recently, hospitals have been implementing patient portals to bedside technology systems, such as tablets, to facilitate inpatients adoption of patient portal systems (Aljabri et al., 2018). This effort led to researchers showing how patient portal use during hospital stay showed patients' and caregivers' improved understanding of medications and communication with the care team (Kelly, Hoonakker, & Dean, 2017; Winstanley et al., 2017). At the same time, further support and research efforts are necessary regarding the types of information patients and caregivers would need to know, the appropriate amount and level of information about their ongoing care process, and potential emotional burden on patients and unnecessary interruption to clinicians' work for ensuring such adoption to be successful (Mishra et al., 2018; Park & Chen, 2016; Walker, Menser, Yen, & McAlearney, 2018). Even fewer have focused on the emergency care setting (Vardoulakis et al., 2012; Wilcox, Lu, et al., 2010; Wilcox, Morris, et al., 2010). Thus most existing HIT systems do not provide information to patients during hospital stays or emergency visits, where patients experience unmet needs in terms of receiving situational information in real time. Patients' information needs are not supported by current workflow in hospital care.

We conducted a follow-up study in the same ED to examine the details of how patients experience this information-deprivation environment, where they had to manage information, yet have no access to it, during their ED stay. Specifically, our study examined the information sources that patients and their family caregivers used, types of information breakdowns patients faced in the process of receiving their care, and coping behaviors they created to better handle information breakdowns and assist with their own care (Park & Chen, 2016, 2017). We identified four types of information breakdowns resulting from the patients' lack of information access and information support in the ED. Patients experienced breakdowns when (1) information sources were not accessible to them; (2) too much information was provided to them all at once; (3) information updates were not delivered in a timely manner; and (4) information-related care planning was uncertain and constantly changing. Our study further revealed that many patients and caregivers produced coping mechanisms to deal with these breakdowns. Patients and their caregivers approached any available ED staff and/or observed contextual cues to access information; they constantly reported and reminded their providers of their wait and care conditions to receive timely updates; and they proactively performed guesswork and made alternative plans to better prepare for any contingencies (e.g., working on different backup plans in case they ended up being confined to the ED). While patients initially developed these strategies to accommodate their basic information needs, these strategies later improved the overall care quality in the ED by expediting part of the ED care process, aiding providers' care tasks and workflow, and potentially enhancing patient safety.

Our study found that these behaviors are, in fact, coping strategies that patients use to proactively adjust to the ED, a place where there is limited information support to address their needs. Patients developed these strategies by actively projecting and modifying their expectations and behaviors through interactions with health-care providers, monitoring their situational surroundings in the ED, and communicating with others in their social network. We argue that the kinds of coping strategies the patients developed, how the strategies were developed, the resources or tools needed to implement the strategies, and the specific situations evoking these strategies, should inform the design practices of future systems and policies for emergency care and other similar care environments.

Designing workflows and designing for workflows are interrelated, because they are part of designing the ED work practice essentially—that is, artifacts used, systems, people with various roles, physical layout, policy, etc., are all part of the workflow and closely interact with each other in practice, and so cannot be designed for one or the other in isolation. HIT researchers and designers need to be mindful about adverse impacts or unintended consequences in designing sociotechnical systems in health-care settings. These systems are not only affecting primary users but also the secondary, peripheral, or potential users eventually. All these design challenges related to HIT in EDs is further complicated by the need for HIT to support interorganizational workflows. The success of health management, especially for patients with chronic illness admitted to the ED, depends on interorganizational workflows.

Understanding interorganizational workflow in ED care

HIT and its interplay with workflow has been a key area of study of design efforts because this interplay is an important determinant of high quality of safe care delivery. The boundary of care delivery goes beyond ED settings and involves other settings. Hence, understanding interorganizational (or cross-institutional) workflows are important as health-care services become more distributed.

In case of children with acute asthmatic events, although ED care may be common, the treatment of asthma is mainly managed by their primary care provider, at school, where the child can use an inhaler under supervision of the school nurse, and through many health-related activities (such as medication use and monitoring of symptoms) in daily living settings such as home, camping, library, gym, playground, and shopping mall.

In case of the elderly with HF, besides ED, primary care, specialty HF and other clinics, the daily living setting may be a nursing home, the individual's home or a community setting such as a restaurant or gym. People who are involved with care may be a home nurse, various clinicians in long-term or assisted care facilities, friends or family members.

In both cases, workflow in the diverse settings listed above should be connected (Ozkaynak et al., 2016). The concept of workflow is also applicable to the daily living setting. If there is a disconnect among workflow, a gap occurs (Ozkaynak et al., 2018). This gap can lead to poor patient outcomes due to nonadherence. Not only should EDs be connected to other settings, but also each of these settings should be connected to each other. People who are involved in health-related activities include clinicians with different scopes of practice and nonclinicians. HIT can be a key to connect these settings to ensure seamless information exchange.

These diverse settings present challenges as well as opportunities. Challenges include interorganizational workflows being loosely coupled, lack of information exchange, and conflicting objectives. Opportunities associated with interorganizational workflows include availability of rich, complementary information, and more integrated care opportunities.

The role of the patient is central in interorganizational workflow, as the patient is the most obvious denominator across all the diverse settings in which health-related activities take place. The patient should not only be a partner in decision-making but also a data generator and user of HIT. Workflows may need to be redesigned to incorporate the more active participation of the patient.

Contextual inquiry is particularly effective in understanding interorganizational workflows. Studying interorganizational workflow is methodologically challenging since it takes place across diverse settings. Patients are critical collaborators since they are the common denominator at each step of the workflow. However, clinicians at multiple settings as well as patient proxies should be involved to ensure that there is no disconnect between these settings. Since usually there is no expert in each setting, the design team should include participants from each setting.

Conclusion and recommendations

Design can improve workflow directly and indirectly. Moreover, workflow studies can inform various HIT and organizational design efforts. As summarized in this chapter, both design and workflow communities have benefited from each other, and these benefits can translate into better patient and organizational outcomes. Both workflow and design researchers and practitioners can benefit from more collaboration. Collaboration in research can focus on (1) development of user interfaces to capture and analyze workflow-related data; (2) development of workflow methodologies to link design approaches and patient and organizational outcomes; and (3) development of theoretical frameworks to link workflow and design. Workflow and design practitioners can focus on applying various qualitative and quantitative methods that are already used in the research community in a more agile manner. Moreover, development of nimbler ways to integrate workflow studies into design initiatives can improve relevant outputs.

Codesign and contextual inquiry provide rich information opportunities to design better workflow and design interventions that improve workflow. However, collaboration between workflow and design experts can also benefit from rich quantitative data available in clinical settings. Workflow and design communities can utilize sophisticated quantitative approaches (such as machine learning) that are fed by EHR and other data sources to obtain necessary information to make care delivery more individualized. Moreover, the design problems that involve multiple organizations may require experts in business models to ensure sustainability of the suggested solutions.

Interinstitutional workflow is inevitable in care delivery as care is provided in more specialized clinics and as daily living environments become more central places for health-related activities. More systematic design studies are needed to ensure seamless health management.

References

Aarts, J., Ash, J., & Berg, M. (2007). Extending the understanding of computerized physician order entry: Implications for professional collaboration, workflow and quality of care. *International Journal of Medical Informatics*, 76(Suppl. 1), S4–S13. Available from https://doi.org/10.1016/j.ijmedinf.2006.05.009.

Akinbami, L. J., Moorman, J. E., & Liu, X. (2011). Asthma prevalence, health care use, and mortality: United States, 2005-2009. *National Health Statistics Reports* (32), 1–14.

Aljabri, D., Dumitrascu, A., Burton, M. C., White, L., Khan, M., Xirasagar, S., ... Naessens, J. (2018). Patient portal adoption and use by hospitalized cancer patients: A retrospective study of its impact on adverse events, utilization, and patient satisfaction. *BMC Medical Informatics and Decision Making*, *18*(1), 70. Available from https://doi.org/10.1186/s12911-018-0644-4.

Barnum, C., & Dragga, S. (2001). *Usability testing and research*. Needham Heights, MA: Allyn & Bacon, Inc.

Bergs, J., Lambrechts, F., Simons, P., Vlayen, A., Marneffe, W., Hellings, J., ... Vandijck, D. (2015). Barriers and facilitators related to the implementation of surgical safety checklists: A systematic review of the qualitative evidence. *BMJ Quality & Safety*. Available from https://doi.org/10.1136/bmjqs-2015-004021.

Bickmore, T. W., Pfeifer, L. M., & Jack, B. W. (2009). Taking the time to care: Empowering low health literacy hospital patients with virtual nurse agents. In: *Paper presented at the proceedings of the SIGCHI conference on human factors in computing systems*, Boston, MA.

Campbell, E. M., Sittig, D. F., Ash, J. S., Guappone, K. P., & Dykstra, R. H. (2006). Types of unintended consequences related to computerized provider order entry. *Journal of the American Medical Informatics Association*, *13*(5), 547−556. Available from https://doi.org/10.1197/jamia.M2042.

Carayon, P., Wetterneck, T. B., Alyousef, B., Brown, R. L., Cartmill, R. S., McGuire, K., ... Wood, K. E. (2015). Impact of electronic health record technology on the work and work-flow of physicians in the intensive care unit. *International Journal of Medical Informatics*, *84*(8), 578−594. Available from https://doi.org/10.1016/j.ijmedinf.2015.04.002.

Carayon, P., Wetterneck, T. B., Hundt, A. S., Ozkaynak, M., DeSilvey, J., Ludwig, B., ... Rough, S. S. (2007). Evaluation of nurse interaction with bar code medication administration technology in the work environment. *Journal of Patient Safety*, *3*(1), 34−42. Available from https://doi.org/10.1097/PTS.0b013e3180319de7.

Chung, J., Ozkaynak, M., & Demiris, G. (2017). Examining daily activity routines of older adults using workflow. *Journal of Biomedical Informatics*, 82−90. Available from https://doi.org/10.1016/j.jbi.2017.05.010.

Courtney, K. L., Demiris, G., & Alexander, G. L. (2005). Information technology: Changing nursing processes at the point-of-care. *Nursing Administration Quarterly*, *29*(4), 315−322.

Crowley, K., Mishra, A., Cruz-Cano, R., Gold, R., Kleinman, D., & Agarwal, R. (2018). Electronic health record implementation findings at a large, suburban health and human services department. *Journal of Public Health Management & Practice*. Available from https://doi.org/10.1097/PHH.0000000000000768.

Cyert, R., & March, J. G. (1992). *A behavioral theory of the firm* (2nd ed). New York: Blackwell.

deMarrais, K. B. (2004). Qualitative interview studies: Learning through experience. In K. deMarrais, & S. D. Lapan (Eds.), *Foundations for research: Methods of inquiry in education and the social sciences* (pp. 51−68). Mahwah, NJ: Erlbaum Associates.

Demiris, G. (2012). New era for the consumer health informatics research agenda. *Health Systems*, *1*(1), 13−16. Available from https://doi.org/10.1057/hs.2012.7.

Denton, C. A., Soni, H. C., Kannampallil, T. G., Serrichio, A., Shapiro, J. S., Traub, S. J., & Patel, V. L. (2018). Emergency physicians' perceived influence of EHR use on clinical workflow and performance metrics. *Applied Clinical Informatics*, *9*(3), 725−733. Available from https://doi.org/10.1055/s-0038-1668553.

Ellsworth, M. A., Dziadzko, M., O'Horo, J. C., Farrell, A. M., Zhang, J., & Herasevich, V. (2017). An appraisal of published usability evaluations of electronic health records via systematic review. *Journal of the American Medical Informatics Association*, *24*(1), 218–226. Available from https://doi.org/10.1093/jamia/ocw046.

Eysenbach, G. (2000). Consumer health informatics. *British Medical Journal*, *320*(7251), 1713–1716.

Faiola, A., & Holden, R. J. (2017). Consumer health informatics: Empowering healthy-living-seekers through mHealth. *Progress in Cardiovascular Diseases*, *59*(5), 479–486. Available from https://doi.org/10.1016/j.pcad.2016.12.006.

Hadi, K., & Zimring, C. (2016). Design to improve visibility: Impact of corridor width and unit shape. *HERD: Health Environments Research & Design Journal*, *9*(4), 35–49. Available from https://doi.org/10.1177/1937586715621643.

Han, Y. Y., Carcillo, J. A., Venkataraman, S. T., Clark, R. S., Watson, R. S., Nguyen, T. C., ... Orr, R. A. (2005). Unexpected increased mortality after implementation of a commercially sold computerized physician order entry system. *Pediatrics*, *116*(6), 1506–1512. Available from https://doi.org/10.1542/peds.2005-1287.

Harrison, M. I., Koppel, R., & Bar-Lev, S. (2007). Unintended consequences of information technologies in health care—An interactive sociotechnical analysis. *Journal of the American Medical Informatics Association*, *14*(5), 542–549. Available from https://doi.org/10.1197/jamia.M2384.

Henry, J., Pylypchuck, Y., Searcy, T., & Patel, V. (2016). Adoption of electronic health record systems among US non-federal acute care hospitals: 2008-2015. *ONC Data Brief*, *35*, 1–9.

Holtzblatt, K., & Jones, S. (1993). Contextual inquiry: A participatory technique for system design. In D. Schuler, & A. Namioka (Eds.), *Participatory design: Principles and practices*. Hillsdale, NJ: L. Erlbaum Associates Inc.

Huh, J., Kwon, B. C., Kim, S. H., Lee, S., Choo, J., Kim, J., ... Yi, J. S. (2016). Personas in online health communities. *Journal of Biomedical Informatics*, *63*, 212–225. Available from https://doi.org/10.1016/j.jbi.2016.08.019.

Huh, J., Le, T., Reeder, B., Thompson, H. J., & Demiris, G. (2013). Perspectives on wellness self-monitoring tools for older adults. *International Journal of Medical Informatics*, *82*(11), 1092–1103. Available from https://doi.org/10.1016/j.ijmedinf.2013.08.009.

Institute of Medicine Committee on Quality of Health Care in America. (2001). Crossing the quality chasm: A new health system for the 21st century. Washington, DC: National Academies Press (US), Copyright 2001 by the National Academy of Sciences. All rights reserved.

Jang, H., Ozkaynak, M., Ayer, T., & Sills, M. R. (2019). Factors associated with first medication time for children treated in the emergency department for asthma. *Pediatric Emergency Care*, Published Ahead of Print. Available from: https://doi.org/10.1097/pec.0000000000001609.

Jaspers, M. W. M., Steen, T., Bos, C. V. D., & Geenen, M. (2004). The think aloud method: A guide to user interface design. *International Journal of Medical Informatics*, *73*(11–12), 781–795.

Jencks, S. F., Williams, M. V., & Coleman, E. A. (2009). Rehospitalizations among patients in the Medicare fee-for-service program. *The New England Journal of Medicine*, *360*(14), 1418–1428. Available from https://doi.org/10.1056/NEJMsa0803563.

Jessee, M. A., & Mion, L. C. (2013). Is evidence guiding practice? Reported versus observed adherence to contact precautions: A pilot study. *American Journal of Infection Control*, *41* (11), 965–970. Available from https://doi.org/10.1016/j.ajic.2013.05.005.

Jones, W., Drake, C., Mack, D., Reeder, B., Trautner, B., & Wald, H. (2017). Developing mobile clinical decision support for nursing home staff assessment of urinary tract infection using goal-directed design. *Applied Clinical Informatics*, *8*(2), 632−650. Available from https://doi.org/10.4338/ACI-2016-12-RA-0209.

Kaufman, D. R., Patel, V. L., Hilliman, C., Morin, P. C., Pevzner, J., Weinstock, R. S., ... Starren, J. (2003). Usability in the real world: Assessing medical information technologies in patients' homes. *Journal of Biomedical Informatics*, *36*, 1−2.

Kelly, M. M., Hoonakker, P. L., & Dean, S. M. (2017). Using an inpatient portal to engage families in pediatric hospital care. *Journal of the American Medical Informatics Association*, *24* (1), 153−161. Available from https://doi.org/10.1093/jamia/ocw070.

Koppel, R., Metlay, J. P., Cohen, A., Abaluck, B., Localio, A. R., Kimmel, S. E., & Strom, B. L. (2005). Role of computerized physician order entry systems in facilitating medication errors. *The Journal of the American Medical Association*, *293*(10), 1197−1203. Available from https://doi.org/10.1001/jama.293.10.1197.

Koppel, R., Wetterneck, T., Telles, J. L., & Karsh, B. T. (2008). Workarounds to barcode medication administration systems: Their occurrences, causes, and threats to patient safety. *Journal of the American Medical Informatics Association*, *15*(4), 408−423. Available from https://doi.org/10.1197/jamia.M2616.

Kulikowski, C. A., Shortliffe, E. H., Currie, L. M., Elkin, P. L., Hunter, L. E., Johnson, T. R., ... Williamson, J. J. (2012). AMIA Board white paper: Definition of biomedical informatics and specification of core competencies for graduate education in the discipline. *Journal of the American Medical Informatics Association*, *19*(6), 931−938. Available from https://doi.org/10.1136/amiajnl-2012-001053.

Kushniruk, A., & Nohr, C. (2016). Participatory design, user involvement and health IT evaluation. *Studies in Health Technology and Informatics*, *222*, 139−151.

Lai, A. M., Hsueh, P. S., Choi, Y. K., & Austin, R. R. (2017). Present and future trends in consumer health informatics and patient-generated health data. *Yearbook of Medical Informatics*, *26*(1), 152−159. Available from https://doi.org/10.15265/IY-2017-016.

Le, T., Reeder, B., Yoo, D., Aziz, R., Thompson, H. J., & Demiris, G. (2015). An evaluation of wellness assessment visualizations for older adults. *Telemedicine and e-Health*, *21*(1), 9−15.

LeCompte, M. D., & Schensul, J. J. (1999). *Designing and conducting ethnographic research*. Walnut Creek, CA: Altamira Press.

Lewis, C. (1982). *Using the 'thinking-aloud' method in cognitive interface design* (p. 6). Yorktown Heights, NY: IBM.

Middleton, B., Bloomrosen, M., Dente, M. A., Hashmat, B., Koppel, R., Overhage, J. M., ... American Medical Informatics Association. (2013). Enhancing patient safety and quality of care by improving the usability of electronic health record systems: Recommendations from AMIA. *Journal of the American Medical Informatics Association*, *20*(e1), e2−e8. Available from https://doi.org/10.1136/amiajnl-2012-001458.

Mishra, S. R., Miller, A. D., Haldar, S., Khelifi, M., Eschler, J., Elera, R. G. ... Pratt, W. (2018). Supporting collaborative health tracking in the hospital: Patients' perspectives. In: *Proc SIGCHI Conf Hum Factor Comput Syst, 2018*. Available from https://doi.org/10.1145/3173574.3174224.

Nielsen, J. (1993). *Usability engineering*. San Francisco, CA: Morgan Kaufmann.

Nolan, M. E., Siwani, R., Helmi, H., Pickering, B. W., Moreno-Franco, P., & Herasevich, V. (2017). Health IT usability focus section: Data use and navigation patterns among medical ICU clinicians during electronic chart review. *Applied Clinical Informatics*, *8*(4), 1117−1126. Available from https://doi.org/10.4338/ACI-2017-06-RA-0110.

Norman, D. (1988). *The psychology of everyday things*. Basic Books.

O'Carroll, P. W. (2003). Introduction to Public Health Informatics. In P. W. O'Carroll, W. A. Yasnoff, E. A. Ward, L. H. Ripp, & E. L. Martin (Eds.), *Public health informatics and information systems* (pp. 1–15). New York: Springer.

Oudshoorn, N. (2008). Diagnosis at a distance: The invisible work of patients and healthcare professionals in cardiac telemonitoring technology. *Sociology of Health and Illness, 30*(2), 272–288. Available from https://doi.org/10.1111/j.1467-9566.2007.01032.x.

Ozkaynak, M., & Brennan, P. F. (2012). Characterizing patient care in hospital emergency departments. *Health Systems, 1*(2), 104–117. Available from https://doi.org/10.1057/hs.2012.14.

Ozkaynak, M., & Brennan, P. F. (2013). Revisiting sociotechnical systems in a case of unreported use of health information exchange system in three hospital emergency departments. *Journal of Evaluation in Clinical Practice, 19*(2), 370–373. Available from https://doi.org/10.1111/j.1365-2753.2012.01837.x.

Ozkaynak, M., Brennan, P. F., Hanauer, D. A., Johnson, S., Aarts, J., Zheng, K., & Haque, S. N. (2013). Patient-centered care requires a patient-oriented workflow model. *Journal of the American Medical Informatics Association: JAMIA, 20*(e1), e14–e16. Available from https://doi.org/10.1136/amiajnl-2013-001633.

Ozkaynak, M., Dziadkowiec, O., Mistry, R., Callahan, T., He, Z., Deakyne, S., & Tham, E. (2015). Characterizing workflow for pediatric asthma patients in emergency departments using electronic health records. *Journal of Biomedical Informatics, 57*, 386–398. Available from https://doi.org/10.1016/j.jbi.2015.08.018.

Ozkaynak, M., Jones, J., Weiss, J., Klem, P., & Reeder, B. (2016). A workflow framework for health management in daily living settings. *Studies in Health Technology and Informatics, 225*, 392–396.

Ozkaynak, M., Ponnala, S., & Werner, N. E. (2019). Patient-oriented workflow approach. In K. Zheng, J. Westbrook, T. G. Kannampallil, & V. L. Patel (Eds.), *Cognitive informatics: Reengineering clinical workflow for safer and more efficient care*. Springer, NY.

Ozkaynak, M., Reeder, B., Drake, C., Ferrarone, P., Trautner, B., & Wald, H. (2019). Characterizing workflow to inform clinical decision support systems in nursing homes. *The Gerontologist*. Published Ahead of Print. Available from https://doi.org/10.1093/geront/gny100.

Ozkaynak, M., Valdez, R. S., Holden, R. J., & Weiss, J. (2018). Infinicare framework for an integrated understanding of health-related activities in clinical and daily-living contexts. *Health Systems, 7*(1), 66–78.

Ozkaynak, M., Wu, D. T. Y., Hannah, K., Dayan, P. S., & Mistry, R. D. (2018). Examining workflow in a pediatric emergency department to develop a clinical decision support for an antimicrobial stewardship program. *Applied Clinical Informatics, 9*(2), 248–260.

Park, S. Y., & Chen, Y. (2012). Adaptation as design: Learning from an EMR deployment study. In: *Paper presented at the proceedings of the SIGCHI conference on human factors in computing systems*, Austin, TX.

Park, S. Y., & Chen, Y. (2016). Design opportunities for supporting patient information needs during an emergency visit. In: *Paper presented at the proceedings of the 10th EAI international conference on pervasive computing technologies for healthcare*, Cancun, Mexico.

Park, S. Y., & Chen, Y. (2017). Patient strategies as active adaptation: Understanding patient behaviors during an emergency visit. In: *Paper presented at the proceedings of the 2017 CHI conference on human factors in computing systems*, Denver, CO.

Park, S. Y., Chen, Y., & Rudkin, S. (2015). *Technological and organizational adaptation of EMR implementation in an emergency department* (Vol. 22). ACM.

Park, S. Y., Lee, S. Y., & Chen, Y. (2012). The effects of EMR deployment on doctors' work practices: A qualitative study in the emergency department of a teaching hospital. *International Journal of Medical Informatics, 81*(3), 204−217. Available from https://doi.org/10.1016/j.ijmedinf.2011.12.001.

Patterson, E. S., Cook, R. I., & Render, M. L. (2002). Improving patient safety by identifying side effects from introducing bar coding in medication administration. *Journal of the American Medical Informatics Association, 9*(5), 540−553. Available from https://doi.org/10.1197/jamia.M1061.

Plain, C. (2007). Build an affinity for KJ method. *Quality Progress, 40*(3), 88.

Plsek, P. E., & Greenhalgh, T. (2001). Complexity science: The challenge of complexity in health care. *British Medical Journal, 323*(7313), 625−628. Available from https://doi.org/10.1136/bmj.323.7313.625.

Poissant, L., Pereira, J., Tamblyn, R., & Kawasumi, Y. (2005). The impact of electronic health records on time efficiency of physicians and nurses: A systematic review. *Journal of the American Medical Informatics Association, 12*(5), 505−516. Available from https://doi.org/10.1197/jamia.M1700.

Pype, P., Mertens, F., Helewaut, F., & Krystallidou, D. (2018). Healthcare teams as complex adaptive systems: Understanding team behaviour through team members' perception of interpersonal interaction. *BMC Health Services Research, 18*(1), 570. Available from https://doi.org/10.1186/s12913-018-3392-3.

Ratwani, R., Fairbanks, T., Savage, E., Adams, K., Wittie, M., Boone, E., ... Gettinger, A. (2016). Mind the Gap. A systematic review to identify usability and safety challenges and practices during electronic health record implementation. *Applied Clinical Informatics, 7*(4), 1069−1087. Available from https://doi.org/10.4338/ACI-2016-06-R-0105.

Reeder, B., & Turner, A. M. (2011). Scenario-based design: A method for connecting information system design with public health operations and emergency management. *Journal of Biomedical Informatics, 44*(6), 978−988. Available from https://doi.org/10.1016/j.jbi.2011.07.004.

Reeder, B., Chung, J., Lazar, A., Joe, J., Demiris, G., & Thompson, H. J. (2013). Testing a theory-based mobility monitoring protocol using in-home sensors: A feasibility study. *Research in Gerontological Nursing, 6*(4), 253−263. Available from https://doi.org/10.3928/19404921-20130729-02.

Reeder, B., Hills, R. A., Turner, A. M., & Demiris, G. (2014). Participatory design of an integrated information system design to support public health nurses and nurse managers. *Public Health Nursing, 31*(2), 183−192. Available from https://doi.org/10.1111/phn.12081.

Reeder, B., Le, T., Thompson, H. J., & Demiris, G. (2013). Comparing information needs of health care providers and older adults: Findings from a wellness study. *Studies in Health Technology and Informatics, 192*, 18−22.

Reeder, B., Meyer, E., Lazar, A., Chaudhuri, S., Thompson, H. J., & Demiris, G. (2013). Framing the evidence for health smart homes and home-based consumer health technologies as a public health intervention for independent aging: A systematic review. *International Journal of Medical Informatics, 82*(7), 565−579. Available from https://doi.org/10.1016/j.ijmedinf.2013.03.007.

Reeder, B., Revere, D., Olson, D. R., & Lober, W. B. (2011). Perceived usefulness of a distributed community-based syndromic surveillance system: A pilot qualitative evaluation study. *BMC Research Notes, 4*(1), 187. Available from https://doi.org/10.1186/1756-0500-4-187.

Richardson, J. E., & Ash, J. S. (2008). The effects of hands free communication devices on clinical communication: Balancing communication access needs with user control. In: AMIA Annu Symp Proc, pp. 621−625.

Rismanchian, F., & Lee, Y. H. (2017). Process mining−based method of designing and optimizing the layouts of emergency departments in hospitals. *HERD: Health Environments Research & Design Journal, 10*(4), 105−120. Available from https://doi.org/10.1177/1937586716674471.

Roman, L. C., Ancker, J. S., Johnson, S. B., & Senathirajah, Y. (2017). Navigation in the electronic health record: A review of the safety and usability literature. *Journal of Biomedical Informatics, 67,* 69−79. Available from https://doi.org/10.1016/j.jbi.2017.01.005.

Saitwal, H., Feng, X., Walji, M., Patel, V., & Zhang, J. (2010). Assessing performance of an electronic health record (EHR) using cognitive task analysis. *International Journal of Medical Informatics, 79*(7), 501−506. Available from https://doi.org/10.1016/j.ijmedinf.2010.04.001.

Saleem, J. J., Russ, A. L., Neddo, A., Blades, P. T., Doebbeling, B. N., & Foresman, B. H. (2011). Paper persistence, workarounds, and communication breakdowns in computerized consultation management. *International Journal of Medical Informatics, 80*(7), 466−479. Available from https://doi.org/10.1016/j.ijmedinf.2011.03.016.

Sendlhofer, G., Lumenta, D. B., Leitgeb, K., Kober, B., Jantscher, L., Schanbacher, M., ... Kamolz, L. P. (2016). The gap between individual perception and compliance: A qualitative follow-up study of the surgical safety checklist application. *PLoS One, 11*(2), e0149212. Available from https://doi.org/10.1371/journal.pone.0149212.

Sheehan, B., Nigrovic, L. E., Dayan, P. S., Kuppermann, N., Ballard, D. W., Alessandrini, E., ... Pediatric Emergency Care Applied Research, N. (2013). Informing the design of clinical decision support services for evaluation of children with minor blunt head trauma in the emergency department: A sociotechnical analysis. *Journal of Biomedical Informatics, 46*(5), 905−913. Available from https://doi.org/10.1016/j.jbi.2013.07.005.

Shneiderman, B., Plaisant, C., & Hesse, B. W. (2013). Improving healthcare with interactive visualization. *Computer, 46*(5), 58−66. Available from https://doi.org/10.1109/Mc.2013.38.

Spradley, J. (1979). *The ethnographic interview.* New York: Holt Rinehart & Winston.

Stisen, A., Verdezoto, N., Blunck, H., Kjærgaard, M. B., & Grønbæk, K. (2016). Accounting for the invisible work of hospital orderlies: Designing for local and global coordination. In: *Paper presented at the proceedings of the 19th ACM conference on computer-supported cooperative work & social computing,* San Francisco, CA.

Tang, P. C., Ash, J. S., Bates, D. W., Overhage, J. M., & Sands, D. Z. (2006). Personal health records: Definitions, benefits, and strategies for overcoming barriers to adoption. *Journal of the American Medical Informatics Association, 13*(2), 121−126. Available from https://doi.org/10.1197/jamia.M2025.

Tang, T., Lim, M. E., Mansfield, E., McLachlan, A., & Quan, S. D. (2018). Clinician user involvement in the real world: Designing an electronic tool to improve interprofessional communication and collaboration in a hospital setting. *International Journal of Medical Informatics, 110,* 90−97.

Trzeciak, S., & Rivers, E. P. (2003). Emergency department overcrowding in the United States: An emerging threat to patient safety and public health. *Emergency Medicine Journal, 20*(5), 402−405.

Turner, A. M., Reeder, B., & Ramey, J. (2013). Scenarios, personas and user stories: User-centered evidence-based design representations of communicable disease investigations. *Journal of Biomedical Informatics, 46*(4), 575−584.

Turner, A. M., Reeder, B., & Wallace, J. C. (2013a). A resource management tool for public health continuity of operations during disasters. *Disaster Medicine and Public Health Preparedness, 7*(2), 146−152. Available from https://doi.org/10.1017/dmp.2013.24.

Turner, A. M., Reeder, B., & Wallace, J. C. (2013b). A resource management tool for public health continuity of operations during disasters. *Disaster Medicine and Public Health Preparedness, 7*(2), 146−152. Available from https://doi.org/10.1017/dmp.2013.24.

Valdez, R. S., Holden, R. J., Novak, L. L., & Veinot, T. C. (2015). Transforming consumer health informatics through a patient work framework: Connecting patients to context. *Journal of the American Medical Informatics Association, 22*(1), 2−10. Available from https://doi.org/10.1136/amiajnl-2014-002826.

Vankipuram, M., Kahol, K., Cohen, T., & Patel, V. L. (2011). Toward automated workflow analysis and visualization in clinical environments. *Journal of Biomedical Informatics, 44*(3), 432−440. Available from https://doi.org/10.1016/j.jbi.2010.05.015.

Vardoulakis, L. P., Karlson, A., Morris, D., Smith, G., Gatewood, J., & Tan, D. (2012). Using mobile phones to present medical information to hospital patients. In: *Paper presented at the proceedings of the SIGCHI conference on human factors in computing systems*, Austin, TX.

Vogelsmeier, A. A., Halbesleben, J. R., & Scott-Cawiezell, J. R. (2008). Technology implementation and workarounds in the nursing home. *Journal of the American Medical Informatics Association, 15*(1), 114−119. Available from https://doi.org/10.1197/jamia.M2378.

Walker, D. M., Menser, T., Yen, P. Y., & McAlearney, A. S. (2018). Optimizing the user experience: Identifying opportunities to improve use of an inpatient portal. *Applied Clinical Informatics, 9*(1), 105−113. Available from https://doi.org/10.1055/s-0037-1621732.

Walker, J. M., & Carayon, P. (2009). From tasks to processes: The case for changing health information technology to improve health care. *Health Affairs (Millwood), 28*(2), 467−477. Available from https://doi.org/10.1377/hlthaff.28.2.467.

Wilcox, L., Lu, J., Lai, J., Feiner, S., & Jordan, D. (2010). Physician-driven management of patient progress notes in an intensive care unit. In: *Paper presented at the proceedings of the SIGCHI conference on human factors in computing systems*, Atlanta, GA.

Wilcox, L., Morris, D., Tan, D., & Gatewood, J. (2010). Designing patient-centric information displays for hospitals. In: *Paper presented at the proceedings of the SIGCHI conference on human factors in computing systems*, Atlanta, GA.

Wiler, J. L., Ozkaynak, M., Bookman, K., Koehler, A., Leeret, R., Chua-Tuan, J., ... Zane, R. (2016). Implementation of a front-end split-flow model to promote performance in an urban academic emergency department. *The Joint Commission Journal on Quality and Patient Safety, 42*(6), 271−280.

Winstanley, E. L., Burtchin, M., Zhang, Y., Campbell, P., Pahl, J., Beck, S., & Bohenek, W. (2017). Inpatient experiences with MyChart Bedside. *Telemedicine Journal and e-Health, 23*(8), 691−693. Available from https://doi.org/10.1089/tmj.2016.0132.

Wood, L. E. (1997). Semi-structured interviewing for user-centered design. *Interactions, 4*(2), 48−61. Available from https://doi.org/10.1145/245129.245134.

Yancy, C. W., Jessup, M., Bozkurt, B., Butler, J., Casey, D. E., Jr., Drazner, M. H., ... American College of Cardiology Foundation/American Heart Association Task Force on Practice Guidelines. (2013). 2013 ACCF/AHA guideline for the management of heart failure: A report of the American College of Cardiology Foundation/American Heart Association Task Force on practice guidelines. *Circulation, 128*(16), e240−e327. Available from https://doi.org/10.1161/CIR.0b013e31829e8776.

Yang, Y., Ward-Charlerie, S., Dhavle, A. A., Rupp, M. T., & Green, J. (2018). Quality and variability of patient directions in electronic prescriptions in the ambulatory care setting. *Journal of Managed Care & Specialty Pharmacy, 24*(7), 691−699. Available from https://doi.org/10.18553/jmcp.2018.17404.

Yeow, A., & Goh, K. H. (2015). Work harder or work smarter? Information technology and resource allocation in healthcare processes. *Management Information Systems Quarterly, 39* (4), 763−786. Available from https://doi.org/10.25300/misq/2015/39.4.2.

Zahabi, M., Kaber, D. B., & Swangnetr, M. (2015). Usability and safety in electronic medical records interface design: A review of recent literature and guideline formulation. *Human Factors, 57*(5), 805−834. Available from https://doi.org/10.1177/0018720815576827.

Chapter 14

Design for self-care

Victor P. Cornet[1], Carly Daley[2,3], Luiz H. Cavalcanti[1], Amit Parulekar[2]
and Richard J. Holden[4,5]
[1]*Department of Human-centered Computing, IUPUI School of Informatics and Computing,
Indianapolis, IN, United States,* [2]*Department of BioHealth Informatics, IUPUI School of
Informatics and Computing, Indianapolis, IN, United States,* [3]*Parkview Mirro Center for
Research and Innovation, Parkview Health, Fort Wayne, IN, United States,* [4]*Department of
Medicine, Indiana University School of Medicine, Indianapolis, IN, United States,* [5]*Regenstrief
Institute, Indianapolis, IN, United States*

Introduction

Self-care is the process of acting on one's own behalf to respond to one's
health demands, with the goal of improving or maintaining one's health
(Orem, 2001). The "one" in question can be a patient with a chronic or acute
health condition or a nonpatient (e.g., person managing health). These individuals may perform self-care autonomously or receive help from others,
including informal and formal caregivers; however, the decision to initiate
and maintain self-care behaviors belongs to the individual (Richard & Shea,
2011). Self-care is effortful and demands time and energy. The ability or
capacity to perform self-care is shaped by internal (cognitive, physical, emotional, behavioral) and external (environmental, social) constraints and
enablers (Dean, 1981; Sidani, 2003). Self-care behaviors can be learned,
instructed, or instinctual.

Designing for self-care is challenging because self-care involves multiple
tasks performed by one or multiple agents, including patients, informal caregivers or family members, and various clinical professionals (Klein, 2008;
Richard & Shea, 2011). From a human factors perspective, design for self-
care begins the same way as designing for any other type of work performance: by understanding the internal and external systems' constraints and
influences on agents involved in self-care; the nature of their work including
their tasks, processes, strategies, and goals; and how the combination of systems' structure and work process produces self-care outcomes (Holden,
Schubert, & Mickelson, 2015; Lippa, Klein, & Shalin, 2008). By identifying
needs, problems, and requirements related to self-care performance,

Design for Health. DOI: https://doi.org/10.1016/B978-0-12-816427-3.00014-2

corresponding solutions can be developed and tested. Human factors self-care-related studies have used multiple methods to study self-care performance and have begun to develop and test technological and nontechnological solutions.

Identifying and understanding problems in self-care

We now describe the nature of self-care performance from a human factors perspective.

Actors in the practice of self-care

Fig. 14.1 illustrates the types of individuals who perform or assist in self-care and their specific challenges. While patients are central in the practice of self-care, they do not necessarily perform self-care alone, especially when older or chronically ill. Formal and informal caregivers may assist patients with self-care tasks or even perform tasks on their behalf, for example,

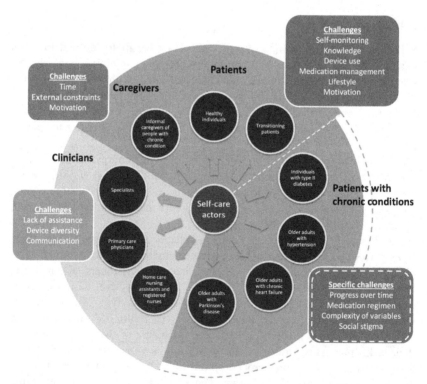

FIGURE 14.1   Actors in the practice of self-care and the challenges associated with each actor group.

by scheduling medical appointments (Holden et al., 2013). Interactions between patients, their social network, and care network are complex and can both facilitate and be a source of tension in the practice of self-care (Beer, McBride, Mitzner, & Rogers, 2014; Cornet, Voida, & Holden, 2017; Valdez & Brennan, 2015).

Types of self-care

The types of self-care performed depend on the actor's health status and goals.

Preventive self-care is performed by people to maintain their health status and prevent acute and chronic diseases. A person can initiate and carry out preventive self-care activities on their own or in concert with health-care professionals. Tasks performed during the process of preventive self-care can include exercise and diet control (Mamykina, Mynatt, & Kaufman, 2006).

Transitional self-care is performed by those recently discharged from a care setting (e.g., hospital) where they received professional health care (Coleman, Parry, Chalmers, & Min, 2006). Transitional self-care is negatively impacted by fragmentation of care and quality of self-care education received pre-discharge and can be improved with patient participation during the discharge process, education, and resources (e.g., support from care-givers, discharge care plans, brochures) (Dyrstad, Testad, Aase, & Storm, 2015; Pollack et al., 2016; Werner, Gurses, Leff, & Arbaje, 2016; Werner, Tong, Borkenhagen, & Holden, 2019).

Self-care for chronic conditions is performed by people, often older adults, with illnesses lasting months or years. To maintain health, avoid associated conditions for which they are at risk, and prevent acute exacerbations or further degradation, chronically ill individuals are recommended by clinicians to perform regular and frequent behaviors such as symptom monitoring, medication taking, exercise, and diet control. Generally, the number of self-care-related tasks increases with condition progression; keeping up with the treatment plan becomes more difficult, and patient and caregiver quality of life may decline. Human factors researchers have studied the challenges unique to specific chronic conditions such as diabetes (e.g., Klein & Lippa, 2012), osteoarthritis pain (Barg-Walkow et al., 2013), chronic heart failure (e.g., Mickelson & Holden, 2018a; Morrow et al., 2006), and Parkinson's disease (e.g., Nunes & Fitzpatrick, 2018).

Components of self-care

Self-care is a naturalistic macrocognitive decision-making process, where decisions are made in "real-life" situations with problems that are ill-defined and complex (Mickelson, Unertl, & Holden, 2016). Patients monitor physical, emotional, mental, and other signs or signals; synthesize or interpret the information; and take action (Daley et al., 2018). They also perform regular maintenance tasks such as taking medication, exercise, and diet management.

Monitoring, interpreting, and acting. Most self-care regimens, whether for wellness or chronic conditions, involve monitoring health signs and symptoms (e.g., weight and pain), interpreting those signs to assess health status, and taking subsequent action (Mickelson, Willis, & Holden, 2015). Interpretation of health status is a crucial step that, if done improperly, can lead to the wrong action or inaction, such as patients delaying treatment for pneumonia when symptoms are present. Over time, individuals learn from their actions, with some patients becoming "experts" who can interpret data and take appropriate autonomous action (Lippa et al., 2008).

Medication management. Over-the-counter and prescription medications are often part of transitional and chronic illness plans of care. Medication regimens can be heavy and complex (e.g., multiple medications and different times; Holden, Schubert, & Mickelson, 2015), placing demands on memory and time (e.g., to refill or prepare) and promoting intentional and unintentional nonadherence (e.g., pillboxes and cabinetry; Mickelson & Holden, 2018a). Good use of artifacts (Mickelson & Holden, 2018b), adaptive strategies (e.g., placing medications in a visible spot and routinizing medication taking; Blocker, Insel, Koerner, & Rogers, 2017), and task distribution (e.g., caregivers refilling medications; Mickelson & Holden, 2013) can address the demands of medication management.

Knowledge acquisition and transfer. Knowledge is indispensable for self-care performance (Klein, Jackson, Street, Whitacre, & Klein, 2013) and lack of knowledge can lead to self-care errors or nonadherence (Dyrstad et al., 2015; Or et al., 2009; Verdezoto & Grönvall, 2015). Health systems offer formal education programs, but these often focus on declarative rather than procedural knowledge, so patients know what to do but not how to do it, especially in novel situations (Klein, 2008).

Physical activity and nutrition. Physical activity and nutrition can promote recovery from acute conditions, minimize the risk of new disease, and delay age-related decline (Warburton, Nicol, & Bredin, 2006). As physical activity and diet are lifelong habitual processes, adherence to new activity and diet recommendations often pose a behavior change challenge requiring specialized interventions rather than simply prescribing the behavior (Abraham & Michie, 2008).

Barriers to self-care performance

Self-care performance is affected by many barriers in the patient work system (Holden, Schubert, & Mickelson, 2015), which must be acknowledged and addressed when designing for self-care (cf. Table 14.1).

TABLE 14.1 Systems barriers to self-care and their effects on process and outcomes.

Examples of barriers to self-care	Possible effects on self-care process or outcome
Person-related barriers. Personal habits; physical, sensory, and cognitive limitations/impairments; lack of motivation	• Forgetting to take medications • Struggling to remove pills from prescription bottles
Task-related barriers. Task properties (complexity, ambiguity, lengthiness); task side effects; task sequencing	• Difficulty in monitoring, interpreting, and acting on subtle or variable vital signs • Joint pain associated with physical exercise or the inconvenience of certain diets • Errors and intentional nonadherence to medication or other self-care recommendations
Tool-related barriers. Poor design of tools (e.g., accessibility, usability); obtrusive tools; lack of access to tools	• Improper use of tools or use at the wrong time • Overreliance on memory and task completion despite available information or tool • Errors and other performance issues in using tools
Context-related barriers. Distraction due to life events and demands; lack of resources; social pressure; physical environment barriers	• Disruption of self-care routines • Inability to perform self-care due to lack of resources

Source: Based on Beer et al., 2014; Cheatham & Wogalter, 2002; Holden & Mickelson, 2013; Holden, Schubert, Eiland et al., 2015; Holden, Valdez, Schubert, Thompson, & Hundt, 2017; Mamykina et al., 2006; Mickelson & Holden, 2017, 2018a; Morrow, Weiner, Young, Steinley, & Murray, 2003; Nunes & Fitzpatrick, 2018; Verdezoto & Grönvall, 2015

Solutions for self-care

Table 14.2 lists examples of self-care solutions, many intended to overcome the barriers listed in Table 14.1.

Emerging trends in design for self-care

Technology has emerged as a convenient means to monitor well-being, symptoms, and other health phenomena. Some solutions, such as mobile applications, intend to help users manage their chronic conditions, such as diabetes (e.g., Kwok & Burns, 2005) or heart failure (e.g., Cornet, Daley, et al., 2017)

TABLE 14.2 Solutions supporting self-care.

Solution	Use	Targeted users
Mobile application	Diabetes management	People with diabetes (Cage, Santos, Scott, & Vaughn-Cooke, 2014; Kwok & Burns, 2005)
	Heart failure management	Older adults with heart failure (Cornet, Daley, Srinivas, & Holden, 2017; Morey, Barg-Walkow, & Rogers, 2017)
	Substance abuse recovery	Matalenas, McLaughlin, Chen, and Daughters (2015)
Computer application/ website	Collaborative medication planning	Older adults (Kannampallil, Waicekauskas, Morrow, Kopren, & Fu, 2013)
	Heart failure management	Older adults with heart failure (Rezai, Torenvliet, & Burns, 2014)
	Information for breast cancer survivors	Breast cancer survivors (Sesto et al., 2011)
	Exercise and diet monitoring	Older adults (Fausset et al., 2013; Preusse, Mitzner, Fausset, & Rogers, 2014)
Paper artifact (worksheet, log sheet)	Collaborative medication planning	Older adults (Kannampallil et al., 2013)
	Comprehension of personal monitoring data	General population (Douglas & Caldwell, 2009)
	Medication instructions	Older adults (Morrow, Weiner, Young, Steinley, & Murray, 2003)
	Medication labels	Older adults (Ng, Chan, & Ho, 2017)
PHRs	Health management/ communication with providers	Patients, providers, and caregivers (Archer, Fevrier-Thomas, Lokker, McKibbon, & Straus, 2011; Thompson, Reilly, & Valdez, 2016), diabetes (Cage et al., 2014)
Wearables	Activity/exercise monitoring	Older adults (Fausset et al., 2013; Preusse et al., 2014)
Media	Communication of health information	People with diabetes (Lottridge, Yu, & Chignell, 2012)
Robots	Self-care assistance	Older adults (Ezer, Fisk, & Rogers, 2009)
Medical devices	Blood glucose monitoring	People with diabetes (Jones & Caird, 2017) and disabilities (Santos, Olumese, & Vaughn-Cooke, 2014)
Education programs	Self-management education	People with diabetes (Klein et al., 2013)

PHRs, Personal health records.

by providing features such as self-tracking, communication with the user's health-care system, and reminders. Wearables and websites are helping people log their diet and physical activity to improve their well-being (Fausset et al., 2013; Preusse et al., 2014). With improved miniaturization and rapid progress in sensor technology in the 2010s, sensors—including those in smartphones, smart homes, and wearables—are enabling continuous and context-aware self-care monitoring without patient intervention (Abedtash & Holden, 2017; Cornet & Holden, 2018). Artificial intelligence and virtual agents or avatars are being used for diagnosis, prediction, and therapy. Robots are another technology with the potential to assist or replace informal caregivers in the performance of activities of daily living (Mitzner, Chen, Kemp, & Rogers, 2014).

A second trend is the democratization of data. Patients' health data, traditionally confined to hospitals and insurer databases, are making their way to patients through public health records, personal medical devices or apps, and other methods (Cage et al., 2014; Jones & Caird, 2017). Secure messaging, shared screen use during clinic visits, and the use of telehealth (e.g., televisits) are collaborative patient–clinician technologies that can enable not only data sharing but also shared decision making and patient–clinician coordination (Valdez, Holden, Novak, & Veinot, 2015).

Third, a number of low-tech and no-tech self-care solutions continue to require better design, including paper documentation, instructions, and labeling (e.g., of medication products) (Morrow et al., 2003); these are especially useful in low-resource settings, among older or less technology-dependent groups, and when safety is paramount (e.g., on warning labels). Other nontechnological interventions for self-care, including those that offer education and skills training, social support, or better transitional care, remain important targets for design.

Design guidelines: supporting self-care

Fig. 14.2 summarizes design guidelines for self-care based on the nature of self-care, associated challenges and barriers, solutions, and trend reviewed above.

Design for self-care components

Effective design should support all three stages, *monitoring, interpretation, and action* and facilitate transitions between steps. For example, self-monitoring can be eased by minimizing data entry through automated processes in smartphones and wearables (Abedtash & Holden, 2017; Cornet & Holden, 2018) and automatic data transmission to health-care delivery organizations (Verdezoto & Grönvall, 2015). In addition to providing generic

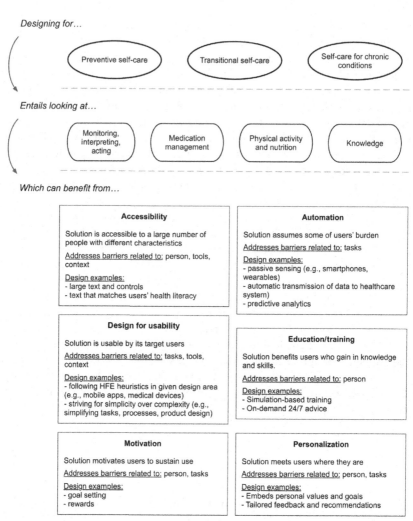

Designing for...

Entails looking at...

Which can benefit from...

FIGURE 14.2   Design guidelines (bottom) addressing self-care components (middle) for different types of self-care (top).

rules and action plans, self-care solutions can provide personalized displays and recommendations (Li, Dey, & Forlizzi, 2011).

Medication management design solutions should go beyond education and skills training, providing better labeling and instruction cards, organization tools such as pillboxes and pill dispensers, and various other technologies for reminding and keeping track of medications, administration instructions, and supply. Solutions could assist in the simplification and facilitation of the medication management process, for example, by minimizing the number of medication administration times or helping patients and clinicians agree on medications that can be deprescribed because they are not efficacious relative to the burdens or risks they place on patients. Solutions should help coordinate the multiple actors involved in medication management.

Knowledge interventions primarily educational in nature produce mixed or underwhelming results (Minet, Møller, Vach, Wagner, & Henriksen, 2010). Novel self-care knowledge design solutions could focus on matching information to personal values and goals, self-reflection, and developing mastery (knowing *how* vs *what*), as well as group support (Riegel, Dickson, & Faulkner, 2016). Knowledge- and skills-focused solutions can include education and skills training classes, or computer-based training software to teach and support problem-solving, explicit knowledge development, and practice applying skills and knowledge in personal contexts (Klein & Lippa, 2012; Mamykina et al., 2016).

Design to overcome self-care barriers

Self-care design solutions should accommodate physical and cognitive abilities, for example, by using larger fonts to address visual acuity or pictograms to address low literacy (Or et al., 2009). Lack of motivation and mood-related conditions such as depressive symptoms inhibit proper self-care (Beer et al., 2014; Holden, Schubert, & Mickelson, 2015; Mamykina et al., 2006; Nunes & Fitzpatrick, 2018). To address motivational barriers, self-care solutions can integrate motivational elements, such as goal-setting and rewards (Cornet, Daley, et al., 2017; Matalenas et al., 2015; Rezai et al., 2014). Designs should have the goal of reducing self-care burden versus adding more work for the patient (Holden, Kulanthaivel, Purkayastha, Goggins, & Kripalani, 2017).

Task-related barriers can be addressed in two ways: (1) simplifying or tailoring self-care tasks and regimens and (2) enhancing patients' capacity and ability to perform their self-care tasks (Holden, Schubert, & Mickelson, 2015; Shippee, Shah, May, Mair, & Montori, 2012). While some aspects of self-care tasks such as medication side effects cannot be simplified or removed, hard-to-operate medical devices and medication regimens established without input from patients are examples of barriers addressable by human factors approaches such as usability testing and user-centered design.

Artifacts should facilitate, not complicate, self-care processes. Self-tracking tools can reinforce interpretation and action, explaining what the measurements mean and clearly suggesting actions (Klein & Lippa, 2012). Technologies should be tailored or customizable (e.g., not suggesting walking for a wheelchair-bound user) (Thompson et al., 2016).

Solutions to address context barriers should use macroergonomic strategies, such as better process and job design, team training and mechanisms of coordination and collaboration, and personalization given the multiple, unique contextual factors affecting each individual.

Case study: designing for heart failure self-care

Heart failure is a highly prevalent chronic disease affecting over 5 million older adults in the United States alone and characterized by a worsening health trajectory and functional impairment. Older adults with heart failure typically also have other diseases and impairments, particularly diabetes, other forms of heart disease, and depression (Chaudhry, Wang, Gill, & Krumholz, 2010; Murad et al., 2015). It is increasingly demonstrated that people with heart failure are at very high risk for cognitive dysfunction, which appears to affect their ability to perform self-care (Currie, Rideout, Lindsay, & Harkness, 2015). Heart failure self-care can slow disease progression, improve quality of life, and prevent or delay acute exacerbations that lead to sudden death or hospitalizations. A typical self-care regimen for people with heart failure includes managing medication; restricting fluid and sodium intake in their diet; sustaining daily physical activity; avoiding smoking and tobacco; monitoring weights, vitals, and symptoms; and responding to changes in symptoms by adjusting behavior, seeking treatment, or in some cases self-adjusting medication dosage (Jaarsma, Cameron, Riegel, & Stromberg, 2017). People with heart failure attend clinical visits, coordinate with health-care professionals and informal caregivers (Buck et al., 2015), and may receive and be managed for implanted electronic devices (Yancy et al., 2016).

Due to the complexity of heart failure self-care, interventions aimed at improving patient-reported and clinical outcomes need improvement. Education alone has been shown to be insufficient (Creber et al., 2016), suggesting interventions need to target multiple barriers of self-care performance, not just gaps in patients' declarative knowledge. We now present how a three-phase user-centered design cycle of formative research, product design, and evaluation can produce promising interventions such as patient-facing technologies for heart failure self-care (Srinivas, Cornet, & Holden, 2017).

Formative research to understand heart failure self-care

To understand a complex phenomenon such as heart failure self-care, a combination of methods is needed to study what kind of self-care is performed, by whom, when, where, why, and how (Novak, Unertl, & Holden, 2016). Many of the methods for quantitative and qualitative data collection and analysis used in other human factors studies in health care are applicable (Carayon et al., 2015). Table 14.3 depicts examples of methods for formative research used in human factors studies of self-care.

TABLE 14.3 Examples of formative research methods used in human factors studies of self-care (including, but not limited to, the ones employed in our case study).

Methods	Sample studies
Data collection	
In-person interviews	Barg-Walkow et al. (2014), Beer et al. (2014), Calvin et al. (2005), Holden, Schubert, and Mickelson (2015), Klein et al. (2013), Klein (2008), Lippa et al. (2008), Mamykina et al. (2006), Mickelson and Holden (2018a), Nunes and Fitzpatrick (2018), Verdezoto and Grönvall (2015)
Questionnaires	Beer et al. (2014), Cheatham and Wogalter (2002), Holden and Mickelson (2013), Mickelson and Holden (2018a), Verdezoto and Grönvall (2015)
Observations	Calvin et al. (2005), Holden, Schubert, and Mickelson (2015), Klein and Lippa (2012), Klein (2008), Mamykina et al. (2006), Mickelson and Holden (2018a)
Test battery	Chin et al. (2009), D'Andrea et al. (2010), Morrow et al. (2003), Yamani et al. (2012)
Review of internet content	Klein and Lippa (2012), Klein (2008), Nunes and Fitzpatrick (2018)
Review of EHR data	Holden, Schubert, and Mickelson (2015), Mickelson and Holden (2018a)
Digital diary	Mickelson and Holden (2017)
Focus group	Verdezoto and Grönvall (2015)
Data analysis	
Thematic analysis/coding	Barg-Walkow et al. (2014), Blocker et al. (2017), Lippa et al. (2008), Mickelson and Holden (2018a), Verdezoto and Grönvall (2015)
Grounded theory methodology	Mamykina et al. (2006), Nunes and Fitzpatrick (2018)
Coding along a framework/model	Beer et al. (2014), Holden and Mickelson (2013), Holden, Schubert, and Mickelson (2015), Mickelson and Holden (2015, 2017)
Work system analysis (workflow diagrams)	Calvin et al. (2005)
Statistical analysis (test/ surveys)	Cheatham and Wogalter (2002), Chin et al. (2009), D'Andrea et al. (2010), Yamani et al. (2012)
Geographical analysis	Ye and Holden (2015)

EHR, Electronic Health Record.

Data collection methods: interviews, observations, and surveys

Interviews based on human factors models, theories, and frameworks allow researchers to understand the work systems and cognitive processes involved in heart failure self-care from the patients' perspective (Daley et al., 2018; Holden et al., 2018; Srinivas et al., 2017). In the Caring Hearts study (Holden, Schubert, & Mickelson, 2015; Srinivas et al., 2017), interview guides were designed based upon the Systems Engineering Initiative for Patient Safety (SEIPS) 2.0 model (Holden et al., 2013), a framework for the comprehension of work systems, processes, outcomes, and adaptations present or occurring in health care for various entities (patients, clinicians, caregivers, or others). SEIPS 2.0 enabled the researchers to devise an interview protocol that targeted the patients' work system—and especially its barriers—shaping self-care performance. In a separate study (Daley et al., 2018; Holden et al., 2018) the interview protocol was developed based on the critical incident technique (Kain, 2003) to elicit information on self-care processes, particularly how patients made day-to-day decisions about their health. Probes were used to explore patients' decision-making in fictitious scenarios and specific past scenarios recalled by the patient, producing richer qualitative data. One advantage of interviews that have over other techniques is their dynamic nature; well-trained researchers can swiftly probe participants to ensure maximum data quality and coverage of the problem, something observations and surveys do not readily allow.

Human factors frameworks can also be used to build standardized survey questionnaires. For example, Holden, Schubert, Eiland, et al. (2015) developed a survey tool to assess barriers to self-care among patients with heart failure presenting in the emergency department. The survey depicted these barriers as products of multiple factors including task, technology, and environment. Using the tool permitted an estimate of the prevalence of systems barriers in this patient population, leading to conclusions such as that personal and organizational barriers are more prevalent than others. It also enabled a comparison across studies using the same survey instrument, for example, allowing a comparison of barriers reported by patients in the United States versus Singapore (Lim et al., 2017).

Direct observations during clinical visits and in patients' homes were conducted as part of the Caring Heart study to more accurately represent the contexts in which people with heart failure conducted self-care (Holden, Schubert, & Mickelson, 2015). These observations included the examination of the areas in their house related to self-care such as kitchens (diet) and bathrooms (medications), artifacts used for self-care, and places where information and documents were kept. Observations helped examine the realities of self-care versus what patients self-reported; for example, observations sometimes revealed nonadherence or hazards not reported in interview responses. Performing observations in naturalistic settings such as homes is accompanied by challenges, including ensuring researcher safety, travel logistics, and privacy concerns, discussed in detail elsewhere (Holden, McDougald Scott, Hoonakker, Hundt, & Carayon, 2015; Valdez & Holden, 2016).

Data analysis methods

Although there are many ways to analyze collected data to aid design (cf. Table 14.3 for examples of methods used in other human factors studies), here we discuss two in particular: personas and cognitive task analysis (CTA).

Personas are archetypes of prospective users of an intervention based on data collected from or about the user population. Personas help designers and others envision and accommodate the variety of users and to understand common attributes present in specific archetypes (Holden, Kulanthaivel, et al., 2017). For example, in the Power to the Patient study, researchers used notes taken during interviews, participant demographics, and survey data to create individual participant profiles and from the profiles developed three decision-making personas: the direction-follower (who prefers clear if-then rules), the investigator (who closely tracks data), and the explorer (who takes risks). In a contrasting approach to personas development, Holden, Kulanthaivel, et al. (2017) used longitudinal survey and medical records data to perform cluster analysis, quantitatively deriving six personas of older adults with heart failure. When investigating human behavior and attitudes in complex social environments, influenced by a multitude of factors, personas can be developed by systematic integration of both quantitative and qualitative methods collected in natural and simulated situations (Holden et al., 2019).

CTA seeks to understand and explain the micro- or macrocognitive processes involved in executing tasks by analyzing data collected about what people actually do in naturalistic settings (Klein & Militello, 2001). Applying CTA to interview data from the Caring Hearts study of older adults with heart failure, human factors researchers were able to characterize the macrocognitive functions performed by patients to manage their medications (Mickelson et al., 2016). A follow-up study used video and photo diary methods to document how older adults with heart failure manage medications; researchers used the multimedia content generated by patients to examine barriers to medication management and adaptive strategies used to overcome them (Mickelson & Holden, 2017). An analysis of interview data from the Power to the Patient study showed how older patients with heart failure monitor, interpret, and act on health-related data, the barriers and strategies at each of these steps, and the involvement of others besides the patient (Daley et al., 2018). Rather than prescribing the ideal process, CTA shows how self-care actually occurs and is therefore a fundamental input into design aligned with the realities of self-care (Valdez et al., 2015).

Designing for heart failure self-care

The findings from the formative research conducted in the Caring Hearts study helped design Engage, an mHealth application prototype promoting self-care knowledge, motivation, and behavior among older adults with chronic heart failure (Cornet, Daley, et al., 2017; Srinivas et al., 2017). The design process started by summarizing the findings from the different analyses of the Caring Hearts dataset (Srinivas et al., 2017). Themes that emerged were the lack of appropriate tools to support monitoring, interpreting, and acting on symptoms; patients' disengagement from self-care because of infrequent disease management or offloading self-care to caregivers; and a lack of knowledge about heart failure (Srinivas et al., 2017). Based on these themes and a review of the literature, the design team generated design requirements and identified features posited to be accepted by older adults that would support long-term self-care (see Table 14.4 for design features in other self-care interventions from human factors studies). After having developed several alternative concepts—for example, a tool to promote goal setting, or a tool to structure patients' clinic visits—the team pursued design of "Engage," a solution to help individuals with heart failure routinize self-care by performing self-care-related self-monitoring, learning, and goal-setting tasks over a 30-day period (Srinivas et al., 2017).

TABLE 14.4 Examples of design features supporting self-care reported in human factors studies (including, but not limited to, the ones employed in our case study).

Feature	Sample studies
Assistance for instrumental activities of daily living	Ezer et al. (2009)
Calendar/time management	Cage et al. (2014), Matalenas et al. (2015)
Communication with health-care system[a]	Cage et al. (2014), Cornet, Daley, et al. (2017), Kwok and Burns (2005)
Education/information[a]	Cage et al. (2014), Cornet, Daley, et al. (2017), Ezer et al. (2009), Lottridge et al. (2012), Sesto et al. (2011), Zachary et al. (2017)
Goal setting[a]	Cornet, Daley, et al. (2017), Matalenas et al. (2015)
Instructions/rules for self-care	Jones and Caird (2017), Morrow et al. (2003), Ng et al. (2017)

(Continued)

TABLE 14.4 (Continued)

Feature	Sample studies
Management (e.g., medication)	Cage et al. (2014), Kannampallil et al. (2013), Rezai et al. (2014)
Motivational messages	Ezer et al. (2009), Rezai et al. (2014)
Personalization/tailoring[a]	Cornet, Daley, et al. (2017), Rezai et al. (2014), Stuck, Chong, Tracy, and Rogers (2017)
Reminders	Cornet, Daley, et al. (2017), Ezer et al. (2009), Rezai et al. (2014), Stuck et al. (2017), Zachary et al. (2017)
Remote collaboration support	Zachary et al. (2017)
Reports (e.g., trends, graphs, or logs of activity, health, weight, and goal progress)[a]	Cornet, Daley, et al. (2017), Douglas and Caldwell (2009), Fausset et al. (2013), Kwok and Burns (2005), Matalenas et al. (2015), Morey et al. (2017), Preusse et al. (2014), Rezai et al. (2014)
Rewards (gamification)[a]	Cornet, Daley, et al. (2017), Matalenas et al. (2015), Rezai et al. (2014)
Social portal/web community	Rezai et al. (2014), Zachary et al. (2017)
Self-tracking (software)[a]	Cornet, Daley, et al. (2017), Kwok and Burns (2005), Matalenas et al. (2015), Morey et al. (2017)
Self-tracking (hardware)	Fausset et al. (2013), Jones and Caird (2017), Preusse et al. (2014)

[a]Indicates feature in Engage.

Evaluating design for heart failure self-care

The Caring Hearts team used traditional human factors evaluation methods to assess the usability and acceptance of the Engage prototype. First, the design team performed expert heuristic evaluation following Nielsen and Molich's (1990) usability heuristics. They identified and fixed interface problems older adults would have faced, such as inconsistent font sizes and overly complex navigation patterns. Next, the interactive prototype was tested with older adults with heart failure and their informal caregivers, in two rounds. In the first round ($n = 5$) participants answered questions about their self-care behaviors (location, use of technology), then used the prototype over a series of set tasks while thinking aloud. In the second round ($n = 10$), participants used the prototype, role-playing the protagonist of fictitious scenarios (Cornet, Daley, et al., 2017), two of which are included in Table 14.5 as examples. Scenarios simulated the daily self-care behaviors of a person with heart failure, mimicking Engage's real-world use context. In both rounds, participants completed System Usability Scale (SUS) surveys and were interviewed about their experience with the prototype and the role Engage might play in their self-care (Cornet, Daley, et al., 2017; Srinivas et al., 2017). The prototype was modified between the two rounds to simplify it and address other usability shortcomings.

TABLE 14.5 Excerpt of the Engage testing protocol for the second round of usability testing. Each participant went through seven scenarios such as the ones in this table in a 90-minute testing session.

Step	Facilitator's script
Introduction	I am now going to tell you about John (*or Jane for female participants*), a 65-year-old man living on the outskirts of Indianapolis. John has been diagnosed with heart failure 5 years ago. He has tried to follow his cardiologist's advice, by walking every day for 30 minutes, keeping his sodium to 2000 mg a day or less, and drinking no more than 64 oz of fluids per day. Also, on his cardiologist's advice, John just started using Engage.
	In this test, you are pretending to be John. You will use Engage just like John would. We will help you by telling you more about what John is doing. As you use Engage, I want you to think aloud (*the facilitator demonstrated the think-aloud technique*). Okay, now I'll go through some scenarios and tell you about John as he goes through four or five days of his life. Pretend time is going by with each little scene we do. Use Engage every day based on what John is doing.
Scenario 1	Now it is the morning of day 1. John measured his weight today, the scale read 165 lbs. He also took his blood pressure and heart rate. They were, respectively, 138 over 80 and 67 bpm. John's family is coming to town today, so he will probably be eating lots of salty foods that his cardiologist does not recommend. His recommended sodium intake is 2000 mg/day, but he expects to really go overboard today. He plans on walking between 30 and 40 min around the neighborhood with his family, as recommended by his doctor. Use Engage to record John's weight and heart rate, set his activity and sodium consumption goals for today.

(Continued)

TABLE 14.5 (Continued)

Step	Facilitator's script
	(*The facilitator let the participant use the prototype.*)
	Postscenario questions
	1. How did you feel about the process of using Engage in this scenario? 2. If this were John's program, how many coins has John earned so far? 3. Was there anything that was difficult or challenging? (If "yes," ask to elaborate)
Scenario 2	It is now close to 5 pm on the same day. John biked for 10 min instead of walking for 30 min as he had originally planned because his family was visiting him today. And, it turned out that John did not really go overboard with consuming sodium. Let Engage know about John's activity and sodium consumption. You may also play other available cards as if you were using Engage yourself.
	(*The facilitator let the participant use the prototype.*)
	Postscenario questions
	1. How did you feel about the process of using Engage in this scenario? 2. How many cards do you have left for this session? 3. Did John meet his long-term goals today? 4. John changed the kind of activity that he ended up doing. Did it cost him a coin/give him a coin/not change anything?

Both quantitative (SUS, time to complete tasks) and qualitative (interviews) measures were useful in their own right: the former for revising the designs, the latter for assessing the relevance of Engage for heart failure self-care. Using a standardized usability scale allowed comparisons to other studies and between rounds of testing. An improvement in the SUS score from 66.3 to 74.9 between the two rounds validated the importance of iterative design and evaluation (Cornet, Daley, et al., 2017). As expected, while task-based testing was adequate for addressing usability issues, scenario-based testing gave a better account of how Engage would be used to support self-care in the participants' daily lives (Cornet, Daley, et al., 2017). Other evaluation methods could have elicited different feedback. For example, having participants use diaries while using Engage at home for several weeks could have improved ecological validity. Table 14.6 lists examples of evaluation methods found in other human factors studies of solutions supporting self-care.

TABLE 14.6 Methods used for the evaluation of solutions supporting self-care.

Evaluation method	Sample studies
Expert evaluations	
Heuristic evaluation[a]	Morey et al. (2017), Preusse et al. (2014), Santos et al. (2014), Stuck et al. (2017)
Cognitive walkthrough	Morey et al. (2017), Stuck et al. (2017), Wood, Chapman, Taylor, Wright, and Scott (2014)
User evaluations	
Task-based evaluation[a]	Cornet, Daley, et al. (2017), Jones and Caird (2017), Kannampallil et al. (2013), Kwok and Burns (2005), Matalenas et al. (2015), Morrow et al. (2003), Ng et al. (2017), Rezai et al. (2014), Santos et al. (2014)
Scenario-based evaluation[a]	Cornet, Daley, et al. (2017)
Researcher-guided walkthrough	Barg-Walkow et al. (2014)
Diary (testing in users' homes)	Fausset et al. (2013), Preusse et al. (2014)
Scales	
System usability scale[a]	Cornet, Daley, et al. (2017), Kannampallil et al. (2013), Morey et al. (2017), Rezai et al. (2014)
NASA TLX[a]	Cornet, Daley, et al. (2017), Kannampallil et al. (2013)

TLX, Task Load Index.
[a]*Indicates the method was used in the evaluation of Engage.*

Conclusion

Self-care is a complex process, in part, due to the multiple actors who often work together, its vastly different purposes (prevention, post-acute care transition, chronic disease management) and types, and the many challenges and barriers in the patient work system and health-care delivery system that must be resolved to accomplish self-care goals. Multiple solutions have been attempted, though the majority were not designed and evaluated following human factors approaches and methods such as the user-centered design cycle of formative research, iterative design, and testing for usability and acceptance. Self-care, like any other example of effortful, goal-driven human activity, deserves to benefit from careful, user-centered design supported by the methods and design guidelines reviewed here and illustrated in our case study.

Acknowledgments

Projects on technology design for heart failure self-care described in the case study were supported by grants from the National Institute on Aging (NIA) (K01 AG044439) and National Center for Advancing Translational Sciences (NCATS) (KL2 TR000446) of the US National Institutes of Health (NIH) and the Agency for Healthcare Research & Quality (AHRQ) (R21 HS025232) to Dr. Holden. The content is solely the responsibility of the authors and does not necessarily represent the official views of NIH or AHRQ.

References

Abedtash, H., & Holden, R. J. (2017). Systematic review of the effectiveness of health-related behavioral interventions using portable activity sensing devices (PASDs). *Journal of the American Medical Informatics Association*, 24(5), 1002−1013. Available from https://doi.org/10.1093/jamia/ocx006.

Abraham, C., & Michie, S. (2008). A taxonomy of behavior change techniques used in interventions. *Health Psychology*, 27(3), 379−387. Available from https://doi.org/10.1037/0278-6133.27.3.379.

Archer, N., Fevrier-Thomas, U., Lokker, C., McKibbon, K. A., & Straus, S. E. (2011). Personal health records: A scoping review. *Journal of the American Medical Informatics Association*, 18(4), 515−522. Available from https://doi.org/10.1136/amiajnl-2011-000105.

Barg-Walkow, L. H., McBride, S. E., Morgan, M. J., Mitzner, T. L., Clarke, E. E., Bauer, D. T., ... Rogers, W. A. (2014). Efficacy of a system for tracking and managing osteoarthritis pain for both healthcare providers and older adults. *Proceedings of the International Symposium on Human Factors and Ergonomics in Health Care*, 3(1), 108−111. Available from https://doi.org/10.1177/2327857914031017.

Barg-Walkow, L. H., McBride, S. E., Morgan, M. J., Mitzner, T. L., Knott, C. C., & Rogers, W. A. (2013). How do older adults manage osteoarthritis pain? The need for a person-centered disease model. *Proceedings of the Human Factors and Ergonomics Society Annual Meeting*, 57(1), 743−747. Available from https://doi.org/10.1177/1541931213571162.

Beer, J. M., McBride, S. E., Mitzner, T. L., & Rogers, W. A. (2014). Understanding challenges in the front lines of home health care: A human-systems approach. *Applied Ergonomics*, 45(6), 1687−1699. Available from https://doi.org/10.1016/j.apergo.2014.05.019.

Blocker, K. A., Insel, K. C., Koerner, K. M., & Rogers, W. A. (2017). Understanding the medication adherence strategies of older adults with hypertension. *Proceedings of the Human Factors and Ergonomics Society Annual Meeting*, 61(1), 11−15. Available from https://doi.org/10.1177/1541931213601498.

Buck, H. G., Harkness, K., Wion, R., Carroll, S. L., Cosman, T., Kaasalainen, S., ... Arthur, H. M. (2015). Caregivers' contributions to heart failure self-care: A systematic review. *European Journal of Cardiovascular Nursing*, 14(1), 79−89. Available from https://doi.org/10.1177/1474515113518434.

Cage, K., Santos, L., Scott, C., & Vaughn-Cooke, M. (2014). Personal health record design preferences for minority diabetic patients. *Proceedings of the Human Factors and Ergonomics Society Annual Meeting*, 58(1), 614−618. Available from https://doi.org/10.1177/1541931214581131.

Calvin, K. L., Casper, G. R., Karsh, B.-T., Brennan, P. F., Burke, L. J., Carayon, P., ... Sebern, M. (2005). Work system analysis of home nursing care and implications for medication errors. *Proceedings of the Human Factors and Ergonomics Society Annual Meeting, 49*(11), 1052−1056. Available from https://doi.org/10.1177/154193120504901111.

Carayon, P., Kianfar, S., Li, Y., Xie, A., Alyousef, B., & Wooldridge, A. (2015). A systematic review of mixed methods research on human factors and ergonomics in health care. *Applied Ergonomics, 51,* 291−321. Available from https://doi.org/10.1016/j.apergo.2015.06.001.

Chaudhry, S. I., Wang, Y., Gill, T. M., & Krumholz, H. M. (2010). Geriatric conditions and subsequent mortality in older patients with heart failure. *Journal of the American College of Cardiology, 55*(4), 309−316. Available from https://doi.org/10.1016/j.jacc.2009.07.066.

Cheatham, D. B., & Wogalter, M. S. (2002). Reported likelihood of reading over-the-counter (OTC) medication labeling and contacting a physician. *Proceedings of the Human Factors and Ergonomics Society Annual Meeting, 46*(16), 1452−1456. Available from https://doi.org/10.1177/154193120204601610.

Chin, J., D'Andrea, L., Morrow, D., Stine-Morrow, E. A. L., Conner-Garcia, T., Graumlich, J., & Murray, M. (2009). Cognition and illness experience are associated with illness knowledge among older adults with hypertension. *Proceedings of the Human Factors and Ergonomics Society Annual Meeting, 53*(2), 116−120. Available from https://doi.org/10.1177/154193120905300202.

Coleman, E. A., Parry, C., Chalmers, S., & Min, S. (2006). The care transitions intervention: Results of a randomized controlled trial. *Archives of Internal Medicine, 166*(17), 1822−1828. Available from https://doi.org/10.1001/archinte.166.17.1822.

Cornet, V. P., & Holden, R. J. (2018). Systematic review of smartphone-based passive sensing for health and wellbeing. *Journal of Biomedical Informatics, 77,* 120−132. Available from https://doi.org/10.1016/j.jbi.2017.12.008.

Cornet, V. P., Daley, C. N., Srinivas, P., & Holden, R. J. (2017). User-centered evaluations with older adults: Testing the usability of a mobile health system for heart failure self-management. *Proceedings of the Human Factors and Ergonomics Society Annual Meeting, 61*(1), 6−10. Available from https://doi.org/10.1177/1541931213601497.

Cornet, V. P., Voida, S., & Holden, R. J. (2017). Activity theory analysis of heart failure self-care. *Mind, Culture, and Activity, 25*(1), 22−39. Available from https://doi.org/10.1080/10749039.2017.1372785.

Creber, R. M., Patey, M., Lee, C. S., Kuan, A., Jurgens, C., & Riegel, B. (2016). Motivational interviewing to improve self-care for patients with chronic heart failure: MITI-HF randomized controlled trial. *Patient Education and Counseling, 99*(2), 256−264. Available from https://doi.org/10.1016/j.cardfail.2015.06.244.

Currie, K., Rideout, A., Lindsay, G., & Harkness, K. (2015). The association between mild cognitive impairment and self-care in adults with chronic heart failure: A systematic review and narrative synthesis. *Journal of Cardiovascular Nursing, 30*(5), 382−393. Available from https://doi.org/10.1097/jcn.0000000000000173.

Daley, C. N., Bolchini, D., Varrier, A., Rao, K., Joshi, P., Blackburn, J., ... Holden, R. J. (2018). Naturalistic decision making by older adults with chronic heart failure: An exploratory study using the critical incident technique. *Proceedings of the Human Factors and Ergonomics Society Annual Meeting, 62*(1), 568−572. Available from https://doi.org/10.1177/1541931218621130.

D'Andrea, L., Morrow, D., Stine-Morrow, E., Shake, M., Bertel, S., Kopren, K., ... Murray, M. (2010). Impact of health knowledge on older adults' comprehension of multimedia health information. *Proceedings of the Human Factors and Ergonomics Society Annual Meeting, 54*(2), 180−184. Available from https://doi.org/10.1177/154193121005400209.

Dean, K. (1981). Self-care responses to illness: A selected review. *Social Science & Medicine. Part A: Medical Psychology & Medical Sociology*, *15*(5), 673–687. Available from https://doi.org/10.1016/0271-7123(81)90091-2.

Douglas, S. E., & Caldwell, B. S. (2009). Improving communication of health status information. *Proceedings of the Human Factors and Ergonomics Society Annual Meeting*, *53*(11), 709–713. Available from https://doi.org/10.1177/154193120905301116.

Dyrstad, D. N., Testad, I., Aase, K., & Storm, M. (2015). A review of the literature on patient participation in transitions of the elderly. *Cognition, Technology & Work*, *17*(1), 15–34. Available from https://doi.org/10.1007/s10111-014-0300-4.

Ezer, N., Fisk, A. D., & Rogers, W. A. (2009). More than a servant: Self-reported willingness of younger and older adults to having a robot perform interactive and critical tasks in the home. *Proceedings of the Human Factors and Ergonomics Society Annual Meeting*, *53*(2), 136–140. Available from https://doi.org/10.1177/154193120905300206.

Fausset, C. B., Mitzner, T. L., Price, C. E., Jones, B. D., Fain, B. W., & Rogers, W. A. (2013). Older adults' use of and attitudes toward activity monitoring technologies. *Proceedings of the Human Factors and Ergonomics Society Annual Meeting*, *57*(1), 1683–1687. Available from https://doi.org/10.1177/1541931213571374.

Holden, R. J., & Mickelson, R. S. (2013). Performance barriers among elderly chronic heart failure patients: An application of patient-engaged human factors and ergonomics. *Proceedings of the Human Factors and Ergonomics Society Annual Meeting*, *57*(1), 758–762. Available from https://doi.org/10.1177/1541931213571166.

Holden, R. J., Carayon, P., Gurses, A. P., Hoonakker, P., Hundt, A. S., Ozok, A. A., & Rivera-Rodriguez, A. J. (2013). SEIPS 2.0: A human factors framework for studying and improving the work of healthcare professionals and patients. *Ergonomics*, *56*(11), 1669–1686. Available from https://doi.org/10.1080/00140139.2013.838643.

Holden, R. J., Joshi, P., Rao, K., Varrier, A., Daley, C. N., Bolchini, D., . . . Mirro, M. J. (2018). Modeling personas for older adults with heart failure. *Proceedings of the Human Factors and Ergonomics Society Annual Meeting*, *62*(1), 1072–1076. Available from https://doi.org/10.1177/1541931218621246.

Holden, R. J., Kulanthaivel, A., Purkayastha, S., Goggins, K. M., & Kripalani, S. (2017). Know thy eHealth user: Development of biopsychosocial personas from a study of older adults with heart failure. *International Journal of Medical Informatics*, *108*, 158–167. Available from https://doi.org/10.1016/j.ijmedinf.2017.10.006.

Holden, R. J., McDougald Scott, A. M., Hoonakker, P. L. T., Hundt, A. S., & Carayon, P. (2015). Data collection challenges in community settings: Insights from two field studies of patients with chronic disease. *Quality of Life Research*, *24*(5), 1043–1055. Available from https://doi.org/10.1007%2Fs11136-014-0780-y.

Holden, R. J., Schubert, C. C., & Mickelson, R. S. (2015). The patient work system: An analysis of self-care performance barriers among elderly heart failure patients and their informal caregivers. *Applied Ergonomics*, *47*, 133–150. Available from https://doi.org/10.1016/j.apergo.2014.09.009.

Holden, R. J., Schubert, C. C., Eiland, E. C., Storrow, A. B., Miller, K. F., & Collins, S. P. (2015). Self-care barriers reported by emergency department patients with acute heart failure: A sociotechnical systems-based approach. *Annals of Emergency Medicine*, *66*(1), 1–12. e12. Available from https://doi.org/10.1016/j.annemergmed.2014.12.031.

Holden, R. J., Srinivas, P., Campbell, N. L., Clark, D. O., Bodke, K. S., Hong, Y., . . . Callahan, C. M. (2019). Understanding older adults' medication decision making and behavior: A study on over-the-counter (OTC) anticholinergic medications. *Research in Social and*

Administrative Pharmacy, *15*(1), 53−60. Available from https://doi.org/10.1016/j.
sapharm.2018.03.002.

Holden, R. J., Valdez, R. S., Schubert, C. C., Thompson, M. J., & Hundt, A. S. (2017).
Macroergonomic factors in the patient work system: Examining the context of patients with
chronic illness. *Ergonomics*, *60*(1), 26−43. Available from https://doi.org/10.1080/
00140139.2016.1168529.

Jaarsma, T., Cameron, J., Riegel, B., & Stromberg, A. (2017). Factors related to self-care in
heart failure patients according to the middle-range theory of self-care of chronic illness: A
literature update. *Current Heart Failure Reports*, *14*(2), 71−77. Available from https://doi.
org/10.1007/s11897-017-0324-1.

Jones, J., & Caird, J. K. (2017). The usability of blood glucose meters: Task performance differences between younger and older age groups. *Proceedings of the Human Factors and
Ergonomics Society Annual Meeting*, *61*(1), 604−608. Available from https://doi.org/
10.1177/1541931213601636.

Kain, D. L. (2003). *Owning significance: The critical incident technique in research.*
Foundations for research (pp. 85−102). Routledge.

Kannampallil, T. G., Waicekauskas, K., Morrow, D. G., Kopren, K. M., & Fu, W.-T. (2013).
External tools for collaborative medication scheduling. *Cognition, Technology & Work*, *15*
(2), 121−131. Available from https://doi.org/10.1007/s10111-011-0190-7.

Klein, G., & Militello, L. (2001). *Some guidelines for conducting a cognitive task analysis.*
Advances in human performance and cognitive engineering research (pp. 163−199).
Emerald Group Publishing Limited.

Klein, H. A. (2008). Adaptation at the edge: When the system is complex, the stakes high, and
the operator novice. *Proceedings of the Human Factors and Ergonomics Society Annual
Meeting*, *52*(4), 309−313. Available from https://doi.org/10.1177/154193120805200424.

Klein, H. A., Jackson, S. M., Street, K., Whitacre, J. C., & Klein, G. (2013). Diabetes self-
management education: Miles to go. *Nursing Research and Practice*, *2013*, 15. Available
from https://doi.org/10.1155/2013/581012.

Klein, H. A., & Lippa, K. D. (2012). Assuming control after system failure: Type II diabetes
self-management. *Cognition, Technology & Work*, *14*(3), 243−251. Available from https://
doi.org/10.1007/s10111-011-0206-3.

Kwok, J., & Burns, C. M. (2005). Usability evaluation of a mobile ecological interface design
application for diabetes management. *Proceedings of the Human Factors and Ergonomics
Society Annual Meeting*, *49*(11), 1042−1046. Available from https://doi.org/10.1177/
154193120504901109.

Li, I., Dey, A. K., & Forlizzi, J. (2011). *Understanding my data, myself: Supporting self-
reflection with Ubicomp technologies.*

Lim, S. L., Chan, S. P., Lee, K. Y., Ching, A., Holden, R. J., Miller, K. F., ... Collins, S. P.
(2017). An East−West comparison of self-care barriers in heart failure. *European Heart
Journal: Acute Cardiovascular Care*. Available from https://doi.org/10.1177/
2048872617744352.

Lippa, K. D., Klein, H. A., & Shalin, V. L. (2008). Everyday expertise: Cognitive demands in
diabetes self-management. *Human Factors*, *50*(1), 112−120. Available from https://doi.org/
10.1518/001872008x250601.

Lottridge, D., Yu, C., & Chignell, M. (2012). Measuring the emotional impacts of multimedia
eHealth. *Proceedings of the Human Factors and Ergonomics Society Annual Meeting*, *56*(1),
1947−1951. Available from https://doi.org/10.1177/1071181312561287.

Mamykina, L., Heitkemper, E. M., Smaldone, A. M., Kukafka, R., Cole-Lewis, H., Davidson, P. G., ... Hripcsak, G. (2016). Structured scaffolding for reflection and problem solving in diabetes self-management: Qualitative study of mobile diabetes detective. *Journal of the American Medical Informatics Association, 23*(1), 129−136. Available from https://doi.org/10.1093/jamia/ocv169.

Mamykina, L., Mynatt, E. D., & Kaufman, D. R. (2006). Investigating health management practices of individuals with diabetes. In: *Paper presented at the proceedings of the SIGCHI conference on human factors in computing systems*, Montreal, QC, Canada. <https://dx.org/10.1145/1124772.1124910>.

Matalenas, L. A., McLaughlin, A. C., Chen, Y., & Daughters, S. B. (2015). Developing a smartphone application for the life enhancement treatment for substance use (lets act): Designing for motivation and feedback. *Proceedings of the Human Factors and Ergonomics Society Annual Meeting, 59*(1), 1100−1104. Available from https://doi.org/10.1177/1541931215591158.

Mickelson, R. S., & Holden, R. J. (2013). Assessing the distributed nature of home-based heart failure medication management in older adults. *Proceedings of the Human Factors and Ergonomics Society Annual Meeting, 57*(1), 753−757. Available from https://doi.org/10.1177/1541931213571165.

Mickelson, R. S., & Holden, R. J. (2015). Mind the gulfs: An analysis of medication-related cognitive artifacts used by older adults with heart failure. *Proceedings of the Human Factors and Ergonomics Society Annual Meeting, 59*(1), 481−485. Available from https://doi.org/10.1177/1541931215591103.

Mickelson, R. S., & Holden, R. J. (2017). Capturing the medication management work system of older adults using a digital diary method. *Proceedings of the Human Factors and Ergonomics Society Annual Meeting, 61*(1), 555−559. Available from https://doi.org/10.1177/1541931213601622.

Mickelson, R. S., & Holden, R. J. (2018a). Medication adherence: Staying within the boundaries of safety. *Ergonomics, 61*(1), 82−103. Available from https://doi.org/10.1080/00140139.2017.1301574.

Mickelson, R. S., & Holden, R. J. (2018b). Medication management strategies used by older adults with heart failure: A systems-based analysis. *European Journal of Cardiovascular Nursing, 17*(5), 418−428. Available from https://doi.org/10.1177/1474515117730704.

Mickelson, R. S., Unertl, K. M., & Holden, R. J. (2016). Medication management: The macrocognitive workflow of older adults with heart failure. *JMIR Human Factors, 3*(2), e27. Available from https://doi.org/10.2196/humanfactors.6338.

Mickelson, R. S., Willis, M., & Holden, R. J. (2015). Medication-related cognitive artifacts used by older adults with heart failure. *Health Policy and Technology, 4*(4), 387−398. Available from https://doi.org/10.1016/j.hlpt.2015.08.009.

Minet, L., Møller, S., Vach, W., Wagner, L., & Henriksen, J. E. (2010). Mediating the effect of self-care management intervention in type 2 diabetes: A meta-analysis of 47 randomised controlled trials. *Patient Education and Counseling, 80*(1), 29−41. Available from https://doi.org/10.1016/j.pec.2009.09.033.

Mitzner, T. L., Chen, T. L., Kemp, C. C., & Rogers, W. A. (2014). Identifying the potential for robotics to assist older adults in different living environments. *International Journal of Social Robotics, 6*(2), 213−227. Available from https://doi.org/10.1007/s12369-013-0218-7.

Morey, S. A., Barg-Walkow, L. H., & Rogers, W. A. (2017). Managing heart failure on the go: Usability issues with mHealth apps for older adults. *Proceedings of the Human Factors and

Ergonomics Society Annual Meeting, *61*(1), 1–5. Available from https://doi.org/10.1177/1541931213601496.

Morrow, D., Clark, D., Tu, W., Wu, J., Weiner, M., Steinley, D., & Murray, M. D. (2006). Correlates of health literacy in patients with chronic heart failure. *The Gerontologist*, *46*(5), 669–676. Available from https://doi.org/10.1093/geront/46.5.669.

Morrow, D., Weiner, M., Young, J., Steinley, D., & Murray, M. D. (2003). Improving comprehension of medication instructions in older adults with heart failure: A patient-centered approach. *Proceedings of the Human Factors and Ergonomics Society Annual Meeting*, *47*(2), 232–236. Available from https://doi.org/10.1177/154193120304700202.

Murad, K., Goff, D. C., Morgan, T. M., Burke, G. L., Bartz, T. M., Kizer, J. R., ... Kitzman, D. W. (2015). Burden of comorbidities and functional and cognitive impairments in elderly patients at the initial diagnosis of heart failure and their impact on total mortality: The Cardiovascular Health Study. *JACC: Heart Failure*, *3*(7), 542–550. Available from https://doi.org/10.1016/j.jchf.2015.03.004.

Ng, A. W. Y., Chan, A. H. S., & Ho, V. W. S. (2017). Comprehension by older people of medication information with or without supplementary pharmaceutical pictograms. *Applied Ergonomics*, *58*, 167–175. Available from https://doi.org/10.1016/j.apergo.2016.06.005.

Nielsen, J., & Molich, R. (1990). Heuristic evaluation of user interfaces. In: *Paper presented at the proceedings of the SIGCHI conference on human factors in computing systems*, Seattle, WA. <https://dx.org/10.1145/97243.97281>.

Novak, L. L., Unertl, K. M., & Holden, R. J. (2016). Realizing the potential of patient engagement: Designing IT to support health in everyday life. *Studies in Health Technology and Informatics*, *222*, 237–247. Available from https://doi.org/10.3233/978-1-61499-635-4-237.

Nunes, F., & Fitzpatrick, G. (2018). Understanding the mundane nature of self-care: Ethnographic accounts of people living with Parkinson's. In: *Paper presented at the proceedings of the 2018 CHI conference on human factors in computing systems*, Montreal, QC, Canada. <https://doi.org/10.1145/3173574.3173976>.

Or, C. K. L., Valdez, R. S., Casper, G. R., Carayon, P., Burke, L. J., Brennan, P. F., & Karsh, B.-T. (2009). Human factors and ergonomics in home care: Current concerns and future considerations for health information technology. *Work*, *33*(2), 201–209. Available from https://doi.org/10.3233/WOR-2009-0867.

Orem. (2001). *Nursing: Concepts of practice* (6th ed.). St. Louis, MO: Mosby.

Pollack, A. H., Backonja, U., Miller, A. D., Mishra, S. R., Khelifi, M., Kendall, L., et al. (2016). Closing the gap: Supporting patients' transition to self-management after hospitalization. In: *Paper presented at the proceedings of the 2016 CHI conference on human factors in computing systems*, San Jose, CA. <https://dx.org/10.1145/2858036.2858240>.

Preusse, K. C., Mitzner, T. L., Fausset, C. B., & Rogers, W. A. (2014). Older adults' changes in intent to adopt wellness management technologies. *Proceedings of the Human Factors and Ergonomics Society Annual Meeting*, *58*(1), 200–204. Available from https://doi.org/10.1177/1541931214581042.

Rezai, L. S., Torenvliet, G., & Burns, C. M. (2014). Increasing patient adherence to home health-monitoring systems. *Proceedings of the International Symposium on Human Factors and Ergonomics in Health Care*, *3*(1), 8–14. Available from https://doi.org/10.1177/2327857914031001.

Richard, A. A., & Shea, K. (2011). Delineation of self-care and associated concepts. *Journal of Nursing Scholarship*, *43*(3), 255–264. Available from https://doi.org/10.1111/j.1547-5069.2011.01404.x.

Riegel, B., Dickson, V. V., & Faulkner, K. M. (2016). The situation-specific theory of heart failure self-care: Revised and updated. *Journal of Cardiovascular Nursing*, *31*(3), 226–235. Available from https://doi.org/10.1097/jcn.0000000000000244.

Santos, L., Olumese, O., & Vaughn-Cooke, M. (2014). Glucometer design for patients with vision and mobility impairments. *Proceedings of the Human Factors and Ergonomics Society Annual Meeting*, *58*(1), 669–673. Available from https://doi.org/10.1177/1541931214581157.

Sesto, M., Wachowiak, R., Tevaarwerk, A., Faatin, M., Heidrich, S., & Wiegmann, D. (2011). Improving employment outcomes of breast cancer survivors: Development of a web-based educational and decision support tool. *Proceedings of the Human Factors and Ergonomics Society Annual Meeting*, 55(1), 1333–1337. Available from https://doi.org/10.1177/1071181311551277.

Shippee, N. D., Shah, N. D., May, C. R., Mair, F. S., & Montori, V. M. (2012). Cumulative complexity: A functional, patient-centered model of patient complexity can improve research and practice. *Journal of Clinical Epidemiology*, *65*(10), 1041–1051. Available from https://doi.org/10.1016/j.jclinepi.2012.05.005.

Sidani, S. (2003). Self-care. In D. M. Doran (Ed.), *Nursing-sensitive outcomes: State of the science* (pp. 65–113). Boston, MA: Jones and Barlett Publishers.

Srinivas, P., Cornet, V., & Holden, R. (2017). Human factors analysis, design, and evaluation of Engage, a consumer health IT application for geriatric heart failure self-care. *International Journal of Human–Computer Interaction*, *33*(4), 298–312. Available from https://doi.org/10.1080/10447318.2016.1265784.

Stuck, R. E., Chong, A. W., Tracy, L. M., & Rogers, W. A. (2017). Medication management apps: Usable by older adults? *Proceedings of the Human Factors and Ergonomics Society Annual Meeting*, *61*(1), 1141–1144. Available from https://doi.org/10.1177/1541931213601769.

Thompson, M. J., Reilly, J. D., & Valdez, R. S. (2016). Work system barriers to patient, provider, and caregiver use of personal health records: A systematic review. *Applied Ergonomics*, *54*, 218–242. Available from https://doi.org/10.1016/j.apergo.2015.10.010.

Valdez, R. S., & Brennan, P. F. (2015). Exploring patients' health information communication practices with social network members as a foundation for consumer health IT design. *International Journal of Medical Informatics*, *84*(5), 363–374. Available from https://doi.org/10.1016/j.ijmedinf.2015.01.014.

Valdez, R. S., & Holden, R. J. (2016). Health care human factors/ergonomics fieldwork in home and community settings. *Ergonomics in Design*, *24*(4), 4–9. Available from https://doi.org/10.1177/1064804615622111.

Valdez, R. S., Holden, R. J., Novak, L. L., & Veinot, T. C. (2015). Technical infrastructure implications of the patient work framework. *Journal of the American Medical Informatics Association*, *22*(e1), e213–e215. Available from https://doi.org/10.1093/jamia/ocu031.

Verdezoto, N., & Grönvall, E. (2015). On preventive blood pressure self-monitoring at home. *Cognition, Technology & Work*, *18*(2), 267–285. Available from https://doi.org/10.1007/s10111-015-0358-7.

Warburton, D. E. R., Nicol, C. W., & Bredin, S. S. D. (2006). Health benefits of physical activity: The evidence. *Canadian Medical Association Journal*, *174*(6), 801–809. Available from https://doi.org/10.1503/cmaj.051351.

Werner, N. E., Gurses, A. P., Leff, B., & Arbaje, A. I. (2016). Improving care transitions across healthcare settings through a human factors approach. *Journal for Healthcare Quality*, *38* (6), 328–343. Available from https://doi.org/10.1097/jhq.0000000000000025.

Werner, N. E., Tong, M., Borkenhagen, A., & Holden, R. J. (2019). Performance-shaping factors affecting older adults' hospital-to-home transition success: A systems approach. *The Gerontologist, 59*(2), 303−314. Available from https://doi.org/10.1093/geront/gnx199.

Wood, S. D., Chapman, R., Taylor, L., Wright, P., & Scott, J. (2014). Identifying latent design issues in mobile products to prevent patient harm. *Proceedings of the International Symposium on Human Factors and Ergonomics in Health Care, 3*(1), 222−229. Available from https://doi.org/10.1177/2327857914031048.

Yamani, Y., Chin, J., Meyers, E. A. G., Gao, X., Morrow, D. G., Stine-Morrow, E. A. L., ... Murray, M. D. (2012). Reading engagement offsets declines in processing capacity for health literacy. *Proceedings of the Human Factors and Ergonomics Society Annual Meeting, 56*(1), 916−920. Available from https://doi.org/10.1177/1071181312561191.

Yancy, C. W., Jessup, M., Bozkurt, B., Butler, J., Casey, D. E., Colvin, M. M., ... Givertz, M. M. (2016). 2016 ACC/AHA/HFSA focused update on new pharmacological therapy for heart failure: An update of the 2013 ACCF/AHA guideline for the management of heart failure: A report of the American College of Cardiology/American Heart Association Task Force on Clinical Practice Guidelines and the Heart Failure Society of America. *Journal of the American College of Cardiology, 68*(13), 1476−1488. Available from https://doi.org/10.1161/CIR.0000000000000435.

Ye, N., & Holden, R. J. (2015). Exploring the context of chronic illness self-care using geospatial analyses. *Proceedings of the International Symposium on Human Factors and Ergonomics in Health Care, 4*(1), 37−41. Available from https://doi.org/10.1177/2327857915041033.

Zachary, W. W., Michlig, G., Kaplan, A., Nguyen, N.-T., Quinn, C. C., & Surkan, P. J. (2017). Participatory design of a social networking app to support type II diabetes self-management in low-income minority communities. *Proceedings of the International Symposium on Human Factors and Ergonomics in Health Care, 6*(1), 37−43. Available from https://doi.org/10.1177/2327857917061010.

Section 3

Special population

Chapter 15

Design for inclusivity

Natalie C. Benda[1], Enid Montague[2] and Rupa S. Valdez[3]
[1]Weill Cornell Medicine, New York, NY, United States, [2]DePaul University, Chicago, IL, United States, [3]University of Virginia, Charlottesville, VA, United States

Human factors (HF) research in the health-care domain tends to focus on the clinical care provided to patients. Previous research has demonstrated that clinical care only explains 20% of health outcomes. The other 80% have been attributed to social determinants of health, such as socioeconomic status, education, social support, and geographic location (McGovern, Miller, & Hughes-Cromwick, 2014). Social determinants of health are conditions under which people are born, grow, live, work, and age (World Health Organization, 2019).

Social determinants of health perpetuate the health inequities found across the world (Marmot, 2005). For example, three African nations reported an average life expectancy of 53 years (Lesotho, Central African Republic, and Sierra Leone), while the average life expectancy in Japan is over 84 years (World Health Organization, 2018). Further, in different geographic areas within the United States, life expectancy varies by over 20 years (Dwyer-Lindgren et al., 2017).

The public health community, led by the World Health Organization, has advocated for improving *health equity*. Whitehead (2000) defines health equity as "the absence of avoidable or remediable differences in health outcomes between groups of people, whether those groups are defined socially, economically, geographically or demographically." A commonly cited framework describes three stages of research for improving health equity. First, health disparities must be measured and documented. Second, the causes for health inequity must be identified. Third, solutions should be provided for reducing or eliminating health inequities (Kilbourne, Switzer, Hyman, Crowley-Matoka, & Fine, 2006). Others have argued that research should not stop at the third stage because solutions should be integrated into the community to improve health equity on a broader level. Therefore a fourth stage of research has been proposed—taking action by implementing multilevel interventions to address systemic drivers of inequity (Thomas, Quinn, Butler, Fryer, & Garza, 2011).

Design for Health. DOI: https://doi.org/10.1016/B978-0-12-816427-3.00015-4

306 SECTION | 3 Special population

The framework for achieving health equity, however, does not explicate the foundational tenet in bioethics of nonmaleficence, or, "first, to do no harm." This tenet is particularly important in health-care design research due to the issue of intervention-generated inequities. Intervention-generated inequities refer to interventions intended to improve health that are of greater benefit to advantaged groups than to disadvantaged groups (Lorenc, Petticrew, Welch, & Tugwell, 2013). Interventions that aim to improve equity for specified communities may also fall short if they are not executed in an informed, responsible manner. Poor cultural sensitivity, identification of power dynamics, and insufficient trust building can hinder the effectiveness of an intervention and even lead to negative consequences for members of the community (Lillie-Blanton & Hoffman, 1995).

This chapter focuses on designing for inclusivity in health care in order to prevent intervention-generated inequities and improve equity in health-care design. Inclusive design involves creating solutions that are accessible to and usable by as many persons as reasonably possible (Keates, 2005).

In extreme situations, failure to consider different end-user groups has resulted in catastrophic events. The use of English instead of the operators' native Hindi language contributed to an industrial explosion in Bhopal, India that led to the death of an estimated 2500 persons and irreparable harm to 10,000 more (Mechkati, 1991). In another incident, US farmers had marked grain unfit for human consumption by dyeing it red, including a warning label (in English), and adding a skull-and-crossbones icon. This grain was shipped to Iraq as animal feed. The Iraqi farmers who received the grain cannot read English, nor did they have the same cultural context to identify that the skull-and-crossbones signaled hazardous material. The farmers washed away the red dye and consumed the grains. Experts estimate that the poisoning led to significant neurological damage in as many as 60,000 people (Bakir et al., 1973).

In the health-care domain, poor design inclusivity can also be dangerous. For example, parents with lower health literacy are significantly more likely to commit dosing errors when administering liquid medication to their children (Yin et al., 2010). Although pictogram-based instructions can reduce dosing errors for parents with lower health literacy, wholly text-based instructions still pervade the market.

The issues described underscore problems of inclusivity and our ethnocentric tendency to design for the "ordinary user," who we presume to be much like ourselves or the persons surrounding us (Kroemer, 2006). Issues in various components of the work system have been found to affect poor design inclusivity. Environmental and organizational factors, including Internet access and health-insurance status, have been demonstrated to reduce access to health-related interventions (Frumkin, 2005; Perzynski et al., 2017). Person characteristics have also been linked to poor adoption/uptake of technology due to racial differences in risk perception, privacy, and trust in the health-care system (LaVeist, Nickerson, & Bowie, 2000; Perzynski et al., 2017; Tieu et al., 2009; Valdez, Gibbons, Siegel, Kukafka, & Brennan, 2012). Physical system characteristics, such as poor usability and technological issues, have been found to have worse effects related to misuse and disuse on traditionally underserved populations (Habibović et al., 2014; Nijland, Van Gemert-Pijnen, Kelders, Brandenburg, & Seydel, 2011; Taha, Sharit, & Czaja, 2014). Further person characteristics including age, literacy, and numeracy have also been demonstrated to impact the effectiveness of technological tools and information technology (Jensen, King, Davis, & Guntzviller, 2010; Tao, Shao, Liu, Wang, & Qu, 2016; Tieu et al., 2009).

The goal of this chapter is to provide best practices and applied examples to instruct HF practitioners (researchers and designers) in creating health-care designs that are inclusive of various populations. Keeping in mind that practitioners may begin with different levels of resources and experiences, we present general best practices and approaches with the following three "levels of involvement":

- Passively related techniques—personas
- Maximum variance sampling
- Community-based participatory research (CBPR)

The chapter should serve as a starting point and practical guide for completing inclusive design research. Kroemer (2006) and Smith-Jackson, Resnick, and Johnson (2013) provide further instruction regarding HF and inclusive design. Although the context of application in this chapter is health care, the approaches are relevant across application domains. This chapter is not meant to be an all-inclusive description of each method, and referential texts are provided related to each approach.

Inclusive design guidelines

General guidelines

Multiple levels of considerations are necessary to create inclusive designs. Fig. 15.1 provides examples of work-system-level components (Holden et al., 2013; Smith-Jackson et al., 2013), design-level components (Valdez et al., 2012), and constructs to ensure inclusive, equitable design (Veinot, Mitchell, & Ancker, 2018).

Fig. 15.1 provides HF practitioners with different levels of considerations grounded in familiar concepts to utilize through the iterative data collection, design, testing, and use process. Fig. 15.1 also demonstrates that the levels of consideration provided are interconnected. For example, access is almost wholly dependent on the design platform, while the design platform choice should be dictated by constraints of the physical environment and the intended users' sensory, physical, and cognitive abilities. Previous

Work System Components		Design Components		Constructs to be Measured	
Component	Question/ Consideration	Component	Question/ Consideration	Construct	Question/ Consideration
Physical environment	Local climate (e.g. desert, tropical)	Design platform	Will the design platform be accessible to the target end users?	Access	Are different end user groups participating/ able to access to the design?
	Broadband access		Are multiple design platforms necessary?		
	Environmental exposure	Functionality	What tasks should to be supported for the target user group?	Adoption/ Uptake	Use metrics – who is using the design or "logging on"?
	Housing status		Will tasks differ across user groups?		
Social, organizational, cultural	Ethnicity			Adherence/ effectiveness	Are there patterns in attrition or disuse over time?
	Gender	Content	Are cultural norms of the user group properly reflected?		
	Religion				
	Government	User interface	What language and literacy level appropriate?		Are there differences in outcome measures between relevant groups of users?
Person/ individual	Sensory capabilities		Can colors and icons be interpreted by the user group?		
	Physical abilities				
	Cognitive abilities				

FIGURE 15.1 Examples of work system (Holden et al., 2013; Smith-Jackson et al., 2013), design component (Valdez et al., 2012), and measurement related considerations (Veinot et al., 2018), for inclusive design.

interventions affecting the environment have involved increasing the access of technologies through widespread broadband Internet access and making more interactions or tools available via 2G connections (i.e., altering the design platform) (Anderson, 2017; Anzilotti, 2016; Latulippe, Hamel, & Giroux, 2017). Similarly, health conditions affecting a person's visual abilities may result in a preference for larger screens, making tablet-based interventions preferable to phone-based interventions (Muskens, Van Lent, Vijfvinkel, Van Cann, & Shahid, 2014). In such designs, it is still important to consider the social, organizational, and cultural information and individual-level characteristics. Multiple studies have demonstrated that creating culturally relevant, contextually situated content improves the effectiveness of design on knowledge and health outcomes (Houston et al., 2011; Montague & Perchonok, 2012; Mosnaim, Cohen, Rhoads, Rittner, & Powell, 2008; Wilkin et al., 2007).

In line with a systems-based approach the interactions between levels of this framework are important to consider. Subsequent sections describe different approaches for inclusive design, and the considerations discussed here remain critical independent of the methodological approach.

Passive techniques: personas

Overview

Personas are descriptive models of users that embody important and realistic user characteristics that must be considered in the design process. A model of a persona is typically a one-to-three paragraph description of a user's personality, characteristics, and use goals related to a specific design problem, often accompanied by a photo for improved realism. From an HF practitioner perspective, personas can be further enhanced through knowledge regarding aspects of the work system, such as social/organizational factors and their interaction with the physical environment.

The use of personas can be helpful in situations where iterative, rapid development is necessary, obtaining sufficient participants for more in-depth forms of user-centered or participatory design is not feasible, or when user testing may require challenging situations for the target participant group(s). For example, one study utilized personas to understand and generate interventions for patient falls, which are dangerous or difficult to recreate, and it may be challenging or harmful for those who experienced the fall to recount what happened (Hignett, Griffiths, Sands, Wolf, & Costantinou, 2013). In another study, personas were used to develop design requirements for alternative augmentative communication (AAC) devices, which help individuals who have trouble speaking and communicating. The use of personas was particularly advantageous in this case because patients requiring AAC devices typically have considerable physical and communicative limitations, making it challenging for them to actively participate in the design process for extended periods of time (Subrahmaniyan et al., 2013). Adlin and Pruitt (2010) and Cooper, Reimann, Cronin, and Noessel (2014), for example, provide detailed methodologies related to the employment of personas in design.

Practical guidance

Triangulate common characteristics to be embodied in the personas created through multiple sources. For example, medical device companies may review characteristics related to their customers to determine the most prominent user groups. The device manufacturer may then also conduct focus groups with customers to understand the needs and characteristics of the key user groups identified through their consumer data. The combination of consumer data and focus group results can then be utilized to develop personas for future design scenarios.

Designate specific user experience leads separate from the product design staff. One common pitfall of persona development is letting the design of a product (as opposed to the problem a product addresses) dictate the personas' makeup. User experience researchers' role is geared specifically toward serving the user, and they will typically be less constrained by the technical aspects of the product design. It is also helpful to have multiple team members involved in the development process, preferably with different roles and backgrounds to mitigate potential biases.

Ensure the persona research and development process is iterative. Persona development and subsequent outputs should be iteratively reviewed with key stakeholders. Related to inclusive design, personas should be reviewed by individuals with cultural competency related to the given user groups to ensure that the depictions are accurate and do not contain any potentially offensive or stereotyped views. Individuals with deep knowledge of the target population could include patient advocates, social workers, or clinicians who frequently treat the given population.

Case study: hospital parking lot redesign for safety and accessibility

Members of an HF team were asked by their health-care system to provide feedback on the redesign of an innercity hospital parking garage with the goals of improving efficiency and ensuring patient safety. The health-care system had a short (2 week) timeline by which recommendations were needed. Signage and parking flow design could not be tested using actual users, as the old designs were in place and under use in the current parking garage. However, the team of HF experts needed a systematic, evidence-based approach to provide recommendations. The team also wanted to provide an approach that could be used by key stakeholders at the hospital for the existing project as well as for future signage and way-finding design projects. The team completed a site visit and multiple phone calls with stakeholders from the hospital (building design, operations, security, patient services, etc.). It was not possible to consult with actual patients, but the director of patient services provided information regarding key patient characteristics to consider in the design. As associates of the health-care system, the HF experts also had experience with the hospital and surrounding area and thus had personal domain knowledge to draw upon.

The experts determined that designs should target those with physical/ cognitive limitations or those in high-stress situations. These limitations and situations relate to dimensions of inclusive design described in Fig. 15.1. The HF team utilized information from the phone calls, site visits, and their personal knowledge of the environment to create a list of specific patient characteristics that should be embodied in the personas. Key patient characteristics identified included limited literacy/English proficiency, reduced vision, reduced mobility, use of alternative format vehicles (e.g., hand operated), and those experiencing high-stress situations. These characteristics pertain both to those who may be at the highest risk for misinterpreting the signage and groups that are prevalent to the patient population of the hospital. The team iteratively designed four different patient personas including an elderly couple with reduced mobility, sight impairment, and some cognitive disabilities; a ride-share driver who speaks English as a second language and has lower literacy related to health-care terminology; a mother bringing a child to the emergency room with a head injury; and a paraplegic woman with a hand-operated vehicle.

In order to provide design feedback, the parking garage and drop-off areas were broken into key decision points where drivers would need to decide when to turn, continue on, stop, exit their vehicle, etc. Each persona had a defined goal destination. Multiple members of the team collaboratively identified the decision points and goal destinations. One team member walked through 14 identified decision points to determine where errors could be made by each persona. Ideally, this walkthrough should be completed with a multidisciplinary group but was not done so in this case due to time constraints of the project and competing demands. The list of potential errors was then reviewed by the larger team, and a series of design recommendations was developed to mitigate the issues identified. Specific recommendations were then presented to the hospital stakeholders to inform the redesign process. One example involved directing patients, caregivers, and visitors to an area where their vehicle would be valeted, a service provided free of charge by the hospital to expedite parking and improve safety. Many people, however, may not be familiar with the process of having their vehicle valeted. The HF team recommended limiting the phrase "valet" and using phrases such as "vehicle drop-off" and "vehicle pick-up" in its place (Fig. 15.2). The team also designed a sign that would provide brief, easy to understand steps for vehicle valet (Fig. 15.3).

Key themes related to the recommendations, some of which are highlighted in the example previously mentioned, included the following:

- Use concise phrasing to facilitate quick reading while driving.
- Use wording understandable to the general public (especially those less familiar with a health-care system).
- Use bright colors that can be easily differentiated in darker areas.
- Avoid colors that may be confused by those with color blindness.

In the scenario described, personas were developed though a site visit and key stakeholder interviews. The use of personas provided a systematic mechanism for devising rapid feedback to improve design inclusivity of a design for operational problems in a hospital environment. A sample persona of the elderly couple (Clarence and Beatrice) is provided. This persona focuses on aspects of the work system important to the design problem at

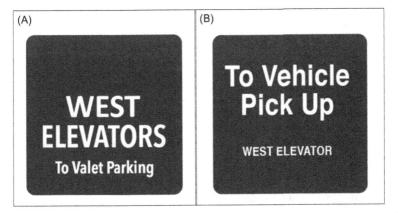

FIGURE 15.2 Example of how the HF experts recommended emphasizing key, easily accessible phrases, such as "vehicle pick up" instead of "valet." The HF experts also emphasized the goal action, "vehicle pick up," instead of the direction of the elevator where the sign was hung, "west elevator." (A) Initial design and (B) HF experts' design. *HF*, Human factors.

FIGURE 15.3 These signs illustrate the human factors experts' recommendations for the valet area where cars needed to stop. For the safety of the valets and pedestrians, the experts recommended multiple large, red signs (valet sign, sign with instructions) and painting the floor of the area red. They also included a sign with concise steps for those not familiar with the valet process (left wall in B). (A) Initial design and (B) HF experts' design. *HF*, Human factors.

hand, an important facet to ensuring personas can be utilized efficiently and effectively (Box 15.1).

Maximum variance sampling

Overview

Maximum variance sampling is another methodology for promoting diverse samples in research- and design-based studies. Maximum variance sampling is a qualitative inquiry technique that involves a wide range of extremes in

BOX 15.1 Sample persona

Clarence (87 years old) is bringing his wife Beatrice (84 years old) to an appointment for a first-time neurology consult for suspected signs of dementia. They live in a suburban area approximately 15 mi away from the city, and this is their first time at this hospital. They still live independently and get around on their own. Clarence still drives but has diminishing eyesight and sometimes has trouble reading signs at a distance. Beatrice uses a walker and becomes easily tired walking long distances. Clarence does not like to leave Beatrice alone as he likes to make sure she can walk to locations safely. Clarence does not use any assistive devices for walking but has trouble with long walks and stairs. He has fallen in the last month, tripping on a lip in the sidewalk.

Photo from Stannah International, www.stannah-stairlifts.com.

terms of participant characteristics in order to represent a diverse population (Cresswell & Cresswell, 2017; Palinkas et al., 2015). For example, if socioeconomic status is a variable of interest, instead of taking an interview of someone from the middle class, hoping they will provide an "average" opinion, a maximum variance approach suggests that interviews should include those from both the lowest and highest levels of socioeconomic status. Patton (1990) describes advantages of maximum variance sampling related documenting "unique and diverse variations that have emerged in adapting to different conditions" and identifying "important common patterns that cut across variations." This approach is typically used when only small or convenience samples are available, and a sample representative of a diverse set of users is desired. Cresswell and Cresswell (2017) and Patton (1990) provide further instruction in maximum variance sampling approaches.

Practical guidance

Engage the community. Once target participant characteristics have been identified, relevant stakeholders, such as community organizations, should be consulted. Recruitment, data collection, and interpretation can be greatly aided by the use of community-based organizations or less traditional mechanisms. For example, one study found that social media can be a helpful tool for obtaining smaller samples for qualitative research studies seeking to engage diverse samples (Valdez et al., 2014). Involvement of community-based organizations can also foster trust with potential participants and provide resources for ensuring whether recruitment and screen materials are appropriate (as described earlier).

Consider your target demographics in designing recruitment and data collection methods. It is important to ensure that recruitment and data collection are appropriate for all targeted groups. This includes ensuring the materials are culturally appropriate, of a literacy level that is understandable for a general population, and that the materials are offered in formats suitable for those with different capabilities (e.g., hearing impairment, sight impairment, different languages, and low-literate individuals). The sampling goals can help determine which of these characteristics must be considered. The conduct of the data collection should remain as uniform as possible, but different variations of data collection tools may be necessary if, for example, participants who speak different languages are sought. In this example, additional resources such as translators may be necessary. It is also important that the research objectives and consenting materials be explained in plain, approachable language as participants may not be familiar with research processes or participation in research studies.

Anticipate and mitigate barriers to participation. Actions should be taken to ensure that potential barriers related to participation are mitigated. This may entail offering compensation, transportation vouchers, Internet access, etc. Informants who help design the recruitment and data collection materials can also help in anticipating potential offerings that may be necessary to not exclude target individuals from participating.

Acknowledge that it may not be possible to reach all target groups. It may, for example, not be possible to find a person of lower socioeconomic status who has utilized a certain type of product, especially if the product is particularly expensive. In these instances, it is okay to have multiple people who may represent a similar demographic (e.g., someone of middle-high socioeconomic status who has used the product). List (2004) asserts that this issue can be addressed, and additional participants that fulfill the same criteria may be recruited. It is, however, important that these participants are different in another way that is relevant to the study (e.g., they have completed different levels of education).

Be clear about the goals and limitations of the study. Maximum variance sampling is not equivalent to completing quantitative studies that are sufficiently powered to test for between-group effects. It also cannot be assured that this type of sampling represents all perspectives that may be related to a given design. However, this approach provides a mechanism that allows for obtaining participants from diverse groups with a small sample size that can provide a broader spectrum of views than other mechanisms such as homogenous, opportunistic, or convenience-based approaches.

Case study: understanding design requirements for health information technology to aid in sharing health information with patients' social networks

Members of a multidisciplinary team led by an HF professional engaged in a series of research projects to determine the patient needs for a health IT that facilitates communication between patients and members of their social network (Menefee, Thompson, Guterbock, Williams, & Valdez, 2016; Valdez & Brennan, 2015; Valdez et al., 2014). To ensure that the design guidelines generated would be relevant across many different types of patients, the team engaged in maximum variance sampling across a range of demographic characteristics. The team determined that a maximum variance sampling approach was an appropriate first step to generating design guidance that could then be refined for specific communities through CBPR approaches. The team conducted three qualitative studies with the goal of obtaining diversity across demographic characteristics such as gender, socioeconomic status, geographic location, age, health status, and race and ethnicity. The first study prioritized variability across self-identified cultural identity, the second study prioritized variability across engagement with online and offline social networks, and the third study prioritized variability across experience living with physical, cognitive, or sensory disabilities. The maximum variance sampling approach prioritized one demographic variable in each of the three studies and sought to attain variability across several other demographic characteristics.

To obtain maximum variance across the study sample, the team first asked the study participants to complete a brief demographic survey. For the studies conducted in person, the survey was provided in a study information packet to all interested individuals in the clinic. For the studies conducted online, the survey link was provided to all individuals joining the study's team Facebook group, which served as platform for recruitment. As the surveys were completed, the team recruited individuals who identified as having demographic characteristics that were not yet well represented in the study sample.

Qualitative data obtained in each study (e.g., interviews, journals, and focus groups) were analyzed in aggregate. In other words, we did not attempt to ascribe specific needs or design guidance to specific demographic characteristics. Rather, the goal of the analysis was to highlight the range of needs represented across the entire sample.

Employing a maximum variance sampling approach resulted in findings that we may not have been able draw from a convenience sample. We highlight a few of these findings in the following paragraphs:

- Participants discussed the need to communicate about their health information to a wide range of social network members including spiritual figures, foster parents, virtual friends, case managers, and members of communities defined by religion, cultural identity, and disability identity.
- Participants discussed that from their perspective, clinicians may be thought of as social network members and not as individuals separate from others in their lives. Such a finding implies that from a patient perspective, health IT focused on communication should not always be separated into technologies that facilitate communication with clinicians and those that facilitate communication with other family members.
- Participants mentioned communicating about health information not only for their own health management, but also as a means of advocating for others living with stigmatized conditions. Such a finding implies that health IT designs may have a broader role to play beyond simply facilitating individual self-management.

Community-based participatory research

Overview

CBPR "focuses on social, structural, and physical environmental inequities through active involvement of community members, organizational representatives, and researchers in all aspects of the research process (Israel, Schulz, Parker, & Becker, 2001)." This approach can also facilitate achieving the fourth level of health equity previously described, taking action and implementing social change (Thomas et al., 2011). However, CBPR-related work can also be challenging, time-consuming, and resource intensive. Further, there are relatively few examples of extending CBPR projects into controlled evaluations demonstrating outcome effectiveness due to issues balancing the need for sustained social improvement with the rigor of research evaluation processes (Wallerstein et al., 2017). Refer to Stoecker (2008) as well as Valdez and Holden (2016) for further guidance related to conducting CBPR work.

Practical guidance

Ask yourself the following questions to determine an appropriate role in the CBPR effort (Stoecker, 2008):

- What is this CBPR trying to do? At what stage in the problem design process are the community members of the project?

- What are my skills that I can contribute to this project, and my realistic constraints for the time and effort I can contribute?
- How much participation from HF practitioners does the community want or need? (Note: In some cases the answer may be none.)

Answering these questions can help HF practitioners determine their involvement as either an *initiator* who organizes a community to diagnose and address an issue, a *consultant* who is commissioned by the community to advise in the research process, or a *collaborator* who combines their expertise with that of the community leader to work unitarily to develop a social change intervention (Stoecker, 2008).

Carefully identify the right members to participate in the team. It is important to give agency and balance to members with community experience, systems design, and patients. Approaches such as maximum variance sampling (described earlier) can be utilized in conjunction with a CBPR approach to ensure that ample input from different subgroups is included.

Allow enough time for team building. Ensure that each team member has provided enough of an overview of their expertise, so there is a shared understanding. When possible, allocate resources for shared trainings. Some communities may have a large amount of distrust, so consider that it may take a significant amount of time for researchers to gain trust from the community.

Organize the research process while working closely with members of the community. Depending on the specific needs of the project, the HF practitioners may also assume additional roles, such as a leader, a community organizer, or educator. A key tenant is that these are not solely research projects but also vehicles for sustained social change that should be designed in full partnership with the community. Throughout the course of the project cycle, it is particularly important to ensure that the community members drive defining the design goals (although this may involve input from the HF practitioner), inform culturally appropriate designs of the research (where applicable), be involved as is possible in the data collection, and own the postdissemination step of acting upon the results of the evaluation with support from the researcher as requested.

Consider and plan for your own safety. Similar to wearing personal protective equipment in a hospital setting, it is important to establish plans for your safety when entering a community environment (Valdez & Holden, 2016). This may include

- having community sponsors help arrange initial visits in community settings,
- ensuring at least two team members are present, at least for initial visits,
- informing other staff or team members not attending the visit of your plans, and
- setting ground rules for safety, such as only entering common spaces in a home (i.e., living room, dining room, and kitchen).

It is also important to ensure team members entering the community set-ting have respectful strategies for declining to do things that may be against research/design or safety protocols. While maintaining respect may seem second nature, responding appropriately without offending community members may be more challenging when put on the spot. For example, if a participant or community member asks you to see something in their bedroom, it is prudent to have prepared responses, such as "My supervisor has instructed me to stay in common areas out of concerns for your privacy." It is also helpful to vet such responses with community sponsors in advance as they may have a better idea of how members of the community would respond.

Case study: improving maternal health outcomes and maximizing patient experience for African American women in Chicago

In Chicago the concerns about poor maternal and infant health outcomes for African American women were a growing public health concern. This case study describes ongoing efforts with community partners to improve inequities in health outcomes for African American mothers and infants to illustrate possibilities in using CBPR throughout the progress of a project.

Rather than developing research questions and approaches to mitigate the problem, HF researchers may begin by conducting a community scan of organizations already working with affected communities and individuals.

To better understand concerns, women in the community could be invited to share their stories about their birth experiences. Women may be contacted by working with community organizations (e.g., faith-based organizations and community health centers) with which the women have established trust. In this scenario, it may be helpful to include persons who have had diverse experiences, both positive and negative. HF experts should also consider that discussing the birthing experiences may be challenging for some women and ensure that the proper mental health and emotional support experts have been consulted before proceeding.

HF researchers could then generate process maps to illustrate the diversity of patient experiences and identify failures from the patients' perspectives. Development of the process maps would benefit from iterative feedback from patients. From here, key stakeholders in the community as well as patients would generate a plan to move forward in addressing the key concerns related to maternal and infant health that were identified. The plan could include more research, advocating for funding, targeted interventions or other initiatives. Contextual design methodologies are often helpful for diverse groups of community members to identify the breakdowns in the system and creatively brainstorm solutions. In these approaches, HF practitioners can facilitate the process or work as a member of the team, while a member of the community or a practitioner with expertise in CBPR facilitates.

Conclusion

Promoting inclusivity in design is critical for advancing design in health and ensuring health equity. HF practitioners are uniquely suited to contribute to the improvement of design inclusivity given our experience in utilizing system-based approaches and incorporating perspectives from diverse users to create usable tools. Various methods may be utilized to enhance design inclusivity, such as use of personas, maximum variance sampling, and engaging in CBPR. Each method has different strengths and may be useful at different points throughout the research process. Independent of the method utilized, best practices for inclusive design include building multidisciplinary teams, engaging members of a community or those with deep knowledge of the target community, and continuing to practice iterative design.

References

Adlin, T., & Pruitt, J. (2010). *The essential persona lifecycle: Your guide to building and using personas*. San Francisco, CA: Morgan Kaufmann Publishers.

Anderson, M. (2017). *Digital divide persists even as lower-income Americans make gains in tech adoption*. Retrieved August 9, 2018, from <http://www.pewresearch.org/fact-tank/2017/03/22/digital-divide-persists-even-as-lower-income-americans-make-gains-in-tech-adoption/>.

Anzilotti, E. (2016). *Visualizing the state of global Internet connectivity*. Retrieved August 9, 2018, from <https://www.citylab.com/life/2016/08/visualizing-the-state-of-global-internet-connectivity/496328/>.

Bakir, F., Damluji, S. F., Amin-Zaki, L., Murtadha, M., Khalidi, A., Al-Rawi, N. Y., & Doherty, R. (1973). Methylmercury poisoning in Iraq. *Science, 181*(4096), 230–241. Available from https://doi.org/10.1126/science.181.4096.230.

Cooper, A., Reimann, R., Cronin, D., & Noessel, C. (2014). Modeling users: Personas and goals the power of personas. In *about Face: The Essentials of Interaction Design*. Hoboken, NJ: John Wiley & Sons.

Cresswell, J. W., & Creswell, J. D. (2017). *Research design: Qualitative, quantitative, and mixed methods approaches*. Sage Publications, Inc.

Dwyer-Lindgren, L., Bertozzi-Villa, A., Stubbs, R. W., Morozoff, C., Mackenbach, J. P., Van Lenthe, F. J., ... Murray, C. J. L. (2017). Inequalities in life expectancy among US counties, 1980 to 2014: Temporal trends and key drivers. *JAMA Internal Medicine, 177*(7), 1003–1011. Available from https://doi.org/10.1001/jamainternmed.2017.0918.

Frumkin, H. (2005). Health, equity, and the built environment. *Environmental Health Perspectives, 113*(5), 2001–2002.

Habibović, M., Cuijpers, P., Alings, M., Van Der Voort, P., Theuns, D., Bouwels, L., ... Pedersen, S. (2014). Attrition and adherence in a web-based distress management program for implantable cardioverter defibrillator patients (WEBCARE): Randomized controlled trial. *Journal of Medical Internet Research, 16*(2), 1–18. Available from https://doi.org/10.2196/jmir.2809.

Hignett, S., Griffiths, P., Sands, G., Wolf, L., & Costantinou, E. (2013). Patient falls: Focusing on human factors rather than clinical conditions. *Proceedings of the International*

Symposium on Human Factors and Ergonomics in Health Care, 2(1), 99–104. Available from https://doi.org/10.1177/2327857913021019.

Holden, R. J., Carayon, P., Gurses, A. P., Hoonakker, P., Hundt, A. S., Ozok, A. A., & Rivera-Rodriguez, A. J. (2013). SEIPS 2.0: A human factors framework for studying and improving the work of healthcare professionals and patients. *Ergonomics.* Available from https://doi.org/10.1080/00140139.2013.838643.

Houston, T. K., Allson, J. J., Sussman, M., Horn, W., Holt, C. L., Trobaugh, J., . . . Hullett, S. (2011). Original research culturally appropriate storytelling to improve blood pressure. *Annals of Internal Medicine, 154*(2), 78–89. Available from https://doi.org/10.7326/0003-4819-154-2-201101180-00004.

Israel, B. A., Schulz, A. J., Parker, E. A., & Becker, A. B. (2001). Community-based participatory research: Policy recommendations for promoting a partnership approach in health research. *Education for Health (Abingdon, England), 14*(2), 182–197. Available from https://doi.org/10.1080/13576280110051055.

Jensen, J. D., King, A. J., Davis, L. A., & Guntzviller, L. M. (2010). Utilization of internet technology by low-income adults: The role of health literacy, health numeracy, and computer assistance. *Journal of Aging and Health, 22*(6), 804–826. Available from https://doi.org/10.1177/0898264310366161.

Keates, S. (2005). *BS 7000-6:2005: Design management systems. Managing inclusive design.* London, UK: BSI Standards.

Kilbourne, A. M., Switzer, G., Hyman, K., Crowley-Matoka, M., & Fine, M. J. (2006). Advancing health disparities research within the health care system: A conceptual framework. *American Journal of Public Health, 96*(12), 2113–2121. Available from https://doi.org/10.2105/AJPH.2005.077628.

Kroemer, K. (2006). *"Extra-ordinary" ergonomics: How to accommodate small, and big persons, the disabled and elderly, expectant mothers and children.* Boca Raton, FL: CRC Press.

Latulippe, K., Hamel, C., & Giroux, D. (2017). Social health inequalities and eHealth: A literature review with qualitative synthesis of theoretical and empirical studies. *Journal of Medical Internet Research, 19*(4), 1–22. Available from https://doi.org/10.2196/jmir.6731.

LaVeist, T. A., Nickerson, K. J., & Bowie, J. V. (2000). Attitudes about racism, medical mistrust, and satisfaction with care among African American and white cardiac patients. *Medical Care Research and Review, 57*(4), 146–161. Available from https://doi.org/10.1177/107755800773743637.

Lillie-Blanton, M., & Hoffman, S. C. (1995). Conducting an assessment of health needs and resources in a racial/ethnic minority community. *Health Services Research, 30*(1), 225–236.

Lorenc, T., Petticrew, M., Welch, V., & Tugwell, P. (2013). What types of interventions generate inequalities? Evidence from systematic reviews. *Journal of Epidemiology and Community Health, 67*(2), 190–193. Available from https://doi.org/10.1136/jech-2012-201257.

Marmot, M. (2005). Social determinants of health inequalities. *The Lancet, 365*(9464), 1099–1104. Available from https://doi.org/10.1016/S0140-6736(05)74234-3.

McGovern, L., Miller, G., & Hughes-Cromwick, P. (2014). Health policy brief: The relative contribution of multiple determinants to health outcomes. *Health Affairs*, 1–9. Available from https://doi.org/10.1377/hpb2014.17.

Mechkati, N. (1991). Human factors in large-scale technological systems' accidents: Three mile Island, Bhopal, Chernobyl. *Industrial Crisis Quarterly, 5*(2), 131–154. Retrieved from http://www-bcf.usc.edu/~meshkati/humanfactors.html.

Menefee, H. K., Thompson, M. J., Guterbock, T. M., Williams, I. C., & Valdez, R. S. (2016). Mechanisms of communicating health information through Facebook: Implications for consumer health information technology design. *Journal of Medical Internet Research*, *18*(8), e218.

Montague, E., & Perchonok, J. (2012). Health and wellness technology use by historically underserved health consumers: Systematic review. *Journal of Medical Internet Research*, *14*(3). Available from https://doi.org/10.2196/jmir.2095.

Mosnaim, G. S., Cohen, M. S., Rhoads, C. H., Rittner, S. S., & Powell, L. H. (2008). Use of MP3 players to increase asthma knowledge in inner-city African-American adolescents. *International Journal of Behavioral Medicine*, *15*(4), 341−346. Available from https://doi.org/10.1080/10705500802365656.

Muskens, L., Van Lent, R., Vijfvinkel, A., Van Cann, P., & Shahid, S. (2014). Never too old to use a tablet: Designing tablet applications for the cognitively and physically impaired determining the design guidelines: Literature review. In: The 14th international conference on computers helping people with special needs (pp. 391−398).

Nijland, N., Van Gemert-Pijnen, J. E. W. C., Kelders, S. M., Brandenburg, B. J., & Seydel, E. R. (2011). Factors influencing the use of a web-based application for supporting the self-care of patients with type 2 diabetes: A longitudinal study. *Journal of Medical Internet Research*, *13*(3). Available from https://doi.org/10.2196/jmir.1603.

Palinkas, L. A., Horwitz, S. M., Green, C. A., Wisdom, J. P., Duan, N., & Hoagwood, K. (2015). Purposeful sampling for qualitative data collection and analysis in mixed method implementation research. *Administration and Policy in Mental Health*, *42*(5), 533−544. Available from https://doi.org/10.1007/s10488-013-0528-y.

Patton, M. Q. (1990). *Qualitative evaluation and research methods*. SAGE Publications, Inc.

Perzynski, A. T., Roach, M. J., Shick, S., Callahan, B., Gunzler, D., Cebul, R., ... Einstadter, D. (2017). Patient portals and broadband internet inequality. *Journal of the American Medical Informatics Association*, *24*(5), 927−932. Available from https://doi.org/10.1093/jamia/ocx020.

Smith-Jackson, T. L., Resnick, M. L., & Johnson, K. T. (2013). *Cultural ergonomics: Theory, methods, and applications*. CRC Press.

Stoecker, R. (2008). Are academic irrelevant? Approaches and roles for scholars in CBPR. In M. Minkler, & N. Wallerstein (Eds.), *Community-based participatory research for health: From process to outcomes* (pp. 107−120). John Wiley & Sons.

Subrahmaniyan, N., Fulcher, K. R., Hutchinson, T. E., Min, H., Seale, J. M., Bisantz, A. M., & Higginbotham, D. J. (2013). Application of personas in the design of augmentative alternative communication devices. *Proceedings of the Human Factors and Ergonomics Society Annual Meeting*, *57*, 1022−1026. Available from https://doi.org/10.1177/1541931213571228.

Taha, J., Sharit, J., & Czaja, S. J. (2014). Usability of an electronic personal health record (PHR) among a diverse group of adults. *Proceedings of the Human Factors and Ergonomics Society Annual Meeting*, 619−623. Available from https://doi.org/10.1177/1541931214581132.

Tao, D., Shao, F., Liu, S., Wang, T., & Qu, X. (2016). Predicting factors of consumer acceptance of health information technologies. *Proceedings of the Human Factors and Ergonomics Society Annual Meeting*, *60*(1), 598−602. Available from https://doi.org/10.1177/1541931213601137.

Thomas, S. B., Quinn, S. C., Butler, J., Fryer, C. S., & Garza, M. A. (2011). Toward a fourth generation of disparities research to achieve health equity. *Annual Review of Public Health*, *32*(1), 399−416. Available from https://doi.org/10.1146/annurev-publhealth-031210-101136.

Tieu, L., Sarkar, U., Schillinger, D., Ralson, J., Pasick, R., & Lyles, C. (2009). Barriers and facilitators to online portal use among patients and caregivers in a safety net health care system: A qualitative study. *Journal of Medical Internet Research, 60*(5), e275. Available from https://doi.org/10.1093/heapro/dan004.

Valdez, R. S., & Brennan, P. F. (2015). Exploring patients' health information communication practices with social network members as a foundation for consumer health IT design. *International Journal of Medical Informatics, 84*(5), 363−374. Available from https://doi.org/10.1016/j.ijmedinf.2015.01.014.

Valdez, R. S., & Holden, R. J. (2016). Health care human factors/ergonomics fieldwork in home and community settings. *Ergonomics in Design, 24*(4), 4−9. Available from https://doi.org/10.1177/1064804615622111.

Valdez, R. S., Gibbons, M. C., Siegel, E. R., Kukafka, R., & Brennan, P. F. (2012). Designing consumer health IT to enhance usability among different racial and ethnic groups within the United States. *Health and Technology, 2*(4), 225−233. Available from https://doi.org/10.1007/s12553-012-0031-6.

Valdez, R. S., Guterbock, T. M., Thompson, M. J., Reilly, J. D., Menefee, H. K., Bennici, M. S., ... Rexrode, D. L. (2014). Beyond traditional advertisements: Leveraging Facebook's social structures for research recruitment. *Journal of Medical Internet Research, 16*(10), e243. Available from https://doi.org/10.2196/jmir.3786.

Veinot, T. C., Mitchell, H., & Ancker, J. (2018). Good intentions are not enough: How informatics interventions can worsen inequality. *Journal of the American Medical Informatics Association*, 1−9. Available from https://doi.org/10.1093/jamia/ocy052.

Wallerstein, N., Duran, B., Oetzel, J. G., & Minkler, M. (2017). *Community-based participatory research for health: advancing social and health equity*. Hoboken, NJ: John Wiley & Sons.

Whitehead, M. (2000). The concepts and principles of equity and health. *Health Promotion International, 6*(3), 217−228. Available from https://doi.org/10.1093/heapro/6.3.217.

Wilkin, H. A., Valente, T. W., Murphy, S., Cody, M. J., Huang, G., & Beck, V. (2007). Does entertainment-education work with Latinos in the United States? Identification and the effects of a telenovela breast cancer storyline. *Journal of Health Communication, 12*(5), 455−469. Available from https://doi.org/10.1080/10810730701438690.

World Health Organization (2018). Life expectancy and Healthy life expectancy: Data by country. Retrieved from https://apps.who.int/gho/data/node.main.688.

World Health Organization (2019). Social determinants of health. Retrieved from https://www.who.int/social_determinants/en/.

Yin, H. S., Mendelsohn, A. L., Wolf, M. S., Parker, R. M., Fierman, A., Van Schaick, L., ... Dreyer, B. P. (2010). Parents' medication administration errors: Role of dosing instruments and health literacy. *Archives of Pediatrics, 164*(2), 181−186. Available from https://doi.org/10.1001/archpediatrics.2009.269.

Chapter 16

Design for global health

Alessandra N. Bazzano[1,2] and Shirley D. Yan[3]
[1]Tulane University School of Public Health and Tropical Medicine, New Orleans, LA, United States, [2]Taylor Center for Social Innovation and Design Thinking, Tulane University, New Orleans, LA, United States, [3]Johns Hopkins Bloomberg School of Public Health, Baltimore, MD, United States

Introduction

This chapter will introduce readers to the field of global health, provide an overview of models used to integrate design into international health programs, and present a global-health design case study.

History of global health

The field of global health is concerned with population level health outcomes, building on prior foundations of tropical medicine and international health, often referred to historically as hygiene. It has always been distinct from medicine, which addresses health at the individual or patient level. Study of tropical medicine developed as colonizers encountered infectious diseases during explorations in Asia and Africa. The discipline aimed to understand unfamiliar illnesses and what could be done to prevent and cure them. In London, England, a call for education in tropical medicine spurred the Colonial Office to begin what would become the London School of Hygiene and Tropical Medicine in 1898, while in Liverpool, a prominent ship owner concerned about the rising rates of tropical disease due to shipping and trade, joined with businessmen to fund the Liverpool School of Tropical Medicine in the same year (Wilkinson & Power, 1998). As borders became more fluid through colonization, wars, and independence in the late 19th and 20th centuries, international health emerged as a new discipline. International health "referred primarily to a focus on the control of epidemics across the boundaries between nations" (Brown, Cueto, & Fee, 2006). The creation of the World Health Organization and other multilateral organizations post—World War II reinforced the importance of controlling diseases across borders. Disease-eradication campaigns were the hallmark of

Design for Health. DOI: https://doi.org/10.1016/B978-0-12-816427-3.00016-6

international health efforts (e.g., hookworm in 1909, yellow fever in 1918, and smallpox in 1958).

As the boundaries of international health moved beyond eradicating disease to prevention, investments were made in programs as a means of not only improving health, but also economic and social development. In the 1950s, national family planning strategies served as economic and social policies to address development through curbing population growth (Bongarts, Cleland, Townsend, Bertrand, & Das Gupta, 2012). Maternal, newborn, and child health also became key to international health programming due to high mortality in these vulnerable groups in low-income countries. Maternal illness was highest in the 1970s and child death highest in 1990s; in recent decades, maternal and child deaths have begun to reduce, as more funding and programs target improved health outcomes (Kassebaum et al., 2014; Wang et al., 2014). The Alma-Ata declaration, adopted in 1978 by the International Conference on Primary Health Care, focused on integrated health programs. The declaration advocated for governments to build stronger health systems by addressing equity and seeking equality through building foundational primary health care for all (Declaration of Alma-Ata, 1978). Other strategies in population health largely focused on so-called vertical programming, concurrent with a disease-focused approach (e.g., stand-alone programming to reduce malaria illness in the population). Increased funding for capacity-strengthening activities for health systems marked transition toward a system-wide approach, reflecting a further shift beyond disease control to focus on health equity for the global population. Stakeholders and institutions involved in international public health have transitioned from using the term tropical medicine to international health, and more recently to global health (Macfarlane, Jacobs, & Kaaya, 2008). Beaglehole and Bonita (2010) provide a succinct description, defining global health as "Collaborative transnational research and action for promoting health for all." From this definition, global health comprises various types of activities (both theory and practice oriented) that require teamwork, and focus on health equity across borders. Global health broadens the scope of tropical medicine and international health by leveraging different sectors to consider wider health challenges for populations (Macfarlane et al., 2008).

Current global-health challenges

At the turn of the 21st century, global progress has been made toward more collaborative approaches to health. The United Nations (UN) guided the global-health agenda through Millennium Development Goals (MDGs) from 2000 to 2015 and Sustainable Development Goals (SDGs) from 2015 to 2030.

At the conclusion of the MDGs, considerable progress had been made: the reduction of under-five mortality since 1990 had been remarkable, maternal mortality had declined by 45% globally, and 37 million lives had been saved due to tuberculosis (TB) prevention, diagnosis, and treatment interventions between 2000 and 2013 (United Nations, 2015). However, more progress still remains to be made, given that many countries failed to meet goals (Institute for Health Metrics and Evaluation, 2017b). At the conclusion of the MDGs in 2015, the UN created 169 targets nested within the overall 17 SDGs, to be achieved by 2030, as shown in Fig. 16.1 (United Nations, 2018).

Substantial funding is directed at improving equity and health outcomes globally. In 2017, 37.4 billion USD of funds were disbursed toward health, which has increased fivefold since 1990 when 7.6 billion USD were disbursed as adjusted for inflation (Institute for Health Metrics and Evaluation, 2017a). These funds consist of contributions from a variety of stakeholders, including countries, multilateral donors, and foundations. Funds for sector-wide approaches and noncommunicable diseases (NCDs) have increased in recent years, but HIV/AIDS, child and newborn health, maternal health, malaria, and TB receive more than half of all funds (Institute for Health Metrics and Evaluation, 2017a) (Fig. 16.2).

As progress is made toward preventing, diagnosing, and curing infectious disease, disease burden has shifted toward NCDs, whose prevalence has been rising rapidly, including in lower income countries. NCDs include cardiovascular disease, cancer, chronic respiratory disease, diabetes, and other chronic illnesses. These account for 71% of deaths globally, killing 41 million people per year, with cardiovascular disease accounting for the largest share at 44% (World Health Organization, 2018). Risk factors for NCDs include lifestyle,

FIGURE 16.1 Sustainable Development Goals (United Nations, 2018).

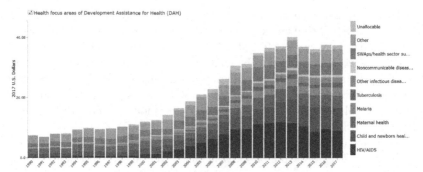

FIGURE 16.2 Development Assistance for Health funds data from the Institute for Health Metrics and Evaluation (Institute for Health Metrics and Evaluation, 2017a).

access to resources, access to health care, and social determinants (World Health Organization, 2018). Many global-health projects are related to social and behavioral change, such as increasing demand for quality health services and influencing social norms. In this context, the last decade has seen the rise of design as an additive approach to improving public-health interventions.

Design in the context of global health

The changing global-health landscape over the last decade has included incorporating strategies from private business (e.g., marketing approaches), along with more private–public partnerships. The movement toward incorporating design in global health may be seen as a feature related to that change. Human-centered design (HCD) emerged from the private sector as a process to integrate the needs of consumers within the product-development cycle, particularly around technology and services. HCD is often considered to have originated from user-centered design (UCD), which was pioneered by Don Norman and colleagues at the University of California, San Diego (Norman & Drapher, 1986). UCD prioritizes the needs and emotions of the end user of a product or service, as opposed to those of the organization creating it, and includes carrying out early testing and evaluation, and designing iteratively, which were not standard practice at the time. These principles are reflected in the definition for HCD that the International Organization for Standardization gives

> *Approach to systems design and development that aims to make interactive systems more usable by focusing on the use of the system and applying human factors/ergonomics and usability knowledge and techniques (ISO, 2015).*

HCD, design thinking, and social design are often used interchangeably to refer to the most common design approaches used in global health. Design thinking is a framework that considers the feasibility and viability of a solution, in addition to desirability and is defined as (Brown, 2008)

"a discipline that uses the designer's sensibility and methods to match people's needs with what is technologically feasible and what a viable business strategy can convert into customer value and market opportunity."

Social design is another way to conceptualize design for improving priority social outcomes, such as health equity (Abrahamson & Rubin, 2012). Instead of using design to encourage people to buy more products, social design relies on design thinking as an additional tool to solve a social challenge. Emotions and empathy are key parts of understanding how to build the best solutions that are attractive and sustainable to people who will be impacted by them or interacting with them. This is quite relevant to global-health work, which often involves improving services or changing behaviors.

Design for global-health guidelines

Several frameworks have been formulated to provide guidelines on design for social change and global-health programming. As early as 2008, a team at the design firm IDEO developed a toolkit to help international nongovernmental organizations to apply HCD to their work. The resulting "Toolkit" launched in 2009 and was updated in 2015 as the "Field guide to human centered design." This updated field guide highlights a three-phase iterative process (IDEO.org, 2015): Inspiration−Ideation−Implementation. Inspiration draws insights from key stakeholders, beneficiaries, or customers about their lives, motivations, and challenges. Ideation incorporates these insights to generate potential solutions for further development, testing, and refining. Implementation sees finalized solutions scaled for impact.

Some organizations, such as Stanford d.school, have more recently eschewed a process-oriented guideline model in favor of emphasizing design abilities that can inform the use of design in teams: navigate ambiguity, learn from others (people and context), synthesize information, experiment rapidly, move between concrete and abstract, build and craft intentionally, communicate deliberately, design your design work (Hasso Plattner Institute of Design at Stanford, 2019).

The UK Design Council, a nonprofit dedicated to improving people's lives through the use of design, describes the double diamond model (see Fig. 16.3) with four stages and it should be emphasized that although these stages seem linear, they involve iteration throughout (Design Council, 2015):

1. Discover insights into the problem.
2. Define the area to focus upon.
3. Develop potential solutions.
4. Deliver solutions that work.

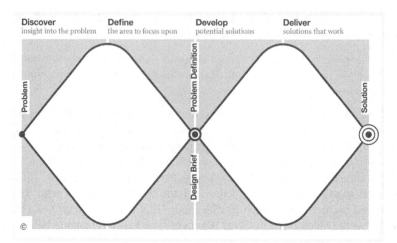

FIGURE 16.3 Double diamond model and the four stages of design (Design Council, 2015).

Underlying these guidelines is the prioritization of end users and benefi-ciaries throughout each stage of the process. Tools to boost empathy within users are utilized to ensure the resulting solution is most appropriate. Rapid prototyping and iteration based on users' or stakeholders' feedback are key features of the design process. The design process leverages data from ethno-graphic methods, interviews, observations, and other qualitative research methodologies to generate insights and ideas. Intuition and feelings, in addi-tion to data, are used in conjunction with stakeholder feedback to develop and identify promising solutions.

Guidelines for applying HCD or design thinking to global health include those developed by DesignForHealth.org, which offers training modules and resources describing the use of design in global health. Introduced by USAID, the Bill and Melinda Gates Foundation, and Dalberg Design (Design for Health, 2018), the DesignForHealth platform provides guidance and practical resources for design. The materials will continue to be expanded and adapted over time to strengthen appropriate application and use of design to advance a shared vision of global health.

Key guidance in the design process for global health suggests the impor-tance of the following common concepts:

- Close and equitable partnership with populations and stakeholders at the heart of the design challenge.
- In-depth discovery and immersion into the world of those intended to benefit from the solution.
- Reframing and redefining the design brief to ensure it meets the needs of all users and stakeholders.

- Rapid prototyping and experimentation with cycles of iteration prior to choosing an intervention.
- Testing and evolution of the proposed solutions or intervention must involve key stakeholders, and sustainability should be an important consideration.
- Documenting the work at each phase and iteration is crucial for transparency, evaluation, and understanding.

Models of applying design to global health in action

The most common model for projects that employ design for global health is to have an expert designer or design team work with health-technical specialists to develop a product, service, or program, through a consulting arrangement. Numerous design firms provide a designer or design team with appropriate specialization and training in social design, industrial design, engineering, or service design to then immerse in the global-health setting for a discrete period of time, using a design brief that details the product, service, challenge, or issue to be addressed. These relationships are often funded by international health donors. The case study at the end of this chapter illustrates one such model, the Adolescents 360 (A360) health program.

Another model is to develop an in-house, dedicated design team, within global-health organizations. For example, UNICEF's Office of Innovation has a mandate to ensure equity and fairness in cocreation and protect the best interests of the end users (UNICEF, 2014). This division identifies, prototypes, and scales technologies and practices that strengthen UNICEF's work for children using new approaches, types of partnerships, and technologies to address nutrition, education, child protection, and health issues including immunization; water, hygiene and sanitation; HIV/AIDS; and humanitarian emergencies. Organizations such as Kaiser Permanente (one of the largest health systems in the United States with 12.2 million members) and the Mayo Clinic in Rochester, Minnesota (which sees more than 1.3 million patients per year) also incorporate HCD to improve quality of care for their patient population through dedicated design teams within the organization (Kaiser Permanente, 2018; Mayo Clinic, 2017).

A variation on developing a dedicated in-house design team in a global-health organization is to diffuse design mindsets and skills to all staff. This includes developing capacity within health organizations to engage in their own design work, particularly in relation to the sustainability of design in the global-health field, which is resource constrained. Medic Mobile is an organization that seeks to improve global-health systems through developing tools and technology at the community level (Medic Mobile, 2018). The design principles espoused by the organization are: designing for the familiar, solving the most important challenges first, and letting the best ideas lead to better solutions. HCD is explicitly applied to all the work done by

Medic Mobile and integrated into the organizational culture and training of staff. Isaac Holeman, cofounder of Medic Mobile, described how in addition to incorporating design into the culture of their organization, they actively seek to strengthen internal research on HCD for global health, particularly around key user personas, design workflows, and practices, as well as implementation documentation, which can be linked with a mechanism of action for design-based global-health projects (Holeman, 2018). Medic Mobile embodies a strong tradition of collaboration between designers, engineers, and ethnographers for global health to be carried forward by intentional and comprehensive implementation research. This collaboration between disciplines allows for larger contributions to the health and medical evidence base.

A final model of utilizing design in global health focuses on bringing together both users of public health services and providers of these services to be codesigners. Broadly, codesign is "the effort to combine the views, input and skills of people with many different perspectives to address a specific problem" (Bradwell & Marr, 2008). The process shifts the power dynamics to participants so that they are part of the design process from the beginning, from identifying the problems, conducting research, and developing solutions (Bradwell & Marr, 2008). Experience-based codesign and accelerated experience-based codesign, which introduces elements from architecture, engineering, and software design, have been utilized in international health quality–improvement projects (Bate & Robert, 2006; Goodrich, 2018). Similarly, "slow coproduction" is an approach to codesign, where patients are seen not only as users but also as coresearchers and cocreators of knowledge about and for their health (Miles, Renedo, & Marston, 2018).

One argument for increasing the use of HCD in global health relates to creativity. In the Stanford Social Innovation Review, Fabricant and Milestone highlighted the importance of "adopting novel approaches to persistent challenges" and described how "Bringing in diverse perspectives and a structured design process helped us uncover new solutions to entrenched challenges, and we believe that other global-health projects, even other sectors, could benefit from using a similar approach" (Fabricant, Milestone, & Qureshi, 2014). Roberts, Fisher, Trowbridge, and Bent (2016) advocate for design thinking within health-care administration, and for "radical collaboration" among health stakeholders. Stanford researchers have even undertaken an fMRI assessment of brain changes occurring after design training, in order to demonstrate that these impact creativity (Saggar et al., 2017). Tracy Johnson, a senior program officer in user experience and innovation at BMGF, notes that design brings a critical creative problem-solving methodology to global health. In the design process, not only are users brought front and center, but different mindsets are also brought to bear that traditionally have not been included in global health (Johnson, 2018). Johnson also proposes that the iterative nature of design has the important potential to derisk the development of effective and desired global-health interventions, so that teams do not move through the project life cycle with one solution, only to find at the end that the solution does not work as intended. Another value of design is in the engagement created by the nature of design processes, where the voices of vulnerable and often overlooked segments of the population (precisely those who may not yet be reached by global-health interventions) are heard, leading to the possibility of more sustainable health interventions. In this way, design can be seen as a blueprint for fostering and structuring deeper collaboration among multidisciplinary teams, including designers, global-health practitioners, technology experts, and social and behavioral scientists, both international and local, in the development and implementation of global-health programs (Johnson, 2018). Anne LaFond (2018), director of the John Snow Inc. Center for Health Information, Monitoring and Evaluation (CHIME), noted that design seeks to bring the development of solutions directly to the community, and tailoring evidence-based programs for communities through this more involved approach is a key strength. Global-health practitioners find that design harkens back to the participatory processes espoused in global health during the 1960s and 1970s, when primary care for all was the priority, and interacting with beneficiaries was considered a key to ensuring individuals have appropriate services and support to adopt recommended health behaviors (LaFond, 2018).

Modern global-health organizations are focused on the scientific evidence base, financial considerations, and measurement of reported outcomes, which may rely on deductive approaches at the expense of engaged transformation potentially provided by design. The organization ITAD recently completed an evaluation of investments in HCD for global health, particularly to improve family planning and reproductive health services in Sub-Saharan Africa. The report highlighted the effectiveness and reach of HCD for developing appropriate solutions (Itad, 2017). However, the report also emphasized the need for commitment and institutionalization of design to be most effective, further cautioning that the application of design to global-health projects is very context specific. Ultimately, the report suggested several important points, among them, the need to promote shared understanding of what can be expected from design-based research; the importance of a well-designed impact study of any such work; establishment of goals for capacity building in design for local and health staff; paying greater attention to the preparation phase; and ensuring that synthesis of insights and the process of prototyping are more inclusive and discursive, explicit, and well-documented. Tolley provided a useful side-by-side comparison of socio-behavioral and design approaches in global health and noted that each has strengths and limitations. Design may allow for more rapid and direct synthesis of findings from field data collection (as there is less focus on an auditable and replicable process), but it is important to not only have design

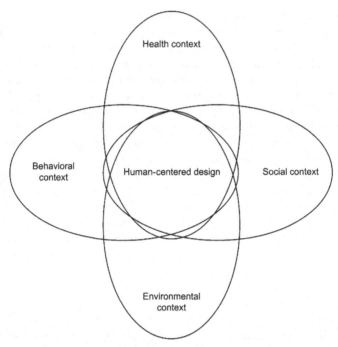

FIGURE 16.4 Intersection of four different domains which intersect for HCD. *HCD*, Human-centered design.

expertise but also health content and public health technical expertise when arriving at solutions through research (Tolley, 2017).

The context and constraints under which an HCD global-health project takes place may determine success—understanding and mapping the contextual, social, and environmental contributors and how they interact are crucial. A one-size-fits-all approach for HCD in global health is not possible because of the varied settings and constraints, nor will it be possible to predict the success of using HCD in differing contexts, but guidance can allow for adaptation to individual settings. The illustration below provides a concept map of domains where design and global health interact with other important domains (Fig. 16.4).

Johns Hopkins University Center for Communication Programs is a global health—practice organization using HCD among other methodologies (Vondrasek, Mills, & Loehr, 2018). Global-health projects incorporating design range from identifying ways to invite at-risk populations for HIV to appropriate programs in Côte d'Ivoire; design strategies and approaches for STI self-testing; how to bring women into prenatal care programs in Mali; and increased adoption of healthy behaviors for newborn health in the Democratic Republic of the Congo. The role of design within global health activities has been formalized within one flagship project Breakthrough

ACTION, which along with its sister project Breakthrough RESEARCH is part of a cooperative agreement with USAID. Two different models have been used thus far by the organization, employing third party consultants, and leveraging the prior experience and training of internal personnel in design to implement activities and build capacity among local teams. Several challenges to using design have been noted. First, participant literacy levels may be a challenge when working in low-income settings, since many design-based activities require writing ideas down. Second, the capacity, time, and availability of local staff to engage in building out prototypes and iterative stages of the design process, while attending to other program demands, has been identified as a challenge. The HCD process has the potential to produce results for programming more rapidly than conventional approaches but may demand more from global-health program staff than other socio-behavioral approaches. Initial hesitation and resistance to adopt design processes on the part of program staff in resource-constrained settings may also be a challenge as these seem abstract to those unaccustomed to working with design.

Case study: Adolescents 360

Launched in January 2016, A360 is a 4.5-year, 30 million USD project that aims to increase voluntary, modern contraceptive use among 250,000 + 15- to 19-year-old adolescent girls in Ethiopia, Nigeria, and Tanzania. A360 is led by Population Services International (PSI), along with a core consortium of partners, and cofunded by the Bill & Melinda Gates Foundation and the Children's Investment Fund Foundation. PSI is a global nonprofit operating in more than 50 countries worldwide, with programs in a range of health areas and services. Their mission is to make it easier for people in the developing world to lead healthier lives and plan for the families they desire, by reimagining health care with the consumer at the center.

The global-health problem

Adolescence is a critical and vulnerable time of transition during which many young women in lower income countries aged 15—19 become sexually active, marry, and start having children. They often do so without adequate information about or access to contraceptive options to delay and space childbearing (Darroch, Woog, Bankole, & Ashford, 2016). Thirty-eight percent of the 252 million adolescent girls living in developing countries are sexually active and do not wish to have a child in the next 2 years. Unmet need for contraception in these countries is much higher among adolescents than older women, with 60% of those in need, or 23 million young women, not using a modern contraceptive method (Darroch et al., 2016). Adolescent development also involves profound changes in social contexts, social roles, and social responsibilities, and there are complex interactions between and among these levels of change (Darroch et al., 2016).

A360 has been implemented in Ethiopia, Nigeria, and Tanzania, and this case study will focus on the work implemented in Tanzania. The population of Tanzania has continued to be predominantly rural despite the increase in the proportion of urban residents over time, from 6% in 1967 to 30% in 2012 (Ministry of Health, Community Development, Gender, Elderly and Children - MoHCDGEC/Tanzania Mainland, Ministry of Health - MoH/ Zanzibar, National Bureau of Statistics - NBS/Tanzania, Office of Chief Government Statistician - OCGS/Zanzibar, & ICF, 2016). Tanzanian cultural practices related to adolescence vary regionally. Girls in Tanzania demonstrate a sense of urgency to secure a stable financial and social future, pursuing small businesses, jobs, and income-generating initiatives to amass personal savings and exert some level of control in an uncertain economic landscape (PSI & IDEO.org, 2015). At the same time, girls acknowledge the heightened risk they are exposed to in this scenario, as pursuit of income, jobs, and security often links to increased exposure to coerced and/or transactional sex. In Tanzania, 23% of adolescent girls are married or are cohabitating, and 56.7% have begun bearing children by the age of 19 (Ministry of Health et al., 2016). However, 27% of women who gave birth by the age of 20 said they would have preferred to have waited until later (UNICEF, 2011). Adolescent girls also experience a third of all abortions in Tanzania (Mpangile, 2003) and there is low contraceptive use.

Adolescents 360 design process

The A360 consortium consisted of youth, professional designers, public-health specialists, adolescent-developmental scientists, anthropologists, and marketers encouraging an interdisciplinary approach to the project. The implementers hypothesized that a fusion of these disciplines combined with meaningful engagement of adolescent girls in all phases of the project could catalyze a series of novel approaches to program design and delivery that could be replicated and scaled by partners and governments in similar settings around the world. Adolescent girls were design and implementation partners in the A360 design process that included four phases of design over a 4.5-year period: inquiry, insights and synthesis, prototyping, and adaptive implementation.

As a diverse group of public health, adolescent-developmental science, anthropological, youth, and design experts, there were tensions that arose during the design process. For example, given team members' diverse backgrounds, concepts of rigor, data, and evidence-based decision-making varied across the team members. To account for each other's backgrounds, a "stop/ start" design process was employed. Through this process, teams created safe, clearly defined periods to fully immerse themselves in creative, expansive design thinking, having confidence that later they would have protected time to "start" the process of applying the evidence base and interrogating ideas generated during the creative design thinking periods. In this way, the teams ensured they balanced creativity and rigorous, evidence-based vetting.

During the start-up phase, A360 prepared its consortium for HCD work through recruitment of staff demonstrating curiosity, creativity, and strong adolescent and youth and sexual and reproductive health (AYSRH) backgrounds; then bringing teams together for a "boot camp" session to establish across the teams a common basic knowledge of the project's disciplinary lenses, as well as the HCD process through which these lenses would be applied. Boot camp covered youth-positive research culture and translating research methods into youth-friendly concepts, user-centered design and social—cultural anthropology, research collection, and data analysis. A360 also conducted a market-landscape analysis and selected segments (socioeconomic, geographic, demographic, gender, etc.) where the gaps are largest between contraceptive use and need.

During the A360 inquiry step, design activities began with literature review as well as design research with youth to generate insights. PSI and partners joined together with local partners and stakeholders to conduct qualitative inquiry for design in partnership with youth to (1) gain in-depth understanding of adolescents' needs, barriers, and motivations to use contraceptives; (2) develop key insights into their lives, hopes, and desires; and (3) identify their key influencers. This process included data collection and observation, in-depth interrogation of insights and their interpretation vis-à-vis the project and youth codesigner perspectives, and insight synthesis to prepare for prototyping. The process centered on creating interventions by, for, and with adolescents, in contrast to typical processes of developing interventions in global health from a purely biomedical research paradigm.

Inquiry teams consisted of recruited youth researchers, implementing and research staff, members of the core A360 project team, and staff from IDEO. org trained in qualitative inquiry for design, along with coordinators and translators. Parents, health providers, young men, and other adults who serve as influencers provided consent to participate in research activities, to facilitate a cultural analysis of how youth sexuality, puberty, and transitions into adult roles are conceptualized. Core principles to establish empathy with research participants included listening to and respecting research participants; cocreating insights; and iterating and adapting in the field based on joint learning.

The A360 Tanzania team held 26 interview sessions with 100 + participants, including married and unmarried adolescent girls, adolescent boys, male partners and husbands of adolescent girls, mothers-in law, fathers and aunties, community leaders, and providers. Consortium members came together for the Insight and Synthesis phase to generate insights from the research. Insights are statements that help point the way forward and drive toward design solutions. Some insights may be novel while others were not, the combination of insights should help launch the team into novel ideas.

Formative research yielded several themes including but not limited to anxiety and uncertainty about how to secure a stable future, contraception and self-identification, motherhood as an achievable dream, isolation and mistrust, and continuing connection of adolescent girls to their mothers. During the insights workshop, the team turned insight statements into "How might we?" questions to trigger innovative thinking toward potential solutions during the Inquiry and Insights phase. The insight synthesis and prototyping phase was a period of continuous idea generation, prototyping, and rapid testing. Findings from the inspiration phase were utilized to rapidly develop culturally salient prototypes grounded in the local context for overcoming identified barriers, and increasing demand for voluntary use of modern contraceptives. Intervention prototypes addressed one or more of the "How might we?" questions that emerged from field research.

Results of the design process

At the end of the research and design period, A360 had identified priority-target segments of the adolescent population (girls aged 15−19) and had developed and validated at least one intervention. In Tanzania, A360 works across several regions and targets both married and unmarried girls with the *Kuwa Mjanja* ("be smart" in Kiswahili) intervention, pairing contraceptive-service delivery with entrepreneurial-skills training, responding to girls' desire for financial and social independence, and the autonomy to shape the course of their lives. *Kuwa Mjanja* was developed to address two insights that emerged from the research: girls seek accurate and trusted sources of information for sexual and reproductive health and greater financial autonomy. First piloted in Mwanza, the program blends contraceptive and life-coaching services for urban and periurban girls, to reframe the narrative about girls and contraception. During the prototyping phase, pretesting and piloting allowed the program to adapt to existing health services.

Through audience-segmentation analysis and iterations, two Tanzanian adolescent girl archetypes emerged around experience in their life trajectories: younger, less-experienced "Faridas," socially dependent on their families and are focused on navigating the social, emotional, and physical changes early adolescence brings; and more-experienced "Bahatis," socially independent girls who have a sense of their goals for their future. Regardless of marital status or sexual activity, messaging was tailored to the audience's life experiences and needs-programming and branding tapped into girls' priorities and curated messaging and services based on two audience groups: financial independence and stability, managing growing responsibility and navigating the transition to adulthood. For Faridas, a "know your body" messaging is emphasized and for Bahati, "know your path." Overall, the brand focuses on a "nanasi" (pineapple) motif as an inspirational and familiar symbol to showcase an archetypal figure for girls to identify with—one who is proud of herself, knows her worth, and is both sweet and strong, knowing her power and her potential. This archetypal figure is paired with the intervention's *nanasi* slogan and song: "We stand tall (we are *nanasi*). We wear crowns as our symbol. We are good girls, we shine. We have decided to dream."

Mjanja Connect, a mobile app, connects girls to the intervention by identifying which archetype they match with through videos and a quiz. Information about contraception is presented, based on priorities, needs, and experiences as indicated in the quiz. Outreach is aided by "Kuwa Mjanja queens," girls with large and active social networks identified by local governments. Outreach events are conducted with public-health facilities, and through service delivery and "clinic days" in public and private facilities. *Kuwa Mjanja* branded sessions during "clinic days" are for girls and their mothers and aunties, as found to be desirable to girls in the "Farida" segment, who desire the support of their mothers in accessing SRH information and services.

Throughout these events, motivational talks using the *nanasi* brand messaging are delivered to girls, and then transition into entrepreneurial-skills training. Youth-friendly trained facilitators discreetly ask girls attending if they would like to receive counseling on life goals, adolescent body changes, and the importance of contraception in achieving life goals. Provision of contraceptive methods is offered at the interest of girls. Health providers involved are identified as youth-friendly and can choose to receive more training on youth-friendly services. After their engagement, girls can rate their interaction; these ratings are made available to other girls in search of providers.

As of September 2018, 80,000 girls received information from *Kuwa Mjanja* events. More than half have adopted contraceptive methods. A360's external evaluation team will conduct process, outcome, and cost-effectiveness evaluations to answer whether voluntary use of contraception among sexually active girls of 15−19 years has increased. These will include pre- and postpopulation cross-sectional surveys with questionnaires that administered face-to-face by female interviewers of similar ages. Study outcomes were assessed after 2 years of prototyping and field work but before the start of implementation. Final assessment will be conducted after 2 years.

Conclusion

The case study illustrated a global-health project with design explicitly incorporated into the heart of the program. Design is being applied more frequently to global-health problems and being used by international actors in order to address issues impacting health and well-being for people in low-income settings. Along with this increased application of design comes a need to understand how it is operationalized in the context of global-health projects, and how designers, stakeholders, and the people intended to benefit from global-health programs work together. This chapter has explored the current state of design as applied to global health, presented models for how it has been carried out, and addressed some of the questions that have arisen for practitioners. It is envisioned that global-health stakeholders will increasingly adopt design-led strategies to close the remaining gaps in achieving health equity.

References

Abrahamson, J. A., & Rubin, V. L. (2012). Discourse structure differences in lay and professional health communication. *Journal of Documentation, 68*(6), 826–851. Available from https://doi.org/10.1108/00220411211277064.

Bate, P., & Robert, G. (2006). Experience-based design: From redesigning the system around the patient to co-designing services with the patient. *Quality & Safety in Health Care, 15*(5), 307–310. Available from https://doi.org/10.1136/qshc.2005.016527.

Beaglehole, R., & Bonita, R. (2010). What is global health? *Global Health Action, 3*. Available from https://dx.doi.org/10.3402%2Fgha.v3i0.5142.

Bongarts, J., Cleland, J., Townsend, J., Bertrand, J., & Das Gupta, M., 2012. Family planning programs in the 21st century: rationale and design. The Population Council, New York, NY. Retrieved from http://www.popcouncil.org/uploads/pdfs/2012_FPfor21stCentury.pdf.

Bradwell, P., & Marr, S. (2008). *Making the most of collaboration: An international survey of public service co-design.* London: Demos.

Brown, T. (2008). Design thinking. *Harvard Business Review, 86*(6), 84–92.

Brown, T. M., Cueto, M., & Fee, E. (2006). The World Health Organization and the transition from "international" to "global" public health. *American Journal of Public Health, 96*(1), 62–72. Available from https://doi.org/10.2105/ajph.2004.050831.

Darroch, J. E., Woog, V., Bankole, A., & Ashford, L. S. (2016). *Adding it up: Costs and benefits of meeting the contraceptive needs of adolescents.* Guttmacher Institute, New York, NY. Retrieved from https://www.guttmacher.org/sites/default/files/report_pdf/adding-it-up-adolescents-report.pdf.

Declaration of Alma-Ata. (1978). *WHO chronicle, 32*(11), 428–430.

Design Council. (March 15, 2015). The design process: What is the design diamond? *Designcouncil.org.uk, News & Opinion.* Retrieved from https://www.designcouncil.org.uk/news-opinion/design-process-what-double-diamond.

Design for Health. (2018). *Design for health.* Retrieved from https://www.designforhealth.org/.

Fabricant, R., Milestone, D., & Qureshi, C. (2014). Human-centered design and the last mile. *Stanford Social Innovation Review, 2014 (Feb 27).* Retrieved from https://ssir.org/articles/entry/human_centered_design_and_the_last_mile.

Goodrich, J. (2018). Why experience-based co-design improves the patient experience. *The Journal of Health Design, 3*(1), 84–85.

Hasso Plattner Institute of Design at Stanford. (2019). *An introduction to design thinking: Process guide.* Retrieved from https://dschool.stanford.edu/about.

Holeman, I. (2018). [*Personal communication through phone interview.*].

IDEO.org. (2015). *The field guide to human-centered design* (p. 192). Retrieved from http://www.designkit.org/resources/1.

Institute for Health Metrics and Evaluation. (2017a). *Financing global health visualization.* Retrieved from http://vizhub.healthdata.org/fgh/.

Institute for Health Metrics and Evaluation. (2017b). *Health related SDGs.* Retrieved from http://vizhub.healthdata.org/sdg.

ISO. (2015). *ISO 9241-210:2010: Ergonomics of human-system interaction Part 210: Human-centered design for interactive systems.* Geneva: International Organization for Standardization.

Itad. (2017). *Evaluation of the Hewlett Foundation's strategy to apply human-centered design to improve family planning and reproductive health services in sub-Saharan Africa.* Retrieved from https://itad.com/wp-content/uploads/2018/07/Itad-HCD-Evaluation_Final-Report_Nov-10-2017.pdf

Johnson, T. (2018). *[Personal communication during phone interview.].*

Kaiser Permanente. (2018). *Fast facts about Kaiser Permanente.* Retrieved from https://share.kaiserpermanente.org/article/fast-facts-about-kaiser-permanente/.

Kassebaum, N. J., Bertozzi-Villa, A., Coggeshall, M. S., Shackelford, K. A., Steiner, C., Heuton, K. R., ... Lozano, R. (2014). Global, regional, and national levels and causes of maternal mortality during 1990-2013: A systematic analysis for the Global Burden of Disease Study 2013. *Lancet, 384*(9947), 980–1004. Available from https://doi.org/10.1016/s0140-6736(14)60696-6.

LaFond, A. (2018). *[Personal communication during phone interview.].*

Macfarlane, S. B., Jacobs, M., & Kaaya, E. E. (2008). In the name of global health: Trends in academic institutions. *Journal of Public Health Policy, 29*(4), 383–401. Available from https://doi.org/10.1057/jphp.2008.25.

Mayo Clinic. (2017). *Mayo Clinic facts.* Retrieved from https://www.mayoclinic.org/about-mayo-clinic/facts-statistics.

Medic Mobile. (2018). *Medic Mobile.* Retrieved from https://medicmobile.org.

Miles, S., Renedo, A., & Marston, C. (2018). 'Slow co-production' for deeper patient involvement in health care. *The Journal of Health Design, 3*(1), 57–62. Available from https://doi.org/10.21853/JHD.2018.39.

Ministry of Health, Community Development, Gender, Elderly and Children - MoHCDGEC/Tanzania Mainland, Ministry of Health - MoH/Zanzibar, National Bureau of Statistics - NBS/Tanzania, Office of Chief Government Statistician - OCGS/Zanzibar, & ICF. (2016). *Tanzania demographic and health survey and malaria indicator survey 2015-2016.* Retrieved from http://dhsprogram.com/pubs/pdf/FR321/FR321.pdf.

Mpangile, G. S. (2003). *Youth-friendly sexual and reproductive health services: An assessment of facilities.* Retrieved from www2.pathfinder.org/site/DocServer/Youth_Friendly_Services_Summary_Assessment_Report_Tanzan.pdf.

Norman, D., & Drapher, S. (1986). *User centered system design: New perspectives on human-computer interaction.* Hillsdale, NJ: Erlbaum.

PSI, & IDEO.org. (2015). *Insights: Conversations with youth, parents, caregivers, and providers with two communities in rural Tanzania.* Retrieved from https://www.psi.org/wp-content/uploads/2019/01/The-Case-of-Kuwa-Mjanja-in-Tanzania.pdf.

Roberts, J. P., Fisher, T. R., Trowbridge, M. J., & Bent, C. (2016). A design thinking framework for health-care management and innovation. *Healthcare (Amsterdam), 4*(1), 11–14. Available from https://doi.org/10.1016/j.hjdsi.2015.12.002.

Saggar, M., Quintin, E. M., Bott, N. T., Kienitz, E., Chien, Y. H., Hong, D. W., ... Reiss, A. L. (2017). Changes in brain activation associated with spontaneous improvization and figural creativity after design-thinking-based training: A longitudinal fMRI study. *Cerebral Cortex*, *27*(7), 3542–3552. Available from https://doi.org/10.1093/cercor/bhw171.

Tolley, E. (2017). *Traditional socio-behavioral research and human-centered: Similarities, unique contributions and synergies*. Retrieved from http://www.theimpt.org/documents/reports/Report-HCD-BSS-Research.pdf.

UNICEF. (2011). *Adolescence in Tanzania*. Retrieved from https://www.unicef.org/adolescence/files/TANZANIA_ADOLESCENT_REPORT_Final.pdf.

UNICEF. (2014). *Innovation*. Retrieved from https://www.unicef.org/innovation/innovation_73239.html.

United Nations. (2015). *The Millennium Development Goals report 2015*. United Nations New York. Retrieved from http://www.un.org/millenniumgoals/2015_MDG_Report/pdf/MDG%202015%20rev%20(July%201).pdf.

United Nations. (2018). *Sustainable Development Goals*. Retrieved from https://sustainabledevelopment.un.org/?menu=1300.

Vondrasek, C., Mills, H., & Loehr, C. (2018). [*Personal communication during video interview*.].

Wang, H., Liddell, C. A., Coates, M. M., Mooney, M. D., Levitz, C. E., Schumacher, A. E., … Murray, C. J. (2014). Global, regional, and national levels of neonatal, infant, and under-5 mortality during 1990-2013: A systematic analysis for the Global Burden of Disease Study 2013. *Lancet*, *384*(9947), 957–979. Available from https://doi.org/10.1016/s0140-6736(14)60497-9.

Wilkinson, L., & Power, H. (1998). The London and Liverpool Schools of Tropical Medicine 1898-1998. *British Medical Bulletin*, *54*(2), 281–292.

World Health Organization. (2018). *Noncommunicable diseases*. Retrieved from <http://www.who.int/en/news-room/fact-sheets/detail/noncommunicable-diseases>.

Further reading

Bazzano, A. N., Martin, J., Hicks, E., Faughnan, M., & Murphy, L. (2017). Human-centered design in global health: A scoping review of applications and contexts. *PLoS One*, *12*(11), e0186744. Available from https://doi.org/10.1371/journal.pone.0186744.

Lister, C., Payne, H., Hanson, C. L., Barnes, M. D., Davis, S. F., & Manwaring, T. (2017). The public health innovation model: Merging private sector processes with public health strengths. *Frontiers in Public Health*, *5*, 192. Available from https://doi.org/10.3389/fpubh.2017.00192.

Chapter 17

Design of health information and communication technologies for older adults

Christina N. Harrington[1], Lyndsie Marie Koon[2] and Wendy A. Rogers[2]
[1]Communication Studies, Northwestern University, Evanston, IL, United States, [2]College of Applied Health Sciences, University of Illinois at Urbana Champagne, IL, United States

The life span of the average person has increased to seeing people living well into their 70s and 80s, placing a considerable demand on health-care technologies and systems to support people in older age. As older adults require more to be able to age successfully and to function independently, their needs for functional assistance grows. The emergence of pervasive and responsive health technologies such as information and communication technologies (ICTs) suggests that there is potential to address the growing health needs of those aging into older adulthood. The challenge, for designers and researchers, however, is understanding the areas of health and well-being that can be supported by ICTs and establishing how to best design health-related ICTs.

This chapter aims to provide a better understanding of the health-technology needs of older adults. Throughout this chapter, we discuss health needs, describe the utility of ICTs as a resource for health management, review the ways that age-related impairments and conditions relate to the design of these technologies, and highlight best practice examples from existing literature.

Health-care needs of older adults

Demographics and age-related health needs

With the vastly growing population of older adults, there is much focus on how health technologies can support health maintenance and daily functioning, both for individuals living with and without chronic disabilities. As the baby-boomer generation ages into older adulthood, the current population of individuals over 65 becomes the largest age subgroup (World Health Organization, 2015) (see Fig. 17.1). This increase in life span places high

Design for Health. DOI: https://doi.org/10.1016/B978-0-12-816427-3.00017-8

Aging around the globe

Share of the population aged 65 or older

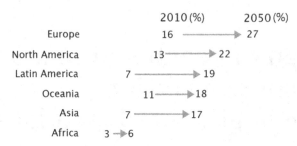

FIGURE 17.1 Demographic projections from 2010 to 2050. *Note*: Caribbean countries are included in Latin America. Source: *United Nations Population Division World Population Prospects, 2012 revision. Retrieved from Pew Research Center.*

demands on health care and technological solutions to support health self-maintenance, as the prevalence of chronic conditions and diseases (i.e., heart disease, diabetes, and arthritis) also increases.

Normative processes of aging cause declines in sensory, physical, and cognitive functioning (Czaja et al., 2019). The ability of older adults to independently perform activities of daily living is impacted not only by age-related impairments in vision, hearing, and mobility, but can be additionally exacerbated by the compound of existing disabilities (Mitzner, Sanford, & Rogers, 2018). For example, an individual living with mobility impairment due to an accident experienced at a young age may experience additional challenges in older adulthood at the onset of vision and hearing decline.

Functional limitations are also seen in instrumental activities of daily living such as medication management, transportation to and from doctor's offices, and other tasks of health self-maintenance (tracking and monitoring of vital signs and overall health status). Oftentimes, older adults report experiencing difficulty with these types of tasks, with many older adults reporting consistent need for support (technological or caregiver) in performance of these tasks (Montaquila, Freedman, Spillman, & Kasper, 2012). As seen in Fig. 17.2, as age increases, older adults report more age-related impairments or preexisting disabilities, having adverse effect on performance of activities of daily living, including health self-maintenance activities (Montaquila et al., 2012).

Technology has the potential to address challenges in health self-maintenance among older adults aging into impairments and disability (Mitzner et al., 2018). However, as the needs of older adults functioning with impairments or disabilities differ from those without, there are different considerations necessary to support various levels of functioning. Applying various modalities to health-care technologies may support these differing

Population aged 65 and over by number of disabilities and age: 2008–12

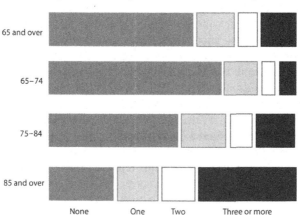

FIGURE 17.2 Number of disabilities by age group as collected from Older Americans 2012: Key Indicators of Well-Being.

needs, but we first must understand the ways in which age-related changes impact design considerations and the types of technologies that would be considered feasible to address these health needs.

Use of information and communication technology for health-care self-management

ICTs provide convenient ways for individuals to store, access, and transmit information and personal data. Use of the Internet as a resource for identifying health symptoms, locating health-care providers, and storing personal health information has become more common among the general population and is critical for improving quality of life for many individuals. These technology solutions, often described as eHealth or mHealth technologies, include systems such as health portals and databases for storage of individual health history, telemedicine devices, electronic learning tools, and mobile health devices. Such technologies have potential to be an advantageous resource for health maintenance and promotion among older adults, with 67% of adults over 65 currently using the Internet and 42% using mobile smartphones on a frequent basis according to Pew Research Center data (Anderson & Perrin, 2017).

The readily accessible nature of many ICTs presents them as a method for bridging the digital gap that has long existed among older adults. In this way use of ICTs may increase independence in health maintenance, where mobile devices and Internet systems serve as personal tools allowing individuals to manage their health at their own discretion through remote interactions with health-care professionals (i.e., telemedicine), potentially eliminating barriers to in-person health care.

Current reports on the use of health-related ICTs find that as of 2013, 71% of older adults are using Internet sources for seeking health information (Fox & Duggan, 2013), with a likelihood that this percentage will increase as older adults become more technically savvy. More specifically, older adults reportedly have an interest in leveraging mobile ICTs for the management of specific health conditions and organizing and keeping up with health appointments (Davidson & Jensen, 2013; Fox & Duggan, 2013). While the percentage of older adults using Internet resources to search for health information is projected to grow, the use of medical messaging and communication has substantially increased (49% of adults over the age of 65, according to the National Poll on Healthy Aging) (Clark, Singer, Solway, Kirch, & Malani, 2018), despite many older adults reporting a preference for in-person health discussions. Understanding the current ways in which older adults use ICTs and potential reasons for nonuse may serve as a useful starting point for designing better ICTs used for health maintenance.

Although there is evidence of the relevance of ICTs as health-care solutions in supporting caregivers, or medical professionals, there is also great potential for the use of ICTs in managing chronic conditions and also maintaining wellness among older adults themselves. Thus we focus on health-related ICTs that have the potential to be used by older adults themselves, instead of those that are used on them by medical personnel.

Chapter scope

To set the stage for useful guidelines for designing health-care ICTs for older adults, the remainder of this chapter focuses on defining the characteristics that impact older adults' use of health-care technologies, the implications of physical and sensory abilities of the older adult population on design, and ways in which this population can be centered in the design process. Employing the user-centered design approach allows for older adults to have an influential role in designing the health technologies they use, and thus we focus on this area of design. By outlining seemingly advantageous design methods for older adults, we hope to demonstrate the value of incorporating these users from the beginning stages of design.

Older Adults' physiological and psychological characteristics related to information and communication technology use

There is great variability within the psychological and physiological profiles of older adults, thus it can be difficult to characterize both of these facets (Allen, 1986). Changes to these systems are an inevitable part of the aging process and should be considered for the design of health-care ICT. Age-related changes impact the perceptual (e.g., visual and hearing), physical (e.g., strength and dexterity), mobility (e.g., balance and coordination), and cognition (e.g., working memory and attention) the most (Birren & Schaie, 2005). Other factors include psychological aspects (e.g., motivation), as life experiences that accompany aging often influence psychological well-being of older adults (e.g., retirement and need for assistance).

It is important to understand how such age-related changes affect one's ability to manage health (e.g., medication management and physical activity engagement), or how appropriately designed technology may moderate these changes to promote autonomous health management, resulting in positive health behavioral outcomes. Designers of ICTs must consider how these changes influence older adults' ability and willingness to utilize health-care technologies. This section will discuss some of functional changes associated with aging and design-related considerations for health-care technologies.

Sensory/perceptual processes/systems

Vision

Age-related vision decline is the most common perceptual change, affecting approximately 15%−20% of adults age 65 years and older, and more than 25% of those over the age of 75 years (Czaja et al., 2019). Vision impairments are a major contributor of physical and mental functionality (Branch, Horowitz, & Carr, 1989) and a strong predictor of future functional decline among older adults (Brennan, Horowitz, & Su, 2005). Specific age-related changes in vision include a higher sensitivity to glare and illumination (moving from dark to bright environments), a decrease in contrast sensitivity, a narrowing of the visual field due to changes in peripheral vision, difficulty recognizing certain colors (e.g., blue), a decline in visual acuity, visual search problems such as difficulty locating a favorite sauce on a grocery store shelf, and a reduction in the speed of visual information processing (Czaja et al., 2019; Pak & McLaughlin, 2010). All these physiological changes and functional issues with the aging eye have major implication for design, as technology presents information to the user through visual displays more than any other sensory process.

To facilitate effortless searching, designers should enhance conspicuity of items, particularly those of importance, or frequent use. Technologies should also be designed to create categories or patterns of similar items. This design process of supporting effortless visual searching is based on one of Gestalt's principles (see Brunswik & Kamiya, 1953), which posits that humans naturally assume objects that are perceived to be close together should be identified as a group or as more similar to one another compared to objects that are further apart (law of proximity). Thus spacing between similar or dissimilar objects is an important design consideration. Similarly, the user should be provided options of higher level categories in one place, and lower level categories in another to reduce effortful searching. For example, when searching online health sites, information should be grouped by condition and then sorted by categories (symptoms, treatments, etc.). An older adult's declining ability to detect contrast, or the ability to identify the difference between light and dark sections of an image, may impact how much attention is devoted to understanding written words or graphics. This may influence the users' ability to understand the information presented. As an example, the presentation of necessary health information from technology sources can serve as a source of support for obtaining information on side effects from medication or reading visual displays of self-monitoring devices.

Hearing

Hearing loss impacts approximately 25%−30% of adults over the age of 65 (Czaja et al., 2019) and the prevalence jumps to 50% by age 85 (Bogardus, Yueh, & Shekelle, 2003). There are a number of physiological changes occurring with aging that contribute to hearing loss, including but not limited to deterioration of receptor hair cells, vascular changes to the inner ear, a decrease in neurons, or even a decline in speed of information processing (see Willott, Chisolm, & Lister, 2001). These physiological changes affect older adults' ability to detect tones, frequencies, and comprehend speech. For example, normal hearing includes acknowledging tones in frequency as high as 15,000 Hz; after the age of 65−70 years, sound above 4000 Hz may be inaudible (Czaja et al., 2019).

Health-care technology utilizes the user's hearing sense by providing auditory feedback or responses. For example, a portable device used to monitor blood pressure may beep with one sound when the reading is obtained successfully, and beep with a different sound when the reading was not successful. Similarly, a health-care application designed to provide medication reminders on a smartphone may make a sound for the alarm, indicating time to take a medication, as well as provide a notification that the alarm has been deactivated.

Age-related hearing changes impact a user's ability to interact successfully with an auditory interface. Designers should consider the proximity of the device's speaker to the user's ear when considering volume settings, as well as any possible interference of background noise. Contrary to popular belief, the resulting sounds are not necessarily required to be louder for older adult users; instead, pitch range should be considered. Low and high pitches are difficult for older adults to identify; thus low to mid-range frequencies are preferable. In addition, succinct prompts are more easily identified, as well as pulsating sound as opposed to sustained frequencies (Pak & McLaughlin, 2010).

Sensory & Perceptual Systems

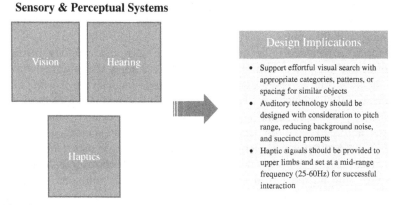

FIGURE 17.3   Design Implications for Sensory/Perceptual Age-Related Changes.

Haptics

Age-related changes to sensory receptors located in various parts of the human body (e.g., joints, muscles and skin) inhibit proprioception and kinesthesis abilities, or the ability of the body to identify joint, limb, body position, and motion to remain coordinated in a given environment (Konczak et al., 2009). These changes impact physical functionality including balance and touch. Among older adults, there is greater variability of haptic control (e.g., maintaining force when grasping an object) and an increase in vibration and temperature thresholds (Czaja et al., 2019). These changes may result in postural instability, vertigo, and prehension difficulty (maintaining consistent motor control). To enable successful interaction with health-care technology artifacts, consider utilizing mid-range frequency levels for haptic signals; frequencies lower than 25 Hz or higher than 60 Hz are difficult to detect. Information provided through vibration should occur predominately for the upper body limbs, and an increase in signal strength with a reduction in other stimuli would serve the older user by lowering the demands on a declining perceptual system (Czaja et al., 2019) (Fig. 17.3).

Cognitive function

Cognitive capabilities allow a user to perceive, comprehend, and carry out appropriate health behaviors based on the information presented by the health-care technology (Pak & McLaughlin, 2010). While some areas of the brain are impacted by age-related physiological changes (e.g., hippocampus and prefrontal cortex), other areas remain relatively intact with aging (e.g., occipital lobe). Thus only certain cognitive capabilities are negatively impacted by aging (e.g., attention, executive functions), whereas others are not (e.g., metacognition and semantic memory). This section will focus on two aspects of cognition that are not only susceptible to age-related decline but are also imperative for interacting successfully with technology: working memory and attention.

Working memory refers to the ability to store and maintain pertinent information (e.g., short-term memory), as well as apply the information with the help of higher level executive processes (Baddeley & Hitch, 1974; Baddeley, 1986; Miyake & Shah, 1999). Variability in working-memory performance is apparent in the aging population and can negatively impact older adults' ability to solve problems, reason, or comprehend language and speech (Czaja et al., 2019). Changes to working memory have many implications for health-care technology design. For example, interfaces should provide the user with no more than seven options at one time (utilizing short-term memory capacity). Options beyond this may result in poor user performance due to memory failure. In addition, pertinent information should be maintained in a display so that the user does not need to remember previous options. Keeping small chunks of task-relevant information available in the display will help in preventing cognitive overload (Pak & McLaughlin, 2010).

Attention is another cognitive function, which may decline due to aging. In this case, older adults struggle with both divided attention—paying attention to multiple stimuli at one time—and selective attention—paying attention to one stimulus while ignoring others. Older adults have less attentional resources than younger adults, causing difficulty ignoring irrelevant or distracting stimuli. The goal of health-care design, then, is to avoid these limitations by reducing the number of display items and making sure the important and useful features draw more attention than irrelevant features. Finally, users should be provided with clear, step-by-step instructions during their interaction with an interface to successfully engage with the technology (Czaja et al., 2019; Pak & McLaughlin, 2010) (Fig. 17.4).

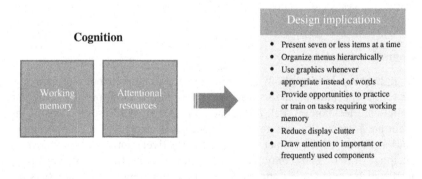

FIGURE 17.4 Design implications for cognitive age-related changes.

Psychological needs

A sense of purpose and control over one's life is integral to the health of the aged
Rodin (1986)

Health-care technology has the potential to not only influence health behavior (e.g., regular health monitoring and accessing pertinent information) but to also impact psychological well-being.

There is a movement in HCI (both for researchers and practitioners) to support technology design that provides users with deeper meaning and happiness (e.g., see positive design; Desmet & Pohlmeyer, 2013; positive computing; Calvo & Peters, 2014). Thus to support well-being and the perception of self-determination (i.e., self-regulation), designers should create technology that fosters the user's basic psychological need for autonomy, competence, and relatedness (Peters, Calvo, & Ryan, 2018; see Fig. 17.4). These three basic needs can serve as a control parameter where the resulting technology can be empirically evaluated and designed for basic need satisfaction, providing others with "usable evidence" (Klasnja, Hekler, Korinek, Harlow, & Mishra, 2017).

Autonomy refers to the need to choose one's behavior and perceive these choices to be self-determined. Health-care technology can support this need by providing the user with options for engagement, requiring assent before proceeding to the next step, and personalizing the experience (see Ford, Wyeth, & Johnson, 2012; Rigby & Ryan, 2018). *Competence* is the need to feel capable and effective when interacting with the environment. Designers can provide the user with intuitive controls and useful feedback, as well as optimally challenging and novel experiences to satisfy the need for competence (see Lomas et al., 2017; Rigby & Ryan, 2011). *Relatedness* is the need to have a sense of belonging and connectedness to others. This need has been found to have a positive impact on longevity, even more than diet and exercise (Kasser & Ryan, 1996). Health-care technology can satisfy this need by promoting active communication between the user and a virtual health-care professional, as well as provide relevant and meaningful feedback from this professional. Supporting these basic needs promotes greater control over older adults' health management as well as overall psychological well-being (Fig. 17.5).

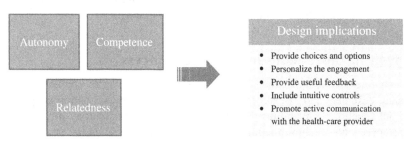

FIGURE 17.5 Design implications for psychological age-related changes.

Guidelines for health-care technology design for the aging population

Health needs of older adults should be considered very broadly—from managing chronic conditions, to maintaining wellness activities, to engaging in social activities that might have a long-term benefit for health. Based on the potential application of ICTs to address health needs of older adults, we provide the following general guidelines for designing health-care technologies for older adults:

- Engage older adults throughout the design process but be certain to consider the specific characteristics of the target users and select representative older adults to participate (i.e., not all older adults are alike). Examples include the following:
  - Older adults living alone and at risk for social isolation
  - Individuals aging with sensory or mobility impairments
  - People who are interested in engaging in physical activity but could benefit from motivation provided by ICT
- Utilize a mixed-method approach to support the iterative design process, which includes:
  - Initial surveys of attitudes and needs to help contextualize new ICT systems for older adults and inform useful system criteria
  - Observations of how older adults perform task workarounds due to functional limitations (ad hoc solutions to challenges) can guide design ideas
  - Usability of the ICT in representative-tasks context is informative regarding use barriers and facilitators in realistic-use situations
  - Long-term evaluation of ICT integration into everyday activities provides insights into benefits as well as potentially unforeseen usage challenges
  - Participatory design following experience with ICT usage may be especially informative for older adults; more novel or robust ideas may emerge as a result of exposure to newer technologies

Just as each individual is unique, each design effort will be unique as well. ICTs have more potential to be effective if derived from systematic, iterative design approaches. The following case studies provide illustrations of ICT design efforts within the context of health care that leverage methods of contextual inquiry, universal and participatory design.

Involving older adults in the design process

Designing technologies that best serve older adults can be challenging, as many designers and researchers operate with a set of biases and assumptions about functional capabilities, access to resources, or technology proficiency. Instances of design-thinking methods, however, suggest that health technologies meant for older adults may benefit from the direct input of older adults themselves (Davidson & Jensen, 2013). Affording older adults the opportunity to engage in the process of designing technologies for their health not only provides designers and researchers with better insight into the needs of these users but may also improve long-term adherence to the technology as an intervention. Involving older adults in the design process also allows us to consider their experiences and perspectives to generate and evaluate relevant ideas to meet health needs and ultimately to implement solutions that are not just innovative but practical for older users.

Physiological and psychological changes experienced during aging play a major role in the perceptions of health needs and resultant use of health ICTs. Thus it is beneficial for those designing health ICTs for older adults to directly center these individuals as potential technology collaborators and not just users, capturing first-hand accounts of individual needs, implementing design considerations with universal benefit, and doing so in collaboration with older adults themselves.

There are many approaches to user-centered design that support innovation for individuals with a wide range of abilities. These approaches begin with identifying and understanding user needs to product testing and evaluation. In the remainder of this section, we discuss various types of user-centered design methods and case studies that highlight how some of the suggested design guidelines have been implemented in the design or evaluation of health-related ICTs and associated support tools.

Contextual inquiry

One of the core underlying concepts of user-centered design is the initial user research that takes place to understand user needs associated with a task. Contextual inquiry is a semistructured user-research method in which researchers and designers can gather information about the context of use of a product or system through questions or observations (Beyer & Holtzblatt, 1998; Holtzblatt, Wendell, & Wood, 2005). Research approaches associated with contextual inquiry may include surveys, interviews, observational studies, focus groups, artifact analysis or field studies, methods that highlight user needs in the context of their environment, or task of study. Contextual inquiry has the benefit of providing in-depth qualitative data that might not be collected in usability testing alone. We discuss two case studies demonstrating the use of contextual inquiry in examining health ICTs from older adults' perspective.

Case study: PRISM

Project overview

Social isolation is a risk factor for negative health outcomes. The Personal Reminder and Information System (PRISM) is a computer system specifically targeted to support social engagement for older adults who lived alone and were at risk for social isolation (Czaja et al., 2015; see Fig. 17.6). The development of the system was guided by survey and focus group interviews with current older adult computer users to ensure that PRISM was designed appropriately for the target population who were above 65, with minimal computer experience, and without current access to a computer. This deliberate and in-depth development process was necessary to ensure that the subsequent randomized clinical trial would provide a valid and reliable assessment of the benefits of the PRISM system to reduce loneliness and increase perceptions of social support, which were the key findings of extended (6 months) use of PRISM, relative to a control condition that received similar information in a booklet format (Czaja, Boot, Charness, Rogers, & Sharit, 2018).

First, to identify the primary features that older adults might want on their computer system, 321 computer users, aged 60−93, were surveyed about the importance of various activities (e.g., socializing) to quality of life; the value of having access to computers and the Internet; and features and information topics that would be of potential value. The information helped

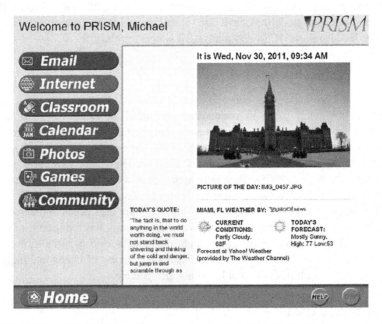

FIGURE 17.6 The PRISM home page. *From Czaja, S. J., Boot, W. R., Charness, N., Rogers, W. A., Sharit, J., Fisk, A.D. et al. (2015). The Personalized Reminder Information and Social Management System (PRISM) trial: Rationale, methods and baseline characteristics. Contemporary Clinical Trials, 40, 35−46.*

determine the selection of features for PRISM, topics for the classroom feature and the community resource guide, and website favorites.

Second, we conducted focus group interviews with a total of 14 users aged 60−85; participants were introduced to the concept of the PRISM system and shown an early mockup via a PowerPoint presentation. They were then asked to comment on the potential value of PRISM, the planned system features and content of the features, and the interface. They were also asked about topics of interest for the classroom features and resources, the screen graphics, the choice of icon, and the functionality of the calendar feature.

Design approach

The design of PRISM was guided by contextual inquiry with individuals from the target age group (over age 60) who were already using a computer. Data from the survey and the focus groups also guided the initial design of the system. Together these methods enabled us to (1) understand how computer systems were used by current older adult users, (2) clarify labels and terminology for PRISM system, and (3) identify potential use challenges with prototype system. While the intended users of PRISM were novice older computer users, this initial research with experienced users provided valuable guidance for the content and features to include in the system. We then conducted heuristic analyses and cognitive walk-throughs of prototype iterations. Moreover, once the system was functional, we conducted extensive, summative user testing with older adults, both to evaluate PRISM and assess the utility of the training materials we had developed for the randomized clinical trial. Together, these efforts yielded a system that could be used effectively by older adults without prior computer experience in their homes (Czaja et al., 2015, 2018).

Lessons learned

- Older adults are willing to use computers for a variety of activities, including accessing health information. Their acceptance and excitement was well illustrated by one participant: "I feel very very fortunate being part of the PRISM program …. I'm lonely and alone and I appreciate the computer so much. It has brought me a lot of the email, a lot of information from the Internet. To pass time, I play the games. And I thank everybody involved with the PRISM program for this opportunity. … I love the email, I can't get out, so I love the email. And when I want some information, I go on Google or Yahoo. And when I am able to sit longer, I like to play the games to keep my mind going …. I think it's very helpful to me … when I was without it for few days, I really really missed it … really did."
- Icons and labels on existing systems may be misinterpreted by older adults. They must be tested for comprehension with representatives of the target user group and mapped onto their knowledge and expectations.

- Surveys and interviews are equally useful in defining design criteria for systems.
- Long-term use of a system designed specifically for older adults can reduce social isolation, which can positively impact health outcomes.

Case study: Aging Concerns, Challenges, and Everyday Solution Strategies

Project overview

ACCESS (Aging Concerns, Challenges, and Everyday Solution Strategies) is a large-scale, mixed-method study investigating user needs of individuals aging with impairments for a range of everyday activities (Remillard, Mitzner, Singleton, & Rogers, 2018). The data collected during the ACCESS study provided a comprehensive user-needs assessment for older adults with long-term vision, hearing, or mobility impairments. Participants aged 60−79 years were recruited into three groups (blind/low vision, $n = 60$; mobility impaired, $n = 60$; deaf/hard of hearing, $n = 47$) and completed questionnaires (demographics, health, functional limitations) and an in-depth interview to assess challenges and current responses to such challenges, with a range of daily activities such as transportation, managing health, or engaging in activities outside of the home. One of the goals of the project was to identify challenges associated with health-care technology and how the participants responded to those challenges using their own methods or strategies, obtaining assistance from others, or utilizing other devices or technologies to support the task at hand.

A thematic analysis illustrated challenges for health-care technology design to assist the older population with their health-care needs. For example, one participant with a long-term hearing impairment reported that when attending health-care provider appointments, a video remote interpreter must be utilized to facilitate communication with the professional. This participant recalled issues with the technology itself, "...Sometimes it is blurry, and I cannot see the interpreter on the screen," and was forced to revert to communication with a "thumbs up or a thumbs down to the doctor."

In addition, challenges related to accessing health-care information were a common issue among participants aging with visual impairments. For example, one participant stated how difficult it was to access information on the Internet related to their health care because they found the "text-to-speech programs frustrating because they are slower than, when I had sight and I could look things up with my eyes," and this task often required assistance from others, "...and that means I have to get somebody who has the patience to sit down and go through it with me."

Design approach

Here researchers implemented contextual inquiry as a way to better understand older adults' approaches to and challenges with personal health maintenance and the technologies that may be used to address those challenges. Data from the ACCESS study provides a snapshot into the potential challenges and responses older adults encounter with regard to their health-care needs, and the results indicate the potential of, and the need to improve the design of, health-care technology for adults aging with sensory or mobility impairments.

Lessons learned

- Improve usability (e.g., speed and accuracy) of screen and device readers.
- Incorporate voice-activated digital assistant devices to guide visually impaired users through health-related Internet searches.
- Health-care monitoring systems are important to one's health (both mentally and physically).
- Details from user interviews provide rich insight into the source of individual challenges.
- Participants often develop their own solutions which can be harnessed to develop tools that will support others experiencing the same challenges.

Universal design

Universal design is a design approach that centers the needs of the widest possible spectrum of users, designs environments and products that can be easily understood, accessed, and used by a wide range of people without specialized adaptations (Center for Universal Design, 2006; Story, Mueller, & Mace, 1998). A widely known user-centered design approach, universal design, emphasizes understanding the needs of a particular population and how those needs can be considered in the design of a product that will also appeal to a larger user base. Universal design is defined by seven principles of design consideration (equitable use, flexibility in use, simple and intuitive use, perceptible information, tolerance for error, low physical effort, and size and space for approach and use; Story et al., 1998), thus both guiding and evaluating products and systems as "good design for all." One of the major underlying concepts of this approach is the consideration and incorporation of accessible features that can benefit all users.

Unlike other specialized approaches to design such as accessible design or adaptation that centers on the functional needs of one or two types of impairment for system use, universal design aims to encompass varying needs of all individuals who desire access to a product or system, regardless of impairment or ability status. This differentiation positions universal design to enhance the quality of life for older adults by creating safer technology interactions that are less stigmatizing and socially isolating (Carr, Weir, Azar, & Azar, 2013). This has great potential to address low usage numbers of health ICTs and increase use among this population. We discuss a case study of universal design used in developing ICTs to improve the health of the aging population.

Case study: A universally designed support tool for exergame use

Project overview

Use of exergames (i.e., video games that simulate exercise) may address barriers to older adults being physically active and exercising. To understand the ways these technologies may encourage and facilitate physical activity, a research team designed a study to evaluate Kinect-based exergames. A sample of 18 older adults tested the usability of the Xbox 360 with Kinect with two existing exergames: *Body and Brain Connection* and *Your Shape Fitness Evolved* (see Fig. 17.7). Researchers assessed participants' ability to understand in-game prompts and to successfully perform various tasks associated with the games to identify usability challenges of the system and the games themselves.

Despite positive perceptions about the use of exergames for physical activity (Barg-Walkow, Harrington, Mitzner, Hartley, & Rogers, 2017), participants identified that there was difficulty in understanding the task demands of the game, particularly discerning between instruction mode and live game play. In addition, participants reported significant difficulty in understanding the concept of on-screen gestures, suggesting that this caused feelings of frustration, and despite the potential of this system to get older adults active, it may cause some users to not want to interact (for additional results, see Harrington, Hartley, Mitzner, & Rogers, 2015). The challenges identified provide direction for the design of a support tool centered on the needs of older users that would potentially alleviate barriers to exergame use.

FIGURE 17.7   Usability testing of Kinect-based exergames.

Design research approach

In the second phase of this research project, researchers addressed usability challenges by developing a universally designed quick-start guide to support the use of the system (Harrington, Hare, & Rogers, 2017). The initial task was to develop a guide wherein exergame users would be provided with diagrams, texts, and images to guide them through using the system. However, the challenges perceived during usability testing made it evident that there was a need to discern the best way to visually communicate and teach gestures to this population. Thus three versions of a paper-based quick-start guide were developed: version 1 featured photo images of older adults performing gestures, version 2 featured animated hands performing gestures, and version 3 featured line-drawn avatar images. This project leveraged an iterative universal design approach that included a needs assessment based on usability data, design criteria mapping, and rapid and iterative prototyping for the form of the guide (see Fig. 17.8). The resulting prototype was then tested with a sample that met the same demographic criteria of generally healthy older adults.

Lessons learned

- Usability data are helpful in discerning that older adults may benefit from off-screen support tool.

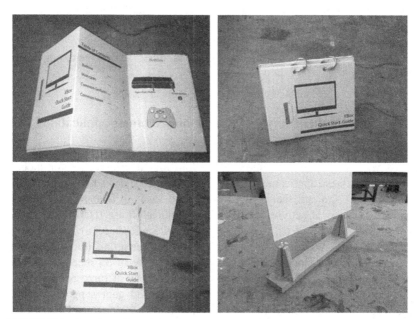

FIGURE 17.8 Iterations of physical quick-start guide prototype from Harrington et al. (2017).

- Support tool should be stand-alone for most convenient use.
- In teaching gesture-based tasks to older adults, there was a preference for line-drawn avatar images as a simpler method to understanding physical movements on paper.
- Use of a quick-start guide has potential to benefit not only older adults but other novice users of exergames and other gesture-based technologies.

Participatory health-technology design

Collaborative approaches to design, such as participatory design, establish an in-depth understanding of older adults' needs and preferences for the design of health technology. Participatory design enables end users to be directly involved in the decision-making process of product conception and development as not just the users of the technology but stakeholders with vested interest in how the product is designed. Researchers suggest that involving older adults as cocreators in the design of a technology, as opposed to just a consumer of that technology, has potential to increase the likelihood of technology adoption by the older adult population (Davidson & Jensen, 2013). Participatory design advocates the voices and input of nontraditional designers in a creative environment. Often, this method requires methodological concessions to make participatory design accessible and friendly to older adult participants, including social and material configuration of spaces and tools. Benefits of participatory design include mutual learning and empowerment of older adult participants, and in-depth understanding of design requirements by researchers. This research area is growing to be a well-established approach to designing ICT and other health technologies for older adults.

Case study: Participatory design of a mobile fitness application

Project overview

As a way to gain insight into useful motivational affordances for mobile health and fitness applications, researchers engaged older adults in participatory design sessions identifying useful and desired features that would encourage physical activity and sustained application use (Harrington et al., 2017; Harrington, Wilcox, Connelly, Rogers, & Sanford, 2018). Participatory design sessions were held as a part of a larger research effort to identify effective behavior-change strategies, where a sample of 39 older adults was given a mobile fitness application that embodied one of three combinations of behavior-change strategies (analytic tracking and goal support, analytic tracking and social support, basic analytic tracking alone) to be used for

10 weeks. Researchers observed physical activity patterns as well as the patterns of mobile application use among the sample, leveraging intermittent follow-ups throughout the study.

Following the 10-week period of using the assigned mobile application, participants who were still enrolled in the study ($n = 29$) engaged in participatory design sessions. Each session began with a final assessment of physical activity and application use patterns. The group was then guided through a discussion of participant experiences, including perceptions of mobile apps. Following this discussion, participants were provided with basic ideation materials (pens, markers, drawing paper, post-it notes) to visually share their ideas for ideal features for future fitness apps. This ideation process was structured by prompts to specifically identify ideal features to encourage application use, ideal features to increase physical activity, and ideal features to appeal to older users. Each prompt was discussed among the larger group for congruent and divergent ideas (Fig. 17.9).

From these sessions, researchers identified that older users envisioned their ideal health and fitness tool to be one that was visually accessible and required low physical effort for data entry and review, assessed health holistically, and evaluated pain. Findings from these design sessions were used to identify potential design recommendations for future mobile fitness applications that targeted older adults. In addition, results of these sessions highlighted the benefit of providing older adults with technology exposure prior to participatory design sessions as one that might better inform codesign of unfamiliar technologies (Fig. 17.10).

FIGURE 17.9 Older adults participating in codesign activities from Harrington et al. (2018).

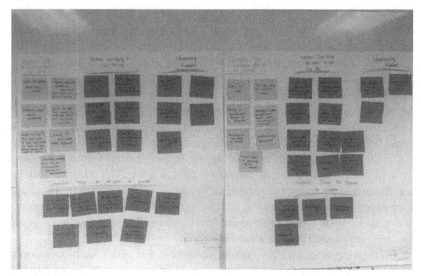

FIGURE 17.10 Brainstormed ICT features from Harrington et al. (2018).

Design research approach

The larger research effort of this case study demonstrated the use of a longitudinal behavioral assessment in which participants were randomly assigned to an intervention in the form of a mobile fitness application and assessed at intermittent benchmarks across the 10 weeks of the study (Harrington et al., 2018). To fully understand the experiences of study participants, researchers administered group interviews that allowed older adults to collaboratively discuss their perceptions of mobile fitness applications and the utility of these technologies for health and activity promotion. The participatory design sessions provided a deep dive into the ways older users envisioned improving future applications, giving researchers insights for ideal application features as well as the value of involving older adults into this part of the design process.

Lessons learned

- Technology experience and exposure supports novel and robust ideas among older design collaborators and engagement in participatory design sessions.
- Providing a wide variety of materials in participatory design sessions may be advantageous for engaging older adults. It is important to consider older adults' familiarity with both design method and medium.
- Participatory design in focus group format helps to fully formulate ideas through dialogue and verbal brainstorming among older adults who may not readily engage in sketching for ideation.

Conclusion

This chapter presents various considerations to be taken when designing ICTs for the older adult population. We review natural age-related changes and illustrate how many common design methods can help designers understand and consider these changes when conceptualizing ICTs for older adults. These methods along with the case studies present best practices for how designers can work toward a more inclusive design process when older adults are the target users of health technologies. Older adults are willing to use health technologies, but they must be designed with consideration for their abilities, limitations, and preferences. Design is a process, and older adults must be included in the process.

References

Anderson, M., & Perrin, A. (2017). *Tech adoption climbs among older adults*. Washington, DC: Pew Research Center. (May 17, 2017) <http://www.pewinternet.org/2017/05/17/tech-adoption-climbs-among-older-adults/>.

Baddeley, A. (1986). Oxford psychology series, No. 11. In: *Working memory*. Clarendon Press/ Oxford University Press, New York, NY.

Baddeley, A. D., & Hitch, G. (1974). *Working memory. Psychology of Learning and Motivation* (Vol. 8, pp. 47−89). Cambridge, MA: Academic Press.

Barg-Walkow, L. H., Harrington, C. N., Mitzner, T. L., Hartley, J. Q., & Rogers, W. A. (2017). Understanding older adults' perceptions of and attitudes toward exergames. *Gerontechnology, 16*, 81−90.

Beyer, H., & Holtzblatt, K. (1998). *Contextual design: Defining customer-centered systems*. San Francisco, CA: Morgan Kaufmann Publishers.

Birren, J. E., & Schaie, K. W. (2005). *Handbook for the Psychology of Aging* (6th ed.). New York: Academic Press.

Bogardus, S. T., Jr, Yueh, B., & Shekelle, P. G. (2003). Screening and management of adult hearing loss in primary care: Clinical applications. *The Journal of the American Medical Association, 289*(15), 1986−1990.

Branch, L. G., Horowitz, A., & Carr, C. (1989). The implications for everyday life of incident self-reported visual decline among people over age 65 living in the community. *The Gerontologist, 29*(3), 359−365.

Brennan, M., Horowitz, A., & Su, Y. P. (2005). Dual sensory loss and its impact on everyday competence. *The Gerontologist, 45*(3), 337−346.

Brunswik, E., & Kamiya, J. (1953). Ecological cue-validity of 'proximity' and of other Gestalt factors. *The American Journal of Psychology, 66*(1), 20−32.

Calvo, R. A., & Peters, D. (2014). *Positive computing: Technology for a better world*. Cambridge, MA: MIT Press.

Carr, K., Weir, P. L., Azar, D., & Azar, N. R. (2013). Universal design: A step toward successful aging. *Journal of Aging Research, 2013*, 1−8.

Centre for Universal Design. *Definitions: Accessible, adaptable, and universal design*. (2006). Retrieved from <http://www.ncsu.edu/www/ncsu/design/sod/(cud/pubsp/phousing.htm>.

Clark, S., Singer, D., Solway, E., Kirch, M., & Malani, P. (2018). *Logging in: Using patient portals to access health information* (2018). Institute for Healthcare Policy and Innovation, University of Michigan. Retrieved from <http://hdl.handle.net/2027.42/145683>.

Czaja, S. J., Boot, W. R., Charness, N., & Rogers, W. A. (2019). *Designing for older adults: Principles and creative human factors approaches.* Boca Raton, FL: CRC Press.

Czaja, S. J., Boot, W. R., Charness, N., Rogers, W. A., & Sharit, J. (2018). Improving social support for older adults through technology: Findings from the PRISM randomized controlled trial. *The Gerontologist, 58,* 467–477. Available from https://doi.org/10.1093/geront/gnw249.

Czaja, S. J., Boot, W. R., Charness, N., Rogers, W. A., Sharit, J., Fisk, A. D., ... Nair, S. (2015). The Personalized Reminder Information and Social Management System (PRISM) Trial: Rationale, methods and baseline characteristics. *Contemporary Clinical Trials, 40,* 35–46.

Davidson, J. L., & Jensen, C. (2013). Participatory design with older adults. In: *Proceedings of the ninth ACM conference on creativity & cognition - C&C 13* (June 2013) (pp. 114–123).

Desmet, P. M., & Pohlmeyer, A. E. (2013). Positive design: An introduction to design for subjective well-being. *International Journal of Design, 7*(3).

Ford, M., Wyeth, P., & Johnson, D. (2012). Self-determination theory as applied to the design of a software learning system using whole-body controls. Proceedings of the 24th Australian computer–human interaction conference (pp. 146–149). ACM.

Fox, S., & Duggan, M. (2013). *Health online 2013.* Washington, DC: Pew Research Center's Internet & American Life Project.

Harrington, C. N., Hare, K. J., & Rogers, W. A. (2017). Developing a quick-start guide to aid older adults in interacting with gesture-based video games. Proceedings of the human factors and ergonomics society annual meeting (Vol. 61, No. 1, 32–36). Los Angeles, CA: Sage Publications.

Harrington, C. N., Hartley, J. Q., Mitzner, T. L., & Rogers, W. A. (2015). Assessing older adults' usability challenges using Kinect-based exergames. International conference on human aspects of IT for the aged population (pp. 488–499). Springer, Cham.

Harrington, C. N., Wilcox, L., Connelly, K., Rogers, W., & Sanford, J. (2018). Designing health and fitness apps with older adults: Examining the value of experience-based co-design. Proceedings of the 12th EAI international conference on pervasive computing technologies for healthcare (pp. 15–24). ACM. <https://doi.org/10.475/1145_4>.

Holtzblatt, K., Wendell, J. B., & Wood, S. (2005). *Rapid contextual design: A how-to guide to key techniques for user-centered design.* San Francisco, CA: Morgan Kaufmann.

Kasser, T., & Ryan, R. M. (1996). Further examining the American dream: Differential correlates of intrinsic and extrinsic goals. *Personality and Social Psychology Bulletin, 22*(3), 280–287.

Klasnja, P., Hekler, E. B., Korinek, E. V., Harlow, J., & Mishra, S. R. (2017). Toward usable evidence: optimizing knowledge accumulation in HCI research on health behavior change. *Proceedings of the 2017 CHI conference on human factors in computing systems* (pp. 3071–3082). ACM.

Konczak, J., Corcos, D. M., Horak, F., Poizner, H., Shapiro, M., Tuite, P., ... Maschke, M. (2009). Proprioception and motor control in Parkinson's disease. *Journal of Motor Behavior, 41*(6), 543–552.

Lomas, J. D., Koedinger, K., Patel, N., Shodhan, S., Poonwala, N., & Forlizzi, J. L. (2017). Is difficulty overrated? The effects of choice, novelty and suspense on intrinsic motivation in educational games. *Proceedings of the 2017 CHI conference on human factors in computing systems* (pp. 1028–1039). ACM.

Mitzner, T. L., Sanford, J. A., & Rogers, W. A. (2018). Closing the capacity-ability gap: Using technology to support aging with disability. *Innovation in Aging, 2*(1), 1–8.

Miyake, A., & Shah, P. (Eds.), (1999). *Models of working memory: Mechanisms of active maintenance and executive control.* Cambridge University Press.

Montaquila, J., Freedman, V. A., Spillman, B., & Kasper, J. D. (2012). *National Health and Aging Trends Study development of round 1 survey weights.* Baltimore, MD: Johns Hopkins University School of Public Health, NHATS Technical Paper #2.

Pak, R., & McLaughlin, A. (2010). *Designing displays for older adults.* Boca Raton, FL: CRC Press.

Peters, D., Calvo, R. A., & Ryan, R. M. (2018). Designing for motivation, engagement and well-being in digital experience. *Frontiers in Psychology, 9.*

Remillard, E. T., Mitzner, T. L., Singleton, J. L., & Rogers, W. A. (2018). A qualitative approach to understanding user needs for aging with disability. In: *Proceedings of the third international conference on universal accessibility in the Internet of Things and smart environments (SMART ACCESSIBILITY 2018)* (pp. 18–22).

Rigby, C. S., & Ryan, R. M. (2018). Self-determination theory in human resource development: New directions and practical considerations. *Advances in Developing Human Resources, 20*(2), 133–147.

Rigby, S., & Ryan, R. M. (2011). *Glued to games: How video games draw us in and hold us spellbound: How video games draw us in and hold us spellbound.* Santa Barbara, CA, US: Praeger/ABC-CLIO.

Rodin, J. (1986). Aging and health: Effects of the sense of control. *Science, 233*(4770), 1271–1276.

Story, M. F., Mueller, J. L., & Mace, R. L. (1998). *The universal design file: Designing for people of all ages and abilities.* Retrieved from <http://design-dev.ncsu.edu/openjournal/index.php/redlab/article/view/102>.

Willott, J. F., Chisolm, T. H., & Lister, J. J. (2001). Modulation of presbycusis: Current status and future directions. *Audiology and Neurotology, 6*(5), 231–249.

World Health Organization. (2015). *World report on ageing and health.* WHO. Retrieved from <https://www.who.int/ageing/events/world-report-2015-launch/en/>.

Further reading

Marsiske, M., Margrett, J. A., Birren, J. E., & Schaie, K. W. (2006). *Handbook of the psychology of aging.* Elsevier.

Report of the Joint American Medical Association-American Nursing Association Task Force on "The improvement of health care of the aged chronically ill" (American Medical Association-American Nursing Association, Kansas City, MO, 1983).

World Health Organization. (2001). *The international classification of functioning, disability and health.* Geneva: WHO.

Index

Note: Page numbers followed by "*f*" and "*t*" refer to figures and tables, respectively.

Printed in the United States
By Bookmasters